Revealing
Prophets

Eastern African Studies

Revealing Prophets

*Prophecy in
Eastern African
History*

Edited by

DAVID M. ANDERSON
&
DOUGLAS H. JOHNSON

James Currey
LONDON

E.A.E.P
NAIROBI

Fountain Publishers
KAMPALA

Ohio University Press
ATHENS

James Currey Ltd
54b Thornhill Square
Islington
London N1 1BE

East African Educational Publishers
PO Box 45314
Nairobi

Ohio University Press
Scott Quadrangle
Athens, Ohio 45701

Fountain Publishers
PO Box 488
Kampala

First published 1995
1 2 3 4 5 99 98 97 96 95

British Library Cataloguing in Publication Data
Revealing Prophets : Prophecy in
   Eastern African History. — (Eastern African Studies)
   I. Anderson, David   II. Johnson, Douglas H.   III. Series
   967.6

ISBN 0-85255-718-3 (cased)
     0-85255-717-5 (paper)

Library of Congress Cataloging-in-Publication Data
Revealing prophets : prophecy in Eastern African history / edited by
   David M. Anderson and Douglas H. Johnson.
      p.   cm. — (Eastern African studies)
   Includes bibliographical references and index.
   ISBN 0-8214-1088-1. — ISBN 0-8214-1089-X (paper)
      1. Prophets—Africa, East—History. 2. Africa, East—Religion.
I. Anderson, David, 1957-   . II. Johnson, Douglas Hamilton, 1949-
III. Series: Eastern African studies (London, England)
BL2464.R38   1995
291.6′3—dc20   94-10527
                                                        CIP

Typeset in 10/12 Baskerville by Colset Pte Ltd, Singapore
Printed in Britain by Villiers Publications, London N3

Contents

Contents

Four

The Frontiers of Prophecy

*Healing, the Cosmos & Islam on the East African Coast
in the Nineteenth Century*

DAVID SPERLING

Five

Modern Zande Prophetesses

MARGARET BUCKNER

Part Two

Colonial Historiographies

Six

Maji-Maji

Prophecy & Historiography

MARCIA WRIGHT

Seven

The Colonial Control
of Spirit Cults in Uganda

HOLGER BERNT HANSEN

Eight

Visions of the Vanquished

*Prophets & Colonialism
in Kenya's Western Highlands*

DAVID M. ANDERSON

Part Three

Prophetic Histories

List of Maps

Preface & Acknowledgements

The ideas around which this book has taken shape first emerged at a conference held at the School of Oriental and African Studies, University of London, in December 1989. The theme of that meeting, organized by Andrew Roberts, David Anderson and Douglas Johnson, was 'Seers, Prophets and Prophecy in East African History'. The conference brought together more than 40 scholars of eastern Africa, mostly historians and anthropologists, who spent two very full days considering some 30 papers on a wide variety of topics related to the role of prophetic figures in the history of the region.

The discussion generated at the conference was enormously stimulating, pushing the boundaries of the subject far beyond the scope of the papers themselves, and offering challenging insights on the need to re-evaluate broader issues of terminology, definition, comparability and historicity. The implication of those discussions was that a major revision in the writing of the history of prophets and prophecy in eastern Africa was called for, and that such a revision might make a significant impact on the current historiography of the region. For this reason, the organizers decided not to seek to publish the conference papers as a group, but instead to take up the most promising themes discussed and use these as the framework around which to commission chapters for a book. This collection is the result.

Of the eleven chapters gathered here, only three survive in any recognizable form from the original conference, whilst the remaining eight have been written specifically for this volume. All of our contributors, bar one, attended the 1989 meeting. This collection thus has a close relationship to a conference, but it is in no sense the proceedings of a conference. We hope it is a stronger and more coherent collection as a consequence.

There are people and institutions who deserve thanks for helping to bring this project to publication. The Nuffield Foundation generously funded the administrative costs of the 1989 conference, and provided additional monies to bring speakers from overseas. The Research Committee of the School of Oriental and African Studies assisted with funds to support those attending the conference from Africa. The hard work of managing the conference was accomplished by Marion Swiny with her customary efficiency, and we were glad to be able to run the conference under the auspices of the Centre of African Studies, University of London. We are extremely grateful to Catherine Lawrence and Claire Ivison for preparing the maps that accompany of the chapters in this volume.

We must also thank those scholars who attended the original conference, but whose work does not appear in this collection. Six of the papers from the conference, all written by anthropologists, have been published together as a special issue of *Africa* (61, 1991), with an introductory essay by David Anderson and Douglas Johnson. We are grateful to the Editor of that journal, Murray Last, for giving us the opportunity to air ideas that have now been built upon in this collection. More generally, we wish to acknowledge that many of the ideas expressed at our first meeting in 1989 have been reworked and incorporated in this collection. The editors are more keenly aware than is usually the case of the sense in which this volume is the result of a corporate effort.

St Albans, Hertfordshire   *David M. Anderson*

List of Contributors

Charles Ambler is Professor of African History, at the University of Texas at El Paso

David M. Anderson is Senior Lecturer in History, at the School of Oriental and African Studies, University of London

Iris Berger is Professor of History, at The State University of New York at Albany

Margaret Buckner is a Research Associate, at Laboratoire d'ethnologie et de sociologie comparative, University of Paris X

Holger Bernt Hansen is Senior Lecturer in Religions, at the University of Copenhagen, Denmark

Douglas H. Johnson is a Research Fellow at St Antony's College, University of Oxford

John Lonsdale is a Fellow of Trinity College, University of Cambridge

David Sperling is Senior Lecturer in History, at the University of Nairobi, Kenya

Richard D. Waller is Assistant Professor in African History, at Bucknell University, Pennsylvania

Marcia Wright is Professor of African History at Columbia University, New York

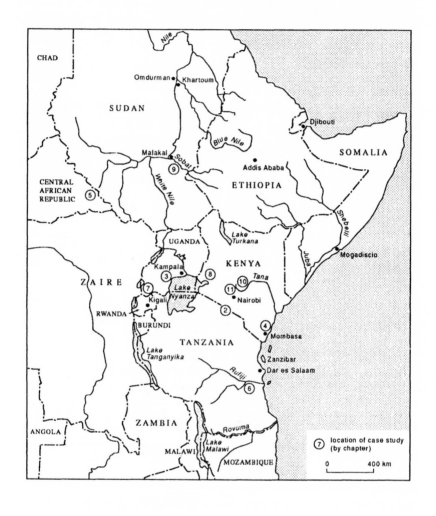

*Map 1   Eastern Africa, showing locations of case studies
(arranged by chapter number)*

One

Revealing Prophets

DOUGLAS H. JOHNSON
&
DAVID M. ANDERSON

Karen Blixen, when out of Africa, used to play a parlour game planning dinner parties of famous persons, living or dead, and imagining their conversations. 'We won't have any prophets,' was her one prohibition, 'for they can't be talked to, they only want to speak'.[1] The authors collected together in this volume would disagree. In trying to recover historical prophets and the history of prophecy we have become aware how stubbornly silent prophets can often be; but we have also found that one of the essential features of prophecy is the extended conversation between prophets and their audiences down through the generations. Far from monopolizing the conversation, prophets frequently have words put into their mouths. And just as Karen Blixen's imaginary conversations consisted of what the famous dinner guest *ought* to have said, so, too, many an obscure figure in the past has become a prophet in the present through a similar process. Insofar as the historical study of prophets must include a disentangling of real from imagined conversations, separating prophets from prophecy, it is a continual rediscovery not only of the past, but of attitudes towards the past, explanations of the present and visions of the future.

The apprehension of prophets as insistent oracles is not uncommon, and in Blixen's reduction of their role to one essential, if simplified, feature she is little different from other modern writers on eastern Africa. The term 'prophet' has more often been applied rhetorically than precisely; in fact its very lack of precision has encouraged its wide application. Almost every people, it seems, has its prophet. But alongside the prophet, however described, we commonly find a host of functionaries with apparently overlapping or related roles. In the corpus of anthropological and historical writing on eastern African societies it is often difficult to appreciate the distinctions that exist from one community to another, between characters who are variously termed 'prophets', 'diviners', 'ritual experts', 'oracles', 'spirit mediums' or even 'witch-doctors'. This indiscriminate use of terms has created a number of obstacles in the way of any comparative study of prophets; for we find that in many cases the only common element uniting a variety of persons or offices is the title 'prophet' imposed upon them in different ethnographies or histories. The purpose of this collection of essays is to move towards a clearer understanding of the history of prophets within the region of eastern Africa, and to give an analytical account of the significantly different forms prophecy has taken over the years from place to place. Because of the confusion of terms that exists in the literature, we must begin with the genealogy of the term 'prophet' itself.

The genealogy of terms in eastern Africa

The Greek word *prophetes* has entered modern European languages mainly through its use in the Old Testament. From the start it has drawn on a double set of images: the oracles of ancient Greece and the Hebrew prophets. In modern ethnography it has been used with overtones of either; therefore it can perhaps be argued that there is no 'incorrect' use of the word prophet, because there is no exclusively 'correct' use. The confusion with which we now have to deal arises less from incorrectness as from an overburdened use of language. We can see this by examining very briefly some variants of prophets found in the social anthropology of eastern Africa.

Evans-Pritchard was one of the first, if not the first anthropologist to adapt 'prophet' to religious figures in eastern Africa when he employed it in his description of the Nuer *guk* in preference to the pejorative 'witch-doctor', then commonly used in administrative writing of the pre-war period. As applied to the Nuer, 'prophet' had a specific meaning, as 'a man possessed by a spirit of some kind . . . prophets have nothing to do with magic. They are the mouthpieces of the Gods.'[2] Evans-Pritchard's own understanding of prophets was influenced by Robertson Smith, whose nineteenth-century description of ancient Semitic life struck a resonant chord with Evans-Pritchard's observations of the twentieth-century Nuer.[3] Evans-Pritchard seems to have been particularly struck by Robertson Smith's description of Isaiah as a political oracle speaking at times of international crisis when Israel was threatened by the world's mightiest empires.[4] Yet Evans-Pritchard's definition was derived from the Nuer context – where magic, divination and prophecy were distinguished from each other – and it was *not* presented as a general definition of African prophets. He later elaborated the Nuer prophets' political and religious roles in separate studies, presenting them on the one hand as organizers of resistance to external threats, and on the other as figures speaking for God to man.[5] This fortuitous separation of the roles in effect provided two different models.

The precision of Evans-Pritchard's language not only reflected the internal distinctions Nuer made, but maintained an analytical distance between other spiritual and religious figures: put simply, Nuer prophets are not comparable to Zande witch-doctors and oracles, nor can they easily be subsumed under the same category. This precision has sometimes been sacrificed in the anthropological search for a broadly-defined set of terms by which appropriate comparisons could be made. Such is the case in Beattie and Middleton's influential collection on *Spirit Mediumship and Society in Africa*, in which an established anthropological terminology is adopted, defining spirit possession as trance interpreted as control by an external spirit, and spirit mediumship as possession by which a person becomes an intelligible 'intermediary between spirits and men'. Not only were prophets placed within this broad definition of spirit mediumship (based partly on Evans-Pritchard's description of spirit possession among the Nuer), but prophecy was bracketed with divination of the future in the figure of the 'prophet-diviner'. Though it is not explicitly stated, what appears to distinguish a diviner from a 'prophet-diviner' is the latter's social and political role, 'especially in the context of rapid social and cultural change'. In this respect the prophets of the Nuer and Lugbara are seen as comparable to the leaders of separatist churches and cargo cults.[6] Middleton elaborated this theme for the Lugbara in his descriptions of the diviner Rembe, who arose outside of the Lugbara 'moral community' (defined as the field of social relations contained within a single social system). He appeared to them as a prophet not only through his innovations in divination and social organization, but in his organizing a response to various crises associated with the advent of colonial conquest.[7] The Lugbara and Nuer prophets are thus made implicitly comparable because of their alleged social and political roles during a period of colonial crisis, even though their sources of inspiration and their activities were quite different.

This seems to be the same criterion Peristiany used when he discovered prophets among the Pokot, where no prophets were previously thought to exist. Peristiany describes his Pokot *werkoyon* as 'a prophet with great magical powers' who claims 'to lead his people in times of danger'. The *werkoi* receive and interpret visions, sometimes of the past or the future, rather in the fashion recently described by Malcolm Ruel for Kuria seers;[8] that is to say the ability to interpret visions is inherent, but the visions themselves are not necessarily direct communications from a spirit or spirits. There seems little here to justify the term prophet at all. Peristiany writes of his encounter with a Pokot *werkoyon* in terms of a magicians' duel, which finds no echoes in the known experiences of either Hebrew or Nuer prophets. Yet the implicit comparison between Peristiany's and Evans-Pritchard's prophets is their place within the political structure. As with Evans-Pritchard, so with Peristiany, the prophet transcends political fragmentation and represents a larger political identity, 'especially during moments of crisis.'[9]

In these two derivations from Evans-Pritchard a figure is a 'prophet' essentially if he meets certain structural and historical criteria, of standing outside or between political segments in a time of externally induced crisis. Not surprisingly this presentation of the prophet as a charismatic leader arising at times of stress to offer a new order, a new vision of society, is much favoured by historians of eastern Africa. Because such visions appear in some respects to be future-oriented, it is the 'diviner' who is most often translated into the prophet, even if only as a 'prophet-diviner'. A clearly stated example of this is John Lamphear's recent account of the role of a 'diviner lineage' in Turkana resistance to British conquest in northwestern Kenya. In the mid-nineteenth century a diviner (Turkana *emuron*, pl. *ngimurok*) of the Meturona lineage, named Lokerio, acquired a wide reputation among Turkana as a 'dreamer'. So successful was he in foretelling the success of Turkana cattle and camel raids against neighbouring peoples during a period of rapid territorial expansion, that he came to be known as the most prominent of the *Ngimurok Aakuj* – 'Diviners of God'. In Turkana explanations of their own history Lokerio is credited with eclipsing the elders as the focus of 'corporate authority' at this time; thus transforming the previous role of the diviner into a more centralizing political authority, with close connections to the military organization of the warrior age-grades. After Lokerio's death (*c.* 1880) other diviners were able to maintain this influence, their new pattern of authority being consolidated by the 'crisis' presented by the beginnings of British conquest

in the early 1900s.[10] Similar accounts, again initially associated with
the upheavals of territorial and sectional wars and then reinforced in
reaction to the British conquest in eastern Africa, have been provided
for the emergence of 'prophetic leadership' among the Maasai and the
Nandi, discussed in this volume by Waller (Chapter 2) and Anderson
(Chapter 8).[11] In the Turkana, Maasai and Nandi examples the role
of the 'prophet' has been presented as innovative in connection with
new political challenges.

Bernardi's monograph, *The Mugwe*, follows a different line, more
like Evans-Pritchard's 'mouthpieces of the Gods'. Here an institution
is described by Meru sources as being like a 'King', a 'Kabaka', an
'Archbishop', and even as a 'queen of the bees', but the ethnographer
translates *Mugwe* as 'prophet, in the sense of a man who, inspired by
God, leads his people'. The subsequent description of various *Agwe*
reveals only one case of a diviner who calls himself *Mugwe* and claims
direct inspiration from God, yet who is seen as distinct from 'the *Mugwe*
proper'. Otherwise all other *Agwe* come from certain families, are
elected and undergo specific training before succeeding to their
hereditary positions. They foster the general welfare by their blessing
and their goodness; therefore they must be persons of outstanding moral
character. The *Mugwe*'s political position in relation to the age-set
system and young warriors was subsequently eclipsed by the new hierarchy of administrative chiefs which the colonial government imposed.[12]
In contrast to the studies of prophets already cited, here is a prophet
who is not called forth by a period of rapid political and social change,
but who goes into decline because of such change. If one were to retain
the Old Testament parallel which Bernardi introduced, one would be
more inclined to call the *Mugwe* a judge or a priest. Each implies the
same principles of heredity, election, training, moral leadership and
safeguarding of tradition which Bernardi describes; yet they neither
require divine inspiration nor exclude it entirely.

Godfrey Lienhardt's treatment of prophets among the Dinka is a
more subtle approach to the study of divine inspiration. Instead of
'prophet' he retains the Dinka term 'man of Divinity' (*ran nhialic*), with
its echoes of 'man of God', one of the older biblical terms for prophet.
Men of Divinity are inspired by both clan and free divinities and are
recognized through the truth of their words, especially by their ability
to bring about an event by saying, or even just thinking it. Unlike
Evans-Pritchard's Nuer prophets, but more like the historical Nuer
prophets than either Evans-Pritchard or Lienhardt knew at the time,
the true man of Divinity among the Dinka is best known for creating

the experience of peace within his community, and for extending that experience of peace across political, territorial and even linguistic boundaries.[13]

Wendy James's study of moral knowledge, religion and power among the Uduk addresses an altogether different problem in relation to spiritual activity: the reception and transformation of the prophetic *idea* as it crosses different frontiers. The Uduk of the Sudan–Ethiopian border have been confronted throughout this century with a variety of demanding theologies (Nilotic, Christian and Muslim), all 'competing sources of power in this political no-man's land'. Nilotic ideas of prophecy were introduced mainly from the Western Nilotic-speaking Meban, neighbours to the Nuer, Dinka and Uduk alike. Their most famous prophet, Leina, bore all the hallmarks of other Nilotic prophets in his direct contact with a divinity and his alleged control over life and death through word and thought. The Uduk, however, perceived him according to their own idioms of life and death. Even while he was alive Leina was seen as a risen spirit, a man who had died and then reappeared in another country. Leina and his acolytes were not received as messengers of a benevolent universal Divinity, but as manifestations of a dangerous power which had to be contained in order to be controlled, mainly through the diagnostic efforts of Uduk Ebony diviners.[14]

The variety of 'prophets' thus found in eastern Africa is indeed bewildering and defies easy amalgamation within a single analytical category. There are prophets who are seized by spirits and prophets who are elected by heredity; prophets who are inspired and prophets who are instructed; prophets who have nothing to do with divination and prophets for whom divination is their daily bread and butter; prophets who are superior to diviners and prophets who are contained by diviners; prophets who combat sorcery and prophets who are themselves sorcerers; prophets who are confined to a single society and prophets who transcend social and political boundaries; prophets who are radical innovators and prophets who are transmitters of tradition; prophets who are brought forth by crisis and prophets who are destroyed by crisis; prophets of war and prophets of peace. It is clear that these studies do not all address the same problems and phenomena. Despite situating prophets in the context of specific periods of change, only a few authors attempt to represent the historical development of prophetic offices, ideas, language or idioms, the interplay between the 'traditional' and the new, the past with the present and the future, which was such a marked feature of prophecy in the ancient world. A brief survey of the genealogy of prophets and prophecy in antiquity will not only reveal the complexity of ideas involved, but will suggest more precise ways in which we can employ these terms in our discussion of Africa's recent history.

The genealogy of terms in classical & biblical scholarship

There was a wide range of divinatory and oracular activity in the Greco-Roman world. Contemporary philosophers made a distinction between technical divination, which was learned through specific training and was applied to the reading of signs, sacrifices, dreams and omens; and natural divination, which came as direct inspiration through the aid of trance, ecstasy or visions. Direct inspiration was associated with, though not confined to great oracular shrines. The cult personnel at these sacred places held the official titles of *promantis*, *hypophetes*, and *prophetes* (fem. *prophetis*): 'announcers', 'spokesmen' or, more technically, the ones who spoke 'in place of or on behalf of the god'. The prophet either interpreted oracular utterances or spoke them in response to stated questions. The questions often concerned the immediate future, but the prophet's utterances were not exclusively predictive; nor were they necessarily made in a state of frenzy. Philosophic opinion was divided over whether the god enhanced the prophet's mind through a divine spark, or suspended the prophet's reason altogether. The earliest depictions of Apolline oracles indicate controlled trances; attributions of ecstasy seemed to have increased only later, especially in the early centuries of the Christian era.[15]

The general term *mantis* was applied to all forms of diviner, soothsayer, seer and prophet. Mantic activity included both technical and natural forms of divination: those who manipulated lots and read signs as well as those who were in direct contact with a deity. While not every mantis was a prophet, every prophet was a mantis.[16] The term prophet acquired a more generalized application in non-religious contexts, so that philosophers were sometimes described as the prophets (spokesmen or interpreters) of nature.[17] Thus a nuanced language of prophecy was available to post-exilic Jewish scholars when they began to translate and comment upon their own scriptures in Greek.

There is clear evidence in the Old Testament of a wide variety of mantic figures in ancient Judaism. What is not so clear are the distinctions between them. There are separate terms for seer or visionary (*ro'eh* and *hozeh*), diviner or soothsayer (*qozem*), holy man or man of God (*ish-ha'elohim*), and one who is either called by God or announces the message of God (*nabi'*). There is considerable debate about which of these figures acted independently and which were part of public, urban, court or Temple cults; whether there was a clear distinction between central and peripheral inspiration; or whether the different terms referred to specific social and territorial types, as between nomadic and settled communities or the northern and southern kingdoms. The term *nabi'*, which now carries clear overtones of the lone, usually ecstatic, social and political critic, originally described the institutional prophet connected to the sanctuary and court in monarchical times, not a 'charismatically independent' figure. There is also considerable disagreement over whether the Hebrew prophets were ecstatics, and if so which ones and in what form.[18]

The variety of social roles of these mantic figures has been obscured very largely through the editorial process of the Deuteronomic writers during the Babylonian exile. Deuteronomy contains what Blenkinsopp calls 'a first sketch for a doctrine of prophecy', which emphasizes prophecy as a native Israelite phenomenon modelled on the ministry of Moses. Moses becomes retroactively the supreme prophet (the 'man of God'), though he is unique since he is the only one to whom God spoke face-to-face (Numbers 12: 6–8). Subsequent prophets are presented in the Deuteronomic mould as being concerned with the law and the covenant in a direct line from Moses. Prophetic books were also claimed as sources of history, and a knowledge of *the past* and the inspired interpretation of past prophecy soon became firmly associated with the prophetic calling.[19] Our biblical sources thus contain evidence of considerable editing and rewriting by later generations to make past prophets fit new theories of history.

The development of ideas about prophets in Judaism took place as part of a centuries' long dialogue and debate between classical paganism, post-exilic Judaism and early Christianity. The Jewish adaptation of *prophetes* in their own translations of Hebrew Scripture began as early as the second century BC. The selection and classification of prophetic writings as canonical continued well into the early Christian era, after the second century AD. Throughout this period Jewish authors were well versed in the Greek philosophic texts concerning prophecy. In the second and third centuries AD the language of Greek prophecy and pagan oracles became the language of communication and debate between pagan, Jewish and Christian communities concerning prophecy, revelation and ideas of a supreme god: not only in the

Christian polemics which turned the philosophers' and oracles' own words against them, but within the mixed urban populations of Greek Asia. This was not only part of the Christian appropriation of Jewish prophetic imagery and pagan religious language, it was also a continuation of the Jewish historiographic effort and refinement of their own prophetic writings.[20]

Thus, at an early stage conflicting ideas about prophecy were discussed in the same terms and language. This was particularly marked in Jewish and early Christian theology, which drew on the same corpus of Scripture, but classified them in different ways. A recent study by John Barton suggests that in Judaism 'prophets' at one time incorporated *all* authors of Scripture, not just those now identified as the canonical prophets – the 'duly authorized successors of Moses' whose expertise was derived from their command of the past rather than from their knowledge of the future. Out of this came the prophets as *tradents*, transmitters of tradition, the teachers of moral law. The Christian identification of prophets, however, emphasized prophets as predictors, looking forward to, and therefore justifying the Messiah. The authority of the ancient prophets rested not just on their antiquity, nor on their bearing witness to God's will, but on the fulfilment of their predictions in the person of Jesus Christ. Prophecy 'in the characteristically Christian sense' came to mean 'predictions about the fulfilment of God's promises.' Christian prophecy became increasingly concerned with apocalyptic texts, with 'prophecy = prediction' being 'a more or less self-evident equation for most of Christian history'. Barton goes further than this in concluding that all post-exilic reconstructions of prophecy (Christian as well as Jewish) masked irreconcilable differences under the single term 'prophet'. The modern tendency to assume that challenge, protest and moral seriousness were recognized as the distinguishing marks of prophecy in all ages exhibits a lack of 'a sense of historical perspective or cultural change'. In his view, the canonical prophets and the *nebi'im* cannot be equated; either one or the other can be called 'prophets', but not both. He is willing to accept the possibility that the 'classical' prophets were not prophets at all, but 'lone geniuses whom any generic title belittles.'[21]

Islam builds upon both Hebrew and Christian traditions of prophecy, but confines prophets firmly to the pre-Islamic past. In Islam it is said that the books of the prophets are there, but they have been altered and are therefore incorrect. Muhammad, alone, gave God's words unaltered and is the Seal of the Prophets. He represents the culmination rather than the fulfilment of prophecy. Islamic prophecy, therefore, is not concerned with prediction, but with fitting the past into an historical pattern which is related to Muhammad's revelation.[22] This presents students of modern Islam with some problems of terminology. Clearly there are figures in the prophetic mould who followed Muhammad, yet religious sensibility requires that they are not labelled as 'prophets'.

The above summary helps us to understand why there is such a widespread disagreement and misunderstanding of the terms prophet and prophecy, even when drawing models from the same Old Testament sources. There are strong images associated with different traditions and modes of interpretation of sacred texts, and scholarly models are frequently built uncritically on these images. Ideas of apocalypse and millenarianism associated with charisma, crisis, social critique and social marginality still dominate many discussions of prophecy outside the biblical context. One Old Testament scholar has complained of modern meanings of 'prophet':

> The emphasis may be on prediction, emotional preaching, social activism, or the power to enlighten, to communicate insight, as with the leader of a cult group. The older meaning of biblical interpreter, in use among the Puritans of the sixteenth and seventeenth centuries, has survived among evangelicals, though here the stress is generally on millenarian and apocalyptic interpretation. Rather curiously, the term is also quite often used of millenarian cults by sociologists of religion. In no case is a preferred connotation based on a critical-historical and typological study of the phenomenon in the Hebrew Bible.[23]

If the terms 'prophet' and 'prophecy' are to retain any descriptive power and analytical value in historical literature, then they must be used with care. Otherwise no author can assume that the terms will automatically be understood as intended; nor can readers be sure of an author's intent. In the section which follows we will attempt to detach 'prophet' from some of the predominant ideas and images which now surround it in history and the social sciences. We will then outline our own approach to the study of prophets, before analysing specific themes which arise from this collection of papers.

Charisma, crisis & social critique

It should already be clear that neither prediction nor ecstasy were defining characteristics of prophetic figures either in the Greco-Roman world or in pre-exilic Israel. It also should be clear that apocalyptic visions of the future and millenarian aspirations apply only to very few prophets in antiquity and assumed commanding importance mainly through the Christian appropriation and interpretation of prophecy. The refashioning of the past to fit a prophetic model, or the editing of prophetic texts to more nearly reflect the processes of history may distort what we know or can ever know about what prophets did in their own times; but these are integral parts of any prophetic tradition which reflects seriously upon prophecy. The study of prophets must include the study of prophecy; and the study of prophecy incorporates later interpretations as well as contemporary reactions. The edited images of the past have had a profound impact on scholarly interpretations, not only of the history of Hebrew prophecy, but of analogous episodes and movements throughout the world.

Robertson Smith's contribution to the study of Hebrew prophets was to recognize that they spoke to their own, rather than to some future time. He took the prophetic books as accurate representations of .their times, and accepted many post-edited perceptions of crisis as contemporary. This acceptance of crisis has been central to many other interpretations of Hebrew prophecy and forms part of Max Weber's influential sociological theory of charismatic leadership. In Weber's discussion of types of authority – traditional, charismatic and bureaucratic – charismatic leaders appear as revolutionaries who break with tradition. In their pure form they are free from family and social ties as well as economic interests. Their call appears to come from out of nowhere, and their success is measured to the extent that they can persuade enough followers of their charisma and bind that following to their authority. Successful charismatic leadership dispenses with old rules, creates new obligations and brings about a radical reorientation of attitudes and values. The stimulus to the rise of charismatic authority is usually found in a crisis involving conflict and suffering.[24] Weber's interpretation of the prophets in ancient Judaism emphasizes the religious message of the prophets, but it is a message which emerges in times of internal social critique or, more particularly, in the world politics of the great powers which threatened Israel. But for that 'the prophets could not have emerged'.[25]

Weber's presentation of an ideal type of charismatic leader very quickly leads to contradictions when applied to specific figures whose biographical details survive. It is now generally agreed that the prophets of Israel were not free from traditional constraints and certainly performed within known traditions concerning inspiration and prophetic language. 'The prophets are neither lone wolves nor bearers of any absolutely anti-traditional and anti-institutional charisma; rather charisma and tradition are bound to one another and permit no more than theoretical differentiation'.[26] Many who have struggled to retain charisma as an analytic category have become aware of these difficulties. A recent collaborative study of African Islam attempted to apply charismatic authority to the analysis of 'a particular style of exemplary leadership, saintly or prophetic', and felt that on the whole it 'seemed to conform to the Weberian ideal type in some basic respects: a miracle at the point of origin, recognized by a clientele in the grip of profound social crisis'. Yet there are important divergences as well. None of the alleged Muslim charismatics broke from Islamic tradition; all were informed about (and tried to adhere to) the legal texts of the *shari'a*; and all were profoundly worldly, especially in economic matters. A further difficulty arises with the identification of 'crisis'. It was in the interest of reformist leaders to assert a crisis which justified their intervention; yet in many cases they did not *respond* to a crisis but worked hard to *create* a crisis. The figures under study clearly did not conform to the ideal type, and were qualified as the 'not quite charismatic'.[27]

Dorothy Emmet observed that if Weber's definition of charismatic authority is applied to prophets, it would have to be restricted 'to a type of messianic or millenarian preacher or revolutionary', and this would exclude the Hebrew prophets.[28] Weber was, in fact, less interested in the analysis of specific charismatic leaders than in the study of charismatic movements in general. His perception of crisis as fundamental to such movements is shared by many historians; thus the motivating engine of crisis continues to drive on where Weber's theory of charismatic authority will not operate. There is a respectable tradition in historical writing of defining millenarian leaders as prophets, which has also served to further reinforce and limit the perceived role of the prophet to that of 'crisis leader'. In millenarian studies prophecy is linked with the religion of the oppressed and the socially marginal. It is thus almost exclusively confined to social and political critique. This is the case in Keith Thomas' discussion of religious prophecy in seventeenth-century England, which he interprets in terms of radical political propaganda and validating myths which mask a break with tradition.[29] Here, the label 'prophet' offered protection from the oppression of a dominant political and religious dogma: a 'prophet', as divinely inspired, was above the written word of Scripture, and could therefore operate as a critic of society with relative impunity from prosecution.

In his study of 'prophets of rebellion', Michael Adas discarded the charismatic formulation as being ambiguous and fundamentally circular, providing little analytical precision. In rejecting charisma Adas adopted the term 'prophet', although in doing so he acknowledged the problems presented by his chosen terminology. Adas is careful to define prophecy in terms of millenarian visions, and to further confine his comparative cases to those in which violence against foreign (colonial) domination played a prominent role, and where prophet-led rebellion can be characterized as having been inspired by an urge for social 'revitalization'.[30] The notion of revitalization, which Adas borrows from Anthony Wallace,[31] is underpinned by a strong call for moral restoration, and in this sense reflects the tone of the canonical prophets. While Adas's portrayal of anti-colonial prophets has obvious echoes in the many prophets who emerged in eastern Africa to inspire, organize and lead resistance to colonial conquest around the turn of the present century, it is important to emphasize the moral aspect of the prophetic message. Are the prophets of rebellion highlighted by Adas true moralists, as is generally claimed of such Old Testament prophets as Amos and Isaiah, whose role in life was to invoke and pronounce a particular moral code as divinely received? Or are they individuals who are placed in the role of moralist *by* the rebellion itself, and therefore who define the moral code *for* the rebellion?

The attribution of millennial concerns to some prophets may, of course, be accurate. But we must not confine our study of prophets and prophecy to times of crisis, social disadvantage, radical action and millenarian expectations, nor strain the evidence to provide recognized prophets each with their own crisis. What these sociological and historical models propose is that the situation defines the prophet. We suggest, on the contrary, that the prophet may define the situation.

Prophets revealed

We have so far identified two central problems from the wide-ranging anthropological and historical literature of prophets and prophecy in eastern Africa. The first concerns the haphazard and indiscriminate use of terms and the misleading comparisons that this has fostered. The second is the significant emphasis given to the study of prophets in the context of political crisis or radical social action. To deal with the first we must adopt a more cautious terminology and become sensitive to specific differences rather than generalized similarities. To deal with the second we must make an effort to locate prophets in their social contexts, and to understand how social perceptions of prophets and prophetic actions change over time.

Douglas H. Johnson & David M. Anderson

It will be useful if we approach a new understanding of 'prophet' by first introducing three general terms: mantic, prophetic idiom, and prophetic tradition. The prophet makes declarations through inspired speech, but these concern public, and not just private matters. The manner of inspiration and form of pronouncement will vary according to the idioms available to the prophet or which the prophet refines or creates, and according to the tradition (expectation) within which a prophet operates. Our contributors do not all adopt this terminology, but we suggest that the employment of these distinctions will allow a more meaningful comparison and discussion of the cases they offer, from which we draw our main examples.

First, *mantic* as a generic term is already commonly used by biblical and classical scholars, although admittedly with various shades of meaning. Here we follow Nora Chadwick's use whereby mantic refers to the possession, cultivation and declaration of *knowledge*, whether of the future or of the commonly unknown present or past.[32] This can include diviners, healers, seers (those endowed with insight) and prophets. It encompasses both inherent powers and learned skills. It is not limited to divination or prediction, and replaces the overly-bureaucratic terms 'spiritual' or 'ritual' experts, whose ranks have often been opened to those with no clear association with a spirit or a rite, or no obvious expertise.

Second, while the term prophecy can be understood to mean inspired speech, this can be enacted through a variety of *prophetic idioms*: religious or spiritual modes of behaviour which become established through the inspiration or activities of prophetic figures. Such idioms can change over time as a direct result of the example a successful prophet may provide, the changes in perception which new events might create, or through an exposure to new idioms from different religious traditions. Other mantics will also operate within their own idioms, and it may be the case that one type will sometimes appear to behave like another: but it is important to recognize the idiom within which the practitioner is socially located.

The activities of certain spirit mediums in relation to external definitions of prophecy offer examples of this overlap. In his analysis of the Holy Spirit Movement in northern Uganda, led by the spirit medium Alice Lakwena, Tim Allen has convincingly argued against the interpretation of Lakwena as a prophet.[33] Rather, he demonstrates that Lakwena functioned within a local tradition of spirit mediumship, widely recognized and understood as such, and fully in keeping with the practices of other female mediums, although given an eclectic character by Lakwena herself. In this volume, Iris Berger's study of spirit mediums in the pre-colonial interlacustrine region (Chapter 3) further illustrates the ways in which an existing and socially pervasive idiom can emerge into greater prominence in response to historical events without necessarily altering the indigenous understanding of the tradition which underpins it. The confusion of terms in this region evidently arises directly from colonial (and Christian) interventions. Holger Hansen (Chapter 7) offers an analysis of conflicting colonial interpretations of what many European administrators and missionaries believed to be revolutionary (and therefore subversive and politically threatening) spirit movements. Nyabingi, in common with other mantic-led movements in Uganda, was described in 'anti-establishment' terms by the colonial government, although it seems to have corresponded (like the Holy Spirit Movement) more directly to a local idiom of spirit mediumship.[34] We therefore see that there can be distinct idioms and traditions of spirit mediumship, of divination, or of healing, as well as those of prophecy; and that internal definitions are likely to be more helpful than externally imposed categories in differentiating between them.

Implied meanings in the ideas and categories imported by Europeans, and frequently passed on to African communities as part of the colonial or Christian message, continue to direct scholarly discussion of mantic phenomena. The heightened language of colonial internal security reports, with their excited references to anarchy, liberation, secret societies and even terrorism, are often given positive values by scholars of anti-colonial resistance. The colonial officer's nightmare of a subversive secret society easily becomes the post-colonialist's millenarian dream. In the rush to sanctify anti-colonial resisters and to rescue their ideology from hostile propaganda, scholars run the risk of rehabilitating the wrong 'prophet', as was done with Kinjikitile and the Maji Maji rising (Wright, Chapter 6). This does not mean that we should overlook or deny the influence of European, Christian or Islamic categories upon African mantic practices. Rather, in recognizing them we should examine the ways in which they may have interacted with indigenous idioms and traditions and contributed to the debates concerning moral knowledge and moral action.[35]

New religions offer their own moral codes which often demand the prohibition of indigenous mantic practice. Colonial legislation often combined Christian and rationalist principles in attempting to redefine good and evil for African subjects. Even in the era of 'indirect rule' long-established practices 'repugnant' to 'civilization' were outlawed by state or church. This had a profound impact on mantic figures, especially in their continuing elaboration of ideas of moral knowledge and moral behaviour – a striking example being the Uduk Ebony diviners in the Sudan.[36] Anti-witchcraft legislation was frequently employed to suppress certain types of mantic activity, as with Nyabingi in colonial Uganda (Hansen, Chapter 7), or with the poison oracles among the Azande in colonial Sudan. Margaret Buckner (Chapter 5) documents some relatively recent changes in Zande mantic practices which are a direct response to legal interventions. She illustrates the complex possibility of a radical innovation (a new prophetic idiom where none had previously existed) being presented within a recognizable tradition (of death and resurrection experiences), despite several contradictions. Here, again, the particularities of a case seem to defy simplistic comparisons at a general level.

In addition to the indirect borrowings from colonial moral codes as a result of legislation and political intervention, there were direct bor-rowings from either Christianity or Islam. In many parts of eastern Africa the term *nabi* was introduced by both Islam and Christianity through the medium of Swahili. It provides a new term by which people can emphasize distinctions between prophets and prominent seers or diviners. In the case of the Kuria a refinement is currently made bet-ween the 'prophets' (*abanaabi*) of the past and the 'seers' (*abarooti*) of the present, even though the term *abanaabi* is not contemporary with the mantic persons it now describes.[37] The question arises whether the restriction of *abanaabi* to figures in the past came about through an appreciation of the essentially historical uses of *nabi* in both the Bible and the Qur'an.

While the notion of prophetic idioms allows for the coexistence of several forms of prophetic inspiration, and stresses the possibility of change over time, our third term draws attention to the continuity of prophetic practices: *prophetic tradition* refers to a community's percep-tion and apprehension of a prophet and prophetic activity, the confirma-tion of forms of prophetic behaviour through the expectations of the community. Most importantly, a prophetic tradition acts as a template against which the retroactive recognition of prophetic figures may be accepted or confirmed, both for those who did consciously work to estab-lish their own prophetic idiom and those who did not. The prevailing perception of a prophetic tradition often fosters the deliberate imitation of previously established patterns of behaviour by successive prophets.

The force which prophetic traditions can exert is illustrated by two examples from practising Muslim communities where, of course, orthodoxy insists that no modern prophets can arise. Muslim mantics may imitate the prophet Muhammad, but they cannot claim inspiration equal to his. Some, such as Sayyid Mahammad 'Abdille Hasan of Somaliland, followed the well-established paths of Sufi mysticism, combining disciplined asceticism and study to obtain insight into the Qur'an.[38] A less orthodox claim was put forward by the Sudanese Mahdi, Muhammad Ahmad. He was also influenced by Sufism, but his pronouncements followed visions and dreams in which he communicated directly with the Prophet Muhammad and assorted Sufi saints. The Mahdi's successor, the Khalifa Abdallahi, claimed a third tier inspiration when he reported visions in which he received the Mahdi's instructions after the latter's death. Both the Mahdi and his Khalifa adapted the Qura'nic model of Muhammad's visitations to suit their specific political circumstances and religious claims. In bolstering his less widely-acknowledged religious authority, however, the Khalifa Abdallahi also co-opted the dreams of others and retained a few 'professional seers' within his entourage and publicized their confirmatory visions.[39]

The assignment of our recommended terminology shifts the emphasis away from broad comparisons of form or function, and instead stresses the possibility of historical change and the reinterpretation of the role of a prophet as well as the meaning of prophecy through time. In short, we must avoid imposing any particular 'doctrine of prophecy' (to return to Blenkinsopp's phrase above) for eastern Africa, and recognize the existence of different types of prophetic figure. To do this we have to examine the history of prophets more closely, paying particular attention (as we have already suggested) to the ethnographic constructions of 'prophets'. This 'ethnographic archaeology' – the excavation of terms and ideas within each society – is a common feature of several of the essays which follow, focusing attention upon *internal* (as distinct from imposed or external) definitions of types of mantic.

This brings us finally to the definition of *prophet*. We suggest, to begin with, that this is an inspired figure. However, not all inspired figures should be known as prophets. It is necessary to separate the prophet from the diviner who is visited by dreams, the seer who reveals the unknown, the spirit medium who communes with those beyond to bring messages to the living. Thus, for the Maasai, Waller (Chapter 2) elaborates the vast range of *loibonok* (mantic) activity and argues that only certain *laibon* can be acknowledged to have any genuine prophetic powers. Even then, *laibon* prophets might still be suspected of involvement in sorcery, and this would separate them categorically from Nuer prophets who are renowned for their anti-sorcery activities. Similarly, mantic categories expressed among the Kalenjin-speaking peoples of Kenya's Western Highlands reveal a set of related and sometimes overlapping practitioners, with marked historical change in the internal understanding of categories in the recent past promoted by the incursion of Maasai influences. Nonetheless, clear internal distinctions are applied to those few mantics who are perceived to have been inspired for the guidance of the wider moral community (Anderson, Chapter 8). Along the Kenya coast there are a number of different types of mantics – Muslim and non-Muslim – whose diagnostic powers stem from an ability to interpret different types of signs. Though these mantics are often involved in some form of prediction, their practices are principally divinatory and therapeutic (Sperling, Chapter 4). The strong local presence of the Islamic understanding of prophecy as firmly confined to the past may in fact have reinforced the separation of prediction from prophecy among Muslim Swahili.

In our view – which is supported by the internal definitions proposed by many communities in eastern Africa – a prophet *must* be concerned with the wider moral community at a social or political level. The moral community which is the prophet's concern is that community whose members have reciprocal moral obligations to each other. (Here we have adopted a more fluid and less exclusive community than implied by Middleton, in keeping with the way historians now approach the study of social relations within and between communities.) Moral communities can and do extend across political boundaries and need not be defined exclusively by kinship, language, ethnicity or territory. The bounds of a moral community are not necessarily fixed; indeed, periods of dramatic expansion or contraction of those bounds, when moral relations are most likely to be disputed, are precisely those times when a prophet's activities are given the highest profile and have their greatest impact upon political and social affairs. This returns us to the idea of the relationship between prophets and crisis, exemplified in eastern Africa by the role attributed to Kinjikitile in the Maji Maji rising of 1905. But, as Marcia Wright notes (Chapter 6), our knowledge of Kinjikitile – who appears to have been only a minor figure – has been framed entirely by the rebellion. Thus history may remember the prophet principally in relation to crisis or change, and such events may well be crucial in the development of an individual prophetic career, but this does not define the prophet as being *solely* concerned with crisis.

The moral authority of the prophet carries force *because* it is believed to be inspired by a divinity or other source of spiritual or moral knowledge that influences the destiny of the community. The utterances of prophets need not always be directly predictive: they will also encompass commentary upon the past, and may be interpreted as offering guidance on the regulation of social and political practice in the present. This more pervasive relation sustaining the moral community places the prophet in a social context that is much broader than mere reaction to crisis: the prophet is also a barometer of social and political behaviour. It is in this latter role that a prophet can respond to the 'prophetic moment', to use Marcia Wright's terms (Chapter 6), and becomes the 'commissioning agent' of action without necessarily being the formulator of a new ideology.

Inspiration from higher or external authorities can offer the prophet some protection from those whom his commentary might criticize. This was true for the pre-exilic prophets of ancient Judaism, and also for the glut of so-called prophets found at times of political upheaval in seventeenth-century England. For a prophet to operate, and for prophecy to have any meaning, there must be a community who is willing to listen and prepared to respond. In Africa, however, colonial governments were not willing members of such audiences and were reluctant to be equal partners in any dialogue. Despite their legal and political interventions in local moral debates, they held themselves apart from the moral community within which prophets operated. Insofar as an audience both *recognized* and *bestowed* authority on a prophet by engaging in dialogue, the very act of listening granted a legitimacy to prophets which governments, for the most part, wished to withold. Thus the monotonous regularity with which colonial governments responded through repression.

The suggestion that prophecy should be connected to the notion of a moral community is not without its difficulties in eastern Africa. Both Maasai and Kalenjin commonly perceive their *loibonok* and *orkoiik* as operating 'beyond' the moral community they seek to serve. They are, in Paul Spencer's description, 'outsiders' whose authority often stands in direct opposition to that of the elders.[40] In some circumstances, mantic figures might even be involved in a struggle with the elders to gain the moral high ground – to claim the right to moral judgement of community actions and behaviour.[41] Prophets, therefore, do not hold a monopoly on moral judgement, although the most successful can achieve this. They are likely to be challenged by rival prophets, and by 'dissenters' or 'disbelievers' within the wider community. To stand 'outside' the community – whether through living at a distance in a forbidding or hostile part of the land, or by being perceived as standing above the moral rules governing the behaviour of 'ordinary' persons through contact with a higher being (the source of inspiration) – does not necessarily exclude the prophetic figure from a role in shaping the moral community. However, in the case of the *loibonok*, we would need to be satisfied that the individuals were perceived as having a real moral authority over the community. Richard Waller's disaggregation of the *loibonok* indeed suggests that many did not have any such recognition.

Something must therefore be said about the process of prophecy, which (contrary to Karen Blixen's expectations) is a dialogue between prophet and audience. Robin Lane Fox has shown how question and answer at oracular shrines did contribute to the philosophical discussion of the nature of a supreme god in the first three centuries AD. Robert Carroll has brought the process of question and answer to the fore in his analysis of Israelite prophecy, although he errs (we think) when he states that prophets both asked the questions and provided the answers and were *always* intolerant of scepticism.[42] Prophets not only provide answers to their own questions, they respond to questions put to them. Scepticism is something that all prophets must deal with, and it is through scepticism that prophetic pronouncements are progressively refined. Thomas Overholt's model of prophetic activity is built on this type of response. As he puts it, 'a prophet speaks in a concrete historical situation and elicits a response from his audience on the basis of their judgements concerning what he says about it'. A mark of a prophet's authority is his 'ability to clarify and articulate what the people who follow him have themselves begun to feel about their particular situation. His utterances are experienced as having explanatory power.' This explanatory power is maintained through the prophet's assimilation of the audience's response, producing further revelations, presumably by putting questions to his own source of inspiration.[43] Prediction can play a role in this process, in that prediction provides a way of verifying or falsifying prophets' larger claims, demonstrating whether or not they really do know the truth. Predictions of the immediate future can also be a way of influencing events, expressing a particular stance which the prophet wants the community to adopt.[44] It can also be the case that prediction is remembered where other prophetic commentary is forgotten precisely because prediction can be verified by history.

The study of prophets is thus essentially historical, not structural. To understand prophecy the prophet must be identified as an individual and located in time and space. Historical context gives life to prophets by emphasizing their engagement in *real* events, and the location of the various meanings attached to prophecies through history allows us to evaluate changes in the power, authority and significance of prophecy. The biographical study of prophets offers one way of moving towards a more historical (and less structural) analysis. But any biographer is likely to encounter a series of different or even conflicting versions of both the prophet and prophecies. This point is illustrated in Douglas Johnson's account of the prophecies variously recounted concerning Ngundeng and the battle of Pading (Chapter 9),[45] and in the layered and multiple interpretations of Waiyaki discussed here by John Lonsdale (Chapter 11). Yet it must be stressed that alternative versions of a prophetic life need not imply contradiction. Versions of a prophet's life, along with the meaning attached to prophecy, will vary according to the perspective of the audience. Biography can allow us to see more clearly what it is that prophets actually *do*, but it can also expose the changing evaluations put upon prophecy by the wider community. The place of the prophet in society can be ambiguous and can change over time, and it should not be surprising to discover that a wide variety of activities and roles are encompassed within the life of a single prophet.

In this respect there has perhaps been a tendency in all literature on mantics to emphasize the mystical and to ignore the prosaic. Prophets are surely mystical characters, but even mystics must eat. All mantics, not least prophets, provide services for which they are paid, whether in kind or cash. Gifts are left at shrines for the priestess or guardian of the oracle; medicines prescribed by the diviner or healer following divination, must be paid for before they can be administered; livestock must be delivered to the diviner or witch-finder after the case has been investigated but before a verdict is issued; and in some cases in eastern Africa, it has even been known for politically powerful mantics to exact a regular tithe from the community. Mantics therefore capitalize (quite literally) upon opportunity. They provide a service which others may hire at a charge. Some are sedentary, and will be visited by petitioners within their geographic constituency, whilst others are itinerant, touting their services from place to place. That mantics move in search of new constituencies relatively often is revealed by the many histories of prophets and diviners which portray them as 'foreigners' or recent arrivals from another community. In short, the mantic is ultimately selling a skill and must find customers. Mobility and flexibility are therefore common characteristics of the most successful and durable of mantics.

Flexibility often implies the combination of a number of mantic roles by a single individual, and this can add a further complication to the definition of categories. It is not impossible, for example, for a diviner to become a prophet, and in the categories of the Maasai *loibonok* and the Kalenjin *orkoiik* it is evident such distinctions have become blurred at points in the past and in relation to particular individuals (see Waller, Chapter 2 and Anderson, Chapter 8). When such shifts take place validating myths may be constructed around the transformation to offer an explanation that fits locally accepted ideas of category, activity, role and status.[46] More commonly, a mantic who aspires to the status of prophet might have to entertain the humbler arts of divination in order to make his living. Reputation can only be gained through experience over time, and so there can be many a prophet who was once known as a diviner. Just so, according to Scripture, did Samuel make a living as a seer prior to persuading Saul to become king of Israel.

While such transformations must be fully acknowledged, there remain important distinctions between different types of mantic that are recognized within eastern African communities. Oracles who speak, diviners who reveal and prophets who foretell are separate categories widely reflected in the internal definitions employed throughout the region. Even where powers seem to overlap, internal definitions often comprehend important differences that might not be immediately observable to the outsider. For example, while many categories of mantic are held to have powers of revelation and prediction, like prophets, they are understood to perform these tasks by different techniques. Indeed, some barriers between categories are extremely difficult to cross legitimately because the 'powers' are held to be technically different. Among many communities the most fundamental divide exists between powers that are inherited and powers that can be learned or acquired. Where specific lineages or clans are associated with mantic abilities, as in the example of Maasai, 'powers of the head' are passed from generation to generation, all members of the line being assumed to have the potential to mantic authority. Prophecy is most commonly a 'power of the head', for it implies foresight and, like the seer, the prophet's predictions may involve dreams and inspiration. Even where such powers may be manifested through some mechanical aid – the reading of entrails, the tossing of sandals, or even the use of a divination gourd – it is the authority of the 'powers of the head' and not the physical technique employed that determines the outcome. Contrast this with mantic skills that can be learned, the 'powers of the hands' for which the initiate may even have been formally apprenticed. These arts have nothing to do with inheritance or with divine inspiration, but rather the power lies in the skill of manipulating the hands in order to give an appropriate outcome. The use of mechanical aids is here essential, for a poorly skilled practitioner will be unable to manipulate the gourd, stones or sandals effectively. Thus, internal distinctions hinge not simply upon whatever device or method is employed by the mantic, but on how the power is *understood* to be derived.

It must be noted that prophecy has a dynamic quality which is crucially absent in all other mantic practices, especially learned techniques. Prophecy is invariably open to interpretation and manipulation in its contemporary setting, and also through time as the words of the prophet are carried forward from one generation to the next and each seeks to validate or refute the prophecies. Although it may be believed to be divinely inspired, prophecy can therefore never be taken as Holy Writ – it is always open to contestation. This is, of course, what gives prophecy its potency in historical reconstruction. The retroactive validation of prophecy is what gives the prophet historical resonance, illustrating the manner in which prophecy must work *through* time. Prophets may predict the future, yet their words also reveal things about the present and the past. Their knowledge of time precisely connects all three, and offers the seamless web of explanation and justification that individuals and communities often seek of their own lives and histories. We would accordingly argue that what is done with the words of the prophet is historically more important than what those words might actually have been. Hence, the relative lack of data on what prophets in eastern Africa might actually have *said* does not invalidate them as significant historical figures; nor is the lack of an authentic prophetic voice any barrier to the exploration of the historical importance of prophecy.

Where Ambler's account of the enduring but shifting memory of prophets in central Kenya (Chapter 10) illustrates the validity of the above point, Johnson provides a specific example of the variations in the textual forms the accounts of prophecies may take (Chapter 9). Social context, political perspective and the passage of time all here work to provide differing accounts of the same prophecy. The biblical and classical studies that we have already discussed suggest that similar variations in original texts and oral accounts were either amalgamated or ignored in the compilation of our received writings of the 'Ancient Prophets', and that they were sometimes added to by subsequent generations who wished to reflect a particular contemporary interpretation of the words of the prophets. This 'layering' of interpretations creates many complexities for the historian in dealing with prophets and prophecies, but the rivalries, shifts and manipulations it throws up are the very stuff of history. Lonsdale's account of the constructions, deconstructions and reconstructions of the story of Waiyaki (Chapter 11) offers a dramatic and potent example of the effect of this 'layering'. To understand such changes, the historian has to excavate each layer of meaning with considerable care.

The excavation of meaning from the histories of prophets and prophecies should enable us to move away from the oversimplified notion that connects prophets only with crises. The chapters gathered in this volume each endeavour to reconstruct a broader and more carefully contextualized history of prophets and their prophecies; many also look beyond the particular crisis that brought the prophetic figure into historical focus. The book is arranged in three parts. The first section deals with prophetic idioms, the four chapters here demonstrating the interaction of different mantic categories in space and time. The second section offers three chapters on colonial representations of prophets, to show the way that descriptions and interpretive categories were imposed from outside the African cognitive system. The final section offers three chapters which focus upon the histories and interpretations of specific prophets, set in their own contexts.

Each of the contributors here has treated prophets and prophecy historically, yet several writers also acknowledge that the meaning attached to prophetic figures has a relevance for current politics in eastern Africa. Politicians and activists throughout the region still look to prophetic traditions, garnering interpretations of the past in order to provide the validation of prophetic wisdom and heroes for different communities in the present. Waiyaki remains a potent political symbol in central Kenya, and the interpretation to be put on his life is still hotly disputed. In the Western Highlands of Kenya, Koitalel enjoys a similarly ambiguous status. Both Waiyaki and Koitalel, along with Kinjikitile and Mekatilile have been translated from their roles as regional figures onto a wider stage, presented by some as symbols of nationalist heroism. Perhaps the most poignant of all reminders of the enduring political power of historical prophetic figures is the act of the guerrilla commander in Southern Sudan's civil war who, in 1989, placed large quantities of ivory around the Mound of the Nuer prophet Ngundeng, invoking the power, authority and blessing of the prophet upon his own endeavours and marking a symbolic link between the struggles of the past and the struggles of the present.[47] For Ngundeng's modern devotee, even though the future is always uncertain, the conflicts of the past are known and understood and can be recalled to make statements about the present. The prophet might be long dead, but the power of prophecy lives on.

Notes

1. Judith Thurman, *Isak Dinesen. The Life of a Storyteller* (New York, 1982), p. 388.
2. E. E. Evans-Pritchard, 'The Nuer: tribe and clan', *Sudan Notes and Records*, 18, i (1935), p. 55.
3. E. E. Evans-Pritchard, 'Some reminiscences and reflections on fieldwork', in

Witchcraft, Oracles and Magic among the Azande, abridged by Eva Gillies (Oxford, 1976), p. 241.

4. W. Robertson Smith, *The Prophets of Israel and their Place in History* (London, 1897), pp. 295, 331.

5. E. E. Evans-Pritchard, *The Nuer* (Oxford, 1940), and *Nuer Religion* (Oxford, 1956).

6. J. Beattie and J. Middleton, 'Introduction', *Spirit Mediumship and Society in Africa* (London, 1969), pp. xvii, xxiii.

7. J. Middleton, chapter 5 of *Lugbara Religion. Ritual and Authority among an East African People* (London, 1960); 'The Yakan or Allah Water Cult among the Lugbara', *J. R. Anth. Inst.*, 93, i (1961); 'Spirit possession among the Lugbara', in Beattie and Middleton, *Spirit Mediumship*; 'Prophets and rainmakers: the agents of social change among the Lugbara', in T. O. Beidelman (ed.), *The Translation of Culture* (London, 1971).

8. M. Ruel, 'Kuria Seers', *Africa*, 61, iii (1991).

9. John G. Peristiany, 'The ideal and the actual: the role of prophets in the Pokot political system', in J. H. M. Beattie and R. G. Lienhardt (eds), *Studies in Social Anthropology* (Oxford, 1975), pp. 188–9, 196–9, 210–2. The roots of Peristiany's confusion are clearly evident in his discussion of 'Religion and Magic' in an earlier monograph, *The Social Institutions of the Kipsigis* (London, 1939), especially pp. 224–7 (see Anderson, Chapter 8).

10. John Lamphear, *The Scattering Time: Turkana Responses to Colonial Rule* (Oxford, 1992), pp. 29–38; 'Aspects of Turkana' leadership during the era of primary resistance', *J. Afr. Hist.*, 17, ii (1976).

11. J. L. Berntsen, 'Maasai age-sets and prophetic leadership: 1850–1910', *Africa*, 49, ii (1979). For the wide array of powers which members of the Maasai *loibonok* deploy, see Elliot Fratkin, 'The *loibon* as sorcerer: a Samburu *loibon* among the Ariaal Rendille, 1973–87', and Paul Spencer, 'The Loonkidongi prophets and the Maasai: protection racket or incipient state?', both in *Africa*, 61, iii (1991). For a recent discussion of the Nandi case, see David M. Anderson, 'Black mischief: crime, protest and resistance in colonial Kenya', *Historical Journal*, 35 (1993). For a comparison from elsewhere in Africa, see J. Peires, *The Dead Will Arise: Nongqawuse and the Great Xhosa Cattle-Killing Movement of 1856–7* (Berkeley and London, 1989).

12. B. Bernardi, *The Mugwe – A Blessing Prophet: A Study of a Religious and Public Dignitary of the Meru of Kenya* (Kisumu, 1989), especially pp. i–iii (originally issued as *The Mugwe: The Failing Prophet*, London, 1959).

13. G. Lienhardt, *Divinity and Experience: The Religion of the Dinka* (Oxford, 1961).

14. Wendy James, *The Listening Ebony: Moral Knowledge, Religion and Power among the Uduk of Sudan* (Oxford, 1988), especially pp. 182–206.

15. D. E. Aune, *Prophecy in Early Christianity and the Ancient Mediterranean World* (Grand Rapids, 1983), chapter 2, especially pp. 23–4, 28–35, 47–8. R. Lane Fox, *Pagans and Christians in the Mediterranean World from the Second Century A.D. to the Conversion of Constantine* (London, 1986), pp. 183–4, 204–5, 211–15.

16. Aune, *Prophecy in Early Christianity*, pp. 23, 29.

17. J. Lindblom, *Prophecy in Ancient Israel* (Oxford, 1978), pp. 27–8.

18. See especially: J. Blenkinsopp, *A History of Prophecy in Israel* (London, 1984), pp. 17–18, 25, 36–7, 87; K. Koch, *The Prophets. Vol I, The Assyrian Period*, trans. Margaret Kohl (London, 1982), p. 16; B. Lang, *Monotheism and the Prophetic Minority: An Essay on Biblical History and Sociology* (Sheffield, 1983), pp. 68–70; Lindblom, *Prophecy in Ancient Israel*, pp. 33–4; D. L. Petersen, *The Roles of Israel's Prophets* (Sheffield, 1981), pp. 27–30, 40–6, 54, 58, 63, 71, 75–6, 78–9, 85; J. R. Porter, 'The origins of prophecy in Israel', in R. Coggins, A. Phillips, M. Knibb (eds), *Israel's Prophetic Tradition* (Cambridge, 1982), pp. 13–15, 18, 20–4.

19. Blenkinsopp, *A History of Prophecy in Israel*, pp. 22–3, 142–3, 158, 188–90, 254–6.

20. J. Barton, *Oracles of God: Perceptions of Ancient Prophecy in Israel after the Exile* (London,

Douglas H. Johnson & David M. Anderson

1986), chapter 1. See also: Lindblom, *Prophecy in Ancient Israel*, p. 29; R. Lane Fox, *Pagans and Christians*, pp. 257-60, 388-90.

21. Barton, *Oracles of God*, pp. 14-15, 20-2, 44-55, 266-73.

22. For this understanding of the role of prophecy in Islam we are indebted to the late Peter Lienhardt.

23. Blenkinsopp, *A History of Prophecy in Israel*, p. 36.

24. Max Weber, *The Theory of Social and Economic Organisation*, trans. and ed. by A. M. Henderson and Talcott Parsons (London, 1964), chapter 3 'Types of Authority', especially pp. 359-63. H. H. Gerth and C. Wright Mills, *From Max Weber: Essays in Sociology* (London, 1948), pp. 52, 246-50.

25. Max Weber, *Ancient Judaism*, (Chicago and London, 1952), pp. 114-16, 267-8.

26. Lang, *Monotheism and the Prophetic Minority*, pp. 67-8, 113.

27. Donal B. Cruise O'Brien 'Introduction', in D. B. Cruise O'Brien and C. Coulon (eds), *Charisma and Brotherhood in African Islam* (Oxford, 1988), pp. 2-11.

28. D. Emmet, 'Prophets and their societies', *J. R. Anth. Inst.*, 86, i (1956), p. 16.

29. K. Thomas, *Religion and the Decline of Magic: Studies in Popular Beliefs in Sixteenth- and Seventeenth-Century England* (Harmondsworth, 1973), pp. 165, 175-8.

30. M. Adas, *Prophets of Rebellion: Millenarian Protest Movements against European Colonial Order* (Cambridge, 1987), pp. xx-xxi.

31. Anthony Wallace, 'Revitalization movements', *American Anthropologist*, 58, ii (1956).

32. N. Chadwick, *Poetry and Prophecy* (Cambridge, 1952), pp. xiii-xiv.

33. Tim Allen, 'Understanding Alice: Uganda's Holy Spirit Movement in context', *Africa*, 61, iii (1991).

34. For Nyabingi see Elizabeth Hopkins, 'The Nyabingi cult of southwestern Uganda', in R. I. Rotberg and Ali A. Mazrui (eds), *Protest and Power in Black Africa* (New York, 1970).

35. There are, of course, numerous movements within Africa which self-consciously operate within the Christian tradition of prophecy and employ or adapt Christian prophetic idioms. These mainly fall outside the scope of this collection, but a number of stimulating studies have fruitfully explored such prophets and movements within both their Christian and their African contexts; two of the most notable being B. G. M. Sundkler, *Bantu Prophets in South Africa*, 2nd ed. (London, 1961), and Wyatt Mac-Gaffey, *Modern Kongo Prophets. Religion in a Plural Society* (Bloomington, 1983).

36. James, *The Listening Ebony*.

37. Ruel, 'Kuria Seers', pp. 346-8, 351-2.

38. Said S. Samatar, *Oral Poetry and Somali Nationalism: The Case of Sayyid Mahammad 'Abdille Hasan* (Cambridge, 1982), pp. 193-4.

39. P. M. Holt, *The Mahdist State in the Sudan 1881-1989: A Study of its Origins, Development and Overthrow*, 2nd ed. (Oxford, 1970), pp. 105-6, 138-41.

40. Paul Spencer: *The Maasai of Matapato: A Study of Rituals of Rebellion* (Manchester, 1988); 'The Loonkidongi prophets and the Maasai'.

41. Anderson, 'Black mischief'.

42. R. P. Carroll, *When Prophecy Failed: Reactions and Responses to Failure in Old Testament Prophetic Traditions* (London, 1979), pp. 77-83.

43. T. W. Overholt, 'Prophecy: the problem of cross-cultural comparison', in B. Lang (ed.), *Anthropological Approaches to the Old Testament* (Philadelphia and London, 1985), pp. 64-6, 78.

44. Blenkinsopp, *A History of Prophecy in Israel*, p. 75. Lang, *Monotheism and the Prophetic Minority*, p. 62.

45. And with Ngundeng and other prophets in *Nuer Prophets: A History of Prophecy from the Upper Nile in the Nineteenth and Twentieth Centuries* (Oxford, 1994).

46. Ruel, 'Kuria Seers'.

47. D. H. Johnson, 'Fixed Shrines and Spiritual Centres in the Upper Nile', *Azania*, 25, 1990, p. 53; and *Nuer Prophets*, Chapter 9.

Part One

Prophetic
Idioms

Two

Kidongoi's Kin

Prophecy & Power in Maasailand

RICHARD D. WALLER

According to Maasai myth, the first *laibon*,[1] Kidongoi, was found as a child wandering on the Ngong Hills by a *murran* who took him home and looked after him. Later, when the child revealed his extraordinary powers of foreknowledge and miracle-working, his alarmed benefactor gave him to another, whose clan, Laiser, he joined. Kidongoi's descendants, often referred to as the House (*Enkang*) of Supeet or Mbatiany, came to form their own sub-clan, the Inkidongi, and have prophesied for Maasai sections ever since.[2]

A belief in prophecy and divination is widespread among the Maa-speakers and their neighbours. The rise of the Inkidongi *laibons* among the Maasai, although almost a paradigm case of the expansion of prophetic power, is only one example, and even in Maasailand the Inkidongi had their rivals. This chapter examines the '*laibon* tradition' by looking first at the special characteristics of prophetic power and influence among the Maasai and then suggesting an interpretation of the development of one prophet group, the Inkidongi, in the context of rivalry between practitioners within what was a highly fluid, entrepreneurial and competitive field of opportunity. Finally, it considers briefly other prophets in Maasailand and sketches in the wider background of an enduring but adaptable tradition of prophecy in the region.

Insiders & outsiders: types of power in Maasailand

The starting point for the discussion is Fosbrooke's observation that *laibons* are an incompletely assimilated element in Maasai society.[3] They are outsiders in two senses. Literally, they were immigrants. The genealogical traditions of all major prophet lineages – not just those of the Inkidongi – emphasize alien origins. They came from 'somewhere else'. Kidongoi himself is sometimes thought to have dropped from the sky, and other founding prophets are given similarly vague origins.[4] Significantly, few are believed to have emerged from within the community itself and it is likely that alien origin, whether real or not, is a necessary characteristic of *laibons* and an important attribute of their power.

Metaphorically, *laibons* are outsiders because they operate outside the moral and social boundaries of the community. As ordinary Maasai see it, *laibons* are amoral and anti-social beings. They live apart from ordinary people (*ilomet*), conduct their affairs secretly and are unrestrainedly competitive. Rivals are 'like two shopkeepers living in the same place' and their jealousy is deadly, both to themselves and to others caught up in their feuds.[5] These traits are emphasized both in their own traditions, where they are part of a discourse of power, and in the reflections of their clients, who regard them with a mixture of fear, resentment, cynicism and contempt.[6] They are magnified by the deliberate cultivation of the ambiguous and abnormal in dress and behaviour by some *laibons* and in the implicit parallels drawn between them and the semi-human cannibal figures of Maasai folk tales.[7] Like images of the Ndorobo, the 'mirror in the forest', the popular conception of *laibons* is something against which Maasai values can be defined. In the sense that it marks them off from ordinary people, it is again both a manifestation and a source of power. At the same time, however, as Spencer points out, this conception represents something that is not 'wholly alien to Maasai'. It is an exaggerated projection of the selfishness and individualism which is an essential part of Maasai patriarchy but which, if carried to extremes, can destroy the community. In this sense, like the ogres, *laibons* are the dark and private side of everyman.[8]

Given that the *laibons are* outsiders in these two senses, and that much of their influence springs from their eccentric and ambiguous position, how were they able to establish themselves in Maasailand? We may begin by surveying briefly other sources of paranormal power available to the Maasai. The main power to bless or curse lies with the elders,

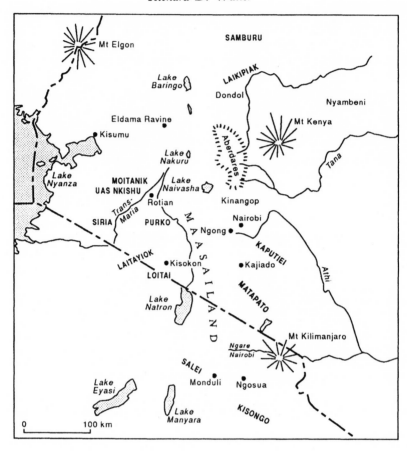

Map 2   Maasailand

acting either as individual household heads disciplining their families or corporately as 'fathers' and seniors acting to restrain their juniors and to maintain continuity and stability within the community. Blessings and at least the threat of a curse are not unusual in themselves and are often invoked in ceremonies. There are also 'lucky' or, better, propitious (*sinya*) lineages and individuals whose presence and blessing at ceremonies are thought to be particularly efficacious or auspicious. It is from such families, for instance, that the 'ritual leader' (*olotuno*) of the age-set, who must be of 'pure' and blameless descent, is selected. In the past, the blessing of propitious elders may also have been sought for raids.[9]

Also operating within the community are possessors of more specialized expertise or enhanced power. These included rainmakers who belonged mainly to one lineage, *il Kiporon*.[10] The role of the rainmakers appears to predate the emergence of the *laibons* (who were not especially concerned with rain) and they may have exercised wider authority in the past. In the mid-nineteenth century, Krapf referred to the figure (or perhaps office) of '*olkibroni*' as the main ritual leader of the Maasai. His account is confused but appears to equate '*olkibroni*' with '*oleibon*, the chief sorcerer', who was above ordinary *laibons*. Similarly, Kersten, who visited Kisongo in 1862 but who may have simply repeated Krapf's information, described '*orlkibroni*' as a community war leader who destroyed enemies by magic but also made rain and acted as 'High Priest' in peacetime. Kersten's account, too, suggests that there were other *laibons* in Maasailand. It is possible that the two accounts reflect one stage in a process of transfer or merging between rainmaker-ritual experts and diviner-prophets which ended in the subordination or suppression of the former. From the later nineteenth century, '*olkibroni*' disappears from travellers' accounts, to be replaced by *laibons*.[11]

Elders, rainmakers and, in a minor way, healers (*inkaikok*) all wielded power within, and on behalf of, the community of which they were part. Three more ambiguous types of power existed outside, however: prophecy, divination and sorcery. All three are interrelated and all three are associated, though not exclusively in the last case, with *laibons*. Sorcery can be distinguished from the other two by virtue of the fact that it is always negative in both intention and effect. It represents the extreme of asociality, jealousy and lack of restraint, and is something which Maasai fear and find difficult to deal with. The blast of the sorcerer (*esakutore*) can be contrasted with the 'just' curse (*oldeket*) of the elder. Sorcerers (*il asakutok*) act secretly for themselves or for clients out of motives of malice and greed: the elders' curse should be pronounced openly, with restraint and in the public interest.[12] Although the sorcerer might be anyone, there is a clear connection between his activities and some of the known or suspected activities of *laibons*. Indeed, some *laibons* were notorious for their skill and predisposition as sorcerers and there seems little doubt that the fear of sorcery was part of their public image.[13]

Divination and prophecy are often found together, but they are different activities and are thought to be manifestations of different powers. Most prophets in Maasailand are also diviners, though not all diviners have the power of foresight. Divination is essentially a mechanical skill, rather than a product of direct inspiration, and can, in theory, be learned by anyone. In Maasailand, it involves the interpretation of stones and other objects shaken from a horn or gourd (*enkidong*) and piled and counted according to a complicated numerology which involves concepts of propitious or 'whole' numbers and combinations. The precise system followed varies, especially between different prophet families. Inkidongi use a pure numerology involving only black and white pebbles, but other families supplement this with the interpretation of objects used as markers, each with its own significance. Some prophets, of the Tunai family in Siria for example, do not use *enkidong* at all or have taken it up 'recently'. Divination may be done publicly at the request of formal deputations or privately for the *laibon* himself or for individual clients.[14]

Prophecy, by contrast, is always public and is usually communicated formally to deputations. Foreknowledge may come either spontaneously in dreams or through self-induced trances. Surviving examples of prophecies, those that have been preserved encapsulated in tradition or memory, are of two broad types. Some are general allusions to, or warnings of, events in the future, chanted or shouted out by the prophet under inspiration, with advice on how the people should respond. Mbatiany's famous prophecies announcing the coming of cattle plague and the whites are in this form.[15] Others are war prophecies, sought by deputations of *murran* and produced, as it were, 'to order', together with appropriate charms. Usually, they include a comprehensive curse on the enemy, in the form of a highly allusive and abusive song (*oloipirri*), and a detailed but obscure set of instructions for the conduct of the raid. The instructions (*imodeta*) specify where enemy stock will be found, what route the raiders must take to find it and what steps will be necessary to carry the enterprise to a successful conclusion.[16]

Foresight is a power 'of the head', hereditary in the male line. All members of the major *laibon* families, Inkidongi and others, have claimed this inherent power, but only some choose, or are chosen, to exercise it. Of these, again, only some will have their powers validated by the community. Their prophecies are accepted as 'correct' or 'good' in the judgement of others – 'when he speaks of something, it happens'. Since prophetic utterance is always couched in highly ambiguous and conditional terms and is not susceptible to inquiry and proof, it may be retrospectively ratified or quietly forgotten depending on the current standing and reputation of the prophet. An example is the interpretation of *imodeta*. If a raid goes badly, it may be accepted that the fault lay with the *murran* who trangressed the letter of the instructions rather than with the prophet himself. Otherwise, the penalty for bad prophecy might be death at the hands of an enraged following, believing that their prophet had betrayed them. There is, thus, considerable flexibility in the exercise and recognition of prophetic power, and scope both for competition between rival purveyors of prophecy, who can and do denounce each other as charlatans, and for manipulation by the clientele, who ultimately decide by bestowing their patronage on one rather than another.[17]

The range of powers is completed by those of the blacksmiths. Like *laibons*, smiths are seen as outsiders, though they now appear to have neither a separate tradition of migration nor a separate lineage structure. Like *laibons*, too, they and their powers are viewed ambivalently by other Maasai. They are both dangerous and powerful but also avoided and ostensibly despised, since their presence contaminates. They also have a powerful curse, connected with the symbols of their profession, which they may use if provoked or invoked, but they neither divine nor prophesy.[18]

There are two obvious ways of contrasting the types of experts and their particular powers reviewed here. *Laibons*, sorcerers and smiths are outsiders as opposed to elders, rainmakers, healers and propitious persons. The power to bless or curse and the ability to manipulate divining stones are general powers which may be wielded by many and which usually have a local focus. Rainmaking, iron smelting and prophecy, however, are or were exclusive powers belonging only to specific groups. Further, all three are public powers whereas the others may be put to private use. What marks *laibons* off from other experts in Maasailand is their range of expertise and the way that their powers cross categories, public and private, general and exclusive. Although they are themselves outsiders, they have been able to penetrate inside the community through their cultivation of a following (*ol kipaaret*), both in private practice and in public function. Moreover, through their ability to manipulate images of otherness and to play on fears and uncertainties, they have turned exclusion into influence. As one elder put it, 'if we did not have Loonkidongi, we would not need Loonkidongi'.[19]

By focusing on the *laibons'* ability to expand the range of their powers, to incorporate elements from other fields of power and to create a role for themselves, we can return to the question of how prophets, the Inkidongi *laibons* in particular, established themselves among the Maa-speakers. I have argued elsewhere that the Inkidongi may have gradually displaced or subordinated other types of practitioner in an attempt to create a monopoly of influence.[20] Here, I wish to look more closely at the internal organization of the prophets and at their relations with the Maasai community after they had established themselves. The discussion that follows adds a historical dimension to the analyses of Spencer and Fratkin, which are based largely on contemporary observations and data.

The available sources, however, are scanty for the crucial period of expansion and permit little more than speculation. They also, it may be argued, bear clear marks of having been reinterpreted to create a homogeneous 'official version' – what I have called elsewhere the 'myth of the Inkidongi'. Nineteenth-century Maasai traditions may be read with or without the insertion of the *laibons* and there are indications that different versions have been joined or conflated. In particular, episodes of sorcery and the supernatural are not fully integrated into the secular tradition of expansion. The impression of reworking is confirmed by a comparison of versions of the wars of the 1890s of which both Inkidongi and '*ilomet*' versions survive. The latter remove the fratricidal struggle within the Inkidongi from the centre of the picture and replace it with a theme more consistent with an elders' view of events. The 'myth of the Inkidongi' has as its centre-piece a genealogy of prophetic succession linking the 'historical' prophets like Supeet and Mbatiany directly with the apical ancestor, Kidongoi. This may have been developed independently of the rest of the myth. Its form is shared by other, non-Inkidongi, prophet lineages whose version of events in the nineteenth century is otherwise different. The myth as a whole, however, provides an explanation of the authority and powers of the Inkidongi. It gives historical depth to their claims, places them centrally within the main traditions of Maasai expansion and demonstrates the infallibility of their prophecies and, therefore, their superiority over all other *laibons* as inheritors of a prophetic Great Tradition.[21]

The rise & fall of the Inkidongi

John Berntsen has proposed what is essentially a three-stage historical model of expansion, ascendancy and dispersal to account for the rise of the Inkidongi in the nineteenth century. My own account, although mainly in agreement, differs somewhat in its perspective and emphasis. The analysis presented later in this chapter stresses the limitations of the prophets' role among the Maasai, the individualism and opportunism inherent in prophetic leadership and the ambiguity of the prophets' authority. Thus, a model which describes the 'rise and fall' of a prophetic institution is too neat and determinist to encompass the complex and uncertain relationship between prophets and their audience. Further, the notion – which Berntsen rightly treats very cautiously – that the apparent hegemony of Mbatiany represented a stage in a movement towards some embryonic state among the Maasai, which was then reversed by disaster and colonial rule, arises from a fundamental misunderstanding of the nature of prophecy and power in Maasailand.[22]

At first, the Inkidongi were settled as a community at Ngosua near Monduli in the territory of the Kisongo. The community was well-established, before the middle of the nineteenth century, in a strategic spot, with access to permanent grazing and water and close to a major trade route, but its claims to prophetic leadership seem to have been confined to the southern Maasai and the influence of the *laibons* may have been purely local. However, during the period of rapid Maasai expansion in the Rift Valley region, from perhaps the 1830s to the 1870s, some form of wider co-ordination between different and dispersed Maasai sections was necessary if they were to support each other in occupying and defending new territory and in fighting off challenges from other Maa-speakers. *Laibons*, whose prophetic claims were both universal and exclusive, were able to fill this role and, in a sense, colonize a vacant political 'niche'. They were themselves outsiders, and therefore able to operate both above and between sectional aggregations, and their expertise as purveyors of charms and directions for raiding appealed particularly to the *murran* who were the spearhead of territorial expansion. The prophets of the Ngosua community were thus able to expand the range of their influence and to develop their functions as war-leaders to the point where the Inkidongi *laibons* Supeet and his successor Mbatiany, having defeated other Maa-speakers and *their* prophets (notably the Laikipiak prophet Koikoti) through their charms and prophecies, are credited with 'ruling' (*aitore*) the Maasai. Indeed, Berntsen suggests that sections, and the Maasai community as a whole, came to derive their corporate identity from their allegiance to the *laibons*. Conversely, if a prophet failed or was defeated, his following lost its focus and was dispersed.[23]

Once they had established and defined their role essentially as war-prophets, the *laibons* began to absorb or incorporate pre-existing sources of power and to adapt themselves further to the perceived needs of their clientele among the Maasai. The incentive, and to some extent the resources, to play a greater role in Maasai affairs derived from the development of the *laibons*' position as 'lay' as well as 'spiritual' patrons. As they acquired cattle as their share of the proceeds from successful raids, *laibons* were able to enlarge their households, admit dependents and extend their local influence through hospitality. This kind of investment buttressed their position in Maasai society and publicized their success as prophets.[24] It also, however, made them vulnerable by exciting jealousy and promoting rivalry between practitioners, and it was this weakness that apparently led to their downfall.

Inkidongi ascendancy was precarious and short-lived. It is not clear, for example, to what extent the northern Maasai sections ever accepted Inkidongi hegemony, and even in the south Mbatiany's sway was never unchallenged.[25] Mbatiany himself died just before the major crises of the 1890s, and his wider influence died with him. His successors had to cope both with the dissolution of the Maasai community under the pressures of disease, famine and intersectional warfare and with disputes among the Inkidongi themselves. With the onset of epidemic disease among the cattle herds, the Ngosua community began to disperse and Inkidongi prophets, perhaps for the first time, settled among other Maasai sections. As the Ngosua community began to break up, a dispute between two of Mbatiany's sons for the prophetic 'succession' split the Inkidongi into two main factions. One claimant, Senteu, was supported primarily by the Loitai and by at least some of the senior Inkidongi. The other claimant, Olonana, settled near Ngong with the eastern Maasai sections until he was driven by Senteu's Loitai raiders to join the Purko in the Naivasha area. At this point, after the disastrous losses inflicted on the Maasai community by rinderpest and smallpox in 1891–2, the succession dispute among the Inkidongi was subsumed within the larger struggle between the Loitai and Purko alliances for control over the diminished resources of Maasailand, an indication of how the relationship between the *laibons* and the wider community was changing. Although the wars among the Maasai in the 1890s are often attributed to the rivalry of Olonana and Senteu, their course was shaped and their outcome determined first by the patterns of sectional opposition and alliance among the *laibons'* potential followings and then by the politics of British and German conquest in the region. Both *laibons* were, in a sense, captured by their clients and their private interests were subordinated to the public interests of the constituencies for whom they practised.[26]

By 1902, the Loitai had been defeated and Senteu's following dispersed. The prophet himself came to live quietly near his rival and under British supervision. Later, he moved back to Loita and established a new Inkidongi community in Kisokon. Olonana, meanwhile, had sought to capitalize on the victory of his following and on his influence with the newly-established British administration to consolidate his position as the recognized *oloiboni kitok* and 'Paramount Chief' of the Maasai. The limits of his authority, and the underlying fallacy of the notion of prophets as a potential 'ruling institution', were quickly demonstrated, however, when Olonana attempted to invade the sphere of competence of the elders in such matters as the choice of age-set spokesmen.[27]

Olonana died suddenly in 1911. His son, Seki, inherited his father's official position but little of his authority. He was largely disregarded by the elders and was bitterly at odds with Senteu, whom he and his brother Kimoruai, carrying on the family feud, accused of having caused their father's death through sorcery and of alienating their supporters. Although Olonana's descendants retained a following and developed a community around Ngong, Senteu's family were independently powerful in the southwest, and the Kisongo in Tanganyika now separately recognized Parrit, another son of Olonana.[28] An uneasy accommodation was reached within *Enkang e Mbatiany* and between it and the Maasai. Maasailand was divided up into territories or domains and sectional clientages, each in principle 'ruled' by a single *laibon*. This helped to regulate internal conflict but, at the same time, limited the spread of Inkidongi influence as a whole and created the conditions for further fragmentation within the prophet lineages. The *laibons* moved back into the interstices of power, somewhat more than the itinerant prophets and diviners described by Fischer, but very much less than members of a 'priestly' ruling class.[29]

Richard D. Waller

Establishment & opportunists: the internal organization of the Inkidongi

Three linked themes underlay the development of the Inkidongi *laibons*: the management of competition between rival prophets within the lineage, and the emergence of a hierarchy, not only among the Inkidongi themselves but also within the wider 'expert community'; the dynamics of reciprocity between the prophet and his clientele; and the sometimes tense and ambivalent relationship between *laibons* and elders, which set limits to the prophets' authority. An examination of each will help us to consider more generally the relationship between prophecy and its social context in Maasailand. This in turn will present a more nuanced picture of development than is provided by the simple linear sketch of 'rise and fall'. From the end of the nineteenth century, these themes emerge with greater clarity than before because of the high degree of competitiveness in the 'field' at a time of extreme social dislocation, and because the sources allow us more insight into the processes by which prophets built individual clientages and competed with one another to win a following.

Like other similarly marginal but powerful figures, *laibons* derived their authority from the possession of a property or power (in this case prophecy, 'the power of the head') that was arcane in its origins and manifestations and restricted to the members of a particular group, but which was not unique to any individual and which could even be claimed or counterfeited by others.[30] This created a contradiction in their position which can be expressed as a double paradox. Prophets multiply, but the essence of their function is that they should be rare. To remain effective, their inherent power must be concentrated, yet it is constantly being diffused through inheritance.[31] Thus, since outlets for prophecy were necessarily restricted both by circumstance and by the need for any would-be prophet to command an audience, control of the 'market' was constantly threatened by oversupply. As Gellner puts it pithily, 'too much *baraka* [was] chasing too little saintly function'.[32] To prevent 'overcrowding' in the field which would threaten both the individual status and the collective authority of the *laibons*, it was necessary to restrict the actual spread of power while still maintaining the principle of inheritance which legitimated it. Thus, while all Inkidongi have the inherent ability to prophesy, only some will become *laibons*. The working out of this exclusionary proposition through a complex process of private choice and public recognition in effect created a stratified prophetic 'establishment', access to whose upper levels was reserved only for the chosen few who could also justify their position by displaying the attributes of a 'real *laibon*' or *oloiboni kitok*. However, expressed in these rather schematic terms, the response of the Inkidongi to the contradictions, opportunities and constraints of their position implies a level of intention which must, in practice, have been hard to articulate and maintain. It is, therefore, important to bear in mind that being a successful *laibon* involved *ad hoc* compromise and accident as much as long-term planning and a consistent ideology.

The odds against success were high. At any time, only a few even of those closest to the actual concentration of power, the sons of a recognized *laibon*, could lay effective claim to the prophetic inheritance and expect to practise on a large scale. Olonana, for example, had either nine or fifteen sons but only four became *iloibonok kitok*. Nkaruiya, his cousin and an active prophet himself, had twenty sons. Four 'had *enkidong*' (i.e. practised as diviners) but only one achieved the status of *oloiboni kitok*. Those beyond that charmed circle had even less chance of recognition except as minor local diviners and purveyors of charms. Genealogies reflect the realities of power and there was a constant pruning of the branches of the Inkidongi family tree as junior and collateral branches were effectively excluded from consideration. Consequently, as ordinary Maasai observed, competition was fiercest between brothers.[33] Great importance was attached to the father's 'choice' amongst his sons, since it was he who was responsible for directing the flow of prophetic power in the next generation by presenting chosen sons to the sections who would subsequently consult them. 'Great prophets' (*iloibonok kitok*) were often consulted by more than one section and, although they might have preferred to appoint a single successor so that the concentration of prophetic power was handed down intact, in most cases their following was divided amongst different sons. Often a father would allow favoured sons to participate in his dealings with clients in order to test their fitness, indicate his choice and enable successor and following to begin to establish a working relationship.[34]

The prophetic succession was, in fact, settled by a combination of predestination, choice and manipulation. Although nomination of a successor was the prerogative of the father, it was expected that he would be guided by dreams in which were revealed the signs by which he would know the 'chosen one'. His choice would later be confirmed by magical tests and private rituals which marked the passing of the prophetic inheritance from father to son. There were no fixed rules of succession by seniority in the prophet's household, and the choice might appear quite arbitrary. Neither Mbatiany nor Olonana and Senteu, nor Senteu's successor Simmel, were eldest sons.[35] Succession was thus both open and, in a sense, predetermined at the same time. Moreover, the father's choice might be overridden, as one reading of the story of Olonana and Senteu suggests. Here, Mbatiany is tricked into bestowing his blessing and powers on Olonana rather than on Senteu, his favoured son (*ol kirotet*), in a manner reminiscent of the story of Esau and Jacob. The tradition, which exists in different and sometimes conflicting versions, is complex and has several levels of meaning. Apart from its immediate function as propaganda in the intersectional wars of the 1890s, it appears to be a way of reconciling the elements of ascription and achievement in the election of prophets.[36]

Ultimately, it was the following that validated the choice of prophet by publicly recognizing his authority. 'A *laibon* has to prove himself to be a *laibon*. It is not [just] a matter of being appointed'.[37] Proof lay in the success of the *laibon* in gathering and keeping clients. Thus, *laibons* proposed but their clients disposed. Despite their customary ratification of the *laibon*'s nomination, sections and clients could and did change their allegiance for a variety of reasons, both practical and political. As one Enkidongi put it, displaying a cynical awareness of the realities of manipulation and power in the relationship, 'people come to a *laibon* because he is famous and powerful; and if they hear of a more famous one, they will leave the one and go to the other'. And even an established *laibon*'s control over his clientage might be threatened by opportunist rivals.[38]

However, a too obviously manipulative attitude to their prophets or too blatant a disregard for the sanctity of the prophetic inheritance embodied in the notion of the father's choice and the predestination of the 'chosen one' would undermine the special moral authority of the prophet's utterance and the efficacy of his instructions. The following statements, intended to be both descriptive and prescriptive, indicate how the contradiction in the relationship between prophets and their following might be reconciled. In a general way, they echo the discourse on free will and predestination implicit in the story of Olonana and Senteu:

> Some sons are chosen . . . They all [divine] but only those who prophesy correctly are chosen by the Maasai . . . The father announces to the Maasai which sons he has chosen and they [the Maasai] start giving them [the sons] cattle . . . Whenever you are appointed by your father to a section, that section will be pleased with you and bring you cattle. Then you bless them and give them charms. You must always prophesy well and prophesy truth. God makes it come true and then the people are pleased with you . . . The sons who are not chosen can do nothing . . . They cannot go and fight the ones who are chosen. [But] even if a father does not choose a son, he can

still rise to be a *laibon* – even if he has not been appointed . . . The real *laibons* are only those who were appointed by their fathers. No-one who was not appointed became *oloiboni kitok* . . .[39]

Although this text comes from a senior practising Enkidongi, the ideas expressed are generally accepted as normative by ordinary Maasai elders. Whatever the realities of the relationship, they were always decently cloaked in a public rhetoric of acceptance and agreement – despite the cynical subtext evident both in traditional accounts and modern discussion. It was this accommodation, however fragile, between the special and intrusive power of the prophets and the secular authority of the community elders that made the creation of a prophetic establishment possible and which perhaps distinguishes the Maasai Inkidongi as a group from more idiosyncratic prophets elsewhere.

Given the important part played by the Maasai themselves in the transference of the Inkidongi prophetic inheritance, how did sons begin to attract the notice of their father's clients? Fathers might well favour a particular son and make their preference public, but Berntsen has argued convincingly, on the basis of a detailed analysis of successions, that the age-set to which the successful claimant belonged was often crucial. A son who belonged to the age-set that were senior *murran* at the time stood a much better chance of being 'chosen'. In the case of the succession to Senteu's position in 1933, for example, the inheritance went to a younger claimant, Simmel, who belonged to Il Derito who were then senior *murran*. Two older brothers who had appeared earlier to be in the running belonged to Il Dareto, a set which had retired from *murran*hood by the early 1930s.[40] There was thus a form of positional succession which shifted over time from one possible inheritor to another as both claimants and their potential followings matured and progressed through the age-grades. The thesis is an elegant one that has the merit of linking the developmental cycles of Inkidongi and *ilomet* and of focusing by implication on the relationship between prophet and warriors. It is strengthened by the observation that the sponsors of the senior *murran*, the senior elders, wielded the greatest authority within the community. If the succession was consistently passed through alternate sets, then their own chosen prophet and age-mate would be handing over to one of their protégés. A claimant who satisfied these criteria, and who had also cultivated good relations with the *murran* spokesmen of his age, would be in a very strong position – whether or not inspiration entered into the choice.[41]

Berntsen's analysis does not, however, cover cases, such as that of Olonana and Senteu, where several sons belonged to the same age-set;

nor does it explain how a prophet who was consulted by more than one group or section divided his domain. One part of the answer perhaps lies in the structure of patronage, marriage and hospitality in the prophet's homestead. Successful *laibons* had many wives, each of whom was expected to help feed and entertain the husband's visitors and clients. *Laibons* had the right to demand girls without bridewealth from their clients, and the wives of senior prophets often, therefore, came from different sections, reflecting the spread of the husband's influence. When deputations arrived, they would seek out the wife from their own area or clan and this might initiate a relationship between clients and their kinswoman's sons. Loitai, for example, visited Senteu's mother, and it was the Loitai to whom Senteu later turned for support after Mbatiany's death. Olonana's mother was either Kaputiei or Kisongo and she entertained Purko visitors as well. Later, Olonana took refuge with Kaputiei and found supporters in both Purko and Kisongo. Thus succession may have been influenced by matrilateral as well as age-based relations with the clientage.[42]

So far, we have looked only at the upper levels of the prophetic hierarchy, at the 'chosen ones' and *iloibonok kitok*. Most Inkidongi, however, were not 'chosen'. If hierarchy was to be maintained, a place for them, too, had to be found within the prophet community, especially for '*il meipuko*' ('those not picked'), who, as sons of *iloibonok kitok*, were close enough to the centre of power to have nourished ambitions but had been passed over as successors. For them in particular, three main options existed. They might move away and attempt to carve out a place for themselves either by encroaching on the domain of another *laibon* (often by secretly directing raids by 'his' *murran*) or by shifting to another community. I describe these as 'opportunists', as opposed to 'establishment'. Senteu's sons, Nanunuaki and Kone, fit into this category, as do the Maasai *laibons* who infiltrated north into Samburu and Dondol.[43] Ultimately, both Nanunuaki and Kone found a place. Nanunuaki left Loita after Senteu's death and settled across the border (in Tanganyika) as *laibon* for Salei and Laitayiok. Kone, much younger, later directed his ambitions towards becoming a respectable and highly influential elder and was appointed government chief of Loita after Independence.

A less risky and more honourable alternative was to take on the role of elder statesman and councillor to the successful *oloiboni kitok* and to share in the benefits of his position. Olonana was closely associated with his uncle, Nailyang, and his cousin, Nkaruiya, both of whom were sufficiently close to power to have had private ambitions. Tolito, Mbatiany's brother, and later Ngabwel, his son, similarly advised and supported Senteu's family. The *laibons*, 'Lembarsacout' and 'Lengobe' (Nkopei, a younger brother of Supeet), whom Thomson reported as living with Mbatiany at Ngare, Nairobi, may be earlier examples.[44]

Finally, juniors could simply retire into relative obscurity as local diviners and charm-makers. They were referred to as *inkoiantik*, minor practitioners (or *Zauberers* – 'medicine men' – as Merker called them), as distinct from *iloibonok*. They might have a small following in their locality but they usually deferred, at least outwardly, to those more senior in the hierarchy.[45] The varying standing and activities of *inkoiantik* reflected the ambiguity of the prophets' position. Some gained a good reputation locally and, like Ngabwel, were men of influence. Lesalaon, a younger son of Mbatiany, 'did not have a following but people loved him because he was rich and the son of a *laibon*'.[46] Others had more sinister reputations. They acted as receivers of stolen stock, extorted wives and 'gifts' by threats and were suspected of crossing the line into sorcery.[47]

However, although there was plenty of scope for what one administrator described as a 'thriving trade in minor magic', the field, though lucrative, was again crowded – with non-Inkidongi practitioners as well. Some of these were from other Maasai lineages and some were immigrants, especially Kikuyu.[48] Inkidongi regarded such interlopers with disdain and, perhaps, a degree of professional jealousy, for they had neither 'the family nor the qualities'. 'They take it as a trade and they see people getting rich'. Inkidongi attempted to defend their status against such 'opportunists' by defining all other prophets and diviners as illegitimate. Usage of the word *inkoiantik* reflects this since it can imply 'false prophets' or 'charlatans' as well as 'minor practitioners'. Yet Inkidongi were unable to drive others from the field, and indeed, as outsiders and opportunists themselves, they were hardly in a position to do so.[49]

The majority of Inkidongi, however, became neither *laibons* nor *inkoiantik*. Although they belonged to the prophet lineage, they were too far from the centre of power to derive any real benefit from it. Yet their special inheritance could not, by its nature, be absolutely renounced, and they were still somewhat set apart. Moreover, it was the existence of a wider Inkidongi community that supported the active prophets at the centre of the lineage. To see how this community developed and spread, it is useful to look again at Gellner's saints. Gellner posits a spectrum of power and influence among them stretching from those who were active and authoritative to those who were 'saints' in name only.

These had dropped out of the running and become effectively 'laicised'. In a similar way, there were 'lay' Inkidongi, belonging to the Sikirari section living in the region around the prophets at Ngosua. There were also 'latent' *laibons*, closer to power but not practising. 'They were *laibons* but stayed at home with their cattle.' In time, their families would become 'laymen', but they themselves might still perhaps 'reactivate' if they chose and if circumstances were favourable. Gradual 'laicisation' was an informal way of dealing with the paradox of prophetic power. It enabled power to drain away at the edges while still remaining concentrated at the centre.[50]

Vox Dei?: prophets & their followings

Prophets depended ultimately on their followings and on the skill with which they managed them. It was the clients who confirmed the choice of *laibon* and then upheld his authority by accepting and acting on his instructions. Thus, while appearing to hold the initiative, *laibons* had to be highly sensitive to the needs and expectations of ordinary Maasai. Prophetic utterance was, therefore, a dialogue between prophet and audience, in which *vox Dei* was an amplified and authoritative version of *vox populi*. *Laibons* who failed to speak with the right voice and gave 'bad [or unacceptable] advice' would be abandoned. Those who succeeded could mould, and act as a sounding-board for, public opinion. Mbatiany, for instance, made his public reputation by calling for unity between different Maasai sections against the threat of the Laikipiak. His predecessor, Supeet, is thought to have played a similarly focal role in the earlier expansion of the Maasai against other Maa-speaking groups like Iloogolala.[51] However, although attention has been largely focused on the leadership that *laibons* provided in moments of crisis, they could only assume this role because they were able to draw on authority built up during more normal times when they advised on and blessed ceremonies, made routine divinations on behalf of deputations and individual clients, and supplied necessary medicines and charms. It was on the success of their ordinary working relationship with *ilomet* that they ultimately relied.

To maintain their influence, *laibons* had to be 'men for all seasons', appealing to different and sometimes conflicting elements in their following. Their interaction with the community encompassed, and was shaped by, many of the potential conflicts which existed within Maasai society at large. This is shown clearly in their triangular relationship with *murran* and elders which dramatized the ambiguous position of prophets as outsiders seeking a way in. The relationship was often tense, depending on the balance of power between elders and *murran*. *Laibons* could exploit the gaps afforded by the elders' fear of sorcery and by their fluctuating control over their wards, the *murran*. There appears to be a strong correlation between the degree of tension existing between *murran* and elders, between rival *laibons* and between *laibons* and elders, all of which tensions vary from section to section within the Maasai community as a whole. Where the elders' control is more secure, the *laibon*'s role is correspondingly restricted and there is less open antagonism between rivals.[52]

Two issues in particular provoked conflict: raiding and the control of promotion through the age-grade system, both of which raised the question of domains and their boundaries. There was obviously a close link between *laibons* as war-prophets, expert at directing raids and protecting the raiders, and the *murran*. Indeed, some observers believed that their powers rested on an alliance with the warriors. Certainly prowess as war-prophets was an important part of the public persona of successful *laibons*, and they competed with each other to provide this service for their clients, boosting their reputations in the process. Directing raids was one way in which an 'opportunist' could break into the establishment monopoly.[53] Successful war-prophets received cattle from the proceeds of raids and extended their personal influence over *murran* to create private retinues of armed followers which they might use against each other. *Laibons*, then, had an interest in the continuation of raiding, partly because their influence over the *murran* required the constant reinforcement of success.[54] However, this interest was potentially in conflict with that of the elders. Elders had probably always been somewhat ambivalent about raiding even though they supported it during the period of expansion in the nineteenth century. With the advent of colonial rule, however, raiding was officially outlawed and went 'underground'. *Laibons* who directed and provided charms for raids were arrested and convicted along with the raiders, while the fathers of *murran* offenders were made liable to heavy stock confiscations. Understandably, the reluctance of elders to countenance independent raiding increased markedly – as did their suspicion of prophets.[55]

The issue was not so much raiding *per se* as control: the control of juniors by seniors. The influence over *murran* that *laibons* sought threatened the control that elders exercised.[56] Elders were concerned with the consolidation of their own authority after a period of turmoil at the end of the nineteenth century from which they, as the then *murran*, had benefited. They now wanted to reassert discipline over succeeding groups of *murran* and to limit the independent authority and activities of the *laibons*. They could enlist the support of the colonial authorities against '*laibonism*' and thus threaten the *laibons*, but *laibons* could in turn exploit the frustrations of increasingly marginalized *murran*.[57] From the elders' point of view, war prophecy now seemed a dangerous extravagance and, although the expertise of *laibons* was still needed, what was required was an orderly succession and division of prophetic power and an end to the 'trade' with the *murran* which threatened social control and the peaceful accumulation of stock wealth. The colonial administration shared the elders' concern, and attempted to distinguish between the authority of establishment *laibons* which could be enlisted in support of the social and political order and the influence of *inkoiantik* and 'opportunists' which could not.[58] *Laibons*, therefore, were caught in the middle, under pressure to face in two directions – towards the elders as responsible public figures and towards the *murran* as charismatic if clandestine war-leaders. As one Enkidongi put it: 'In an argument, the *laibon* loses because he loses the support of the people. If he has no following, he is useless.' Facing the elders, they might lose control over the *murran* from whom they expected to get cattle. For *murran* might well visit a minor figure, whose charms were known to be strong and who was willing to sponsor raids, in preference to an established *laibon* whose views were more in accord with those of the elders. But facing the other way turned them into sinister and ambiguous figures, excluded them from legitimate public authority and also left them open to legal action. Accordingly, *laibons* spoke guardedly with two different voices, depending on the audience – and hoped to keep them separate.[59]

The vulnerability of *laibons* is suggested by the long history of conflict in Loita. Following the death of Senteu, his son, Sankoiyan, was appointed chief. He immediately ran into opposition from factions organized around an alliance between his older brother, Nanunuaki, who had also been passed over as *oloiboni kitok*, but had a sizeable following; and ole Parkiswaa, a spokesman of Il Dareto, who had popular support and aspired to the chiefship himself. Sankoiyan was accused of having 'siezed' the chiefship, of being 'haughty' and a 'wastrel', of supporting *murran* against their elders and instigating raids, and of being a sorcerer. He died suddenly in 1938. After further disputes, ole Parkiswaa was elected two years later, a choice engineered by the leading *il piron* elders or sponsors of the *murran*. Here, clearly, several sensitive issues were joined. Sankoiyan was being attacked as both *laibon* and chief at a time when fraternal relations within *Enkang e Senteu* and between *murran* and elders were particularly tense. Rivalry between spokesmen and *laibon* had a long history in the section. Ole Moti, the former chief spokesman of Il Dareto, had publicly defied Senteu and, it was widely believed, had 'framed' him for the disastrous raid on Meatu which had, in fact, been incited either by Sankoiyan and Nanunuaki or by another 'opportunist', Somai ole Nailyang, or, possibly, by ole Moti himself – who was arrested and then released. Pursued by Senteu's fatal curse, ole Moti defected to the Purko, still enemies of the Loitai, but died horribly before he could lead a Purko raiding party against his former age-mates. Again, these events occurred against the background of tension over the disciplining of *murran*. One of ole Moti's motives in (possibly) turning king's evidence may have been 'jealousy' of Senteu's influence over his *murran*. Meinertzhagen, characteristically, had described Senteu in 1902 as 'a magnificent specimen of the Masai warrior' (Olonana did not impress him) while ole Moti was described in a later report as a 'weedy specimen'. Even earlier, during the wars of the 1890s, there had been friction between Senteu and the then *murran* spokesman, ole Kashu, who had survived to become a highly influential *il piron* elder and a leading 'disciplinarian'. It seems possible that elders siezed the opportunity provided by rivalry between Senteu's sons, the youth of his designated successor and the dubious pasts of the other contenders to settle the long-standing issue of the relationship between *laibons* and elders in the latter's favour.[60]

Control of the passage of social time, symbolized by age ceremonies concerned with the recruitment, promotion and retirement of *murran*, also involved authority and the establishment and maintenance of boundaries between elders and prophets and between *laibons* themselves. Responsibility for the timing and staging of such ceremonies lay with the sponsoring elders of the *murran* age concerned in each section. The prerogative of determining when, where and how ceremonies would be performed was an important and visible aspect of their control over their wards and, indeed, part of their own continuing process of maturation as an age-set. Ceremonies also marked the boundaries of sectional alliances and, in a sense, embodied the community in both space and time.[61]

Laibons also had an important role to play, but its scope was fluctuating and potentially contentious. They provided charms to ward off sorcery at a time of transition when a set was particularly vulnerable, and they were consulted on questions of time, place and ceremonial detail. They might also, if they and the elders wished, 'preside' over the ceremony itself – but very much as honoured if somewhat disquieting guests rather than as sponsors or masters of ceremony. What was significant, however, both to prophets and to their followings, was not actual attendance but the formal deputation (*ol amal*) which preceeded, yet was an integral part of, each ceremony. *Ol amal*, and the gift of cattle that accompanied it, invited a particular *laibon* to confer blessing and protection on the age-set, and, in so doing, publicly recognized or confirmed his standing as *oloiboni kitok*.[62] Ceremonies thus established the prophet's domain, also in space and time, by associating him with one or more sections and age-sets and by setting the seal on his career in public practice.[63]

However, given the notorious 'jealousy' of prophets and their constant need to create and defend their own domains, and to encroach on those of their rivals, ceremonies might mark a time of transition for them as well as for their followings, a time when latent tensions might surface and perhaps be resolved violently. When *laibons* quarrelled over 'cattle and power', this was both an occasion and a cause.[64] In 1916–18, for example, there was tension – almost leading to a repeat of the conflicts of the 1890s – between Senteu and the sons of Olonana over the Eunoto ceremonies of Il Dareto. The Purko sent equal deputations to Seki (the officially 'chosen' successor), to Kimoruai, his brother (the more influential figure) and to Senteu. Although Senteu refused their gift of cattle – and therefore publicly distanced himself from the section – it was widely held that he was, in fact, secretly undermining his rivals' influence and had refused because he wanted 'all or none'. In the event, Kimoruai became *oloiboni kitok* for both Il Dareto and their successors in Purko, but at least one *murran* company (*sirit*) in Il Dareto continued to visit Senteu, then increasingly recognized as the most powerful *laibon* in Kenya Maasailand.[65]

Very little is known about the shape of the ceremonial cycle or about the performance of particular ceremonies, especially the Eunoto ('planting' or promotion ceremony for *murran*), before the 1900s. However, more recent tensions between the claims of *laibons* and of elders suggest that the former may have gradually inserted themselves into what was originally an entirely 'lay' affair, thus creating a permanent role for themselves which did not depend on the fortunes of war. Early accounts make no specific mention of the *laibons*' participation in age ceremonies, and while tradition associates Supeet and Mbatiany with particular age-sets it is unclear what this involved.[66] The first description comes from 1903 when the *murran* of the right-hand circumcision of Il Dwati held an *Eunoto* at which virtually all the major sections were represented. This was followed by the inauguration of a new age-set (Il Dareto) by the Purko and their allies. Olonana presided at the Eunoto as *oloiboni kitok* and received the deputation for the new age-set.[67] His dominance – and the particular interpretation of 'tradition' that underpinned it – was shortly challenged, however, during the next round of ceremonies in 1909–10, when the left-hand circumcision of Il Dwati held their *Eunoto*. Although the ceremony for the northern sections was to have taken place on Kinangop late in 1909, Olonana peremptorily stopped the proceedings on the grounds that it had begun without his sanction and, with the backing of the colonial government, insisted that the *Eunoto* be postponed and held near his camp in the Ngong area – where the Eunoto for the Kaputiei and their allies had already taken place, in August 1909. The elders agreed reluctantly, but it is clear that at least some of them regarded Olonana's intervention as unwarranted and resented his assumption of absolute authority. Colonial officials, who had their own reasons for wanting a move southwards, correctly saw that Olonana's forcing of the issue of control over ceremonial was an attempt to reassert his waning political authority, especially over those sections of Laikipia whose allegiance to him had always been doubtful.[68] Thereafter, the initiative of the *laibon* was sharply curtailed by the combined pressure of elders and administration. While the *oloiboni kitok* could still influence timing, as Simmel did in postponing the Matapato Eunotos in 1940 and 1975, the extent of his general involvement in *murran* ceremony came to depend on his willingness to co-operate with the elders. Whether or not this represented a 'return to tradition' after a period of upheaval is now impossible to determine.[69]

The relationship between the *oloiboni kitok* and the *olotuno* or 'ritual leader' of an age-set suggests the displacement but survival of 'pre-prophet' sources of ritual power. The *oloiboni kitok* confirms but does not initiate the selection of the *olotuno* who is both an 'ideal *murran*' and the official charged with the ritual well-being and discipline of his age-mates. He also acts as a link to the *laibon*.[70] In the past, his role and powers may have been larger. Fischer, for instance, met the '*leitun*' in the Naivasha area. He was possessed of 'powerful magic' and even his 'glance' was dangerous. Merker, however, denies him any 'magical' powers.[71] The ritual connection between *laibon* and *olotuno* is supported by the naming of the age-set. The final name assumed on retirement and consolidation (and, according to Merker, the name taken by the *murran* at Eunoto after the selection of *olotuno*) must be both evocative and propitious. It is selected and announced, in consultation with the elders, by the *laibon*, but it is the *olotuno* who is 'owner of the name' (*olopeny oo nkarna*).[72] A possible interpretation of this sharing of function and responsibility is to see it as the result of a compromise between two sources of authority, evolving over a long period.

Variations of experience: prophets in a wider context

So far, this paper has focused on the Inkidongi, but much of what has been suggested about their establishment, role and dilemmas applies to all prophets in Maasailand. A comparison between the Inkidongi and their rather less well-known fellows may thus sharpen our understanding of the institution in general and helps to widen the context of discussion.

Most Maa-speaking groups have *laibons* living amongst them. In Western Maasailand (Trans-Mara), especially, established prophet lineages, comparable in some ways with the Inkidongi, still exist. Among these are *Enkang e Nchue* in Uas Nkishu, the family of Saaei in Moitanik and the family of Toroni in Siria. All of these lineages produce prophets and diviners who are recognized by the sections amongst whom they are settled and who generally regard themselves as separate from, but equal to, the Inkidongi. Their individual histories and traditions are complex and deserve separate and detailed analysis elsewhere, but it is worth drawing from them three points of general similarity.

These lineages have apical ancestors whose origins are as shadowy as that of Kidongoi himself, and, like the Inkidongi, they have relatively shallow 'real' genealogies. The genealogy of the 'House of Nchue', for instance, begins to have some substance with the figure of Muneria, the first Uas Nkishu *laibon* to whom any traditions are clearly attached and the point of departure for the present lineage of prophets, all of whom claim descent from his 'brothers' or 'sons'. Muneria thus occupies a position, part symbolic and part 'real', analogous to that of Supeet or possibly his predecessor, Sitonik. In fact, the genealogy appears to be more a convenient framework within which different and possibly unrelated prophets have been located, and it may even represent either the remains, or the aborted beginnings, of something like the Ngosua community. Secondly, a similar stress is placed on alien origin. Nchue (or in some versions, Kaamantire) is said to have come from the Mt Kenya area, like Kidongoi, while Nyange, the founder of the family of Toroni, apparently arrived from the borderlands of southwest Kenya, while Kirisua, the founding ancestor of the *Enkang e Saaei*, came from Mt Elgon. In each case the founder was 'adopted' by a particular clan who then discovered his magical powers and recognized him as a prophet. They all, therefore, share with the Inkidongi the attributes of powerful outsiders who are, at the same time, also adopted dependents.[73]

A third point of comparison between the traditions concerns the strong connection between *laibons* and expansion or conflict among their followings. The tradition of Kirisua, for instance, develops from an archetypal episode of 'jealousy' and competition between the *laibons* of two factions or moieties, Uason and Moitanik, among the Uas Nkishu. The *laibon* Muneria is killed by *murran* incited by his rival, Kirisua, on the grounds that he, Muneria, has been tricking or disfavouring them in his advice and direction of raids. The conflict then leads to a split within Uas Nkishu and the defeat and withdrawal of the Moitanik, led by Kirisua. It would appear that the ambivalent identity of the Moitanik is expressed, in part, through these traditions of conflict: belonging to the same original community, yet now separate. There are similar themes in the traditions of the Inkidongi, but these are developed through the construction of the 'myth of the Inkidongi' and its link to the central Maasai traditions of the '*Iloikop*' Wars.[74]

In addition to these established lineages or communities of prophets, the traditions of Western Maasailand also indicate the presence of 'opportunists', some of whom were successful in founding their own communities while others were not. Perhaps the most famous of these was Koikoti ole Tunai who was accepted as a prophet by the Siria. Although other Maasai traditions place him as a defeated rival of Mbatiany, who gave direction to Laikipiak raids, according to Siria traditions, including those of the Tunai family, Koikoti was a prophet from Eastern Maasailand ('Kaputiei') whose origins lay with the Maa-speaking Iloogolala. After the defeat of Iloogolala, Koikoti and his following migrated to Siria and became incorporated into the section as the element still known as 'Kaputiei'.[75] Less successful was Lolgos, of *Enkang e Nchue*, who collected a mixed Uas Nkishu, Damat and Purko following in the Nakuru area towards the end of the last century. Although Lolgos, a refugee from the break-up of the Uas Nkishu community on the Uasin Gishu Plateau, found a niche to exploit in the disturbed conditions of the 1880s, he was unable to weld his following together. He remained exclusively a war-prophet, paid by results, and when his expertise failed his following split and he was murdered by disgruntled Purko *murran*, much as his forbear Muneria had been killed by Moitanik. There were doubtless others who have since largely disappeared from the record.[76] What the careers of such people suggest is that not only were there opportunities for prophetic leadership outside the establishment but also that there were many different sources of power on which to draw.

One source of power was obviously derived from raiding. Another was what Fosbrooke and Berntsen have characterized as 'private practi[ce]', the provision of charms, medicines and other services, including divining, to individual clients.[77] A third source was protection. Prophets came into their own in troubled times when society was dislocated. Their message answered a powerful need for reassurance and action in their following. They might also, however, offer material security by acting as a fixed point around which refugees, displaced by war or famine, could coalesce. The *laibon*'s combination of prescience, external authority and leadership together with his ability to mobilize and direct *murran* – and, therefore, to regain stock – provided a basis for rebuilding communities. Koikoti moved to Trans-Mara with his following and negotiated their acceptance into Siria. Somewhat later, Siria themselves, dispersed by Loitai raids during the 1890s, regrouped in neighbouring Kanyamkago around the prophet Toroni who acted as patron and mediator; as did the *laibon* Murumpi for the Uas Nkishu refugee community at Eldama Ravine. Even Olonana – in contrast with Senteu – rose to power as a refugee leader and ally of the incoming British.[78] Olonana, Toroni and Murumpi were all established prophets working within a familiar framework of expectation. But this kind of patronage could be developed by anyone with the right entrepreneurial skills – self-made prophets indeed. One such was Raurau, who apparently came from 'nowhere' and was accepted as *laibon* by Il Dalalekutuk Maasai and ex-Laikipiak refugees gathered in Meru. His following was eventually absorbed into the mainstream of northern Maasai, but Raurau himself survived as an *enkoiantiki* on Laikipia and then in the south, becoming one of the many local practitioners loosely associated with the dominant Inkidongi hierarchy.[79]

The variety of prophetic experience is confirmed when one looks beyond the Maasai themselves. Samburu and Ariaal have *laibons*, though no single established lineage, but their role is muted in comparison with the Inkidongi. They take no part in public ritual or political leadership and they concentrate on private practice, rather as *inkoiantik* than *iloibonok*. By comparison, Baraguyu have a separate prophet lineage with its own tradition and genealogical structure.[80] There were probably also prophets associated with now defunct *Iloikop* groups, but very little is known about them because *Iloikop* traditions have been preserved only within the dominant Maasai corpus. As antagonists of the Inkidongi prophets, *Iloikop laibons* have been decontextualized, annexed to the 'myth of the Inkidongi' in a process I call elsewhere 'genealogical imperialism' and reformed as images to set off the prowess of Supeet and Mbatiany.[81] Apart from the Uas Nkishu and Baraguyu noted above, only the Laikipiak are definitely known to have had *laibons* of their own. Even here, only one, Koikoti, is mentioned in tradition. However, other sources, when read in the light of what is known about Uas Nkishu for instance, suggest the existence of others, possibly a community, among the Laikipiak and their allies. Chanler, for example, was told that when the Laikipiak were attacked and defeated by the Purko, two of their *laibons* were killed, one (?Donytuli) fled to Nyambeni and three others (?including Raurau) settled in Gathere at the foot of Mt Kenya.[82] The fact that other *Iloikop* groups did not apparently have established prophets is not necessarily suprising since the eastern and northern Maasai sections themselves very probably did not either – at least before the 1870s.[83]

Including other prophets among the Maa-speaking peoples within the scope of the investigation, looking beyond the 'myth of the Inkidongi' and locating prophets in their wider social context reveals a more complex and dynamic picture of established prophetic lineages in the process of formalizing their authority and creating their own legitimacy together with individual 'opportunists' seeking out positions of their own. It also suggests a range of possibilities. If the Inkidongi did not at first enjoy a monopoly of prophetic power in Maasailand, but had to develop and shape their authority in response to the needs both of a particular constituency and of a particular set of circumstances, one might consider how other constituencies and other circumstances could lead to different mutations. It would, for instance, be interesting to pursue the contrast referred to above (p. 45), in the relations between prophets, elders and *murran* in different sections and Maa-speaking groups. Among the Siria, two separate prophetic lineages, those of Toroni and Tunai, have apparently shared authority, under the aegis of the neighbouring Inkidongi in Loita, without competing for followings and in the absence of serious tensions between elders and *murran*. In Uas Nkishu, however, relations between *laibons* both within *Enkang e Nchue* and between them and other 'opportunists' have been notoriously bad. Here, as in Purko and Loitai, the competitiveness of prophets was increased by, and was perhaps in part a response to, a high level of tension between elders and *murran*, especially during the colonial period. However, in Purko, *laibons* had far less influence until quite recently than in Kisongo, where the

Inkidongi first established themselves. In the northern sections a 'Kisongo' pattern of alternating alliances between age-sets is replaced by a generational opposition. To complete the picture, Samburu *laibons* have remained very marginal figures and here again the structuring of clan and age relations is different from that of the Maasai in both form and emphasis, though closer to Purko than Kisongo.[84]

Finally, one can widen the scope of enquiry still further to consider neighbouring (non-Maa) peoples who have, or have had, similar institutions. Among Kalenjin- and Ateker-speaking peoples there are powerful lineages of *orkoiik* (s. *orkoiyot*) or *ngimurok* (s. *emuron*). Tatoga have also had prophets in the past. Small Bantu-speaking groups on the fringes of what became the Southern and Eastern Nilotic world, like Kuria, Zanaki and groups on Mt Elgon, had seers, as Ruel calls them, and so did Kikuyu and perhaps other Mt Kenya peoples. Additionally, there were famous individual prophets among, for example, the Bukusu and Gusii, though these were not apparently operating within an established tradition.[85] Linguistic analysis suggests further that *inkoiantik* ('minor *laibons*') and *isakutok* (sorcerers) – but not *iloibonok* – have deep historical roots in the region and have a fairly wide distribution.[86] Again, there are persistent links in tradition between founding figures in Maasai, Kikuyu and, perhaps, Meru. These take the form of a specific outside point of origin – Kidongoi and Nchue came (in some versions, 'together') from 'Mt Kenya' (or Mathira in Kikuyuland) – and sometimes a 'kinship' relation – Nchue/Kaamantire is connected in some traditions with 'Sancha', a Meru, and one important Kikuyu prophet lineage, the Gatherimu, incorporates 'Sitoni' and 'Thubi' (i.e. Sitonik and Supeet) into its genealogy.[87] Taken together, these traditions and claims evoke a timeless world within which the major prophet families can be located through the relationships between their founding ancestors. Clearly, tradition has both codified and edited reality: but what was that reality?

It is important not to be drawn into adopting a diffusionist position here.[88] There are two separate elements to be considered: the prophet lineages and the prophetic tradition. As it stands, the evidence is entirely insufficient to support any assertion of common origin. The notion of some *ur*-prophet lineage in East Africa seems highly implausible, and, just as we do not have to accept a single 'ancestor' for each of the prophet lineages, we do not have to assume a unified prophetic tradition. One possibility is simply that, as the Inkidongi grew more powerful, other prophets found it expedient to tap into their prestige by claiming kinship; while, at the same time, the 'myth of the

Inkidongi' was expanded to include rivals and potential competitors within a single hierarchy. However, this does not adequately account for the fact that there are historical links which, to some extent, align with these traditional claims. The Kalenjin Talai clan, for example, does seem to have been established by immigrants from Uas Nkishu and to have supplanted existing local lineages.[89] There were exchange and professional relations between Inkidongi and members of *mbari ya Gatherimu*. Nkaruiya and Olonana apparently obtained important ritual 'medicines' from Njao wa Kabacha of Gatherimu who was noted by Hobley as an important Kikuyu *mundu mugo* of the time. Earlier, the (Kikuyu) family of OlolKakwai is said to have provided the special medicines for the Kisongo *Ngesherr* or retirement ceremony. Lolkokwa ole Kashungu, a Kikuyu adopted into the Inkidongi, assisted at the Kisongo Il Dareto *Ngesherr* and Il Derito *Eunoto* ceremonies.[90] There are also close, and more than coincidental, similarities between the divining methods described for Kikuyu, Embu and Maasai.[91]

What this suggests is not a process of diffusion from a single source but a continuous flow of individuals, practices and ideas across ethnic boundaries and through networks similar to those which conveyed more ordinary commodities. The nature of prophecy as an entrepreneurial activity – and the mobility of individuals in search of fame and fortune – might well lend itself to a regional market and to a fairly rapid mutation of ideas and styles of divination and utterance. These small-scale communities were highly eclectic in their search for guidance and authority. Maasai, including Inkidongi, consulted prophets in neighbouring communities as well as their own *laibons*. There were successful immigrant Kikuyu practitioners in Maasailand and Maa-speaking prophets settled in Nandi and elsewhere.[92] Given this degree of interaction, it is likely that something of a common prophetic idiom, adapted in different ways to meet local requirements, gradually spread through the region over a long period. Its spread may have been accelerated at times by 'prophet diasporas', prompted by competition and the dissolution of communities, such as that of *Enkang e Nchue* from Uas Nkishu and, perhaps, that of Laikipiak prophets. The later break-up of the Ngosua community and the migration of the Inkidongi could also be seen in this light, although in this case the diaspora did not move beyond the confines of Maasailand. Thus, traditions of a 'convergence of prophets' may reflect, in symbolic terms, a complex reality of movement, competition, borrowing, experiment, adaptation and replacement within what emerges as a shared and syncretic prophetic tradition.

Richard D. Waller

Conclusion

It is sometimes argued that East African prophets, Maasai *laibons* in particular, might have been able to assume political leadership in the community, especially when times were out of joint, by virtue of their special skills and powers and their interstitial position, and because they offered explanations, answers and, possibly, even a plan of action. However, this approach may be misconceived, derived as it is from a view of prophets isolated from their social and intellectual context and unqualified by reference to neighbouring communities. Certainly the record in Maasailand is one of relative political failure. *Laibons* remained marginal figures. Their authority, externally impressive, was qualified, ambiguous, personal and precarious. It was always exercised in the face of challenges from rivals within what was a highly competitive field of opportunity and in despite of a degree of scepticism amongst their audience. What is perhaps more striking is the fact that they did manage to create and exploit a need for their services and to institutionalize their position and powers.

However, the larger-than-life figures of the great *laibons* still monopolize our attention and block out the dimmer, but no less important, figures of their rivals among the prophets, while the views of their critics and clients among the Maasai need further amplification. Prophets have always had to be good psychologists and image-makers, adept at managing the intuitive rapport between speaker and audience and between practitioner and client. To understand the powerful appeal of prophecy in Maasailand and beyond we must examine not only the overt image of the *laibon* but also the stuff from which it is made, the props that hold it up and the rich tradition of intellectual and moral debate on which it draws.

To survive, *laibons* have always had to adapt to changing styles of presentation and discourse. Today, while still continuing as private practitioners, advising raiding parties and preparing charms for ceremonies, *laibons* have moved into District Council and national politics, into administration and business and into the tourist industry. It is in this last arena that their intuitive and manipulative skills are most obviously apparent. Some Inkidongi have turned themselves into highly visible and successful exemplars and arbitrators of 'Maasai traditional culture' for the West, a role which fits appropriately, if ironically, with their marginality within their own community, but which was foreshadowed during the colonial period by the evident fascination that '*laibonism*' had for British administrators – a form of African Orientalism? To return to Spencer's point, *laibons* represent not only the 'other' but also 'ourselves'. It is their ability to present themselves to outsiders as the (traditional) Other while situating themselves in a current discourse about modernity in their own community, that enables them to continue to prosper from ambiguity and to retain their position as inside-outsiders.[93] It is a self-fulfilling prophecy that where there are sorcerers and raiders there there will also be *laibons*. A modern variant might now add researchers, film-makers and tourists to the list.

Notes

* Earlier versions of this chapter were presented at conference panels in London and St. Louis. I am grateful to the editors and to conference participants for their helpful comments. The chapter is based on material in R. D. Waller, 'The Lords of East Africa: the Maasai in the mid-nineteenth century (c. 1840–c. 1885)', (Ph.D. thesis, University of Cambridge, 1979) ch. 3; but also draws extensively on J. Berntsen, 'Pastoralism, raiding and prophets: Maasailand in the nineteenth century', (Ph.D. thesis, University of Wisconsin-Madison, 1979). I am indebted to John Berntsen for many insights into this aspect of Maasai history and for permission to draw on his unpublished material.

1. There is no entirely satisfactory translation for *oloiboni* (pl. *iloibonok*). Here I follow current usage in anglicizing the Maasai word, but referring more generally to 'prophets'. The name Inkidongi appears to be derived from *enkidong*, the divining gourd or horn that prophets use.

2. Versions of the myth in M(aasai)T(ext)/M/KA6, 11, SK4; A. C. Hollis, *The Masai* (Oxford, 1905), p. 326. Translations of the texts are deposited in Cambridge and Nairobi. For an analysis, see Waller, 'Lords of East Africa', pp. 194–202.

3. H. A. Fosbrooke, 'An administrative survey of the Masai social system', *Tanganyika Notes and Records*, 26 (1948), p. 13.

4. In the case of the Inkidongi and the prophets of the House of Nchue in Uas Nkishu, Kikuyuland or the Mt Kenya area is sometimes claimed as the place of origin – Berntsen, 'Pastoralism, raiding and prophets', pp. 126–7, 133–4; MT/M/UN17.

5. MT/M/KA8. It is said that *laibons* never die naturally and sudden deaths among Inkidongi are usually attributed to the sorcery of rivals. Among the pairs of deadly rivals famous in tradition are Mbatiany and Makoo and Olonana and Senteu. In each case, 'jealousy' led to sorcery, madness and death – MT/M/SK4, KA10; Berntsen, 'Pastoralism, raiding and prophets', pp. 207–10, 331–4; Waller, 'Lords of East Africa', p. 256.

6. MT/M/L1; Waller, 'Lords of East Africa', pp. 245–6; P. Spencer, 'The Loonkidongi prophets and the Maasai: protection racket or incipient state?', *Africa*, 61 (1991), pp. 335–6. Individual Inkidongi are sensitive to such imputations and behave with self-conscious rectitude while somewhat disingenuously deploring the malice of others.

7. Waller, 'Lords of East Africa', pp. 247–8 and references there. The elaborate and somewhat sinister *mise en scène* of reception and consultation at *laibon* homesteads and the mystique associated with their persons enhanced the psychological impact – see e.g. descriptions in G. A. Fischer, 'Am Ostufer des Victoria-Njansa', *Petermann's Mit-teilungen*, 41 (1895), p. 69; E. Johansen, *Führung und Erfahrung*, I (Bethel, nd), p. 245; and J. Adamson, *The Peoples of Kenya* (New York, 1967), p. 234.

8. Spencer, 'Loonkidongi prophets', pp. 340–1, *idem, The Maasai of Matapato; A Study of Rituals of Rebellion* (Manchester, 1988), pp. 225–6.

9. Hollis, *The Masai*, p. 299; A. H. Jacobs, 'The traditional political organisation of the pastoral Masai', (Ph.D. thesis, Oxford University, 1965), pp. 317-9; MT/M/KA15.

10. M Merker, *Die Masai* (Berlin, 1910), p. 22. According to Merker, *il Kiporon* were 'beloved of God for their readiness for peace', a possible reference to propitiousness similar to that of the *olotuno* - *ibid.* p. 312.

11. The word *aibon*, from which *oloiboni* (*laibon*) is derived, refers to both divination and prophecy. For this reason, *laibons* are sometimes referred to as 'prophet-diviners'. J. L. Krapf, *Vocabulary of the Engutuk Eloikob* (Tübingen, 1854), p. 14; *idem*, *Travels, Researches and Missionary Labours* (London, 1860) pp. 362-3; O. Kersten, *Von der Deckens Reisen in Ost-Afrika* (Leipzig, 1869), p. 24. The von der Decken expedition negotiated with two apparently influential *laibons*, one of whom was Supeet, traditionally the 'father' of Mbatiany and *oloiboni kitok* (chief *laibon*) of Kisongo at the time, but neither is specifically referred to as '*orlkibroni*'. Fischer described Mbatiany simply as '*ober-leibon*' - G. Fischer, *Das Massailand* (Hamburg, 1882), p. 28.

12. Spencer, *Maasai of Matapato*, pp. 219-21.

13. Spencer, 'Loonkidongi prophets', pp. 335-41. One such was Koiyaki who apparently terrorized the Kaputiei elders into accepting him as their prophet - Kajiado District, Annual Report (1946) K[enya] N[ational] A[rchives] PC/SP 1/5/3; N. Farson, *Last Chance in Kenya* (London, 1949), pp. 160, 170-1.

14. Berntsen, 'Pastoralism, raiding and prophets', pp. 190-4; Waller, field notes, 1973, 1981.

15. e.g. *Maisha ya Sameni Ole Kivasis Yaani Justin Lemenye* (Nairobi, 1953), pp. 8-10; C. H. Stigand, *Land of Zinj*, (London, 1913), pp. 224-6; S. L. and H. Hinde, *Last of the Masai* (London 1901), pp. 26-7. These prophecies were collected within a decade of the events they describe.

16. MT/M/SK5; J. Berntsen, 'Maasai age-sets and prophetic leadership: 1850-1910', *Africa*, 49, ii (1979), pp. 140-1; Merker, *Die Masai*, p. 93; Waller, field notes, 1973. Some of these cursing songs have come down in tradition - e.g. those exchanged between Mbatiany and the Laikipiak *laibon* Koikoti - MT/M/P7.

17. MT/M/P22; Waller, 'Lords of East Africa', pp. 259-60; MT/M/MK5, LT13, UN20.

18. MT/M/P5, SR4. For smiths generally, see Waller, 'Lords of East Africa', pp. 82-6, and J. Galaty, 'Pollution and pastoral antipraxis: the issue of Maasai inequality', *American Ethnologist*, 6 (1979), pp. 803-15.

19. Quoted in Spencer, *Maasai of Matapato*, p. 221. See also, Spencer, 'Loonkidongi prophets', pp. 336, 339-40 and E. Fratkin, 'The *loibon* as sorcerer: a Samburu *loibon* among the Ariaal Rendille 1973-87', *Africa*, 61 (1991), pp. 318-30.

20. Waller, 'Lords of East Africa', pp. 202-19.

21. *Ibid.* pp. 194-200.

22. In Berntsen, 'Pastoralism, raiding and prophets', esp. ch. 5 and summarized in *idem*, 'Maasai age-sets'. My own interpretation appears in Waller, 'Lords of East Africa', ch. 3. To some extent, our interpretations arise from a difference in research perspective. While Berntsen's view reflects the Inkidongi construction of the past, mine is influenced by the scepticism of their public.

23. Esp. Berntsen, 'Pastoralism, raiding and prophets', pp. 149-54.

24. Discussed in Waller, 'Lords of East Africa', pp. 233-7.

25. Berntsen, 'Pastoralism, raiding and prophets', pp. 183-6, 207-9, 271.

26. 'History of feud between Lenana and Sendeyo' in Ngong Political Record Book, Part B, KNA DC/KAJ 1/2/2; R. Waller, 'Emutai: crisis and response in Maasailand 1883-1902' in (eds) D. Johnson and D. Anderson, *The Ecology of Survival* (London and Boulder, 1988) esp. pp. 75-86, 92-3; *idem*, 'The Maasai and the British 1895-1905: the origins of an alliance', *Journal of African History*, 17 (1976), pp. 540-51. See also Berntsen, 'Pastoralism, raiding and prophets', pp. 305-35.

27. Waller, 'Maasai and the British', pp. 548, 551. Olonana's appointment of ole

Kidongoi's Kin

Koonyo as Purko *murran* spokesman was resisted by many of the most influential elders in the north who proposed ole Kotikosh instead – Laikipia District, Survey of Events, KNA DC/LKA 1/1; MT/M/P35, 43. The fallacy was later officially admitted – G. R. Sandford, *An Administrative and Political History of the Masai Reserve* (London, 1919), p. 3.

28. Memos by McClure, nd. and Crewe-Read, 16 January, 11 October 1911, all in Southern Masai Reserve District Record, DC/KAJ 1/1/1; Masai Province, Annual Reports (1916/17, 1917/18, 1921) PC/SP 2/15/24; Wilkinson to Tate, 13 June 1949, KNA PC/NKU 2/15/24. Largely owing to Seki's incapacity and lack of influence, the office of Paramount Chief was abolished in 1923, and, ten years later, the *laibon* suffered the further indignity of being barred from council meetings for persistent drunkenness – Masai Province, Annual Report (1924); Kajiado District, Annual Report (1933) DC/KAJ 2/1/1. In Tanganyika, however, Inkidongi *laibons* were given official positions as headmen and the *oloiboni kitok* continued to be recognized as Paramount Chief – H. A. Fosbrooke, 'Memorandum re Sociological Survey of the Masai of Tanganyika Territory', KNA DC/NRK 6/1/1.

29. Fischer, *Das Massailand*, p. 28. I owe the concept of the prophet's domain to Paul Spencer, 'Loonkidongi prophets', p. 338. The isolation of the Inkidongi was confirmed, administratively, when they were confined to Kisokon in Loita under police supervision following the murder of the then DC by one of their *murran* in 1946 – Narok District, Annual Report (1946) DC/NRK 1/1/3; *idem*, Handing-Over Report, October 1946, DC/NRK 2/1/1.

30. An analogous case is that of the Berber holy lineages, described by E. Gellner, *Saints of the Atlas* (London, 1969). I have drawn on Gellner's model in what follows.

31. By 1952, there were officially 61 direct living descendants or presumed descendants of Mbatiany alone (of whom 38 were 'sons' of Senteu) – list in Moran Officer to Officer in Charge, Masai Reserve, 9 February 1952, PC/NKU 2/15/24. The problem of dilution was increased by the fact that the prophet lineage expanded not only naturally but also through adoption and clientage. Adoptees and dependents (*il onito*) brought up in, or attached to, a *laibon*'s homestead might later claim biological kinship and set up as minor practitioners in their own right – MT/M/SK5; Berntsen, 'Pastoralism, raiding and prophets', pp. 223–4.

32. Gellner, *Saints*, p. 140. Evans-Pritchard suggested that the Sanussi brotherhood was successful in establishing its influence in Cyrenaica in part because existing 'saintly' lineages had ramified too widely and had become the clients of the groups they advised – E. Evans-Pritchard, *The Sanusi of Cyrenaica* (Oxford, 1949), pp. 51–2, 59–61, 68–70.

33. Sibling rivalry is also embedded in the foundation myth of the Inkidongi through Kidongoi and his 'brother' Moiyaa – Waller, 'Lords of East Africa', pp. 256–7.

34. See Berntsen, 'Pastoralism, raiding and prophets', pp. 195–205. Mbatiany and Senteu (but not apparently Olonana) were both associated with their fathers in this way – T. Kanyangezi, 'Mbatiany, 1824–1889: a biographical study of a nineteenth-century Maasai *oloiboni*', (B. A. dissertation, Nairobi University, nd), p. 34; J. Farler, 'Native routes in East Africa from Pangani to the Masai country and the Victoria Nyanza', *Proceedings of the Royal Geographical Society*, 4 (1882), p. 734.

35. MT/M/KA11, 6; Moran Officer to Officer in Charge, 1 November 1950, PC/NKU 2/15/24; Hinde, *Last of the Masai*, p. 24. Inkidongi thinking reflected the Maasai view that the *paterfamilias* has absolute authority to dispose of his 'possessions', both human and animal, as he thinks fit – see Merker, *Die Masai*, p. 30; Spencer, *Maasai of Matapato*, p. 14.

36. Both 'pro-Senteu' and 'pro-Olonana' accounts of the succession struggle were collected at the time and can be compared with later elaborations in tradition – for full references and analysis, see Waller, 'Lords of East Africa', p. 256.

37. *Ibid.* p. 252.
38. MT/M/SK3. For a discussion of changes of allegiance, see Waller, 'Lords of East Africa', pp. 257-60.
39. MT/M/SK3.
40. Berntsen, 'Pastoralism, raiding and prophets', pp. 195-202; MT/M/SK6, 16. One of the claimants, Nanunuaki, had earlier been his father's 'choice' and had directed raids for his age-mates in Senteu's absence during the early 1920s. Typically, there was bad blood between the three brothers – MT/M/SK15, 16; Masai Province, Monthly Intelligence Report (May 1936) PC/SP 3/1/1.
41. Complimentarity between alternate sets is strongly marked among some Maa-speakers, as is opposition between adjacent sets – see P. Spencer, 'Opposing streams and the gerontocratic ladder: two models of age organisation in East Africa', *Man*, 11 (1976), pp. 153-75. Although Inkidongi were associated with the same age-sets as ordinary Maasai, they held separate ceremonies and did not usually form *manyatas*. They thus remained outside the age-set socially even though they were formally part of it.
42. Fosbrooke, 'Administrative survey', p. 21; MT/M/SK2, 4, 5. Hospitality and marriage among the Inkidongi are discussed more fully in Waller, 'Lords of East Africa', pp. 234-6 and Berntsen, 'Pastoralism, raiding and prophets', pp. 220-4.
43. MT/M/SK16, 17; ADO Loliondo to DC Narok, 30 April 1945, DC/NRK 2/2/3; Waller, 'Lords of East Africa', pp. 209-10; Fratkin, '*Loibon* as sorcerer', p. 320; DC Nanyuki to PC Central, 26 August 1954 and 19 January 1956, PC/NKU 2/15/24.
44. Waller, 'Lords of East Africa', pp. 218, 238-9; MT/M/SK2, 3; Berntsen, 'Pastoralism, raiding and prophets', pp. 203-5; memo. by Crewe-Read, 11 October 1911, Southern Masai Reserve District Record, DC/KAJ 1/1/1; J. Thomson, *Through Masai Land* (London, 1887), pp. 95, 254. These advisers might also be active *laibons* themselves, but they tended to take a broader view of their responsibilities to the Inkidongi 'Establishment'.
45. Merker, *Die Masai*, p. 22. For examples, see Moran Officer to Officer in Charge, 9 February 1952, PC/NKU 2/15/24.
46. Narok District, Annual Report (1939) DC/NRK 1/1/3; MT/M/SK3.
47. See e.g. cases in laibon file: DC/NRK 2/2/3, and Narok District, Special Monthly Intelligence Report, 5 December 1951 and Moran Officer's Report, 8 December 1951, incl. in DC Narok to Officer in Charge, 14 December 1951, PC/NKU 2/15/24.
48. Narok District Annual Report (1925) DC/NRK 1/1/2; H. R. McClure, 'Medicine men and their powers', January 1910, in Southern Masai District Record; MT/M/P2, 11, KA14; 'Notes on Loibonok, 1910-1917' in Ngong Political Record Book, Part B.
49. MT/M/UN24, SK5, 13; Waller, 'Lords of East Africa', pp. 208-9, 249. My interpretation here differs slightly from that of Berntsen who sees the distinction only as a matter of ranking – Berntsen, 'Pastoralism, raiding and prophets', p. 185. The negative distinction serves to emphasize the self-consciously altruistic, and somewhat defensive, image that 'real *laibons*' project of themselves as men 'set apart' to be the protectors and benefactors of the communities they serve. They claim that, despite the wealth it may bring, their skill is not ultimately exercised for profit and complain that the number of 'charlatans' has increased over the years in response to 'commercialisation'.
50. Gellner, *Saints*, pp. 147-8; Waller 'Lords of East Africa', pp. 261-3; MT/M/SK3. For a list of 'latent' *laibons*, see MT/M/P20. Opinions differ as to whether the Sikirari should be regarded as a separate section or as a sub-group of Kisongo and whether all Sikirari were 'lay' Inkidongi. My own data is incomplete but it does suggest that Sikirari differed, at least originally, from other Maasai sections in various ways and that they were seen, and saw themselves, as separate from Kisongo – Fosbrooke, 'Administrative survey', p. 7; Jacobs, 'Organisation of the Masai', p. 321; MT/M/SK3, 4, 13.

51. Berntsen, 'Pastoralism, raiding and prophets', pp. 142, 257–68.

52. These correlations were first suggested by Paul Spencer to whom I am indebted for this and many other insights into the relationship between *laibons*, *murran* and elders.

53. Kersten, *Reisen*, p. 24; Ainsworth to Craufurd, 13 June 1899, KNA Coast Province MP 75/47; Berntsen, 'Maasai age-sets', p. 141; Fosbrooke,˙'Memorandum re sociological survey'.

54. Merker mentions that both Mbatiany and Senteu had 'bodyguards', drawn from Kisongo and Loitai *murran* respectively – Merker, *Die Masai*, pp. 21, 80. See also e.g. MT/M/P27. One informant described raiding as 'like a trade between *laibon* and *murran* – MT/M/DK3, and also MT/M/KE6.

55. R. L. Tignor, *The Colonial Transformation of Kenya* (Princeton, 1976), pp. 75–82. Fines were extended to elders under the provisions of the Collective Punishment Ordinance (1909); and *laibons* prosecuted under the Witchcraft Ordinance (1925). For cases involving *laibons*, see e.g. Narok District, Monthly Intelligence Reports (November 1939) KNA PC/Ngong 1/1/1 (Kone sentenced to 5 years' Hard Labour); Attorney-General files: 2/114 (Raids on Tanganyika) and 4/4911 (Meatu Raid – Senteu deported to Meru for 7 years).

56. See generally, U. Almagor, 'Raiders and elders: a confrontation of generations among the Dassenetch', in K. Fukui and D. Turton (eds), *Warfare Among East African Herders* (Osaka, 1979), pp. 119–47. There is also an interesting structural parallel between the elders and the *murran* on the one hand, and major and minor *laibons* on the other.

57. See e.g. the alleged involvement of Kimoruai s/o Olonana in the *murran* 'riot' at Rotian in 1935 – DC Narok to Officer in Charge, 16 July 1935, PC/SP 6/2/1A – and of Oruma ole Nailyang with the 'rebel' *murran manyata* at Kirtalu in 1936 – DC Narok to ADO Loliondo, 18 and 23 May 1936 and ADO Loliondo to DO Monduli, 2 June 1936, in KNA DC/Ngong 1/1/21.

58. For Maasai views, positive and negative, see e.g. MT/M/LT9, 13 (on Senteu as chief) and transcript of enquiry into prosecution of Konorou ole Senteu under the Witchcraft Ordinance, May 1943, in DC/NRK 2/2/3. For administration views, see e.g. comments on *laibons* generally, Kimoruai, and Senteu (rehabilitated after 1926) in Masai Province, Annual Reports, (1922, 1929, 1933), and on Simmel in Moran Officer to Officer in Charge, 25 June 1950, PC/NKU 2/15/24.

59. MT/M/SK2. See e.g. the predicament of Kimoruai, caught between elders, *murran* and administration in Purko – Narok District, Annual Report (1929) DC/NRK 1/1/2.

60. Reconstruction based on: MT/M/LT3, 4, 6, 7, 11, P38; Masai Province, Annual Reports (1918/19, 1920/21); *idem*, Monthly Intelligence Reports (July–August 1934, May, December 1936, April 1937); Loitai Elders to DC Narok, 15 May 1936, DC/Ngong 1/1/21; Narok District, Annual Report (1940) DC/NRK 1/1/3; *idem*, Monthly Intelligence Reports (January–February 1941); RW Meinertzhagen, *Kenya Diary, 1902–1906* (Edinburgh and London, 1957), p. 30; Chiefs' Records in Ngong Political Record Book, Part B.

61. The best description and analysis is to be found in Spencer, *Maasai of Matapato*.

62. Berntsen, 'Pastoralism, raiding and prophets', pp. 214–9. For examples, see extracts from Kajiado District, Monthly Intelligence Reports (July, September 1951), Moran Officer to DC Kajiado, 18 June 1951 and DC Kajiado to DC Narok, 24 June 1951, all in PC/NKU 2/15/24.

63. Practice varied between sections and over time. Some prophets, Senteu for example, officiated for several sets in succession and for more than one section. Others, like Koiyaki, were consulted by one section only; and some sections, like Siria and Kisongo, preferred to choose different *laibons* for succeeding ages.

64. MT/M/KL11; Berntsen, 'Pastoralism, raiding and prophets', pp. 333–4.

65. Narok District, Annual Report (1916/17) DC/NRK 1/1/1; Masai Province, Annual Reports (1916/17, 1917/18, 1922, 1929); DC Ngong to Officer in Charge, 5, 24, 27

April 1916, DC/KAJ 9/1/1/1; Officer in Charge circular letter, 22 March 1922, Ngong Political Record Book, Part A, DC/KAJ 1/2/1; MT/M/P33, SK16.

66. Merker's account, from the late 1890s, notes the deputation and consultation but little else – Merker, *Die Masai*, pp. 71-2, 77-8. Before this time, it is not clear that the relationship between *laibon* and section had been developed and institutionalized through the ceremonial cycle associated with the age system, though Erhardt was told that 'different parties' selected a 'common leader' – J. Erhardt, *Vocabulary of the Enguduk Iloigob* (Ludwigsburg, 1857) 28.

67. S. Bagge, 'The circumcision ceremony among the Naivasha Masai', *Journal of the Royal Anthropological Institute*, 34 (1904), pp. 167-8. But see Berntsen, 'Pastoralism, raiding and prophets', pp. 326-7 for analysis of Olonana's role.

68. Laikipia District, Annual Reports (1909/10, 1910/11) DC/LKA 1/1; memo. by Crewe-Read, 11 October 1911, in Southern Masai District Record; W. R. McClure, 'District record for the guidance of the officer administrating the Masai Southern Reserve', January 1910, KNA Native Affairs Dept. Ms., 19/iii/47; Girouard to Read, 3 March 1910, P[ublic] R[ecord] O[ffice] CO 533/72; 'Report on Girouard's meeting with Lenana', 2 February 1910 and 'Notes by Collyer on meeting at Kiserian', 24 February 1910, both encl. in Belfield to Harcourt, 6 February 1913, CO 533/116; MT/M/P32, 33. The Eunoto incident is part the much larger issue of the Maasai Moves – see T. H. R. Cashmore, 'Studies in District Administration in the East Africa Protectorate, 1895-1918', (Ph.D. thesis, University of Cambridge, 1965).

69. DC Narok to DC Kajiado, 16 August 1940, DC/KAJ 2/1/7; Berntsen, 'Pastoralism, raiding and prophets', p. 218; DC Narok to Officer in Charge, 2 and 3 April 1929, PC/NKU 2/15/24; MT/M/SK5. According to one tradition, Mbatiany had delayed the circumcision of Il Dalala – W. H. McClure, 'Genealogy of Laibonok', in Southern Masai District Record.

70. The elders prepare a 'shortlist' of names from which the *laibon* makes a final selection using his *enkidong* for guidance – Spencer, *Maasai of Matapato*, p. 145; Merker, *Die Masai*, pp. 73-4; MT/M/SK12, 15, P33.

71. Fischer, *Das Massailand*, p. 44; Merker, *Die Masai*, p. 74. Jacobs suggests that he may have been the only 'ritual expert' before the arrival of *laibons* – Jacobs, 'Organisation of the Masai', pp. 264-5.

72. Merker, *Die Masai*, p. 76; Berntsen, 'Pastoralism, Raiding and Prophets', pp. 87, 102-3. The importance to the *laibon* of the age name as a symbol of a continuing relationship is indicated by the comment of the 'Mondul laibon' [?Mbeiya] on the deputation of Loitokitok *murran* who had come to consult him about their forthcoming retirement ceremony: 'These men are mine and were given their name by me'. The *laibon* asked that they be allowed to remain *murran* until the appropriate moment and offered to guarantee their good behaviour – DO Monduli to DC Kajiado, 10 February 1933, DC/KAJ 2/1/7.

73. MT/M/UN13, 17, 20, SR9, 11, MK6, 8; Waller, 'Lords of East Africa', pp. 198-9.

74. R. Waller, 'Interaction and identity on the periphery: the Trans-Mara Maasai', *International Journal of African Historical Studies*, 17 (1984), pp. 251,277.

75. MT/M/SR7-8, 12-13; Berntsen, 'Pastoralism, raiding and prophets', pp. 261-2.

76. MT/M/UN4, 20; Fischer, 'Am Ostufer', p. 69. Among others were Lekibes, a local *laibon* on Laikipia and 'Donytuli s/o Vomari', whose father was allegedly a Maasai *laibon* who had migrated to Meru – Thomson, *Through Masai Land*, p. 220; L. von Hohnel, *Discovery of Lakes Rudolf and Stephanie*, vol. I (London, 1894), pp. 396-8; W. A. Chanler, *Through Jungle and Desert: Travels in East Africa* (London, 1896), p. 248.

77. Fosbrooke, 'Administrative survey', p. 13; Berntsen, 'Pastoralism, raiding and prophets', pp. 187-9.

78. Waller, 'Interaction and identity', pp. 252, 259-60, 262; *idem*, 'Maasai and the British', esp. pp. 544-5.

79. MT/M/DK5, KE11,P4; Bastmeller to Hardinge, 12 March 1900, encl. in Hardinge

to Salisbury, 15 May 1900, PRO FO 2/287; 'Medicine men 1910' in Laikipia District, Survey of Events; Officer in Charge to DC Ngong, 4 May 1916, DC/KAJ 9/1/1/1.

80. For Baraguyu: T. O. Beidelman, 'The Baraguyu', *Tanganyika Notes and Records*, 55 (1960), p. 253. For Samburu: P. Spencer, *Nomads in Alliance* (London, 1973), pp. 113–5; Fratkin, '*Loibon* as sorcerer', p. 320. Fratkin implies that Samburu *laibons* are really diviners rather than prophets – Fratkin p. 330.

81. Waller, 'Lords of East Africa', pp. 194, 221–5.

82. Berntsen, 'Pastoralism, raiding and prophets', pp. 257–62 (but see above p. 51); Chanler to Royal Geographical Society, 20 September 1893, printed in *Geographical Journal*, 2 (1893), p. 540. Several of the Samburu *laibon* families claim Laikipiak origin – E. Fratkin, 'A comparison of the role of prophets in Samburu and Maasai warfare', in Fukui and Turton, *Warfare Among East African Herders*, p. 55; C. W. Hobley, *Ethnology of the Akamba and Other East African Tribes* (London, 1910), p. 160.

83. Berntsen argues tentatively that 'the unity centered around prophets' gave the Maasai the edge in the '*Iloikop* Wars' (against opponents who had no such overall direction) but this is debatable and he himself emphasizes the ephemeral nature of Inkidongi leadership. The point, an important one, must await further analysis of the socio-political structure of *Iloikop* – Berntsen, 'Pastoralism, raiding and prophets', pp. 149–54, 270–1.

84. MT/M/SR9, 11; Waller, 'Interaction and identity' pp. 262–5; P. Spencer, *Models of the Maasai*, forthcoming; Jacobs, 'Organisation of the Masai', pp. 240–89; P. Spencer, *The Samburu* (London, 1965) esp. ch. 6. Although Fratkin suggests that the greater prominence of prophets in Maasai derives mainly from differences in the ecology of herding and raiding in the two societies, his own analysis points equally to social factors – Fratkin, 'Role of Prophets', esp. p. 66.

85. G. W. B. Huntingford, *The Southern Nilo-Hamites* (London, 1953) (ethnographic summary, but see also Anderson in this volume); M. Tomikawa, 'The migrations and inter-tribal relations of the pastoral Datoga', in Fukui and Turton, *Warfare Among East African Herders*, pp. 20–1,26; M. J. Ruel, 'Kuria seers', *Africa*, 61, iii (1991), pp. 343–53; J. M. Weatherby, 'Inter-tribal warfare on Mt Elgon in the nineteenth and twentieth centuries, *Uganda Journal*, 26 (1962), pp. 203, 209; W. S. and K. Routledge, *With a Prehistoric People: the Akikuyu of British East Africa* (London, 1910), pp. 249–51; G. Wagner, *The Bantu of North Kavirondo* (Oxford, 1949) vol. I p. 212; W. Ochieng, 'Black Jeremiah', *Journal of the Historical Association of Kenya*, 1 (1972), pp. 8–11. Lamphear's account of the 'rise' of the Meturona prophet Lokerio and of the 'opportunist' Lokorijam among the Turkana offers some interesting parallels with the Maasai *loibonok*. Although he terms them 'Great Diviners' (*Ngimurok Aakuj*), it is clear from his informants that they were, in fact, seers – J. Lamphear, *The Scattering Time: Turkana Responses to Colonial Rule* (Oxford, 1992), pp. 29–40.

86. *Enkoiantiki* from proto-Kalenjin source *o:rko:iyo* (modern Kalenjin *orkoiyot*). *Asakut* = 'to bewitch', from proto-Kalenjin *?sa:k/se:k* = 'to do with magic'. Ehret suggests that both these words in Maa are borrowings from sources which must ultimately be southern Nilotic and pre-date Maasai occupation – C. Ehret, *Southern Nilotic History* (Evanston, 1971), pp. 18–19, 76.

87. MT/M/KA11, UN17; Berntsen, 'Pastoralism, raiding and prophets', pp. 133–4; notes on *Uhoro wa Mbatia* in Barlow Papers, Nairobi University Library; K King (ed.), *Harry Thuku: An Autobiography* (Nairobi, 1970) pp. 95–6. One lineage in the Acera clan also claimed a connection with the Inkidongi – G. N. Muriuki, 'A History of the Kikuyu, 1500–1900', vol. I, (Ph.D. thesis, University of London, 1969) pp. 157–8, 320. One Samburu *laibon* family claims descent from 'Sancha' – Fratkin, '*Loibon* as sorcerer', p. 331. 'Sancha' is not known as such in Meru, but 'Komenchue' (?Nchue) does appear in the genealogical traditions of the Mugwe. Like some representations of Kidongoi, the

Mugwe had a tail and a divining horn - B. Bernardi, *The Mugwe: A Failing Prophet* (London, 1959), pp. 48, 51-2, 56-9, 72, 75, 101.

88. I am grateful to Tom Spear for drawing my attention to this tendency in an earlier draft.

89. P. K. arap Magut, 'The rise and fall of the Nandi orkoiyot, c. 1850-1957', in B. G. McIntosh (ed.), *Ngano* (Nairobi, 1969), pp. 95-9.

90. MT/K(ikuyu)2; Chiefs' Records and 'Notes on Loibonok' both in Ngong Political Record Book, Part B; C. W. Hobley, *Bantu Beliefs and Magic* (London, 1922), pp. 184-6; Berntsen, 'Pastoralism, raiding and prophets', p. 135; Fosbrooke, 'Administrative survey', p. 17.

91. Routledge, *Prehistoric People*, pp. 267-8; L. S. B. Leakey, *The Southern Kikuyu Before 1903*, vol. III (London, 1977) pp. 1191-2; G.St.J. Orde Browne, *The Vanishing Tribes of Kenya* (London, 1925), pp. 186-7; Berntsen, 'Pastoralism, raiding and prophets', pp. 190-2; Waller, field notes, 1973, 1981. Kikuyu and Embu diviners, like some Maasai prophets, used special markers as well as pebbles or black beans counted out into heaps.

92. Fosbrooke, 'Administrative survey', pp. 14, 22; Ochieng, 'Black Jeremiah', p. 6; Masai Province, Monthly Intelligence Reports (March 1939) KNA ARC(MAA) 2/3/20/1; MT/M/P2. The DC Narok believed that more than half the minor practitioners were from Kikuyuland - Narok District, Annual Report (1926) DC/NRK 1/1/2.

93. On this discourse, see further T. Spear and R. Waller (eds), *Being Maasai* (London, 1993), pp. 301-2. An example of successful entrepreneurship involved the participation of the then *oloiboni kitok*, Simmel, in the production of 'Disappearing World' films and the widening of his clientele to include whites.

Three

Fertility
as Power

*Spirit Mediums, Priestesses & the Pre-colonial State
in Interlacustrine East Africa*

IRIS BERGER

In his assessment of the literature on religious movements in sub-
Saharan Africa, Terence Ranger analyses the changing trends in
understanding the relationship between religion and politics. Drawing
his examples primarily from East, Central, and Southern Africa, he
argues convincingly that religious ideology and practice during the colonial period require understanding on their own terms, and not simply
as a reflection of anti-colonial sentiment.[1] Absent from his discussion
of popular consciousness, however, is any reference to the ways that
gender has shaped either the meaning and form of religious expression
or the allocation of power within particular groups.

By ignoring the issue of women as historical actors, many critical
aspects of religion are obscured and the opportunity for exploring the
relationship between personal and political life is lost. Studies of spirit
possession and spirit mediumship, in particular, with their frequent
emphasis on reproduction and fertility, draw attention to the potential
for understanding pre-colonial history from a new vantage point. Such
a perspective invites both the reconnection of women's personal
experience with the history of states and lineages, and the historical
analysis of the metaphors of gender that permeate daily religious
experience, oral tradition and conceptions of political power. These
forms of religious expression also involve the more frequently explored
themes of women's collective organization and their responses to a
male-dominated social order. In addition, the study of traditions of

possession and mediumship raises important questions about the development of prophetic idioms.

In seeking to illuminate the issue of gender in East African religious history, *kubandwa* spirit mediumship ceremonies provide a case study with unusual historical depth in which mediumship, prophecy, gender, and politics were closely intertwined. Found throughout the inter-lacustrine region, its deities, rituals, myths, and symbols provided a widely diffused language for conceptualizing spiritual power. Janice Boddy has described the 'culture' of the Hofriyati of the northern Sudan as consisting of 'a plurality of voices orchestrated by common themes, idioms, meanings'.[2] *Kubandwa* provided a similarly varied text that knitted together royal power and women's local ceremonial authority in complex, ambiguous ways; but its basic theme centered on fertility and generativity, whether of individuals, lineages, or states.

Recent research convincingly traces transformations over time in *kubandwa* to the tensions between local and dynastic power.[3] But many questions concerning gender are left unclear. How did women's place in local societies and their ceremonial power change as kings sought to craft a hegemonic religious ideology based on *kubandwa* deities, and how did women maintain some access to religious and political authority under these conditions?[4] Or, formulated somewhat differently, how and why did kings and mediums come to share a common language of spiritual power and how did they influence each other over time? These questions relate to another issue (which this article addresses less fully), of how increasing political centralization and class differentiation reshaped women's lives.

A study of *kubandwa* also raises and illuminates several distinctive issues concerning the history of East African seers, prophets, and pro-phecy. First, it reminds us that, in cases where most prophets were men, the gendered association of religious leadership is just as important to explain and to understand as in situations of female religious pre-eminence. Apparently assuming men's authority as the norm, scholars too often fail to problematize male power.

Second, *kubandwa* helps to illuminate the contexts that generate and sustain both spirit mediumship and prophetism, raising the issue of the different potential for inspired voices and movements in varied political settings. Perhaps not accidentally, southwestern Uganda, the only decen-tralized area in the Lake Region, produced a movement similar to pro-phetic movements elsewhere in East Africa. Centering on the spirit of a former queen named Nyabingi, its leaders amassed considerable personal power that was used, in part, as a counter to both Rwandan and British incursion.

Finally, analysed together, *kubandwa* and its Nyabingi-related off-shoot open up the issue of the boundaries between varied forms of religious expression and power. Although *kubandwa* initiates usually are defined either as spirit mediums, or (in certain cases) as priestesses or priests, those claiming authority through Nyabingi are variously referred to in the literature as priests or prophets. Since Nyabingi worship grew out of and incorporates much of the language of *kubandwa*, a comparative understanding of the two forms of expression helps to address the issues raised in this volume.

Early travellers documented what anthropologists would later confirm: the female predominance in *kubandwa* groups, whether dedicated to the Cwezi deities in western Uganda and northwestern Tanzania or to Ryangombe in Rwanda and Burundi. Writing of Bunyoro, for example, Emin Pasha described the strikingly clad 'Wichwezi sorceresses, a large number of whom are found at the court of every Wawitu prince'.[5] For most women, however, spirit mediumship was a language of local daily life, and its ceremonies reflected a concern with problems of fertility and childbearing. As elsewhere in Africa, since motherhood conferred respect, prestige and adulthood, its unpredictability invited efforts at ritual and symbolic control. In its connection with such individual issues rather than with group social relations, *kubandwa* closely ressembled certain Central African 'cults of affliction'.

To address particular symptoms, such as prolonged illness or an inability to bear children, a diviner might recommend initiation. During this ceremony, which varied in detail from one area to the next, women experienced a symbolic death and rebirth into a new society, superior to the profane and separated from it in many respects. Mediums were given special regalia, taught to communicate with the supernatural world through spirit possession, and instructed in a secret vocabulary, food taboos, and other esoteric knowledge. As in other rites of passage, initiates passed through a liminal period in which they were abused, terrified, and humiliated before symbolically shedding their former personalities and being reborn into a new family. Thus, birth and generativity lay at the heart not only of women's motivation for becoming adepts, but also at the heart of *kubandwa* initiation. The widespread conception of a woman's relationship to the deities as a 'marriage' further emphasized the prospect of fertility.

Only occasional accounts, such as that of Emin Pasha, document the national position of such religious figures. As elsewhere in Africa, colonial rule profoundly disrupted many forms of political power, and European officials were particularly loathe to acknowledge female authority figures. But, throughout the Lake Region, observers wrote of mediums at the courts of kings and local rulers and of itinerant groups of religious specialists. The high level of respect, and sometimes fear, they inspired earned them food and hospitality during their travels. Although the position of these officially recognized specialists varied from place to place, their authority usually rested on their connection with agricultural abundance and healing. Thus, in states where kings and queen mothers were closely identified with agricultural prosperity, women's procreative powers might be harnessed for the national good.

Women's social position also made the potential redressive advantages of *kubandwa* affiliation immediately apparent. In hierarchical societies in which small numbers of cattle-keeping aristocrats exercised power over peasant farmers,[6] women were considered inferior to men of their own class. Those from peasant families worked longer hours than men and all women were expected to be subservient and to obey the dictates of their fathers and husbands. Although a few upper-class women attained considerable wealth and authority, men monopolized political power, judicial rights, the right to inherit cattle and land, and 'indeed, . . . [the right] to independent action outside the walls of the house'. In Burundi, the subservience demanded of women was extreme. According to Ethel Albert, 'Unlike a man, a Rundikazi [Rundi woman] does not speak, nor does she look you in the eye. To each question, she answers *Ndabizi?* How should I know? . . . Whatever she does, she does within the limits of her various feminine roles.'[7]

Through initiation into *kubandwa*, some women could escape temporarily from their subordinate position. The new mystical life of adepts enhanced their social status, allowing them to share in the food taboos of the upper classes on ceremonial occasions and, in some areas, granting them specific privileges and legal immunities. While possessed, women often dressed in men's clothes and experienced the freedom of action normally considered a male prerogative. Furthermore, some mediums might attain continuing prestigious positions as spirit wives and priestesses, enabling them to exercise considerable ceremonial authority with kings and other powerful men. Since the patrilineal and patrilocal kinship systems of the region excluded women from commemoration of their husbands' lineage spirits, *kubandwa* offered women a religious alternative that reflected their specific concerns with fertility and health.

But spirit mediumship and possession cannot be fully analysed in terms of direct practical goals. In helping to decode the richness and the contradictions of such practices, post-modernist anthropologists have illuminated our understanding of African religion. Thus, in criticizing the instrumentalism of I. M. Lewis' analysis of the anti-male content of the *zar* in Northeast Africa, Janice Boddy outlines a complex individual process by which possession may subtly restructure women's perceptions of their experience and the contradictions governing their lives. Although *zar* embodies counter-hegemonic elements, the process of awareness that it may provoke is ultimately creative, imaginative, and individual.[8] This insight probably also applies to *kubandwa*, in which possession gave women a culturally sanctioned dramatic licence that may have altered their lives in ways difficult to pinpoint. It does not, however, negate the argument that some women were able to augment their position in society by becoming spirit mediums.

The rich historical traditions of the Lake Region document, sometimes in coded and ambiguous ways, the lengthy process by which dynasties succeeded one another. Invariably, these legends legitimize the position of the ruling groups that held power in the late nineteenth century. In western Uganda and northwestern Tanzania, the links between *kubandwa* ceremonies and historical texts are immediately evident through the Cwezi. They figure both as the validating ancestors for all legitimate forms of political power and as the collective name for the major pantheon of pre-colonial *mbandwa* spirits. To the south, where religious ceremonies centered on Ryangombe and his followers, traditions expressed the conflicts between kings and deities more openly. But *kubandwa* officials held high positions at court that attested to the close relationship that developed over time between centralized authority and local, female-dominated religious idioms.

Embedded in the Cwezi and Ryangombe legends and in the historical material that illuminates their meaning are clear ideas about women, gender, and political power. The Nyoro dynastic myth begins with two episodes that both turn on kings who manipulate their daughters' reproductive capacities to their own political advantage. First, the king 'of the underworld' Nyamiyonga, whose immense herds of cattle signal his pastoralist origins, sends his daughter to charm a neighbouring king, Isaza, into marrying her. Their son, Isimbwa, impregnates the daughter of Bukuku, a usurper who has mutilated and isolated his offspring to prevent her from giving birth to an ill-omened child. The woman's name, Nyinamwiru, indicates her peasant status. The link with the succeeding Bito dynasty is similarly established through the marriage of Isimbwa's son. Thus, as in many African traditions, marriage forms the primary metaphor for the connections between succeeding groups of rulers and for the relationships between different peoples, in this instance pastoralists and farmers. Throughout, the tradition emphasizes male agency in orchestrating dynastic alliances, all of which turn on the control of women's fertility. By stressing women's regulation of their own reproduction, *kubandwa* represents a counter-hegemonic voice of female control.

Yet even within the traditions, women were more than just passive vehicles for the realization of male political ambitions. Many aspects of the Cwezi legends confirm the idea that *kubandwa* ceremonies represented an ancient idiom of religious power that was adapted and harnessed by successive ruling groups in order to enhance their own authority and to win popular support. Within the groups that represented 'Cwezi' claims, women often were recognized as priestesses and as bearers of religious authority. When Wamara, the last of the Cwezi rulers, retreated, he reportedly designated two royal women to instruct the incoming Bito in the rituals of kingship. Here women figure as reproducers of tradition rather than of kings; but their place in insuring dynastic continuity is equally critical. The ceremonial centre dedicated to Mulindwa, the second Cwezi ruler according to tradition, also included a number of priestesses.

Female power was most pronounced at the shrine on Mubende Hill dedicated to Ndahura, the first Cwezi according to tradition and the god of smallpox. Situated on a ridge nine miles long and presided over by a hereditary priestess named Nyakahuma, the site was a centre of pilgrimage, inspiring the respect of kings and commoners alike. The rulers of both Bunyoro and Buganda sought her advice on a wide range of matters and refrained from fighting against her. Ceremonies at Mubende Hill, which included the ritual sanction of the priestess, were a requisite part of royal accession ritual in Bunyoro. Once again, female involvement in reproducing the dynasty and, by extension, the entire political order, was underlined. Nyakahuma's power parallelled, but was probably less extensive, than that of the priest of Wamara, centered at Masaka Hill.

The three sites dedicated to Ndahura, Mulindwa, and Wamara clearly represented the claims of earlier political and religious leaders within the Bito kingdom. Through the spiritual and political power of both priestesses and priests, new kings sustained their own claims to supernatural validation and to continuity with the past. In this realm, which implies an association with generativity, women's symbolic place was particularly important.

The southern Lake Region differed in important respects from the north. The area had no history of an elitist, priestly religious tradition that might retain the imprint of the powers of pre-dynastic rulers or ceremonial figures, whether male or female. Apart from a few brief recorded episodes of conflict and co-operation between kings and deities, the traditions of the ruling dynasties and those of the *Imandwa* were quite separate. Thus, the story of Ryangombe in Rwanda focused on his contested accession to the kingship of the *Imandwa*. Still, as in the Cwezi tales, Ryangombe produced an heir by marrying a woman he met on his travels. His son, Binego, was a remarkable, larger-than-life figure whose astute advice won Ryangombe his position as king. Women played diverse parts in the tale. Ryangombe's wife was passive, but beneficient, while another woman had her child killed by Binego when she refused to give the infant to him.

The second major episode in the *Imandwa* legends continued the theme of women as vulnerable, but also portrayed them as potentially dangerous. When Ryangombe departed to go hunting, he defied his mother's pleas to postpone the trip because of her prophetic dream the previous night. Each time he encountered one of the omens of which she had warned him, he reminded his companions, 'Do not speak the words of a woman while hunting.' Continuing to flout his mother's cautions, he finally was killed by a woman who had been transformed into a buffalo. Avenging his father, Binego located the woman and her child and killed them both.

In these legends, women are portrayed as possessing remarkable powers of prediction and the ability to transcend normal boundaries between the animal and the human world. But they also exist in a permanent adversarial state with Binego, and with Ryangombe, for whom hunting and women had to be strictly separated. This conflict was in keeping with the common portrayal of the chief *Imandwa* figures as hostile to established norms and conventions and as envisioning themselves, sometimes to their peril, as superior to other supernatural forces, including those embodied both in women and in kingship. Furthermore, by killing a woman and her child in both variants of the tradition, Ryangombe's son Binego helped to establish the counter-tradition of the *Imandwa*; in opposition to the royal association with fertility, Ryangombe's son was a destroyer of women and the new life they created.

The question that follows from this exploration of mythical themes is how they related to the institutional history of *kubandwa* and its relationship to political power in each area. Throughout the Lake Region, spirit mediumship and possession almost certainly formed part of the religious idiom of the area's earliest Bantu-speaking peoples. These beliefs and ceremonies operated within religious contexts centering on creator gods and family spirits. Rituals focused on large numbers of localized, often kin-based deities; on female divinities concerned with agriculture and childbearing; and on other spirits connected with natural forces, particular places, and specific occupations. Ceremonies also might honour the spirits of deceased clan heads and rulers whose renown dated back a number of generations and whose worship had diffused outside of their own family or local groups. Many such deities later were incorporated into the comprehensive mythologies of the Cwezi or Ryangombe.

In the north, however, but not in the southern area, temple-centred ceremonies led by formally trained priestesses and priests co-existed alongside more democratic forms of spirit mediumship. Such observances remained integral to religious practice in Buganda at the end of the nineteenth century, as indicated in descriptions of the healing powers attributed to the medium of Mukasa, the god of Lake Victoria.

> It is more than a month back, that we first heard of the intended journey to Rubaga (the capital) of one of the most noted Gods . . . in Uganda, for the purpose of curing the king. This spirit is named Mukasa, and he is supposed to be the chief deity of the Victoria Nyanza on which lake he has his dwelling. The spirit has gone by the name of Mukasa for generations back and takes up his abode in some witch of great power or medicine woman. All the people, and especially the boatmen and islanders, hold this medicine woman possessed by the evil spirit Mukasa to work miracles, and the report spread that she was going to cure the king by speaking a single word only. The chiefs, especially the older and more influential of them, hailed her coming, and began to make every preparation to receive her with honour.[9]

Highly regarded clan priestesses in Toro, which broke away from Bunyoro in the early nineteenth century, also exemplified the northern elitist practices. Able to communicate with one or two of the group's Cwezi spirits, they directed the construction of shrines, advised on their maintenance, offered prayers on periodic visits to homesteads, and invited initiates, singers, and musicians to participate in rituals. Priestesses usually shared the direction of ceremonies with the most important local medium.[10] Thus, women embodied both spiritual and administrative authority in religious matters, while also providing symbolic links between the state and local communities. But, once again, the ultimate source of their power lay in their association with reproduction, without which kin groups would die out.

Despite the differences between priestly and democratic religious forms, both may owe their origin to the practice of dedicating girls and women to the deities as spirit wives. The wide distribution of this custom and its lack of correlation with other traits suggests its long ancestry. Those consecrated to the gods in this manner were forbidden to marry and had to remain chaste for the duration of their lives. Such 'wives', dedicated to deceased kings or to other spirits, often on behalf of noble families, usually acted as priestesses or shrine caretakers rather than as mediums. As representatives of major deities, they were potentially powerful, although the description below suggests vulnerability as well. An early source from Rwanda described such a situation:

> Kayonza wishes to offer a young girl since he is ill and the diviner recommended this remedy to him. This consists of taking a young bahutu girl, bringing her to Kilala and offering her as a wife to Lyangombe so that he will refrain from torturing with illness the person who has brought him this gift. This practice is very common among batusi chiefs and on every hill there are a certain number of these young girls; no one wishes to marry them any more for fear of the spirit; they wander from family to family among the batusi who accept them as companions.[11]

Similar practices were common throughout the region. In Bushi, in eastern Zaire, family heads commonly dedicated girls to the divinity Muhima and in Buganda many priestesses, including those of Wamala and Mukasa, were attached to particular temples and separated permanently from men. Their power with the Ganda king was amply documented in the late nineteenth century. Nyakahuma, the medium and priestess of Ndahura's temple at Mubende in Bunyoro and Mukakiranga in Burundi, the 'wife' of the major deity, occupied similar positions. Mukakiranga's central role in the annual national sorghum festival suggests that her position evolved from women's ritual importance in ensuring agricultural prosperity.

In different ways once again, the power that all these women represented connected back to their association with life and human continuity. In the case of 'spirit wives' who were required to remain chaste, an important person could redirect a woman's powers of fecundity to a deity on his own behalf. Mukakiranga's position was similar, but writ on a national rather than on an individual scale. The priests and mediums of Mukasa, Wamala, and Ndahura, all represented as the healers of disease, possessed the gift of revitalization, also fundamental to the continuity of life.

The major religious changes of the latest dynastic period lay in the enlargement of scale that created national religious beliefs based around Wamara and Ryangombe and in the ideological ascendance of these deities over earlier women's spirits. Evidence of the latter transformation in the north comes from the crucial division between 'black' and 'white' spirits, usually explained as the difference between the 'white' Cwezi and the 'black' non-Cwezi servants and foreigners. The other important dividing line within the spirit world, however, that between male and female deities, also was correlated with the black–white dichotomy. In J. W. Nyakatura's list of male and female spirits and mediums, for example, all the major Cwezi are male identified. Significantly, though, lineage-based Bakiga, with no 'Cwezi' overlay, retained the term *emandwa zabakazi*, 'spirits of the women', for the local equivalent of *kubandwa*.

These distinctions suggest that at some point in time, probably during the early struggles against centralized rule, formerly female ceremonies were reinterpreted and reshaped, probably by local politico-religious figures. This process involved elevating one group of deities to the status of 'Cwezi' and ideologically demoting others, including the women's spirits, to the point where the Nkore terms for black and white deities might be translated respectively as 'malignant' and 'benevolent'.

The effect of this reconstruction was two-fold. First of all, it moulded into a unified group a number of hitherto unrelated divinities, probably as a way to forge ideological cohesion against incoming Bito and Hinda rulers. Secondly, it transformed the older distinction between women's and men's ceremonies into a Cwezi/non-Cwezi dichotomy. In doing so, the religious tradition associated with women was demoted to a secondary, and sometimes unfavourable position, whereas the male-associated Cwezi gained spiritual and political hegemony.

Yet the actual place of *kubandwa* adherents in local community life varied from one area to the next, depending on the complex historical relationship between royal power and family power. In Bunyoro, for example, the elevation of the Cwezi and their family mediums in association with a centralized ruling class corresponded with a decline in the significance of territorially compact lineages, their associated ghosts, and the family heads who controlled their worship. By the nineteenth century, Cwezi adherents formed a powerful religious organization that cross-cut kinship boundaries and enhanced women's authority in local affairs. Nyoro group mediums, most commonly women, held such high status that household heads had to treat them respectfully at all times. Informants derive their title, *nyakatagara*, from the verb *okutagara*, 'to be free to do what one likes, to be privileged'. Although John Beattie doubts the accuracy of this etymology, the implication is plain.[12] Considering the content of *kubandwa* ceremonies, the collective power of mediums suggests that women may have been relatively independent in controlling their own fertility and sexuality.

The situation to the south was rather different. In keeping with the state's lesser power in Nkore, lineage heads remained important locally and usually acted as the Cwezi mediums for their families. This lineage orientation may account for the low degree of cohesion among initiates and probably left female mediums relatively disempowered by comparison with male lineage heads. Within this context here and in neighbouring Rukiga, where family heads also acted as *emandwa* leaders, solidarity among initiates was low and women became avid followers of new religious movements that emerged during the late nineteenth and early twentieth centuries.

Evidence from this decentralized political system suggests that the issue of women's political and religious authority may be more complex than previous analysis has suggested. Historians often argue that women's power has diminished with the growth of states and the emergence of pronounced class divisions in society.[13] Yet, in Africa at least, another critical element of this analysis may be the relative position of lineage heads. In Rukiga, it is possible that a climate of great insecurity, particularly in face of growing Rwandan expansion in the late nineteenth century, may have reinforced the power of heads of families and thereby undermined women's authority as expressed in *emandwa* ceremonies. Although this hypothesis is necessarily speculative, it suggests that the sources of male power in the family require as much emphasis in seeking to illuminate the origins of inequality as power over women exercised through the state. The issue of family heads is particularly pertinent in political systems in which centralized authorities tended to relate to their subjects not as individuals, but through the mediation of kinship groups. Furthermore, as suggested in the discussion of Bunyoro, the terrain on which this control was exercised, either tightly or loosely, was sexuality and reproduction. This insight suggests that some theorists, in focusing their examination of the effects of class and state formation mainly on women's social and economic roles have overlooked or underplayed the fundamental issue of control of fertility, both personal and, more broadly, in relation to the strength of lineages and states.

Nonetheless, the importance of centralized power should not be underestimated. In Buha, for example, a collection of small, frequently splintering states, much less powerful than Burundi to the north, ceremonies commemorating Kiranga maintained a strongly female orientation and, although both sexes might undergo initiation, Kiranga usually was represented by an old woman.[14] In addition, ancient female agricultural deities remained central religious figures.

In the more powerful, centralized kingdoms of Rwanda and Burundi, where the scope of *kubandwa* was national, women's power was attenuated. Spirits lacked any attachment to particular families, initiates dedicated to a single deity might be possessed by all of them, and a universalist ideology addressed itself to members of all classes. Although this democratic orientation might have made religion a force of social cohesion in these hierarchical kingdoms, such class integration occurred only in Burundi, where ceremonies might include people of different ranks. Rwandan rituals, by contrast, were more exclusive.

In Burundi, however, the imprint of female power and that of earlier ruling families coincided in the figure of Mukakiranga, the wife of Kiranga (Ryangombe). She played a major part in the great national ceremony of *umuganuro*, a yearly spiritual renewal of the kingdom in which everyone participated. Together with the king, she presided over one section of the ritual and filled a crucial role throughout. According to one early European observer:

> She and the king are equals and hold Burundi in common. The king is the visible chief of it. Kiranga incarnates himself in his wife and, through kubandwa or initiation, she becomes Kiranga in person.[15]

The royal standing accorded to Mukakiranga clearly derived from her connection with earlier sources of power in the area. The annual sorghum festival over which she presided was part of an older political tradition and she came from the highly regarded Jiji clan, which also furnished other royal ritualists and controlled the dynastic tombs. As kings devised myths and ceremonies that proclaimed their priority over Kiranga, she lost her independence and became a royal official. Yet she retained her place as an integral aspect of royal power. Once again, it is important to stress that her unique importance rested on her association with the fertility of the land.

Rwanda differed from other states of the region because the Tutsi dynasty was established in the central part of the country before the Ryangombe areas to the south were incorporated. Although it is possible to trace the historical relationships between kings and *emandwa* in greater detail than elsewhere, the implications of this national process for gender relations remain obscure. But comparison with the closely related states of Burundi and Buha suggests that, with growing royal power, the authority of priestesses or mediums associated with agriculture and fertility disappeared. By the late nineteenth century, *emandwa* representatives, all of whom were men, had become thoroughly integrated into the state's ruling institutions and ceremonies. There was no local counterpart of Mukakiranga.

On a local level, the power of the *emandwa* over non-initiates and of their deities over family spirits also reflected the nationalization of *kubandwa*. Although *kubandwa* operated within an extended family context, the lack of a clearly defined local authority in charge of ceremonies, whether a family head or a religious specialist, suggests that lineage authority was deeply eroded. The religious ascendancy of the state was expressed, as in Nkore, by contrasting the supremacy, benevolence, and protectiveness of the *emandwa* with the inferiority and malevolence of the family ghosts, *abazimu*. Unlike the *emandwa*, family spirits were equated with misfortune and injury and required ritual purging. Acknowledging the greater power of the followers of Ryangombe, they might request that their descendants honour the *emandwa* to which they had been dedicated on earth. Thus, in both the political and the religious spheres, the strength of the two 'kings' by the late nineteenth century (the *mwami* and the representative of Ryangombe), seems to have subordinated all independent authority, including that of women. Here the issue was not rulers who had harnessed women's reproductive and curative powers by controlling female religious specialists, but rather kings who, themselves, had come to embody the country's fertility.

The relative absence of archaic ceremonial features and of ancient deities in Rwanda, which elsewhere bore the imprint of women's ritual powers, illustrates the tendency in the country's religious practices for the new to displace the old completely. Similarly, in the twentieth century, rapid Christianization led to a swift decline of *kubandwa*. In this inflexibility, Rwanda contrasted with Bunyoro, where the national pantheon both during the colonial period and in earlier centuries had provided a continuing means to adjust religious beliefs to changing social and political contexts. In twentieth-century Bunyoro, for example, countless new deities were embraced within the context of older *mbandwa* ceremonies. The newcomers included such disparate influences as 'Europeanness' and its invariable ally, military tanks, 'Swahiliness', and European medicine. Significantly, however, it was men who played the major role in these adaptations.

In both northern Rwanda and southwestern Uganda, women's

openness to new religious beliefs in the late nineteenth and early twentieth centuries suggests that where *kubandwa* became increasingly identified with national ideology in the context of male-dominated political institutions (Rwanda) or with male family heads (Rukiga), women sought new religious messages that more distinctly reflected their concerns. Most prominent among the proponents of a new order were the priestesses of Nyabingi.

Arising in southwestern Uganda in regions where family heads had eclipsed female religious authorities, her worship apparently began when the Shambo kingdom was defeated (sometime between c. 1750 and c. 1800). After the death of Kitami, the reigning queen, she came to be venerated as Nyabingi, through a process of deification similar to that of the Cwezi. (One legend speaks of her as the ruler of an ancient kingdom populated only by women). Kitami's veneration originated in the efforts of Shambo pastoralists to mobilize in defence of their territory. By the nineteenth century, however, Nyabingi worship was most prevalent among cultivators and many women sought empowerment through her spirit. During this period, when Nyabingi's followers were predominantly female and many women became *bagirwa* (interpreted most often as priestess/priest, or more problematically as prophet), she was perceived as a divinity concerned primarily with fertility and motherhood.[16]

Other changes occurred later in the nineteenth century, as more men became Nyabingi priests. Some of them began to rise to prominent positions within their own families and to use their authority to acquire wealth and political power. As this process continued, Nyabingi worship was transformed from a source of fertility to a means of enhancing the power of traditional household and lineage elders. Despite this shift, women were sometimes able to take advantage of the powers of priesthood. Thus, when Muhumusa, who claimed to be the wife of the Rwandan king Rwabugiri, fled from Rwanda into Rukiga in 1905 after a royal succession dispute, she declared herself a Nyabingi *mugirwa* in a blatant effort to gain political support.

She followed a pattern already established a quarter-century earlier by another Rwandan woman who claimed to personify Nyabingi. As an outsider who based her powers on involuntary possession, Rutakira Kijuna's primary appeal lay in curative skills centering on advice, remedies, and predictions.[17] She was described in Rukiga as:

> A mysterious woman, possibly from the country of Bahima [who] arrived in Rukiga. She was accompanied by hundreds of worshippers and ordered that she be taken to Kyante where she wanted a temporary court . . . It is

said that she was 'Ekyebumbe' who could appear and disappear and could cause anything to happen. All the Bakiga feared to approach her for fear of death or other misfortune which could easily arise from being associated with such a personality. She was worshiped by many Banyarwanda but not at first by the Bakiga. After some time her fame grew wide and high, spreading like fire until King Rwabugiri IV of Rwanda came to learn about it. He ordered his representative in Bufumbira to investigate.[18]

The investigation proved fatal. Once Rutakira Kijuna's 'almost royal power' was confirmed, Rwabugiri had her killed. The story parallels those of earlier contests between Rwandan kings and Ryangombe. Nyabingi's predecessor also suffered death in some variants of the traditions, but the cause was usually more indirect. Although gender may be a factor in these different outcomes, they probably owe more to the immense power of Rwandan kings by the late nineteenth century.

As the character of Nyabingi worship changed, so did the religious preferences of women in southwestern Uganda. By the 1930s and 1940s, many had converted to Christianity. Yet, women's tendency to shape religion to their own needs again found expression through a widespread Christian revival movement.[19] For some women, the impetus to commit themselves to a new Christian community was precipitated by the desire to meet new norms of family and personal life; but for others, the movement responded to the older pressures around fertility and childbearing that had long provided a critical dimension of women's religious life and had offered female spiritual leaders a basis for empowerment.

The history of the Lake Region suggests that *kubandwa* and succeeding offshoots such as Nyabingi worship provided women with varied forms of ceremonial and political authority. As democratically structured groups through which women expressed their concern with fertility and health, *kubandwa* is probably very old. Equally ancient are women's leading roles in communal ceremonies to insure the fertility of the land and their dedication to local deities as 'spirit wives'. In northern areas of western Uganda, with more elitist religious practices, women assumed some positions of priestly power alongside men.

As the relative power of kings and lineage heads changed over time, initiates and political figures adjusted their relationships with each other. In areas where states grew stronger and more centralized, kings sought to use these forms of authority and legitimation for their own ends, and, where possible, to subordinate the independent power of religious representatives. They were only partially successful, however. Many priestesses had their ritual and political autonomy recognized, and at times when states, lineages, or both were relatively weak, women's claims to religious authority and their collective organization left them significant power in local areas. But this authority was fragile in the face of competing claims from both kings and male lineage heads, and women's association with life, fertility and healing always risked being harnessed on behalf of others. Only at times when states, family heads, or both were relatively weak did strong, collective, local women's organization allow them to control their own reproductive powers.

Thus, in relation to centralized authority, *kubandwa* provided a continuing language of political and religious power that was accessible to women as well as to men. The reformulation of this tradition by Nyabingi *bagirwa* from the eighteenth century onward simply underscores its importance as a primary cultural idiom, as well as the range of possibilities that a belief in spirit possession offered those seeking to bolster their personal position. This history also demonstrates that gendered notions of women's association with fecundity were central to local conceptions of power.

The inclusion of Nyabingi raises the issue of various types of religious specialization, while also casting another light on women's ceremonial powers. Specifically, one must ask to what extent Nyabingi represented the further development of an existing tradition of spirit mediumship, rather than the manifestation of a discrete prophetic idiom. Focusing on the difference between *emandwa* and Nyabingi ceremonies, Elizabeth Hopkins draws attention to the public nature of *kubandwa*, experienced by all initiates, as opposed to the mystery and 'high dramaturgy' of Nyabingi rituals.[20] This distinction applies also to that between the democratic and the priestly ceremonial traditions of the northern Lake Region. In this respect, and in their elitist relationship to those seeking remedies for individual crises, Nyabingi 'prophets' were nearer to priestesses or priests than to mediums. Yet both priestesses and mediums had established positions of power that were widely recognized in their communities; while speaking the inspired language associated with Nyabingi, many ordinary *bagirwa* settled into similar positions. But the idiom also lent itself to the periodic ascendancy of flamboyant, highly political figures (like Muhumusa), who brilliantly manipulated the possibilities of prophetism for their own temporary political advantage.

Thus, boundaries among prophetism, mediumship, and priesthood are difficult to delineate, in part because of their proximity to each other, all based on a belief in individual possession by spirits and in a common idiom of spiritual power. But the problem of definition is a deeper one, since the differences among these forms seem to reside less in clearly definable inherent qualities than in changing relationships, both individual and collective, between religious specialists and particular historical contexts. Based on a common language, mediumship, priesthood, and prophetism represented a continuum of possibilities for religious and political expression and leadership that both women and men might draw upon at various moments of either personal or societal distress. The only clear distinction seems to be that movements associated with 'prophetism' tend to involve more individualistic, less institutionalized expressions of power.

Perhaps more useful than trying to define a series of formal boundaries, however fluid, may be to turn our attention to Marcia Wright's idea (this volume) of 'prophetic moments' that present individuals with the possibility of varied religious responses, some more favourable than others to amassing followers for largely political purposes, some more favourable than others to the leadership of either women or men, and some more favourable than others to transforming authority born of crisis into stable positions. At least in the interlacustrine region, primarily home to expansive centralized states, dynastic changes seem to have occupied a primary place in generating such moments. But the highly individualistic authority of prophets and their propensity to gather followers for political ends, meant that royal figures eventually found ways either to contest or to neutralize prophetic power. The language of religious authority thus took shifting forms as periods of more gradual transformation followed moments of social crisis.

In discussing the periodization of religious change, Terence Ranger draws attention to Wyatt MacGaffey's and J. M. Janzen's idea of a 'tradition of renewal' that in Central Africa transcends the artificial divisions of time into pre-colonial, colonial, and post-colonial periods.[21] In their continuous efforts to maintain control of their lives in male-dominated societies, women in the Lake Region found in *kubandwa* a similar tradition, one that was remarkably adaptable and in which their primacy was generally recognized. Although political and social transformations over which they had little control might periodically diminish their authority in particular societies, women usually found a way to regenerate their prior claims in the form of new deities or new religions in which they could assert their continuing concern with health and fertility and their right to a share in the language and structures of religious and political power.

Iris Berger
Notes

1. Terence O. Ranger, 'Religious movements and politics in sub-Saharan Africa', *African Studies Review*, 29 (1986), pp. 1–69.
2. Janice Boddy, *Wombs and Alien Spirits: Women, Men and the Zar Cult in Northern Sudan* (Madison 1989), p. 7.
3. This is the major theme of my own work, *Religion and Resistance: East African Kingdoms in the Precolonial Period* (Tervuren, 1981) and of Peter Schmidt, *Historical Archaeology: A Structural Approach in an African Culture* (Westport, Conn., 1978).
4. In an earlier article, 'Rebels or status-seekers? Women as spirit mediums in East Africa', in Nancy J. Hafkin and Edna Bay, *Women in Africa: Studies in Social and Economic Change* (Stanford, 1976), I analysed *kubandwa* with reference to I. M. Lewis' ideas about spirit possession as a form of female protest against male domination.
5. G. Schweinfurth *et al.*, *Emin Pasha in Central Africa: Being a Collection of his Letters and Journals* (London, 1988), p. 285. Unless otherwise indicated, this essay is a reformulation of material from Berger, *Religion and Resistance*.
6. Kiga was the only non-centralized area in the region.
7. Both quotes come from Ethel Albert, 'Women of Burundi: a study of social values', in Denise Paulme (ed.), *Women of Tropical Africa* (Berkeley, 1963), pp. 180–1. She extends her conclusions to cover Rwanda as well as Burundi. There is little evidence that the situation was substantially different in other areas, although the strong aristocratic culture of these two kingdoms might have created a distinct environment.
8. Boddy, *Wombs*, pp. 339–45.
9. Letter from George Litchfield to Mr Wright, Rubaga, Uganda, 3 January 1880, Archives, Church Missionary Society, Letters of George Litchfield, Nyanza Mission, c/A6.0 15/1–23.
10. Brian K. Taylor, 'The social structure of the Batoro', (M.A. thesis, University of London, 1957), pp. 198–200.
11. White Fathers, 'Diare, Isavi', 6 January 1903.
12. John Beattie, 'Group aspects of the Nyoro spirit mediumship cult', *Human Problems in British Central Africa*, 30 (1961), pp. 15–18.
13. See, for example, Karen Sacks, *Sisters and Wives: The Past and Future of Sexual Equality* (Urbana, 1982) and Gerda Lerner, *The Creation of Patriarchy* (New York, 1986).
14. J. Van Sambeek, 'Croyances et coutumes des Baha', 2 vols., (unpublished manuscript, Kabanga, 1949), pp. 56, 59.
15. Julien Gorju *et al.*, *Face au royaume hamite du Ruanda: le royaume frère de l'Urundi* (Brussels, 1938), p. 45.
16. This interpretation of Nyabingi draws heavily on J. Freedman, *Nyabingi: The Social History of an African Divinity* (Tervuren, 1984).
17. Elizabeth Hopkins, 'The pragmatics of ritual identity: prophet and clan in a changing imperial field', unpublished paper presented at the Seventh Satterthwaite Colloquium on 'African Religion and Ritual', 20–3 April, 1991, p. 9. I am grateful to the author for sharing this work with me.
18. Zakayo Rwandusya, 'The origin and settlement of people of Bufumbira', Donald Denoon (ed.), *A History of Kigezi in Southwest Uganda* (Kampala, 1972), p. 138.
19. See Catherine Robins, 'Conversion, life crises, and stability among women in the East African revival', in Benetta Jules-Rosette (ed.), *The New Religions of Africa*, (Norwood, NJ, 1979).
20. Hopkins, 'Ritual identity', p. 9.
21. Ranger, 'Religious movements', unpublished version, presented at the 28th Annual Meeting of the African Studies Association, New Orleans, 23–6 November, 1985, pp. 61–2.

Four

The Frontiers
of Prophecy

*Healing, the Cosmos & Islam on the East African coast
in the Nineteenth Century*

DAVID SPERLING

This chapter seeks to examine the nature of mantic activity as practised on the East African coast in the middle of the nineteenth century. At that time the prophetic traditions of Islam and Christianity were both known on the coast. The Islamic tradition had been present for centuries, and its interaction with African mantic practices is the main topic under examination here. The Christian tradition, absent since the Portuguese withdrawal from Mombasa in 1729, had reappeared in 1844, when Johann Ludwig Krapf, an ordained minister of the Church Missionary Society, took up residence in Mombasa. In 1846, Krapf moved several miles inland to establish a mission station among the Rabai, one of the Mijikenda peoples.[1] The Christian understanding of prophecy had little direct impact on the peoples of the coast at this time, but it did colour the way in which local practices were described in those contemporary documents which have come down to us and form our main sources.

The Mijikenda had by this time been in contact with Muslims (mainly the Swahili) for several centuries. For the period before Krapf's arrival, little is known about the nature of Muslim influence among the Mijikenda. With Krapf there began a period of remarkable testimony, which lasted for some ten years until failing health forced him to return to Europe in 1853. From the mission station at Rabai, Krapf travelled extensively throughout Mijikenda country, observing their customs and rites, and recording his observations in journals and letters. Concerned about Islam as a rival religion, he noted the presence of Swahili Muslims among the Mijikenda, and wrote down numerous details about their influence and practices. During the years 1844–53, Krapf also devoted a great deal of time to the study of the Swahili language, in which he developed an intense interest. In his *Dictionary of the Suahili Language*,[2] he illustrates the meaning of words with examples from everyday Mijikenda and Swahili life, and includes innumerable descriptions and explanations of their customs. Thus Krapf came to be a unique witness. A missionary bias is evident in his writings; nonetheless they give us valuable information about Mijikenda–Swahili relations and about Muslim influence among the Mijikenda at the time.

The correspondence and journals of two other Church Missionary Society missionaries, John Rebmann (who arrived in Mombasa in 1846) and John James Erhardt (who arrived in 1849), also contain information about Muslims and Islam among the Mijikenda. In 1857, under threat from Maasai raids, the Rabai Mission was abandoned for some two years. When Rebmann returned to Rabai in 1859, he (and other missionaries who joined him later) became preoccupied with administering the mission, dealing with runaway slaves, and other material problems. From then on, the correspondence of the Rabai Mission deals mainly with these matters, and only occasionally gives useful information about Mijikenda customs and about Islam among the Mijikenda.

The Mijikenda & the prophets of God

By the middle of the nineteenth century, very few Mijikenda had become Muslim. Charles New, who came to Ribe as a Methodist missionary in 1863, commented on the infrequency of Mijikenda conversion to Islam: 'Now and then a man quarrels with his friends or tribes folk, goes to the coast, and asks to be admitted to the company of the faithful, but the great body of the people remain unaffected by Muhammadanism.'[3] The early missionaries were struck by the fact that the Mijikenda had generally resisted Islam:

It is remarkable that Mohamedanism has not made more progress.[4]

They [the Mijikenda] are pure heathen. It is a remarkable fact that though they have been associating with the Muhammadans of the coast for centuries, Islamism has made scarcely any impression upon them.[5]

They cling tenaciously to their heathen customs.[6]

Krapf soon found that his efforts at evangelization had almost no effect on the Rabai and other Mijikenda peoples. Part of the reason for his failure, as Krapf saw it, was the fact that the Mijikenda had little notion of a high God or of reward and punishment in an afterlife: '. . . the Wanica have scarcely any idea of the existence of a Supreme Being and the future state of man'.[7] In Krapf's experience, the very language of the Mijikenda lacked a term to express the concept of God: 'When I asked them their notion of a Supreme Being, they used perfectly atheistical expression . . . the term they use for God, "Mulungu", signifies properly "the heaven or the starry firmament"'.[8] At Ribe, New experienced similar problems. Like Krapf, he considered that the word *Mulungu* (in Swahili *Mungu*),[9] though inadequate, came the closest to expressing the idea of God for the Mijikenda; commenting on its meaning, he noted:

> Their notions of the Supreme Being are so exceedingly crude . . . you have to use a term Mulungu, in speaking to them of God, which conveys to them ideas which are altogether opposed to the Divine Being; indeed it is a question whether they do not often mean, by this term, nothing more than material heavens or thunder.[10]

What seems to have bothered Krapf and New was the fact that the Mijikenda did not distinguish between God's divine spiritual nature and the earthly material effects of his creative power. Krapf expressed this in his *Dictionary* entry for the word *Mulungu*: '. . . heaven and God, or supreme being, of which the African heathen have a faint idea. The heathen mind in rising to the idea of a supreme being stands still, as it were, when contemplating the heaven, and thus confounds the creator and the creature.'[11] The Mijikenda, it seems, did not perceive *Mulungu* as a spiritual being, nor did they recognize *Mulungu*, or any other being, as omnipotent. Indeed, according to New, the Mijikenda viewed the spirits of deceased persons to be equally important, if not more important than *Mulungu*: '. . . they do not think Mulungu more than equal, if not inferior to, the 'koma' – the spirits of the departed.'[12]

Evangelization among the Mijikenda was also hampered by their contact with Muslims. Krapf found that Mijikenda who lived closer to Mombasa were less attracted to Christian teaching than those living farther away.[13] Prior exposure to Islam constituted 'a considerable barrier to the introduction of Christianity', not because the Mijikenda had become Muslim but because they showed no interest in Christianity, regarding it as another form of Islam: 'whenever we are speaking of Christ to the Wanika, they think that Christ was our prophet in the same way as Muhammed was the prophet of the Swahili.'[14] Elsewhere, New wrote: 'You speak of Jesus Christ, Son of God, they stare in blank astonishment, incredulous . . .'[15]

The fact that the Mijikenda perceived a non-theist universe made them unreceptive to the monotheistic prophetic tradition.[16] The prophets of God were strangers in Mijikendaland, not just by reason of their foreign origin, but because they were alien figures claiming incredible authority.

The Mijikenda cosmos & Islam

To Krapf's mind, the Mijikenda had resisted Islam because of their preoccupation with the material world:

> Their chief aversion to religion arises from their worldly mindedness.[17]

> I can now better understand why these tribes did not fall prey to Mohammedanism. Every thought on things that are above is nonsense in their eyes.[18]

> Materialism and worldly propensities find a powerful ally in this aversion to Muhamedanism.[19]

Mijikenda 'materialism' did not exclude belief in an afterlife or a world of spirits. The world of spirits, including the spirits of deceased persons (Swa. *koma*),[20] was of great importance to the Mijikenda, but it was a realm whose very being belonged to the material world. The world of Mijikenda spirits was not so much a spiritual world as an extension of the material world, in which the spirits though invisible were as vividly present as the material things of the earth. The Mijikenda saw immortality as lived out on earth; departed spirits, like men, were tied to this world:

> They have a faint idea of man's immortality since they believe that the departed father or mother or relative lives somewhere in the sky, or in the grave, or in a grove, or in their former plantations, and that he must be appeased with food.[21]

More specifically, the Mijikenda believed that the happiness of departed spirits, like that of their living relatives, was connected in a special way to the principal village or town (Swa. *kaya*) where they had enjoyed life before death:

> The capital town or village (*kaya*) is thought especially to be the place where the *koma* resides – hence the natives bury their dead usually in the vicinity of the *kaya* by the wayside. The Wanica will carry a dead man from a great distance of 3 or 4 days to bury him near the capital . . . they believe there to be more happiness for the *koma* in the vicinity of the capital than elsewhere.

This belief binds them to the capital, the centre of their union which they deem necessary lest they lose all patriotric feeling by their being scattered abroad on their lonely plantations. All their festivities . . . all their consultations, everything is transacted in the *kaya* where the *koma* are. We may not wonder why they consider their dead people still attached to this place . . . where there is always some eating and drinking and other merriments. There is the heaven of the Wanika, at which their mind grasps.[22]

Resistance to Islam clearly stemmed from the deep internal strength of Mijikenda cosmology: their notions about life and life after death, and the religious customs and practices derived from those notions. Within the Mijikenda cosmos, living persons and the deceased were inextricably linked in a single world which was centred on the *kaya*. There, in the *kaya* of the living, were buried the ancestors whose pleasure or displeasure (benevolence or malevolence) determined the course of events; there, too, were buried the powerful charms that protected all members of society. A real communion of Mijikenda existed, binding together the dead and the living. As Erhardt observed, this bond was their defence against Islam: '. . . if the Wanika as a community were not so bound together how could it be explained that Islamism has made so little impression on them as a body'.[23]

Misfortune & the power of spirits

Notwithstanding deep religious differences between the Mijikenda and the Swahili, they shared a belief in the existence of a genre of spirits called *pepo*,[24] quite different from the *koma* spirits of deceased persons. *Pepo* were invisible (though able to appear in a variety of forms), lived in the world, and had power over men. The Mijikenda were preoccupied with the influence of *pepo* in all facets of life, attributing such ills as headaches and ulcers, and all kinds of misfortune, to their capricious power. Krapf mentions the case of a Mijikenda man whose wife had been made 'unfruitful' by an evil spirit,[25] and even such apparently chance happenings as falling from a coconut tree were attributed to a displeased spirit, whom one had to placate promptly by making an offering.[26] Endemic ill health, more than anything else, produced constant concern about how to combat the power of spirits. When traditional techniques of healing failed, the Mijikenda often turned to the missionaries for help. Over a period of one year, from, August 1849 to September 1850, Erhardt estimated that he had given medicine to some 200 persons.[27] The Mijikenda were so vexed with problems of sickness that Rebmann advised the Church Missionary

Society that 'the new missionary ought to be a medical man or possessing a good knowledge of medicine'.[28]

As for the Swahili, they were heirs to the centuries-old Islamic belief in the existence of an order of intelligent spiritual beings (called in Arabic *jinn* and *shaitan*[29]) distinct from men and angels, but created by Allah and subject to His power and judgement.[30] Soon after arriving in Mombasa, Krapf experienced this belief first-hand, when he witnessed a communal attempt to rid the town of evil spirits (*pepo*):[31]

> . . . many people of the town are seized with fever. The learned declared that the pepos or evil spirits to which the origin of diseases is ascribed, must be banished immediately by means of continual processions through the streets . . . crowds of people went processioning through the town, singing and dancing by day and night. Medicines were thrown on the streets to the purpose of casting out the devils. Twice we were requested by the Governor Ali Ben Nasser [sic] to allow the expedient ceremonies in our house.[32]

Krapf came to the conclusion that the Swahili believed in evil spirits even more strongly than the Mijikenda did: 'The superstitious views of the natives concerning demons and evil spirits are disgusting as well as unfathomable to a sober-minded man. The Muhammedans go in many respects far beyond the fancies of the heathen.'[33]

In addition to the efforts made to placate or dispel the *pepo*, the Mijikenda made frequent offerings to the *koma* spirits of the dead. Not all *koma* were equally important or powerful, but no *koma* was so unimportant that it could be ignored. The Mijikenda perceived a whole range of spirits of the dead: from the *koma* of founding ancestors,[34] to whom sacrifices would be offered at prescribed times of national importance or crisis, to the *koma* of more immediate relatives who were likely to cause personal as well as general distress.

It was common practice for individuals and families to make offerings to the spirits of deceased relatives. Krapf was told that it was the custom 'to put tembo [palm wine] and mahindi [maize], mixed up with water, upon the graves of their dead people as soon as the corn was grown on the fields to a certain height, in order to induce the koma, or shade of the dead, to cause rain to fall upon the parched plantations of the living children and relations'.[35] Both Krapf and Rebmann observed many instances of Mijikenda offering food and drink to *koma* spirits: 'maize and palm wine left on the graves of the deceased as an offering' and 'people offering rice and tembo to the *koma* for the express purpose of getting rain.'[36] Krapf described one such ceremony in detail:

This morning we were called upon by a woman who carried a small vessel in which there was a mixture of maize, rice and water to make a dedication to the koma on the grave of a dead relation. On pouring out the mixture she implored the koma, 'O koma, I offer thee this that thou mayst make rain and cause the seed I have sown in my plantation to grow for it will not grow without thee.' It is evident that the Wanika believe that the koma stays in the grave, or in the clouds and elsewhere, and that he has the power of causing rain and other temporal blessing . . . though they represent the koma as the shade of a departed man, yet they believe that having left the body he has a somewhat supernatural power . . . and must be implored and appeased by an offering before he will give rain. Some say that the koma does not eat nor drink what is placed before him, but is satisfied with merely seeing it, and with the readiness of the offering relatives.[37]

Uganga: healing & sacrifice

If spirits were the cause of sickness and misfortune, sacrifice was the cure. Indeed, the offering of sacrifice (Swa. *sadaka*) to the spirits was so frequent that Krapf called it 'the chief sacrament of these heathen which binds them together'.[38] At times, the elders would lead the people in the ceremonies of sacrifice: 'The chiefs made again a sadaka. A sheep of a black colour was slaughtered, the blood was sprinkled upon the ground and a prayer was offered to the purport that rain may fall, and that a certain sick man, for whom the sadaka was chiefly intended, might be healed.'[39]

At other times, the protagonists in the offering of sacrifices were the *waganga*. The Swahili word *mganga* (pl. *waganga*) is derived from the root-*ganga*, which means 'to bind up', 'to fasten together', or 'to mend', what is broken or injured. By extension, *-ganga* has become a generic term for healing, and the word *mganga* is used for persons who practise healing. *Mganga* is often translated in English as 'medicine-man', but the translation fails (aside from its primitive connotations) to convey the attributes and scope of *uganga* (the practice or art of being a *mganga*), which embodies a wide range of procedures, including such diverse practices as herbal medicine, sacrifices or offerings, exorcism, divination, and the use of charms to prevent or dispel misfortune.

Krapf had little respect for the *waganga*, whom he considered for the most part to be charlatans: 'shrewd and designing men who in their cunning calculations work upon the credulity of their ignorant countrymen'.[40] He noted that the Mijikenda paid for treatment 'in fowls, sheep, goats, bullocks, cloth, money, &c., according to their means, the nature of the sickness, and the agreement made previously with the *mganga*, who is generally a man of great shrewdness'.[41] Krapf was particularly critical of Muslim *waganga*, who he felt were motivated principally by the prospect of financial gain: '. . . they traverse as sorcerers the Wanika-land and offer their black arts to the deluded heathen for an enormous price'.[42] Nevertheless, he had cause to admit that the *waganga* were not altogether sham; on one occasion he mentions how he was treated for sores on his legs, and the 'native cure worked'.[43]

While acknowledging the expertise of the *waganga* in the medicinal use of plants and herbs, Erhardt and Krapf were sceptical about their power over spirits. Erhardt distinguished between two kinds of healing, medicinal and 'spiritual':

> . . . it must be said that the waganga are men who have aspired above their countrymen . . . having made out certain properties of plants, etc . . . it is not yet quite clear to us whether the waganga think indeed they have some influence upon the supposed evil spirits, or whether they ascribe the healing effect solely to their medicines.[44]

In his *Dictionary* entry for the word *mganga*, Krapf made a similar distinction between what he considered medicinal and 'superstitious' cures:

> . . . a native physician, who pretends to cure sickness by means of superstitious ceremonies, charms, &c., which he combines with remedies which have in a degree truly medicinal qualities, a circumstance which sustains the belief of the natives in his art, since he often succeeds in a cure by means of the medicinal plants, root, &c.[45]

The disbelief expressed by Erhardt and Krapf towards 'supposed evil spirits' and 'superstitious ceremonies' reciprocated the incredulity of the Mijikenda towards missionary preaching. And yet, evil spirits and the healing practices of the *waganga* were as real and important for the Mijikenda as God and Jesus Christ were for the missionaries. The Mijikenda and the missionaries differed in their perception of cosmic forces and causality. They attributed disorder (sickness and adversity) to quite different agents, and consequently disagreed about the therapy required to re-establish order (health and well-being).

The influence of Muslim healers

Though early European missionaries used the word *mganga* indiscriminately to refer to both Mijikenda and Muslim healers,[46] an important feature distinguished the Muslim from the Mijikenda *mganga*: use of the written word. The Mijikenda *mganga*, no matter how prestigious and efficacious his treatments, was unlettered, whereas the Muslim *mganga* had read and studied books in order to learn his skills. The Muslim *mganga* treated the same kinds of disorder as his Mijikenda counterpart, but he did so following procedures described in written texts; the Mijikenda *mganga* followed methods transmitted and learned orally.[47]

Because a Muslim healer was learned, he might be called *mwalimu* (pl. *walimu*) as well as *mganga*. Krapf translates *mwalimu* as 'a learned man, teacher',[48] without giving other meanings. Elsewhere in Krapf's writings, there is evidence that the word was used to refer to Muslim healers. When describing the steps taken to rid Mombasa of evil spirits, Krapf mentions 'the learned', almost certainly translating into English the Swahili word *walimu*, used in this case to refer to the Muslim *waganga* of Mombasa town.[49]

The common belief of the Mijikenda and Swahili in the power of evil spirits allowed a pervasive Muslim influence among the Mijikenda in the field of healing. Muslim *waganga* were considered especially efficacious at appeasing and controlling spirits and preventing misfortune. At Ribe, New noted how the Mijikenda 'often resort to the incantations of the Waganga in order to expel the evil spirit'.[50] Erhardt noticed that 'medicine is sought for avidly', and that 'Suaheli waganga' were 'well paid' for treating Mijikenda.[51] Muslim healers regularly took part in Mijikenda ceremonies of propitiation; at a burial ceremony at Rabai, Rebmann witnessed an offering of 'two fowls . . . slaughtered by some Muhamedans, who are generally the leading persons in the performance of such ceremonies of the Wanika . . . some blood of the fowl was allowed to drop into the grave'.[52]

Rebmann noticed another common aspect of Muslim and Mijikenda healing practices, the use of amulets and charms: 'Muhamedans and heathens would fain remove all sickness and every other evil by charms.'[53] New had similar first-hand experience of the use of charms for healing: 'A man has arrived today all the way from Kauma . . . suffering from a pulmonary complaint, covered from head to foot in charms.'[54] Muslim *waganga* would approach the missionaries trying to procure paper: '. . . in the forenoon a Muhamedan brought a fowl to exchange for paper . . . to write amulets or charms'.[55] The strong mystique attached by the Mijikenda to writing undoubtedly arose because of the use of written charms by Muslim healers.[56] Krapf observed that the Mijikenda 'are naturally afraid of books and writing',[57] and the Muslims 'make the poor pagans believe that every piece of paper contains . . . charms'.[58] On one occasion, a Mijikenda man came to Krapf wanting paper 'to make a *hirizi*, that is, a talisman to be used as a medicine against the devil and the headache of his wife'.[59] From Krapf's description, the man evidently believed that the very substance of paper (without any writing on it) was apt to effect a cure.

Perceiving the unknown: omens, divination & dreams

The Mijikenda and the Swahili received or acquired knowledge about what was hidden from ordinary perception through omens, divination and dreams. The three sources differed in the way they imparted knowledge and in the kind and level of knowledge conveyed. Belief in the validity of these sources of knowledge constituted yet another affinity between the Mijikenda and the Swahili, which they did not share with the Christian missionaries who, in keeping with the tone of contemporary Christian theology, were generally intolerant of folk beliefs in omens, divination and the interpretation of dreams.

Krapf gives several examples of phenomena popularly regarded as omens:

> . . . the Suaheli (who are Muhammedans) will return from their projected journey if they should meet a one-eyed man or if they should stumble in the outset of the journey. In like manner the pagan Wanika will abandon a journey when they see a bird which is considered not to be an auspicious one.[60]

> . . . if one meets on the road with a man of red complexion, it is a bad omen, and the traveller will return home; but if he meet with a person of black complexion, he will go on, rejoicing at the good omen.[61]

Popular omens, which conveyed unsolicited information, could be experienced and understood by anyone. More obscure phenomena such as the flight of birds required the assessment of a *mganga* versed in the art of augury, what Krapf called 'uganga wa kutazamia niuni', literally '*uganga* of observing birds'.[62] The leader of a caravan (*mkurugenzi*) was usually skilled in the art of augury, and was '. . . at the same time the *mganga* of the caravan, and by means of charms and other superstitious ceremonies [he] directs the march of the travelling party'.[63]

The practice of divination, an intentional search for the unknown, was reserved exclusively to the *waganga*. Krapf's description of divination ceremonies underscores the distinction between Mijikenda and Swahili techniques. The Mijikenda *mganga* used natural objects, such as sticks or seeds from trees, whose manipulation (allowing them to fall onto the ground, measuring or counting them) enabled him to infer the unknown:

> The *mganga* takes the *mburuga* fruit from a little bag and counts the grains four times. When he finds the same number at every counting he considers the sickness not dangerous, but if the number is unequal he suspects evil.[64]

Swahili *waganga* also used natural substances, as in the practice of *kupiga ramli*, which Krapf translates as 'to perform tephramancy', a form of geomancy using ashes.[65] But Swahili divination involved writing and the interpretation of letters or numbers:

> The Swahili physicians (waganga) on being consulted by a sick person write a number of figures on a board called bau (or ubau) which they measure under curious gesticulations, and then tell the patient the cause and remedy of the disease.[66]

Dreams transmitted a kind of knowledge quite distinct from either omens or divination, because of the direct role played by the *koma* spirits of the dead. Krapf makes various references to dreams as a means of communication between the spirits of the dead and the living: 'The natives believe that when dreaming one is in connection with the *koma* of a person who died long ago. They believe that the *koma* is the *kifuli* (shade) of a dead person . . . the shade shows one things in dreams. The shade of the living and of the dead person meet together and give each other news.'[67] Dreams could indicate precise instructions from the *koma*: '. . . the *koma* sometimes appears to a relative in a dream, in which the *koma* gives him orders with regard to sacrifices and offerings in order to avoid public calamities'.[68]

Though anyone could receive a personal communication through a dream, specific 'visionary persons' seem to have acted as mediums for the *koma*. On several occasions Krapf refers to a 'dreaming woman':

> . . . there is a Mnika woman on the plantations who orders all the sadaka which are made in the country. She pretends that the koma or shade of a departed Mnika appears and speaks to her in a dream. On awaking, she raises a sudden cry at night, which her neighbours who may hear it, do respond by asking her, 'tell us, what shall we do? what shall we offer? what is the koma's command?' Then she makes known the wishes of the koma by saying, 'he wants a black sheep, or a red hen, and such and such a quantity of palm-wine and rice, etc. Make haste in offering the sadaka.' . . . The woman is said to eat and drink very seldom or to eat only mud or mire, in consequence of which, she is thought to render herself disposed for the inspiration of the koma. When she dies, another person of her capacity is sought in her stead.[69]

In this case the blood is sprinkled on the grave of that relative whom the dreaming woman (who ordered the sadaka to be made in consequence of the apparition of the koma in the dream) may have pointed out.[70]

Many persons go to a still greater distance after a lapse of 8 to 10 years and dig out some parts of the remains of the dead relative, and bury these on the grave-yard of the capital. In burying them there, they offer a *sadaka*. Such a proceeding is observed as soon as the dreaming woman, or any other visionary person, declares that the *koma* has demanded in a dream that the relative who died and was buried at such and such a place must be fetched and buried near the capital.[71]

Another group of persons whose expertise gave them insight into the unknown were the rainmakers. Krapf attributed their success to their ability to interpret natural phenomena. Their crime, as he saw it, was that of professing to influence the course of natural events by the offering of a *sadaka*:

It is incredible what reliance the Wanika place in their rain-makers, who belong to a separate family which transfers the secret of rain-making from the father to his children, who derive a certain benefit from their countrymen – wherefore the family takes great pains to keep up its public renown. These shrewd imposters from long experience know much about the phenomenon of the sky, clouds and winds, etc., and by this means they predict that rain will shortly fall – wherefore they order a sadaka to be made. When rain actually falls, all honour is given to them.[72]

Seeing into the future

In spite of a shared belief in supernatural access to the unknown, the cosmological principles underlying Swahili and Mijikenda thought were not altogether similar. The dissimilarity emerges when we examine their attitudes towards causality and knowledge of the future.

According to Aquinas (who draws on Aristotelian principles in elaborating his Christian treatise on prediction), the future can be known in two ways, either in itself or in its causes. Only God knows the future in itself; men can at best know the future in its causes.[73] Knowledge of the future in its causes is of three kinds, depending on the degree of certainty of the causes known. First, when the known causes are certain, that is, when they 'necessarily and always produce their effect, then future effects can be foreknown and foretold with certitude, for instance, as when astronomers predict coming eclipses'. Secondly, in the case of causes that do not produce their effects necessarily, but 'do so for the most part and rarely fail, their future effects can be foretold, if not with certainty at least by some probable conjecture, as when, for instance, meteorologists by examining the heavenly bodies forecast rain or drought'. The third kind of foreknowledge is the least certain, for it depends on wholly contingent causes, that is, on causes which 'can go either way'.

In the monotheistic traditions of Christianity and Islam, the notion of prophecy denotes speaking and acting under the guidance of an omnipotent God. The prophets of God are able to know the truth, and so far as this enables them to see the future in itself, they do so not through their own powers, but through the special gift of divine inspiration not granted to other men. As far as we know, there were no Swahili or Mijikenda who claimed the gift of knowing the future in itself. Only once does Krapf refer to what might be considered this kind of prophecy: 'There are many prophecies (as they call them) afloat among the Suahelis that when certain events shall take place, the European will come and take their country.'[74] Unfortunately we do not know the Swahili word Krapf was translating as 'prophecies', and in the absence of details or other references, his statement remains obscure. It may infer a belief in the predictability of contingent future events, or such 'prophecies' may simply have been, as Krapf implies, the popular talk of the time.

The Swahili did believe in the predictive quality of dreams. Krapf gives one of the meanings of the word *agua* as 'to predict, e.g., *kuagua ndoto*, to predict, to foretell by a dream'.[75] The Swahili also believed one could obtain knowledge of the future through the practice of *falaki* (from the Arabic *falaq*), which Krapf described as 'the science of heavenly matters = astronomy, astrology'; to practise *falaki* was 'to foretell or prognosticate by the stars'.[76] Since the course of events was related to the movement of the stars, in itself known and predictable, aspects of the future could also be known. In this, the Swahili were simply professing knowledge of the future in its known causes (the observed regular movement of the stars). Such knowledge did not imply that future events were predetermined or knowable with certainty, for causality as perceived by the Swahili involved the interplay between cosmic forces (signified by the movement of the stars) and the free action of men and spirits, who were agents of causality within the larger cosmic order. By contrast, the Mijikenda had to contend, not with the cosmic influences of an ordered universe, but with spirits whose capricious nature gave the future a rather more arbitrary character. To the extent that the wishes and intentions of spirits could be known, however, it was possible to counter and even forestall their action.

Thus, the Swahili and the Mijikenda seem to have believed not in the absolute predictability of future events in themselves, but in the ability of gifted persons (the astrologer, the *mganga*, the diviner, the healer, the rainmaker) to know the causes influencing the course of events in specific circumstances. Knowing the causes already at work, whether spirits or cosmic forces or both, such persons were able to designate the most fitting course of action. Their diagnostic or oracular knowledge of causes gave them a special capacity to influence the future, by introducing another cause onto the scene, thereby mitigating, if not controlling, the existing causes.

This attitude comes out clearly when Krapf considers the Swahili practice of *tabiri*. His *Dictionary* entry for *tabiri* reads: 'to soothsay, to tell fortune'. Krapf then gives an example: '*kutabiri muaka kwa juo* [*chuo*], to prognosticate the coming events of the year from the book (e.g., rain, dearth, war, sickness, &c.). The prognosticator appoints also the *sadaka* [sacrifice] which is to be made by the people in order to avert the impending calamities.'[77] The Mijikenda cast their rain-makers in the same divinatory role of obtaining advance knowledge, and therefore, through the appropriate *sadaka*, being able to influence the course of events.

Such gifted persons were indeed seers by virtue of their ability to see the future in its causes. Their powers of perception seemed to transcend time and space; they were able to discern forces which were not apparent, and understand realities beyond the reach of other men. They knew the medicinal effects of plants and herbs, they saw beyond the visible world into the domain of the spirits, and in the movement of the stars they comprehended the workings of the very cosmos.

Their power of foresight stemmed from an understanding of causality, in particular the causes of disorder. They perceived the hidden causes that threatened to disrupt well-being, as well as the past causes of present adversity, and so could foresee the future (beneficial) effects of prescribed remedies. Their prescriptions, such as *sadaka* and the use of charms, could be preventive as well as restorative, for they were able to grasp the relationship of present circumstances to past causes and of present causes to future events.

Therapeutic knowledge

What can we conclude about prediction and mantic activity? Evidently, the ability of the Swahili and the Mijikenda to share diagnostic and predictive practices was based on a common cosmology, in spite of having contrasting religious beliefs. For Muslims the power of God was never absent from diagnosis and healing, yet prediction by itself had never been essential to Muslim *prophecy*, and here cannot be interpreted as forming part of a local Muslim prophetic tradition. For the Mijikenda, prediction was part of a matter-of-fact approach to any number of problems of the unknown, both spiritual and natural. On the whole, we are left with the impression that most forms of nineteenth-century divination and diagnosis were essentially technical rather than inspirational, involving learned methods of assessment ('powers of the hands') rather than inspired interpretations ('powers of the head').

Predictive practices, whether Swahili or Mijikenda, all seem to have had two aspects in common: knowledge (the perception of causes) and healing (the restoration of well-being). Krapf hints at the connection between knowledge of the future and healing in his *Dictionary* entry for the Swahili word *agua*, for which he gives two meanings: '(1) to treat medically, to make medicine for one, to attend to a sick person; (2) to predict, to foretell by a dream.'[78] Krapf goes on to explain that *muaguzi* (the noun agent derived from the root *agua*) '. . . may be rendered a medical man, or a foreteller, a prophet'. The meaning of the word *uaguzi* (the action of *agua*) is given by Krapf simply as 'prophecy', a translation based no doubt on his essentially Christian equation of prophecy with prediction. Not satisfied that he had understood the connection between healing and prophecy, at the end of the dictionary entry Krapf comments: 'Both terms, *muaguzi* and *uaguzi*, require further examination.'[79]

Indeed, the two aspects of prediction, knowledge and healing, are so closely linked that they appear as two components or dimensions of a single diagnostic phenomenon or spectrum. The essence of such diagnosis seems to lie in what we might call therapeutic knowledge. Knowledgeable in their power to perceive causes, seers become healers as they use their knowledge to heal. Their therapy extends to all levels of society and to all aspects of life. The seer combats illness of all kinds, from the distress of an individual to the evil afflicting a whole society in the form of an epidemic, a drought, or conquest by foreigners. In the presence of affliction and disorder, the seer is the restorer of health and order.

Notes

1. Mijikenda is a twentieth-century name used to refer to nine distinct peoples (Chonyi, Digo, Duruma, Giriama, Jibana, Kambe, Kauma, Rabai and Ribe) who live in the

coastal hinterland to the north and south of Mombasa. In the eighteenth and nineteenth centuries, the Mijikenda were known as the Wanika, or Wanyika, that is, the people of the Nyika (the region inland from the coast). There is evidence that the Wanyika originally comprised more than nine peoples, eventually coalescing to form the present-day Mijikenda.

2. Dr L. Krapf, *A Dictionary of the Suahili Language*, (London, 1882). While in East Africa, Krapf compiled the draft manuscripts of what was to become his dictionary. After returning to Germany in 1853, he went on to prepare the dictionary for publication. Though not published until 1882, the dictionary reflects Swahili usage of the middle of the nineteenth century, some thirty years earlier.

3. Charles New, *Life, Wanderings and Labours in Eastern Africa*, (London, 1873), p. 102. Times of famine were an exception. Then, Mijikenda are said to have gone to Mombasa and become Muslim: 'In time of famine, which occurs sometimes, many a Wonica is glad to turn Mohamedan to save his life from starvation, but he frequently throws off the compulsory yoke when the time of affluence has returned.' Krapf to the Lay Secretary, 25 September 1844, Church Missionary Society archive, University of Birmingham [CMS], CA5/016/28.

4. Rebmann's Journal, entry for 9 February 1848, CMS, CA5/024/52A.

5. New, *Life, Wanderings and Labours*, p. 102.

6. New to Barton, 24 November 1863, *United Methodist Free Churches Magazine* [UMFCM], VII (May 1864), p. 339.

7. Letter of Dr J. L. Krapf, Mombasa, 2 September 1844, to Richard P. Waters, Esq., Consul of the United States, Zanzibar, Fort Jesus archives, ref. 920 KRA. For the name Wanika, see footnote 1 above. Krapf usually spells the name Wanica, and sometimes Wonica.

8. Krapf to the Lay Secretary, 14 July 1846, CMS, CA5/016/62.

9. For a discussion of the origin, meaning and usage of the words Mulungu and Mungu, see P. J. L. Frankl, 'The word for "God" in Swahili', *Journal of Religion in Africa*, 20, 3 (1990), pp. 269–75.

10. New to Barton, 23 April 1864, *UMFCM*, VII (September 1864), p. 612.

11. Krapf, *Dictionary*, p. 266.

12. New to Barton, 23 April 1864, *UMFCM*, VII (September 1864), p. 612. New's observation is echoed in the statement by a Kimbu elder (when asked why the Kimbu pray to the ancestors rather than to the supreme being) that 'the ancestors *are* the supreme being'. Aylward Shorter, *African Christian Theology* (New York, 1977), p. 103.

13. 'Those Wanikas who have much intercourse with the Muhamedans at Mombas are according to the experience of Dr. Krapf less arrestable to the Gospel than those Wanikas who live at a greater distance from Mombas.' Rebmann to Venn, 27 June 1846, CMS, CA5/024/2.

14. Rebmann to the Secretaries, 27 October 1847, CMS, CA5/024/51.

15. Letter of C. New, Mombasa, 23 April 1864, *UMFCM*, VII (September 1864), p. 612.

16. The notion of monotheism was, however, according to Krapf, being fostered among African peoples by contacts with Muslims; commenting on the religious beliefs of the Kamba, Krapf wrote: 'They have however a very faint idea of a Supreme Being, especially those Wakamba who have seen the Muhamedans on the coast.' 'Rev. Dr Krapf's Journal descriptive of a Journey made to Ukambani in November-December 1849', CMS, CA5/M2/296.

17. Krapf's Journal, entry for 19 September 1847, CMS, CA5/016/172.

18. Krapf to Lay Secretary, 20 January 1848, CMS, CA5/016/71.

19. Krapf's Journal, entry for 19 March 1845, CMS, CA5/M1/547.

20. Krapf explains the meaning of the word *koma* as 'a man who died and who is believed to exist in the grave'. Krapf, *Dictionary*, p. 168.

21. Krapf's Journal, entry for 17 January 1847, CMS, CA5/016/171.

22. Krapf's Journal, entry for 4 August 1847, CMS, CA5/016/172.

23. Erhardt to Venn, 22 September 1852, CMS, CA5/09/9.

24. The Swahili word *pepo* is a generic term for spirit; in addition, Krapf mentions numerous other terms to designate specific kinds of spirits: dungumaro, jinni, kizuka, koikoi, mahoka, milhoi, shetani, zimui. Krapf, *Dictionary*, pp. 54, 118, 165, 166, 195, 227, 432.

25. Krapf's Journal, entry for 6 April 1847, CMS, CA5/016/171.

26. Krapf's Journal, entry for 15 May 1847, CMS, CA5/016/171.

27. Erhardt wrote: '. . . their healing knowledge is very limited, wherefore often they cannot remove those evil spirits and people often call . . . at last on the Msungu [sic] (white man) to try also his art.' Erhardt to Venn, 24 September 1850, CMS, CA5/09/3.

28. Rebmann to Venn, 15 December 1858, CMS, CA5/024/34. Several years later, New expressed the same feeling: 'I wish we had a medical missionary. I never was so besieged for medicines.' Letter of C. New, undated (probably July-August 1869), *UFMCM*, XIII (January 1870) p. 68.

29. The words *jinni* and *shetani* have come into Swahili from the Arabic words *jinn* and *shaitan*. Krapf distinguishes between the two Swahili words: the *jinni* is 'an evil spirit which is believed by the natives to dwell in water, while the *shetani* is thought to reside only on the mainland, especially in the wilderness'. (Krapf, *Dictionary*, p. 118.)

30. For a summary of Muslim beliefs and attitudes in this regard, see the entries *Djinn* and *Shaitan* in the *Shorter Encyclopaedia of Islam* (Leiden, 1961), pp. 90–91, 523–24.

31. Though *pepo* can be either good or bad, the experience of the Mijikenda and Swahili as observed by Krapf led him to stress the evil aspect of their nature; thus he translates the word as 'evil spirit' or 'demon'. Krapf, *Dictionary*, p. 302, 408. Rebmann reached the same conclusion: a *pepo* was 'an evil spirit supposed to cause sickness and other calamities'. Rebmann's Journal, entry for 12 February 1848, CMS, CA5/024/52A.

32. Krapf to the Lay Secretary, 13 August 1844, CMS, CA5/016/26.

33. Krapf, *Dictionary*, p. 118. Earlier, Krapf had written: 'The Muhamedans of Mombasa outdo the Wanica in superstitious views and practices.' Krapf's Journal, entry for 26 March 1845, CMS, CA5/M1/574.

34. That is, those ancestors described by Durkheim as 'named figures of authority'. Emile Durkheim, *Les Formes élémentaires de la vie religieuse*, (4th edition, Paris 1960), pp. 405–8.

35. Krapf's Journal, entry for 17 January 1847, CMS, CA5/016/171.

36. Krapf's Journal, entry for 17 January 1847, CMS, CA5/016/171 and Rebmann's Journal, entry for 23 February 1848, CMS, CA5/024/52A.

37. Krapf's Journal, entry for 4 August 1847, CMS, CA5/016/171.

38. Krapf's Journal, entry for 29 April 1847, CMS, CA5/016/171.

39. Krapf's Journal, entry for 22 April 1847, CMS, CA5/016/171.

40. Krapf's Journal, entry for 10 May 1847, CMS, CA5/016/171.

41. Krapf, *Dictionary*, p. 224.

42. Krapf's Journal, entry for 26 March 1845, CMS, CA5/M1/575. Other evidence, though scanty, seems to confirm that *uganga* was profitable; New once met a sick man who 'had spent all his substance on the *waganga* to no purpose'. Letter of New, undated (probably July–August 1869), *UFMCM*, XIII (January 1870), p. 68.

43. Krapf to the Secretaries, 20 January 1848, CMS, CA5/016/071.

44. Erhardt to Venn, 24 September 1850, CMS, CA5/09/3.

45. Krapf, *Dictionary*, p. 224.

46. Another Swahili word, *tabibu (derived from the Arabic tabib)*, has the same meaning as *mganga*, but was less widely used. Krapf notes the Arabic derivation of *tabibu* and gives its meaning as '(= mganga), physician, doctor'. Krapf, *Dictionary*, p. 352.

47. In Krapf's time, very few non-Muslims were literate, and the distinction between Muslim and non-Muslim healers seems to have been unambiguous. Today, the

phrase *uganga wa kitabu*, that is, 'the art of healing by the book', is used to distinguish Muslim from non-Muslim healing practices, the 'book' in this case being the written text(s) used by the Muslim healer. With the spread of literacy among many of the coastal peoples of East Africa, Muslim and traditional methods of healing have come to merge and overlap. In a study of divination in Dar es Salaam, out of a total of 45 Zaramo diviners Swantz counted nine Muslim *walimu* and 36 traditional diviners; of the 36 traditional diviners, however, nine were using written texts and were mixing traditional with Islamic methods. Lloyd Swantz, *The Medicine Man among the Zaramo of Dar es Salaam* (Uppsala, 1990), pp. 66–79.

48. Krapf, *Dictionary*, p. 259.
49. Krapf to the Lay Secretary, 13 August 1844, CMS, CA5/016/26. For the full text of the passage, see p. 88 above.
50. New to Barton, 24 November 1864, *UMFCM*, VII (1864), pp. 339–40.
51. Erhardt to Lay Secretary, 24 September 1850, CMS, CA5/09/3.
52. Rebmann's Journal, entry for 10 January 1848, CMS, CA5/024/52A. Though Muslim healers were considered effective at dealing with spirits, they had no apparent power over the ancestral spirits of the *kaya*, nor is there any evidence that they took part in major *kaya* rituals.
53. Rebmann's Journal, entry for 21 April 1850, CMS, CA5/024/50. The Swahili tradition of healing, including the use of charms or amulets, contained much that belonged to the legacy of classical Muslim medicine. For which, see Edward G. Browne, *Arabian Medicine* (Cambridge, 1921), pp. 11–12.
    Some Mijikenda are said to consider certain kinds of charms so powerful that one is protected by them even when breaking a taboo. See L. P. Gerlach, 'Some basic Digo conceptions of health and disease', pp. 9–34, in proceedings of a symposium on 'Attitudes to health and disease among some East African tribes', held at Makerere College, Kampala, December 1959.
54. Letter of New, undated (probably July-August 1869), *UFMCM*, XIII (January 1870), p. 68.
55. Rebmann's Journal, entry for 21 April 1850, CMS, CA5/024/50.
56. Charms made or used by Muslims contain Qur'anic texts in one form or another. Such charms are basically protective, but their magic force can also be productive. See A. J. H. Prins, 'Islamic maritime magic: a ship's charm from Lamu', in H. J. Gerschat and H. Jungraithmayr (eds), *Wort und Religion: Kalima na Dini* (Stuttgart 1969), pp. 294–304. Parkin notes how non-Muslim Giriama *waganga* increase their repertoire by buying written charms from Muslim *waganga* in Mombasa. David Parkin, *Palms, Wine and Witnesses*, (London, 1972), p. 40.
57. Krapf's Journal, entry for 22 April 1847, CMS, CA5/016/171.
58. Krapf to Lay Secretary, 20 November 1846, CMS, CA5/016/64.
59. Krapf's Journal, entry for 19 April 1846, CMS, CA5/016/170. The Swahili word *hirizi* is derived from the Arabic *hirz*, which has the same meaning.
60. Krapf, *Dictionary*, p. 62.
61. Ibid. p. 218.
62. Ibid., p. 62. Krapf also found that the Kamba practised augury: 'How much they are attached to the practice of augury I have mentioned.' 'Rev. Dr Krapf's Journal descriptive of a Journey made to Ukambani in November–December 1849', CMS, CA5/M2/296.
63. Krapf, *Dictionary*, p. 236.
64. *Mburuga* is a Mijikenda word for the name of a tree whose fruit (of the same name) was used by Mijikenda *waganga* for divining. Krapf, *Dictionary*, p. 217.
65. The Swahili word *ramli* is derived from the Arabic word *raml*, meaning 'sand'. A characteristic Muslim method of divination is geomancy, called *darb al-ramli* or *'ilm al-ramli*, literally, 'knowledge (or science) of the sand'. The process usually involves taking up sand, placing it at random in columns (which are given names), and then

interpreting the values assigned to various combinations of the columns. Krapf translates *ramli* (spelled by him *ramle*) as 'divination with ashes', but does not give details about the procedure followed. Krapf, *Dictionary*, p. 314.

66. Krapf's Journal, entry for 20 May 1847, CMS, CA5/016/171.
67. Krapf, *Dictionary*, p. 276.
68. Ibid., p. 168.
69. Krapf's Journal, entry for 11 May 1847, CMS, CA5/016/171.
70. Krapf's Journal, entry for 22 April 1847, CMS, CA5/016/171.
71. Krapf's Journal, entry for 4 August 1847, CMS, CA5/016/172.
72. Krapf's Journal, entry for 10 May 1847, CMS, CA5/016/171.
73. The ideas and quotations of this paragraph are taken from St Thomas Aquinas, *Summa Theologiae*, 2a2ae,95, I.
74. Krapf's Journal, entry for 26 January 1847, CMS, CA5/016/171.
75. Krapf, *Dictionary*, p. 4.
76. Ibid., pp. 61-2.
77. Ibid., p. 352. Krapf's system of orthography used the letter 'j' for the sound which is today invariably transcribed as 'ch'; thus, he writes *juo* instead of *chuo*. The book referred to is not named, but could have been *Sa'at al-Khabar*, an anonymous text still in use among the Swahili.
78. Ibid., p. 4.
79. Ibid.

Five

Modern
Zande Prophetesses

MARGARET BUCKNER

The vocabulary Evans-Pritchard used to describe various aspects of witchcraft, oracles and magic among the Zande of central Africa has been widely applied or adapted in anthropological studies of dissimilar peoples, in East Africa as well as in other parts of the world. Returning for a fresh look at the Zande in the context of divination and prophecy is thus useful as a reminder of Evans-Pritchard's original analysis of divination and oracles.

In addition, this Zande case offers an exceptional opportunity for the historical observation of the disappearance of one kind of diviner, the witch-doctor, and the emergence of women 'prophetesses', which will be the focal point for this chapter. In the late 1920s, Evans-Pritchard was witness to some of the remaining traces of pre-colonial Zande society in Southwestern Sudan. Furthermore, he supplemented his own observations with a quantity of texts taken down from elderly informants who had grown up in pre-colonial days. We therefore have a fairly complete portrait of 'ideal' traditional Zande society as it existed before the arrival of European colonial administrators and missionaries. I should stress that all the texts I have gathered from older Zande in the Central African Republic during the 1980s fully corroborate Evans-Pritchard's major theses concerning the Zande conceptual world. I do not hesitate therefore to base an overview of traditional Zande society on his works.[1]

Evans-Pritchard chose to express Zande terms in a language familiar to his readers. He selected English words which he then systematically used in one-to-one correspondence with Zande terms. Thus, 'witchcraft' corresponds to *mangu*, 'magic (or sorcery)' to *ngua*,[2] 'witch-doctor' to *binza*, and so on. It is important to remember, therefore, that when he uses 'witchcraft' in the Zande context, the connotations are those of Zande *mangu*, rather than those of witchcraft elsewhere. In short, Zande witchcraft is held to be an innate power to injure others which emanates from a physical organ in the witch's abdomen. Magicians (and sorcerers), on the other hand, use substances and outward actions to attain their ends. Although similar means of divination are employed in both cases, this distinction is of great importance in seeking to understand Zande social behaviour. As Evans-Pritchard explains:

> Azande believe that some people are witches and can injure them in virtue of any inherent quality. A witch performs no rite, utters no spell, and possesses no medicines. An act of witchcraft is a psychic act. They believe also that sorcerers may do them ill by performing magic rites with bad medicines. Azande distinguish clearly between witches and sorcerers. Against both they employ diviners, oracles, and medicines.[3]

Zande consult 'oracles' and 'diviners' to determine who or what is doing them harm. Evans-Pritchard uses the word 'oracle' to translate 'techniques which are supposed to reveal what cannot be discovered at all, or cannot be discovered for certain, by experiment and logical inferences there from'.[4] The major Zande oracles were: *benge*, the poison oracle; *iwa*, the rubbing-board oracle; *mapingo*, the three sticks oracle; and *dakpa*, the termite oracle. Zande has no generic word for 'oracle', but the verb *soroka* is used with these techniques, best translated as 'to consult an oracle'. The source of the power of oracles is in the object or material substance of the oracle itself, or in the plants eaten by the operator. Zande oracles are not mediums; they take the inanimate pronoun, and are not personified.[5] Oracles were (and are) extremely important in daily life to determine the cause of calamity, and to indicate whether a given activity would be propitious or not. Furthermore, the poison oracle (*benge*) played an essential role in witchcraft cases. Monopolized by the nobles, it was rules of evidence, judge, jury and witnesses all rolled into one.[6]

Evans-Pritchard's working definition of 'divination' is 'a method of discovering what is unknown, and often cannot be known, by experiment and logic'. He names two sources which inspired human diviners: 'medicines' (*ngua*), and ghosts (*a-toro*), which correspond respectively to witch-doctors (*a-binza*), by far the most common Zande diviner, and ghost-diviners.[7]

I would like to underline a distinction between 'prophecy', in the sense of foretelling future events, and 'divination', in the sense of indicating the presence of witchcraft (or sorcery), whether past, present, or future. Thus, 'divination' overlaps 'prophecy' in the sense of foretelling the outcome – the success or failure – of an intended activity depending on whether or not witchcraft will intervene. Diviners and oracles are not asked general questions, such as 'what does the future hold?', but rather they are asked yes/no questions concerning specific situations which may or may not be affected by witchcraft (or sorcery) during a given activity, and this they seek to know only to be able to protect themselves by avoiding or counteracting the harmful source before it has a chance to act.[8] Evans-Pritchard occasionally uses the verb 'prophesy' in the sense of predicting, but only in the sense of revealing 'mystical' forces soon to be at work, and so-called 'prophecies' are actually warnings that witchcraft will interfere with a given plan of action. The word 'prophet' is absent from his descriptions of traditional Zande society.

Since Evans-Pritchard's field work among the Zande, a new character has entered the scene:[9] *Nagidi*, women who have functions which are both 'religious' and 'divinatory'. They are called 'prophetesses' in the local French. (*Bagidi*, their male counterparts, also exist, but as they are usually only assistants to the *Nagidi* in their religious functions, or at least were so originally, I here continue to use the pronoun 'she'.) Unfortunately, I have not been able to carry out systematic research on the subject, so can offer here only a brief sketch of some of the most basic features of the *Nagidi*, to lay the groundwork, so to speak, for further investigation.

During trips to Zandeland in the southeastern corner of the Central African Republic, I have often noticed the 'native' Zande church, Nzapa Zande, and have even met its founder, Awa Marie, who lives in a village just outside Zemio. It seems to me to be a 'normal' or at least understandable consequence of three-quarters of a century of Christian missions, and of Zande society coming to terms with the invading modern world. Awa, and other women 'priestesses' or 'prophetesses', *Nagidi*, are 'chosen' by 'God' to direct congregations in His honour. Many of their teachings parallel Christian doctrine; the rituals and songs, at least in appearance, are if anything more 'Christian' than those of the Christian missionaries. Many a Zande village is nowadays divided into three sections rather than the usual two: besides worrying about each other, the Catholics and the Protestants now have a Nzapa Zande faction to contend with.

Besides their religious function proper as leaders of Nzapa Zande congregations, these women can 'see' the 'mystical' reasons or causes for misfortune, including the guilt or innocence of suspected witches. Their ability to do so, like their religious knowledge, is said to come from God. A few people have also told me that their visions are associated with 'genies', animal-like creatures which live near streams. An elderly Zande gave the following description of Zande oracles:

> Here among us, in Africa, the thing that was most common in the past among our forefathers was *benge*, consulted by putting it into the mouths of chickens. But nowadays that no longer exists. What we use today is this: we cut the neck of a chicken, while addressing it [*sima ru*], so that if the answer to the question is 'yes', the [dying] chicken falls with its left wing topmost . . . Also, we go to the *Nagidi*. One goes there and explains the matter, and she sees a dream [*masumo*] about it. If you are not the guilty party, she says, no, it's not you. And if it is you who are responsible, the dream tells her that as well.

It seems that these women had no conscious desire to become *Nagidi*, but were 'chosen' by *mbori* ('God'). They have undergone unique psycho-physical experiences, often including episodes of simulated death or near-death, followed by a sort of resurrection or reawakening from death, after which they have special powers of divination and seeing, and are transmitters of the word of God. Many people have told me that because these women have been in communion with God during their (so-called) death, they have special powers that come from Him.

Here is a summarized account given by a Zande man (a member of the Nzapa Zande congregation in Nguyo) on how two such *Nagidi* were 'chosen', the first being Awa Marie herself, the founder of the Nzapa Zande sect:

> God seized her in Finzani [a village 9 km from Zemio], where she was staying with her father. God didn't seize her through illness that made her sick; he made rocks rain down upon her until she died. After remaining dead for a while, she awoke. They took her to the *gendarmes'* office where the commander was. They took her to the hospital, but the doctor examined her in vain: he found no sign of illness. They sent her home, and she began to teach her religion [*pa mbori*] to all of us. We still follow it in the same way.

He tells of the experience of Nasunga Marie, the *Nagidi* in Nguyo:

> God didn't seize her through sickness either. He seized her and threw her to the ground, where she lay senseless for a long while. My father himself [the village chief] came to pray over her. He lifted her, and as he did she began speaking the word of God. And so it [her religion] continues today.

Boniface Ngbondo, a Zande doctoral student in Paris, was present at two *Nagidi* 'seances' in August 1989 in the westernmost regions of Zandeland. The following excerpts, presented here with his kind permission, are adapted from his descriptions of cases he personally observed; the first four in the Zande quarter of Bangassou, the last three in Rafai. For the present purposes, only brief summaries suffice to indicate the questions put before the *Nagidi* and her answers.

I.   A schoolgirl, mother of a child, fails her exams several times. Unbeknownst to her parents, she decides to go to join the father of her child, who resides in Bangui, the capital. But the latter lets her know that he wants nothing to do with her. She consults the *Nagidi* to find out why she has been failing her exams, and why her husband/fiancé rejects her.

Response: According to the *Nagidi*, the girl had quarrelled with her mother, who then cursed her daughter. The *Nagidi* says the evil curse would be alleviated if the daughter begged her mother's forgiveness.

II.   A woman does not get along with her brother, with whom she resides. She asks the *Nagidi* if their discord is the result of a curse.

Response: According to the *Nagidi*, there are two causes: first, their dead mother's ghost has long been angry because the man mistreats his sister; and second, the man has never made the proper offerings (*tuka*) to his mother's ghost. The *Nagidi* advises the man to stop mistreating his sister, and to appease his mother's ghost with an offering.

III.   A man has accused his sister-in-law of bewitching her husband, who has been seriously injured in a hunting accident. She then consults the *Nagidi* to uncover the true culprit.

Response: Rather than proclaiming her innocence, the *Nagidi* indeed accuses the woman of having pronounced malicious words against her husband, which then caused her husband's accident. She would be cleansed by a public confession (*kusa pai*).

IV.   A woman whose son is seriously ill consults the *Nagidi* to discover the cause of his illness.

Response: The sick man had started to wear a charm to protect himself while he worked. Having then lost his job, he should have gotten rid of the charm. Since he did not, the charm changed its function from protecting life to destroying it.

V. A man threatened his wife with a knife for having left him, and also her parents because he believed they gave her bad advice. (The reporter is confused as to who actually posed the question, the man or the woman.)

> *Response*: According to the *Nagidi*, the man had asked *mbori* ('God') to never have children because he would be incapable of raising them. *Mbori* heard his prayer and rendered his wife infertile. She then left him to try to have a child with another man. In order to 'erase' his plea to *mbori*, the man was ordered to sweep out the cult's courtyard for one month.

VI. The mother of a sick baby brings it to the *Nagidi* to determine the cause of the illness.

> *Response*: According to the *Nagidi*, the baby is sick because of an insufficiency of blood, as indicated by a whitening of the skin and eyes. She recommends that the woman take her baby to the hospital.

VII. Three months ago, a man bought a new gun, but has never yet succeeded in killing an animal with it. Every animal he shoots at manages to escape, and yet he is an excellent shot. He asks the *Nagidi* the cause for his failure to kill game with the new gun.

> *Response*: This case had actually been presented two weeks previously, but was suspended until the object in question, the gun, could be brought from the man's village over 30 km away. The first response given by the *Nagidi* was that the man refused to pay the seller of the gun what he owed him. The seller had sworn that as long as the buyer hadn't paid his due, he wouldn't kill a single animal with the gun.

The following summary offers yet another example of the type of intervention in which *Nagidi* (and *Bagidi*) are involved. It was given by one of the elders called in to judge a case which I personally observed during my last stay in Zandeland in 1988.

> S seduced D's wife, who fell ill. As the illness continued for a long time, they interrogated her, to seek the reason for her illness; she confessed her love affair with S. Then she died, and S was held responsible. D, in his hatred for S, said to himself that since his own wife had died as a result of her affair with S, he (D) would seduce S's wife and kill her; she would suffer in the same way as his own wife had suffered. So, D seduced her, and

directed magic (*manga sino*) against her, and she subsequently died. Her family took the affair to court, where D was formally accused: since S had gone after his wife and she had died, therefore D had 'poisoned' S's wife so that she would also die. We elders were called to judge the affair. After hearing the case, it was determined that D was guilty. S's wife's family demanded that D be imprisoned. They rehashed the affair, trying to decide whether to imprison him or to order to pay a fine to S's wife's family in compensation. The chief guarded him while oracles were consulted. D's guilt was confirmed either by *iwa* or *bagidi*. [It had not yet been decided whether he would be imprisoned or fined.]

Finally, I happened upon a case in Zemio in which a *Nagidi* was the final 'judge' in a 'murder' trial. A man was accused of having changed into a water genie (*kpiri*) and causing a man to drown in a village 50 miles north. A huge crowd was gathered outside the hut where *Nagidi* had sequestered herself to render a verdict. In front of the hut was the suspect, his hands tied behind him and two *gendarmes* by his side. Among the crowd were several high functionaries, including, at least for part of the time, the assistant governor, the mayor, and the police chief, waiting to cart the suspect off to prison in case of a guilty verdict.

As I stated earlier, in calling these *Nagidi* 'prophetesses' I am merely following the lead of the local inhabitants. As these particular examples show, whether the questions refer to the past, present, or future is irrelevant; what is important is the 'evil' influence which can be 'seen' and revealed by the *Nagidi*, who thus seems to resemble the 'seer'; one who 'sees' into the heart of the matter. But, as I will argue later, what justifies the vernacular appellation of 'prophetess' is the source of the *Nagidi's* inspiration and the 'religious' intent of their words.

To what extent is it possible to trace the origin of the *Nagidi* to traditional figures in Zande society? Let us turn back to two possible forerunners of the *Nagidi*: ghost-diviners and witch-doctors.

Our ideas about 'ghost-diviners' are obscure. In his definition of divination, Evans-Pritchard includes *a-boro a-toro*, or ghost-diviners, but unfortunately mentions them only briefly in *Witchcraft, Oracles and Magic*, and not much more substantially elsewhere:

> There are in Zande society persons who divine through communion with ghosts of the dead, whereas the witch-doctor is fatidical in virtue of medicines.

> Ghost-diviners eat medicines to put them in contact with ghosts.

> Ghost-diviners are people who are able to communicate with the ghosts of the dead, usually through dreams, and are generally women.[10]

In his short survey of the phenomenon, Evans-Pritchard describes how three women became ghost-diviners. In the first example, the ghost made Nabaru dream that men were carrying the corpse of her father, who was away at war. She awoke, and at dawn 'people came bearing the corpse of her father. Messages from the ghosts came to her ever afterwards.'[11] In the second example, Naakadumu went fishing, and caught a crab and a frog. She returned home, and put them into a pot of water on the fire. When the water got hot, the crab escaped from the pot, and ran and entered a hole at the head of the stream. Naakadumu reached into the hole to seize the crab, 'when it cried out aloud like a man'. Horrified, she ran away shrieking and fell into a chasm. People came and beat a drum, and after a while she came out and they all returned home. 'She refused all food, but she ate flies for food. The ghosts continued ever afterwards to trouble her'.[12]

> The third woman, Nambua, said that, 'She died and they dug a grave for her and everyone wailed. Her soul went forth and appeared at the place of ghosts. She was just looking about when all her relatives collected and made a circle around her. It was her mother who said to her, 'what have you come here for? Get up and go whence you came. Go away quickly.' She departed from amongst these people and her eyes at once opened. Everyone ceased wailing and she began immediately to wake from death and recovered completely.[13]

It is significant that these 'ghost diviners' of old underwent a sort of 'initiation'. The first woman was struck by her father's death (rather than her own); the second fell into a chasm; the third underwent a sort of 'death, burial, and resurrection', very similar to that described for the *Nagidi* of modern times.

Several early missionaries have also written about what could also be called 'ghost-diviners', but the discussion is complicated by the similar translation of two different Zande terms: *a-toro*, or 'ghosts of the dead', and *a-girisa*, often translated as 'evil spirits'. Very different appreciations have been given for these two terms. First, Evans-Pritchard says that *a-toro* 'are benevolent beings, at least as benevolent as a Zande father of a family, and their occasional participation in the world they have left behind them is on the whole orderly and conducive to the welfare of their children'.[14] As opposed to these 'ordinary ghosts', the *a-girisa* are the evil ghosts of dead witches, who 'show a venomous hatred of humanity'. He states that neither he nor Major P. M. Larken have heard much of them in the Sudan, though Mgr. Lagae describes them among the Zande of Zaire; he does not suggest that they are dead witches.[15]

Father Giorgetti, in contrast, makes rather much of *a-ira-a-girisa*, which are either evil spirits or the souls of dead witches; he describes in depth the 'hysterical' behaviour of those possessed by the *a-girisa*. Of special interest to us here is his statement that 'under the influence of these spirits, [the possessed] predict the future, and for this, are paid'. He cites a Zande text dated 1928: 'Afterwards, . . . he says that he has been to where God is, that he knows all things, that he knows who the witches are, that he knows what people will do in the future.'[16]

Father Giorgetti also, however, describes certain *a-ira-toro*, who are believed to have been in contact with spirits beyond the grave: they suffer from a strange inexplicable illness, or show symptoms such as unexpected prolonged fainting spells that give the impression of death. The Zande think that during the hours when they were unconscious, they were in fact with the spirits of the ancestors. He continues, translating a Zande text, 'people say that the *ira-a-toro* is capable of knowing the evil acts committed by living persons, because he has been to where the ghosts of the ancestors live with God.' Father Giorgetti also states that both these personages have become rare or extinct: 'Today, if the *a-ira-a-girisa* are out-dated, so much the more so are the *a-ira-a-toro*. Only the elders beyond 50 years of age can give information about them.'[17]

Given these different accounts of Zande spiritual entities, it is perhaps impossible to clearly state exactly what Zande believed at the turn of the century. But we can at least safely say that there was some sort of belief in people – women, according to Evans-Pritchard, Lagae, Philipps (cited by Evans-Pritchard), and Larken – who had special 'prophetic' powers visited upon them by the ghosts, usually after some sort of psychological crisis or illness, often simulated or temporary death. Certain people (whether *a-ira-a-toro* or *a-ira-a-girisa* is not always clear) have, during simulated death, visited the spirits of the ancestors (who according to Father Giorgetti's account live with God), and they can thus reveal spiritual actions.

How far is it possible to say that the *Nagidi* of modern days are more or less direct descendants of these women ghost-diviners? In spite of their many striking similarities, one crucial difference, at least, separates them: whereas the ghost-diviners were inspired by ghosts (but not exclusively in Father Giorgetti's account), the *Nagidi* receive their visions from a God-like *mbori*. Whereas 'the ghosts of the dead cannot be appealed to as arbiters of morals and sanctions of conduct, because the ghosts are members of kinship groups and only exercise authority within these groups',[18] the *mbori* of today is indeed perceived of as not only morally just and good, but also as omniscient. This indicates a profound shift in the Zande notion of *mbori*, which we will examine shortly.

A second personage from which *Nagidi* seem to have inherited certain functions are the witch-doctors (*a-binza*), who had an important and often underestimated role in traditional Zande society. Witch-doctors were 'a corporation of diviners who are believed to diagnose and combat witchcraft'.[19] Evans-Pritchard describes their functions as those of a diviner who exposes witches,[20] a magician who 'thwarts them',[21] and a leech, who 'repairs the ravages of witchcraft'.[22] 'Every witch-doctor is a professional indicator of witchcraft.'[23] 'In both roles [diviner and leech] his task is the same – to counteract witchcraft. As a diviner he discovers the location of witchcraft, and as a leech he repairs its ravages.'[24]

Witch-doctors revealed crimes of witchcraft, and their revelations were subject to confirmation by the poison oracle. A significant feature of witch-doctors is that they intervened before death, rather than after. When someone died, the case was taken to the prince's oracle. It could therefore be said that witch-doctors had a greater role in collectively thwarting and reducing the threat of witchcraft than in punishing actual cases of witchcraft or bringing about vengeance. Along this line, oracles and magic in general are secret, private acts, and must be kept hidden from others, lest witchcraft interfere with their efficacy. Witch-doctors, in contrast, held their seances in public crowds, actively seeking out witchcraft in order to thwart it, and were not at all threatened by it.[25] Thus, a function which was uniquely theirs was that of actively fighting against witchcraft. The fact that merely revealing witchcraft was not their primary function, but that this revelation was accompanied by collective anti-witchcraft action, helps account for the witch-doctors' popularity (or even their very existence), in spite of their low rating among Zande oracles: they were tied for third place with the rubbing-board oracle for reliability.[26]

The witch-doctors's source of power was plants (*ngua*; 'medicines').[27] Those who desired to become witch-doctors went through a long apprenticeship in which they learned which plants to eat and how to prepare them properly. This knowledge had to be paid for, as did the services of the witch-doctor, since, as is generally true in Zandeland, payment determined the efficacy of magic.[28] Witch-doctors underwent an initiation ceremony, described in great detail by Evans-Pritchard, involving symbolic 'death, burial, resurrection'.[29] Most interestingly, Evans-Pritchard relates how the few existing myths accounting for the origins of witch-doctors and their powers involve women. According to two of these myths or legends, the first witch-doctor was a woman; and the medicines eaten by witch-doctors originally came forth from a woman whose belly was cut open upon her death.[30] We will later return to this point.

A witch-doctors' seance was a true public spectacle, with frantic, wild dancing to the beat of drums, a singing chorus, and amazing feats, all of which never failed to attract a crowd.

Several witch-doctors gathered together at the homestead of the host for at least an entire day of dancing and divination. As with oracles, names of possible witches were presented by the client, and from these the 'witch' was chosen.[31] The dual function of the witch-doctor was reflected in the way he expressed himself during the seance. The manner of his anti-witch declarations was 'truculent . . . overbearing . . . browbeating . . . braggart'; whereas when uttering 'prophecies', he used 'the voice of a medium who sees and hears something from without . . . disconnected sentences . . . a dreamy, far-away voice . . . like men talking in a trance, or . . . in their sleep'.[32] The witch-doctors' 'visions' of witchcraft could also come from gazing into water, or a divining pot.[33]

Perhaps a major, underlying raison d'être of the witch-doctor is that he alone, during his seances, enacted a 'public affirmation of the existence of witchcraft', which, in a society where the only evidence of witchcraft was through oracles, could have been crucial. One could argue, then, that witch-doctors were the physical, concrete evidence of witchcraft, since, after all, witches are not visible as such. Evans-Pritchard sums up this important ideological role of the witch-doctors:

> Witch-doctors have always been part of Zande culture. They figure in the oldest traditions of their nation. Their seances occasion one of the few types of social gatherings outside family life, and from an early age children have taken part in them as spectators, chorus, and drummers. Azande do not consider what their world would be like without witch-doctors any more than we consider what it would be like without physicians. Since there is witchcraft there are naturally witch-doctors . . . A seance of witch-doctors is a public affirmation of the existence of witchcraft. It is one of the ways in which belief in witchcraft is inculcated and expressed.[34]

It is most interesting to note the several features which are common to both the witch-doctors of the past and the *Nagidi* of the present.[35] They both undergo an initiation which can be grossly summarized as successive death, burial, and resurrection. The types of matters for which they are consulted are strikingly similar (one major exception being 'homicide'); compare 'the situations in which a man might summon witch-doctors to his assistance – sickness, failure in hunting, indecision in agricultural activities, barrenness of wives, social difficulties of various kinds, especially with relatives-in-law and princes', with the examples included above for the *Nagidi*. They pronounce publicly after long deliberation whether a name placed before them is guilty or innocent of 'mystical' wrong-doing. Their decisions are based on 'largely unconscious mental activity'. They each have specialized social functions; they have prestige, are respected as enactors of 'good magic' or morally good judgements. Both witch-doctors and *Nagidi* function respectively as such only in ritual situations; otherwise they live normal lives, among family and neighbours. They each wage a 'battle of two spiritual powers': the witch-doctor between his own magical powers (derived from medicines) and witchcraft; the *Nagidi* between supernatural powers derived from 'God' and witchcraft and sorcery. They each have 'acquired' rather than 'innate' powers. They each carry out what is perhaps the sole public affirmation of belief in mystical notions. A final connection between witch-doctors and modern women 'prophetesses' derives from the few myths mentioned above. Madina, a woman who was found living in a hole in the rocks, is said to have founded the corporation of witch-doctors. There was also a woman, Semeni, whose belly was cut open after her death and disclosed several important medicines now used by witch-doctors.

There are also several important differences between these two personages. The witch-doctor's source of power is 'medicines'. *Nagidi*, on the other hand, receive their power from 'God' (and are also sometimes associated with genies and ghosts). Witch-doctors actively fight witchcraft in wild, public spectacles, with dancing, drums, songs and incredible feats. *Nagidi* deliberate alone, often isolated from others. Witch-doctors chat and joke among themselves, show no awe or reverence for their magic, while *Nagidi* are religious cult leaders, showing great respect for God and His word, which they in turn reveal to their followers. Witch-doctors never divine about homicide cases,[36] and their verdicts are confirmed by oracles. *Nagidi* can be called on in important cases, including a homicide, to confirm or deny what lesser oracles or judges have decided. Witch-doctors always exact payment (indeed, as with all Zande magic, if they are not paid, they will not be effective). The *Nagidi* ask for no direct payment (though 'penance' can involve work for the Nzapa Zande cult). Witch-doctors enact a 'public affirmation of belief in witchcraft'. *Nagidi* affirm a more general belief in mystical notions which seem to be less and less inclusive of witchcraft (*mangu*) *per se*, and more and more of 'sorcery', and 'genies' (such as *a-kpiri*).[37]

I would like to suggest that the demise of the witch-doctors and the rise of the *Nagidi* are perhaps two aspects (among others) of a general, on-going process of change in Zande society, a process which includes (among others), an upsurge in magic (as opposed to witchcraft), and a shift in the Zande notion of *mbori*.

It seems probable that magic has long been increasing in variety and in importance among the Zande. The Zande penchant for borrowing and their interest in foreign things have far from hampered the introduction of foreign magic.[38] Long before the coming of the Europeans, the Vungara expansion which incorporated numerous foreign peoples was responsible for the introduction of various new 'medicines'. It might even be possible to suggest that, relative to witchcraft (*mangu*), a great deal of Zande magic, in particular 'bad' magic (Evans-Pritchard's 'sorcery'), is relatively new. This increase in 'bad' magic has perhaps been parallelled by a semantic shift. *Ngua*, which properly means plant or tree, refers to all substances or acts which have what we would call magical power.[39] A new opposition seems to be emerging: *dawa*, Arabic for medicine, is increasingly employed to refer to only 'good' medicinal plants, in contrast to *ngua* ('bad') poisonous plants. *Mbe-ngua*, 'owner of magic', a term which used to be neutral, meaning someone acquainted with medicinal plants and herbs, now has strong negative, even fearsome connotations, and refers almost exclusively to 'sorcerers'.

As Evans-Pritchard remarks, there is no real mythology about the efficacy of medicines and magic[40] – this is true in particular for 'bad', magic. Although the Trickster tales abound with magic, they indeed include only the 'good' forms (rain medicine, medicine to open up a rock, to keep a fire from coming near, etc.). There are virtually no allusions to magic used for retribution, vengeance or malevolence.

It would thus be possible to suggest that in Evans-Pritchard's time, many, if not most, 'medicines' were borrowed. It must also be pointed out, however, that Evans-Pritchard did his research in the easternmost Zande province, and, perhaps, the least conservative one. His account of the Zande in Gbudwe's province of the 1920s is thus a description of the Zande region where the increase in magic was probably most pronounced, where the clash between witchcraft and witch-doctors, on the one hand, and magicians and sorcerers on the other, was already 'upsetting the cart' of Zande beliefs, a situation which may account for some of the numerous contradictions and discrepancies in Zande explanations of their own phenomena.

It is most difficult, of course, to assign specific causes for the increase in magic in Zandeland. It would be all too easy to simply write it off as resulting from colonial administration. It is reasonable to state, however, that although changes brought on by colonial administration did not spark the creation of magical means of retribution and punishment, it certainly accelerated, or gave new impulse to, this process. In particular, the closing of the borders, which made the procurement of *benge* difficult, and the breakdown of the princes' authority to decide and punish crimes of witchcraft, drastically altered the traditional methods of divination and punishment of witches.[41] The princes and their oracles no longer had the final say in the designation and sentencing of witches; the traditional means of witchcraft accusations and vengeance was removed. In this void there seem to have been two reactions: first, a recrudescence of magical means to protect oneself from witches and 'sorcerers' (with perhaps increasing emphasis on the latter), to punish witches and 'sorcerers', and to wreak vengeance; and, second, which we will not spend time on here, very forcible extortions to bring about confessions of now otherwise unprovable crimes, a phenomenon attested by Evans-Pritchard,[42] and also by my own informants in the Central African Republic.

The decline of the authority of the Vungara princes and their *benge* under colonial rule thus seems to have played a part in the recrudescence of new magical means, including those of 'secret societies', both for protective and for punitive measures.[43] Evans-Pritchard summarized the role of colonial influence in the increase of magic:

> Many other of their medicines have been borrowed within the memory of living man. The process continues today probably partly because an era of peace has favoured diffusion; partly because the power of medicines lies in their novelty, a sense of distance and unfamiliarity endowing them with prestige; and partly because many legal and moral sanctions have been replaced by magical ones. Thus vengeance can now only be accomplished by magical means. Also men who would have brought cases in which they had a claim for redress before the princes in the old days, but who cannot obtain redress in present-day courts for various reasons, either must abandon all hope of restitution or trust to magic to obtain it. Indeed, European governments have themselves become objects and agents of magic; for protective medicines are often asked to guard their owners against imprisonment and punitive medicines are often asked to bring imprisonment on wrongdoers. In fact, far from magical practices having diminished since European conquest, all evidences point to a remarkable increase of

medicines. Belief in witchcraft, oracles, and magic seems to be as strong as ever it was, and even among the younger generation there is no marked tendency to discard the faith of their fathers.[44]

Just as calamity and failure are attributed to mystical wrong-doing, so is success attributed to special magic. Evans-Pritchard observed that 'great success in an undertaking is an indication of the possession of powerful medicines. . . . [Zande] are inclined to attribute unusual success to special magic'.[45] Nowadays, perhaps even more than ever, success is due to magic. A good harvest, a successful hunt, an excellent grade on an exam, a promotion, are all attributed to magic. It would even be possible to speculate a relationship between an increase in magic and an increase in social and economic inequality.

Returning to our discussion of witch-doctors, although Evans-Pritchard suggests other reasons for their decline (i.e. they gradually became too densely concentrated, in part due to imposed government settlements),[46] it is possible that on the whole their demise corresponds to an increase in the individual use of magic for personal retribution and vengeance. But vengeance magic in itself cannot fulfill the functions of the witch-doctors. Whereas witch-doctors were collective fighters of witchcraft, 'generally . . . magical actions concern only the welfare of an individual'.[47] Witch-doctors were patronized by the princes, while 'princes and courtiers . . . are even contemptuous of much of the magic in Zande culture'.[48] Witch-doctors inspired admiration, and had much prestige, but 'magicians have no great prestige in Zande society'.[49] The witch-doctors dance was a common, if not required, event prior to collective undertakings, whereas 'magic is seldom an essential part of a social activity'.[50]

Thus, the gap left by the decline of the witch-doctors was not filled by magic. It is all the more interesting, therefore, that these are some of the very areas in which witch-doctors and *Nagidi* share common features. *Nagidi* fight against evil (witchcraft and 'sorcery') through their religious teachings. They do not act in secret, but hold a sort of 'public seance' during which belief in mystical notions are confirmed. They hold great prestige. Through prayer and ritual during religious services, they offer collective prayers for the common good. Finally, besides dealing with lesser matters such as continued failure in hunting, barrenness, and so on, they offer public trials for witchcraft and sorcery.

The second major change accompanying the rise of the *Nagidi* occurred more gradually, and, it would seem, almost imperceptibly: the shift in the notion of *mbori*, a word often translated as 'Supreme Being' or 'God'. In the past, *a-toro* (ghosts) and *mbori* (Supreme Being) seem to have been associated; they were spooky notions, to be appealed to, to be appeased, to be feared in the event of transgressions:

> There can be no doubt that Azande do not clearly distinguish between the Supreme Being and the ghosts of the dead when performing the ceremony and that they think of them both together as the object of their ritual.[51]

Furthermore, both *mbori* and *a-toro* are associated with heads of streams.[52] Even today, elderly informants, though well aware that *mbori* was not the Christian 'God' he is nowadays, give confusing accounts as to what he actually was. In examining utterances in which the term appears (especially in texts dating from the 1920s), it becomes obvious that pre-Christian *mbori* was not a personified moral source, nor omnipresent, nor omniscient. The word took the non-human animate pronoun *ru*, could be pluralized, and was used with both principal forms of Zande 'possessive': *ga*, and *se* (used, for example, with body part terms), the use of which reflects the attributes of the notion referred to. *Mbori* (like the *a-toro*, or 'ghosts') could not be a moral, impartial judge: the 'Supreme Being . . . [was a] vague influence . . . not cited . . . as the guardian of moral law'.[53] The word, in its pre-missionary contexts, could as easily (or more easily!) have been translated as 'fate' or some such impersonal equivalent.[54]

With the Christian missionaries, and their ideological offspring, the Nzapa Zande sect, *mbori* takes on the meaning of a Christian 'God'. Only now has 'God' become *ko* (he), rather than *ru* (it), a personified, morally good, impartial, omnipresent, omniscient Supreme Being; a 'Christian' God, in other words, who can see into a person's soul and know whether or not he has committed an evil act. Furthermore, with the Christian religion and the notions of God and sin and personal redemption, we find that free will and individual responsibility for acts are emphasized.

The emergence of 'prophetesses' can be seen as both a development of existing Zande spiritual idioms and an innovation of Christianity. The death-burial-resurrection experience which bequeaths new powers of insight is something the Zande were already familiar with, not only as something sought (as with the *binza*) but as something unbidden (as with the *a-ira-a-toro* and the *a-ira-a-girisa*). A concern with revealing 'bad' actions and reaffirming public notions of 'good' behaviour was also present in the activities of the witch-doctors. What has changed is the nature of the source of inspiration, and here the Christian transformation of *mbori* to the omniscient, morally good God has facilitated the development of figures who, like those early Christian prophets inspired by the Holy Spirit, can see into the human soul and see evil. That those with the new gift of prophecy are women rather than men is also partly explicable through the old idioms associated with 'ghost diviners'.

In closing, I can but offer a general proposition, perhaps worthy of pursuit. Zande diviners, particularly witch-doctors, belonged to a society in which belief in witchcraft was pervasive. It seems that nowadays there is an upsurge of magic and magical beings which vie with, or even displace, witchcraft *per se*, at least as can now be observed in actual, individual accusations. The activities of witch-doctors, diviners and fighters against witchcraft, are collective. The threat of witchcraft is a collective concern; witch-doctors act for the common good, in a public setting; they 'clear the air of witchcraft'. Magic, by contrast, and especially the newer forms of punitive, vindictive magic, is carried out through private actions, for individual pursuits. In sum, witch-doctors are sought to keep things from happening, whereas ('bad') magic seeks to make things happen. Furthermore, the Christian religion (and, in many important ways, the Nzapa Zande of the *Nagidi*) with its omniscient God and a focus on free will and individual responsibility for acts, seems to be at direct odds with witchcraft and the world of witch-doctors, who were involved in collective prevention and revelation rather than individual retribution.[55]

Notes

1. E. E. Evans-Pritchard, *Witchcraft, Oracles and Magic among the Azande* (Oxford, 1937). The Zande, numbering less than one million, inhabit the regions of the Nile-Zaire watershed, and are divided among the modern nations of the Sudan, the Central African Republic and Zaire. Their language belongs to the Ubanguian branch of the Adamawa-Ubangui family (Greenberg's Adamawa-eastern). I use the Zande plural prefix *a-* only in Zande contexts (in italics).

2. This is one of the rare cases where Evans-Pritchard deviated from a direct correspondence between English and Zande terms. He took into account moral values and named *wene ngua* ('good magic') simply 'magic', while *gbegbere ngua* ('bad magic') he translates as 'sorcery'. He also often uses 'medicines' for *ngua* in the 'good' sense. Here, I use 'magic' or 'plants' to translate *ngua*.

3. Evans-Pritchard, *Witchcraft, Oracles and Magic*, p. 21.

4. Ibid., p. 10.

5. Ibid., pp. 320–1. Cf. also p. 465.

6. Ibid., p. 267. See especially p. 288: 'The Prince's oracles reveal matters of tribal importance, judge criminal and civil cases, and determine whether vengeance has been enacted for death'. And again at p. 86: 'the only act of witchcraft that is legally recognized by punishment meted out to a witch is the crime of murder. This must be proved by a verdict of a prince's poison oracle'. Cf. also pp. 85, 293.

7. Ibid., p. 11.
8. Ibid., pp. 45, 148–9, 340–1. And at pp. 90–1: 'Threatened misfortune or illness (by witchcraft) is the equivalent of actual misfortune or illness, and inspires the same behaviour.' Cf. also pp. 93, 98, 134, 347–8.
9. Although I personally observed *Nagidi* only in the Central African Republic, I have heard accounts of them in Zaire, and they also exist in Obo, very near the Sudanese border.
10. Respectively, ibid., pp. 157 and 441; E. E. Evans-Pritchard, 'Zande theology', *Sudan Notes and Records*, 19 (1936), reprinted in *Essays in Social Anthropology* (London, 1962).
11. Evans-Pritchard, 'Zande theology', p. 183.
12. Ibid., pp. 183–4.
13. Ibid., p. 184.
14. Evans-Pritchard, *Witchcraft, Oracles and Magic*, p. 39.
15. C. R. Lagae, *Les Azande ou Niam Niam* (Brussels, 1926), pp. 39, 64–6.
16. F. Giorgetti, *La Superstizione Zande* (Bologna, 1966), p. 247, my translation.
17. Ibid., pp. 247–52.
18. Evans-Pritchard, 'Zande theology', p. 110.
19. Evans-Pritchard, *Witchcraft, Oracles and Magic*, p. 11.
20. Ibid., pp. 149, 168, 185, 187–8, 258.
21. Ibid., p. 149.
22. Ibid., pp. 193, 234.
23. Ibid., p. 257.
24. Ibid., p. 149, Cf. also pp. 488–90.
25. Ibid., pp. 163–4: 'Moreover, the witch-doctor functions at these seances not only as an oracular agent but also as a fighter against witchcraft, . . . by his dances he wages immediate war on witches . . . To those present a seance is a very good show which is amusing to watch . . .' And at p. 258: '[Witch-doctors'] chief value is that they generally clear the atmosphere of witchcraft . . . [J]oint undertakings . . . and the interests of the district are at stake . . . Witch-doctors . . . act as ritual skirmishers to report on and counter the mystical forces in opposition.'
26. Ibid., p. 149.
27. Ibid., p. 51: 'The Zande witch-doctor exercises supernatural powers solely because he knows the right medicines and has eaten them in the right manner. His prophecies are derived from the magic inside him. His inspiration does not spring from the Supreme Being or from the ghosts of the dead . . . He relies on medicines for visions of witchcraft and for indications of direction.' Cf. also pp. 178, 205, 211, 227, 229.
28. Ibid., pp. 159–60, 209–13, 490.
29. Ibid., pp. 240–2.
30. Ibid., p. 195.
31. Ibid., pp. 154, 158–61, 170–2, 177–206.
32. Ibid., pp. 167–70.
33. Ibid., pp. 156, 244.
34. Ibid., p. 194.
35. All material in this paragraph is drawn from Evans-Pritchard, *Witchcraft, Oracles and Magic*, especially pp. 164, 175, 195, 251 and 253. For facility, the present tense is used for the temporal comparison in this and the subsequent paragraph.
36. Ibid., p. 258.
37. Letters from Zemio often include news of recent *kpiri* (a sort of 'man-turned-water-monster') attacks: 'Unfortunately we have been much saddened by further drownings. In the effort to punish the guilty parties, many innocent persons are suffering in prison.' From a missionary, 24 September 1989.
38 Evans-Pritchard, *Witchcraft, Oracles and Magic*, speaks of 'the curiosity and tolerance Azande express towards foreigners and their habits, and the readiness with which they borrow from them objects and ideas . . . [I]n conformity with ideas associated

everywhere with magic Azande think that medicines used by foreign witch-doctors are more powerful than any they possess today.' (pp. 277–8).

'. . . The power of medicines lies often in their novelty, a sense of distance and unfamiliarity endowing them with prestige . . . [T]here is a tendency to attribute all medicines to conquered and foreign peoples . . .' (pp. 445–6).

39. Cf. Ibid., p. 469.
40. Ibid., p. 442.
41. Ibid., p. 128: 'British rule . . . does not permit direct vengeance on a witch, nor accept the legality of paying compensation for an imaginary crime . . . But today a witch is never accused of a crime . . . All is vagueness and confusion . . .' Cf. p. 322.
42. Ibid., pp. 267–8.
43. Ibid., p. 513: 'In so far as the magic of the [secret] associations is not redundant it is directed against the vagaries of European rule. Azande, faced with a power they can neither stand up against not avoid, have found in magic their last defence. New situations demand new magic, and European rule which is responsible for the new situations has opened up roads into neighbouring countries which can supply the new magic.' See also, Douglas H. Johnson, 'Criminal secrecy: the case of the Zande "Secret Societies" ', *Past and Present*, 130 (1991), pp. 170–200.
44. Evans-Pritchard, *Witchcraft, Oracles and Magic*, pp. 445–6. Cf. also p. 467.
45. Ibid., pp. 444.
46. Ibid., pp. 183–4, 202.
47. Ibid., p. 424.
48. Ibid., p. 425.
49. Ibid., p. 428.
50. Ibid., p. 434. If the witch-doctor no longer dances his dance of divination (*a-vure*) in Zande villages, we can at least be consoled by the fact that he lives on in the Trickster tales. Several of the Trickster tales incorporate the characteristics and behaviour and legends of witch-doctors, though modern (especially young) narrators are ignorant of the past existence of witch-doctors. For example, Evans-Pritchard says that according to the little existing mythology concerning witch-doctors, Madina's (the founder of the witch-doctors' corporation) son Nzoropoi caused birds to fall about him like rain by his dancing and singing. The story involving Yangaime (as recounted by Evans-Pritchard, Gore, Lagae and Van den Plas, *La Langue des Azande* [Brussels, 1921], and as told to me), relates the exact same event, but the form of a typical Trickster tale. Ture the Trickster's very appearance corresponds almost point by point with descriptions of ancient witch-doctors, complete with feathered hat, hide-bag, anklets and horns, and his exploits are often those described for witch-doctors (in particular, the dance of divination). By 'reading' these tales with an interest in their mythological and legendary aspect, we can gain a better view of the past world of the Zande witch-doctors.
51. Evans-Pritchard, 'Zande theology', p. 187.
52. Ibid., p. 189. The souls of the dead were believed to reside in ravines at the heads of streams.
53. Ibid., p. 110.
54. In his personally annotated copy of *Witchcraft, Oracles and Magic*, Evans-Pritchard systematically replaced 'supernatural' with 'mystical', as though he wished to remain as vague as the Zande with regard to the notion of *mbori*. One could go even further and suggest that, not only is the concept of a godlike Supreme Being a fairly new concept for the term *mbori*, but that the term itself was borrowed relatively recently perhaps from the Mangbetu. This would account for its often being confused with 'genies' and ghosts, its appearing with different possessive forms, and the very different accounts by various observers. For one thing, a corresponding word (and

accompanying concept) has never existed among the neighbouring and closely-related Nzakara.

55. Eric de Dampierre, *Un Ancien Royeume Bandi du Haut-Oubangui* (Paris, 1967), has discussed the relationship between diviners and prophets among neighbouring Ngbangi peoples:

'The prophet appears under two aspects: that of universal wife-giver and that of witchfighter. In the latter role, he tends to take the place of witch-doctors, whose shamanistic rituals he ceases to perform: thus removing the need for a public. In both these roles the face of the individual, the new man, pierces through.' (p. 567).

'There is a negative correlation between the presence of diviners and oracles in a society and the advent of prophets.' (pp. 568–9).

These observations beg further discussion.

Part Two

Colonial Historiographies

Six

Maji Maji

Prophecy
&
Historiography

MARCIA WRIGHT

The Maji Maji Rebellion in southeastern German East Africa has been recognized since its outbreak as an anti-colonial rising of great extent, intensity and consequences. Its phases were ably summarized by John Iliffe in a seminal article published in 1967, when he wrote: 'Maji Maji, as a mass movement, originated in peasant grievances, was then sanctified and extended by prophetic religion, and finally crumbled as crisis compelled reliance on fundamental loyalties to kin and tribe.'[1] The present review of the historiography of Maji Maji concentrates on the background events and outbreak of the rising in late July 1905, paying attention to the economic context glossed as 'peasant grievances' and 'prophetic religion', summary expressions that require renewed analytical attention in light of accumulating scholarship and new perspectives on protest, ideology and religion. With the aid of analyses based on primary research, and of comparative studies of resistance and leadership in popular movements, this chapter re-examines proximate causes and the interrelationship of grievances and prophetic vision and agency. The intention is not only to stress the need for a reconsideration of the initiation of the Maji Maji rebellion, but also to offer some interpretive guidelines.

Two heuristic devices will be employed to cluster the two contending focuses of attention in a way that will, it is hoped, allow for a richer analysis. The first will be the concept of a *prophetic moment*, as one of a conjuncture of new and old in which old beliefs are reshaped to suggest a course of action to a profoundly troubled society. The momentousness can be thought of as an urgent sense of the present need and possibility for an epic resolution. It is sometimes characterized as millenial. The idea of a prophetic moment can be pursued in the absence of prophetic religion in the sense of an established form where prophets recur as recognized critics of belief and practice calling for purification. The second, concomitant concept is of a prophet or religious figure as a *commissioning agent*, validating the grievances of the afflicted, providing a ritual of incorporation and sanctioning oppositional mobilization. Such agents need not necessarily be the authors of an innovative ideology.

The modern literature on Maji Maji achieved a precocious clarity as documented and developed in the Department of History at the University of Dar es Salaam between 1967 and 1972. The effort was led by John Iliffe, succeeded by Gilbert Gwassa, encouraged by Terence Ranger as Head of the department and extended by Lorne Larsen. The two major Dar es Salaam theses with major bearing were Gwassa's in 1973 and Larsen's in 1976.[2] A campaign to gather oral testimony in 1968 and 1969 generated a fund of source materials, some contained in a widely circulated mimeographed volume. Although a series of pamphlets was projected, only two appeared. Gwassa and Iliffe's edited pamphlet, *The Records of the Maji Maji* included oral data gathered by Gwassa in Matumbi country in 1966 and 1967, as well as an excellent sample of documents.[3]

This research, mobilizing undergraduate as well as graduate students, occurred in an initially very favourable political environment, the newly independent Tanzania of the 1960s. Julius Nyerere had declared in 1956 that Maji Maji anticipated the unity of the nationalist struggle. While he stressed a mainly spiritual quality, de-emphasizing the violence, magic and oathing that were currently being represented as the hallmark of the Mau Mau struggle in Kenya, he also acknowledged certain lessons from defeat:

> The people fought because they did not believe in the white man's right to govern and civilize the black. They rose in a great rebellion not through fear of a terrorist movement or a superstitious oath, but in response to a natural call of the spirit, ringing in the hearts of all men, and of all times, educated and uneducated, to rebel against foreign domination. . . .
> The struggle against the Germans proved to our people the futility of trying to drive out their masters by force.[4]

The historiographical recognition of Maji Maji as a charter event in national history crystalized as early as 1972 and has remained virtually unchallenged at home or abroad.[5] It is not the facts and combination

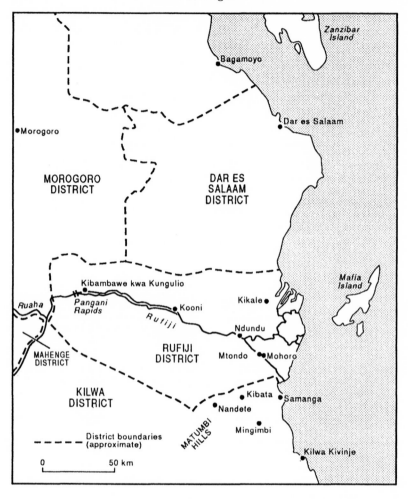

Map 3   Maji Maji in Rufiji

of causes so much as the lessons to be drawn from its achievements and defeats that have been continuously debated in Tanzania.[6] While satisfaction with the newly minted explanations and sequencing of Maji Maji was doubtless at play, there were objective obstacles to systematic pursuit of the topic through oral history. In particular, this resulted from the closure of southern Tanzania to research, owing to its role until 1975 as a place of strategic settlement and a staging point for Frelimo's liberation war against the Portuguese in Mozambique.[7]

Meanwhile, Maji Maji has been absorbed into the received history of African resistance to colonial domination. No other rebellion is mentioned as many times and in as many chapters in volume 7 of the *UNESCO General History of Africa*, covering the period 1880–1935.[8] Understandably, it is also seen as comparable to other rebellions by people confronting the generalizing intention and consequences of colonialism. Walter Rodney put it into the category of famous anti-colonial resistances including, among others, the Bailundu revolt in Angola and the Bambatha rebellion in South Africa. These comparisons deserved to be pursued beyond his bold statement that 'Africans responded aggressively to the attempted dislocation of their economic independence.'[9] What economic independence meant in the region where the Maji Maji outbreak began is a major point of debate, and it is no longer sufficient to see the crisis as the defence of an autonomous subsistence economy against the imposition of cotton 'under the lash' to a people unacquainted with market relations.[10] In taking such a stance Rodney was merely reflecting the superficial treatment of economic causes as presented by Iliffe in his seminal and subsequently canonized work. Iliffe himself, influenced by the research and findings of Lorne Larsen, among others, made an important revision on this score in the late 1970s when he acknowledged that his earlier assumptions that Maji Maji occurred in an area of minimal colonial presence was false and that indeed 'the Maji Maji rebellion was to take place in the one area of the colony which was clearly prospering'.[11] Unfortunately for students of Maji Maji, this statement is placed in an earlier chapter and is not brought to bear upon the major synthesis of Maji Maji that occupies an entire chapter of *A Modern History of Tanganyika*.

Writing on religion during the colonial era, K. Asare Opoku compares Maji Maji with the resistance surrounding Nyabingi spirit mediums in Rwanda and Uganda because they each combined a belief in religion and magic.[12] Nyabingi has continued to command attention and Maji Maji can fruitfully be compared and contrasted with the 1912 Nyabingi revolt.[13] Nyabingi also provides a valuable contrast, for its spirit mediums figured in repeated episodes of resistance, whereas in Maji Maji the mediums of Bokero never again took the lead or rallied the people.

That this particular struggle also warrants consideration in a more global framework of comparative studies was appreciated by Michael Adas who, in *Prophets of Rebellion*, places it alongside cases from India, Burma, Java and New Zealand.[14] All these revitalization movements, Adas contends, arose in times of accelerated change, accompanied by the emergence of new groups, the improvement of some and the perceived diminution of others. The movements have their specificities, yet are comparable in claiming to assert indigenous as against foreign values, and 'whatever form they take, the central aim of revitalization movements is to provide meaningful ideologies, codes of behavior, and systems of social interaction that will allow their adherents to overcome the feeling of deprivation and sense of disorientation'.[15] The religious framework in German East Africa was supplied by the Bokero cult, whose spirit mediums provided the rallying and legitimating message.

The teachings of prophets ought not to be treated as separate from or prior to a popular ferment but rather as galvanizing disparate sources of mass sentiment into a focused movement. This commissioning role arises out of the complex prophetic moment. The salience of this kind of analysis will be confirmed as we amplify evidence about the economic preconditions and exercise of colonial authority in the period from 1898 to 1905 and see a culmination in the months prior to the outbreak of the rebellion. When popular receptivity, the commissioning message and the season of tax collection and cotton harvest came together, rebels took the offensive. Ideological commissioners rarely figured in the field of battle. Kinjikitile, the spirit medium in the foreground of all studies of Maji Maji, had been detained several weeks before the outbreak of the war and was martyred by execution in its first days. The transitory role of Kinjikitile and his curtailed involvement in the actual events of armed conflict and defeat allowed his reputation to flourish both in popular lore and in formal scholarship.

Gwassa's question was not why Maji Maji occurred, since it was given for him that the underlying cause was colonial oppression which he treats in the undifferentiated way that was characteristic at the time. Since this oppression was felt elsewhere without such counteraction he sought to explain how rebellion happened *where* it did. His answer was wrapped around the person of Kinjikitile, who in mid-1904 had become possessed by the spirit Hongo, an emissary of the superior spirit Bokero, whose ritual centre was near some rapids on the Rufiji River. During the year prior to the outbreak of Maji Maji, Kinjikitile received many pilgrims at his headquarters, Ngarambe, on the northwest slopes of the Matumbi Hills. His message was that the ancestors would come back and were gathering at Bokero's. No wild predators would menace people under their protection. The medicine he offered could make its users immune to white weapons, and anyway the white men were weak. Africans were freemen, not slaves.[16]

According to Gwassa, phase one of Kinjikitile's preparations involved a whispering campaign, calling on people to anticipate a war. Next they were invited to make a pilgrimage to Ngarambe to receive the medicine and appeared in groups often formed like units raised for military defence. Lastly, Kinjikitile sent emissaries to more distant places, each of which would later be involved in the Maji Maji outbreak. In explaining why diverse ethnic groups rallied to a single leader, Gwassa credited the widespread influence of the Bokero cult system, but also leaned heavily on a more abstract common denominator, belief in 'vital force'. The Matumbi acted without Kinjikitile's authorization, for he did not think that the time had yet come.[17] Gwassa concluded about the essential significance of Kinjikitile's short career:

> This did not lie . . . in an invention of the idea of the commands of the divinities mediated through a possessed man, or of the idea of the influence of the ancestors, or of the idea of a war medicine. It lay in his demonstration that these ideas could be combined and above all universalised. . . .
>
> In the end Kinjikitile's movement went down in the defeat of Maji Maji. The future did not lie with a universalised traditional religion. But his message could be re-interpreted in secular terms. The theme of his teaching was 'unity to regain independence'. The echoes of 'Unity and Freedom' in Tanzania's coat of arms were implicit in Kinjikitile's teaching.[18]

Maji Maji does indeed offer an excellent example of protest by a society aggravated by profound change but not yet overwhelmed by the power, ideology and values of the colonial order. The challenge remaining for historians of the movement is to convincingly link prophetic leadership with the disaffected groups who joined the rebellion. How did religion become a source of legitimization for the men of action, frequently individuals with frustrated expectations of improvement within the in-coming order, whose self-interest made them potentially unpopular? How did they manage to become identified with an increasingly generalized class of common people seeking relief from exploitation, popularly understood through the metaphors of life-endangering predatory creatures and ill-health?

A multi-faceted view of social disorientation will not demote the importance of religion or do away with evidence of the pervasive appeal to supernatural elements, but will insist on a closer account of the environment of discontent and in so doing will diminish the explanatory potential of a single prophetic figure or hero.[19] The possibilities of such an interpretation, demonstrated by Lorne Larsen in his study of Maji Maji in the Mahenge region, were not extended to apply to the Rufiji District to the east, at the centre of the activities of the Bokero cult. However, there is now evidence available which will allow such an analysis. Kinjikitile must consequently yield the exclusive place he holds in currently received historiography as the ideological innovator and charismatic leader of Maji Maji, not merely because we have theoretical suspicions that too much might hang on a single individual, but also because the retrieval of a previously neglected account from the very centre of cult activities demands an overall reinterpretation.[20]

A fresh report from the scene

While a variety of studies suggested that the build-up to the Maji Maji rising drew upon a multiplicity of grievances, and rested not merely on the forced cotton growing that has become the standard 'proximate cause', those favouring a religious interpretation became arrested by the figure of Kinjikitile.[21] Gilbert Gwassa has been thanked by Terence Ranger for 'rescuing' Kinjikitile's ideology and religious teaching from the 'garbled accounts of . . . adversaries'.[22] Gwassa's discussion illuminated aspects of cosmology and cult organization and underscored the novelty of the new doctrine with its rhetoric of freedom (as opposed to slavery) and its promise of purification and redemption through accepting a medicine that would make resisters invulnerable to enemy bullets.

The key document for any assessment of the religious ideology of Maji Maji was authored by former junior administrator in the Rufiji District, Otto Stollowsky. His account, published in 1912, anticipated modern scholarship in contending that the religious ideology being propounded in the regions affected by the rising, while conveyed through well-established cult networks, was highly innovative, appealing to and willingly polarizing a people pressed by early colonial demands for tax for labour and for commodities.[23] Stollowsky therefore belonged to neither of the camps discerned among German policy makers by John Iliffe, who wrote of two opposed schools. The first dwelt upon the magic water cult including cohesion and fanatical courage, engineered secretly by witch-doctors and dispossessed headmen utilizing superstition to command obedience. This school, backed by the large, supposedly comprehensive book written by the Governor at the time of the outbreak, Graf von Goetzen, occupied the German political and military right wing. On the other side, liberals and socialists argued that maladministration had led to legitimate grievances, and called for colonial reform.[24]

Stollowsky, like Iliffe, faults Graf von Goetzen for discounting the objective grievances and representing the movement as an outgrowth of superstition, but he suggests that von Goetzen was misled by reports from Kilwa District and overlooked the conflicting record generated by himself and his incompatible superior in Rufiji.[25] The District Commissioner (*Bezirksamtmann*), who arrived in the district head-quarters at Mohoro in February 1905, only a month before Stollowsky himself, was often away or inactive because of illness. He never wished to credit Stollowsky's apprehensions of rebellion and certainly objected to his deputy's activist measures although he could not reverse them.[26] Before acting against spirit mediums, Stollowsky cut off the sale of gunpowder that had been liberal at the time of his arrival. When loafers at Mohoro refused to take work and Arab and European employers complained that labour was unavailable at any price, he told the unemployed youth to sign on or leave town. They decamped.

If the religious network of the Bokero cult was discernable anywhere, it would have been in the Rufiji District. Without doubt, the area of its influence overlapped district boundaries, to the north toward Kilosa, Morogoro and Dar es Salaam. Toward the east and south were Samanga, an important commercial centre, Liwale, the sub-administrative centre and caravan staging point in the middle of rubber-gathering country, and Kibata, the administrative post for the Matumbi Highlands. The first assaults by rebels were at Kibata, Samanga and Liwale, within the Kilwa District, but all the cult centres were within the boundaries of the Rufiji District. The three places alluded to by Stollowsky were Mtondo, several hours to the south of Mohoro, Ngarambe on the southeast extreme of the district bordering the Kilwa sub-district of Kibata, and Kibambwe near the Kibesa shrine on the Rufiji River.

As he took steps to stop the nightly assemblies at Matondo, the young official learned that Nawanga, the woman medium he had arrested there, was only one of 'a large family of magicians who came from the Matumbi Hills' and that her medicine was derived from Ngarambe.[27] Police were therefore sent to bring in Kinjikitile, who by 16 July was in custody at Mohoro. A public trial was to have been conducted on 17 July, before a large number of people who had sub-scribed to the mediums' beliefs, but it was suspended on information that the principal cult priest, a medium called 'Bokero' (after the great snake · god living in the rapids of the Rufiji), had predicted that there would be a great flood and that only blacks gathered on mountain tops would sur-vive, while foreigners, European, Arab, and Indian, would perish.[28] Prior to this great event, magic water would protect people from their enemies and turn their bullets into water. In Stollowsky's interpellation: 'Therefore the natives no longer needed to pay hut tax or grow cotton or collect rubber; they would lead a happy, free existence'.[29]

Stollowsky had 'Bokero' and his son brought to Mohoro, but when they arrived, his superior was once more in charge and, having on a very recent tour issued Bokero a permit to dispense water from the hot-spring as medicine for eye disease, did not appreciate his over-zealous deputy's sweep of cult mediums as fomenters of rebellion. So, after a 'brief and unrecorded interrogation' by the District Commis-sioner, Bokero, like Kinjikitile, sat in jail untried and unsentenced.[30] On 31 July and 1 August, reports came from Samanga that a white settler had been beseiged and that Arabs had been murdered at Kibata. On 3 August, the District Commissioner still refused to prosecute Bokero and Kinjikitile because the connection between them and the violence had not been established. A military tribunal was conducted in public the following day by Captain Merker, commander of the newly arrived army detachment, with assessors including a German settler, the Liwali (a Muslim sub-official), two *jumbes* and an Indian trader. Bokero – father and son – and Kinjikitile were found guilty of promoting rebellion and sentenced to hang at once.[31]

One of Stollowsky's most important statements concerning Kinjikitile was aimed in 1912 to rebut information given by Goetzen. It was not Kinjikitile, he insisted, but Bokero his superior who made the famous speech from the scaffold, acknowledging his leadership in the cause. Stollowsky quoted Bokero's words, as he had recorded them on the day in his diary: 'I am not afraid to die. I was sent by God and will be in Kibambawe again this evening. The black people will all stand together, for my medicine has already reached Kilosa and Mahenge!'[32]

Stollowsky's article contains a passage of such value on the relation-ship between preparation for rebellion and the actual outbreak that it deserves to be quoted at length:

> There is just one more very important fact which must be mentioned here – a fact which is incontestably demonstrated by whole series of investigations recorded in the files in Mohoro – namely the fact (which was also reported

in Mahenge, Kilosa, and Morogoro) that the outbreak of the rebellion definitely did not occur at the intended moment. From Kibambawe the message had gone out to the jumbes that 'the Europeans are like lions, so the black people must all act together against them if they are to be conquered', and thus the whole native population was to be prepared for the idea of rebellion through the propaganda which the magicians had begun to spread. In this way the rebellion could be begun throughout the country as nearly as possible at the one agreed time. I am not certain whether a definite date for this had yet been chosen by them all: the evidence on this matter was very contradictory. It must however be regarded as certain that the outbreak among the Wamatumbi took place entirely on their own initiative. The cause is quite obvious: the arrest of their hongu and of Bokero had lifted the veil on their carefully guarded secret and left them, like it or not, with the choice of either abandoning the plan or carrying it through with force and speed. The traditionally rebellious temperament of the Wamatumbi, which was now completely without guidance, made them choose the latter course.[33]

Two further aspects of Stollowsky's account can be drawn out for their bearing upon modern historiography and new perspectives on the preconditions for Maji Maji. The first of these is his emphasis on border areas as especially conducive to conspiracy. The second is his candidate for the position of mastermind, for he too believed there must be a single ideological innovator. Pursuing his argument that the Pangani rapids shrine was 'the source of agitation', Stollowsky explained why its position in the political geography of colonial administration contributed to this status:

> This is a place remarkably suitable for the intended operations, as the boundaries of no less than five different administrative districts (namely, Dar es Salaam, Rufiji, Kilwa, Morogoro, and Mahenge) run within a relatively short distance of it, and it lies moreover almost equidistant from all the relevant district offices.[34]

The lack of regulation and a positive awareness of the differences of policy as between one district and another thus contributed to the merits of Kibesa as a centre of the intelligence. Other district boundary areas have been shown to be environments for compounded disaffection. By Stollowsky's own account, friction between tax collectors representing Kilwa and Rufiji had led to boundary disputes not far from Ngarambe in April 1905 that remained unresolved in July 1905.[35] Research on the Ngindo and Matumbi in these areas shows that defaulting debtors, failed aspirants for *jumbe*ship and people avoiding taxes came together to make new communities.[36] Men of this background became military commanders in Maji Maji.

One researcher of the post-independence period concurs in seeing frontier zones as hotbeds of dissidence. Concentrating upon the Mahenge District, Lorne Larsen raised a number of new questions about the causes and sequencing of the rebellion and showed that for Mahenge, the economic picture was dominated by the rubber boom. The central part of the district, the site of the most systematic control by administrators, was the least militant. It was at the peripheries, along the southeast border, where friction and rebelliousness came together. Larsen concluded that a religious factor, namely anxiety over witchcraft and the desire for purification, had been heightened by the differential impacts of commercial activity. Fear of witchcraft made for initial receptivity to the protective medicine and this involvement paved the way to readiness to answer a subsequent call to arms against colonialism. Larsen's narrative of the build-up and ramifications of the rubber boom, beginning in the later 1890s, confirmed that the economic background of Maji Maji had been treated superficially in the emergent nationalist synthesis.[37]

The growing demand for and production of rubber in the last decade of the nineteenth century set up a commercial framework in the Kilwa and Bagamoyo hinterlands. The two richest sources of vine-grown rubber were to be found in the Donde area of Ngindo, by 1900 a relatively stabilized place of production and trade, and in the Mahenge District, where the rubber frontier at the turn of the century moved continuously westward, closely followed by tax collectors and varying perceptions of the meanings and implications of new wealth.[38] Larsen's findings provided invaluable detail on the turbulent rubber frontier in Mahenge District from 1898 to 1905, where traders from Bagamoyo competed with those connected with Kilwa. The rubber trade after 1895 also propelled the elaboration of colonial and commercial communications, effectively extending Kilwa's economic hinterland through Ngoni country to the northeastern shore of Lake Nyasa. The most heavily impacted areas, however, were precisely those of the Maji Maji 'outbreak zone'.[39]

Larsen also wrestled with the religious and cultural values of people confronted both by such prosperity as the rubber boom brought and by the official tightening of market regulation and intensified calls for tax and labour on public works. He pointed to the need for a dynamic understanding of social relations:

> First, sufficient cognizance must be taken of the very crucial role played by the *maji* in the area of Ngindo ethnicity, of the leadership role assumed by its distributors in a 'stateless' society, and of the promise it offered to a people whose social relationships were being drastically distorted by new economic demands'.[40]

On the southeastern periphery of Mahenge District bordering Kilwa District, during the year prior to the outbreak of Maji Maji at the end of July 1905, the German administrator was attempting to impose taxes in a special environment of communities which had resettled to take advantage of the ambiguity of colonial authority between one district and another. This flashpoint of rebellion, with its mixed population of Ngindo and Pogoro, was neglected by the university oral history project undertaken in 1968 and 1969.[41]

Stollowsky's boldest speculation concerned a 'guiding spirit' of the anti-colonial movement, 'a single, particularly intelligent mind' working out the plan. Answering his own question, 'Who originally devised the plan for the rebellion, and who were the principal patrons of its political and military organization?', he asserted that Bokero and other spirit mediums were 'very suitable propagandists', broadcasting an ideology that was 'a clever mixture of old superstitions, ancestor worship, and new ideas designed to awaken racial consciousness'.[42] The proposed mastermind was 'the old brigand Hilalio', who had died in March 1905. Stollowsky's sketch of Hilalio's career reads as follows:

> Hilalio . . . used to extort hongo[43] from the caravans and had been expelled by the government from the Ngulu area. A former mission pupil who had been trained as a native priest, he spoke French and Latin reasonably well and was in other ways educated to a level that was unusual among our natives. In the early 1880s he had, so to speak, usurped the throne of Ngulu, using the Christianity in which he had been painstakingly educated as the foundation for his rise to a position of power and domination. From the pious missionary Hilarion there emerged a thoroughly unscrupulous heathen potentate Hilalio, who with unusual dissimulation and cunning had elevated the crudest materialism of the native to despotic dignity. After the establishment of German rule in East Africa, he had been clever enough to show unfailing respect to the stronger power, and so fatten himself at the government's expense. The economy of his kingdom, which had formerly depended on caravan hongo, gradually came to depend exclusively on discreet embezzling of the official hut tax. I am not acquainted with the precise reasons for his eventual transfer from his usurped kingdom in Ngulu to the post of sultan and akida in Kungulio [Kibambawe].[44]

The thrust of the present discussion of the historiography of Maji Maji is to urge multiple causations, not to revert to a single or very few factors. Yet ideological synthesis, as the prophetic message of the Bokero cult adepts surely entailed, does have an intellectual history and it is well worthwhile to consider the conflicts of values and beliefs on the one hand and action and legitimization on the other that were active in the late nineteenth-century environment. To dramatize this thread of history, Hilalio is appropriate not only because of his presence in the vicinity of the Bokero cult centre in the years 1901 to March 1905, but also because he was a quintessential entrepreneur, astute in managing power to his own advantage, exploiting and compounding oppositional forces. In common with early colonial renegades, bandits, and upstart accumulators about whom there is an evolving literature, his relationship with colonial power and popular life was deeply ambiguous.[45]

Whereas Kinjikitile's status as a nationalist icon became secure because so very little was known of him, especially before the years 1902 to 1905, Hilalio was one of those figures who repeatedly stole the limelight on the early colonial stage in the Bagamoyo hinterland. He was a liberated slave, brought up and trained as a catechist by the Holy Ghost Fathers. In 1877 he was sent from Zanzibar to the Mhonda Mission station in Nguru, about sixty kilometers north of Morogoro. He became embroiled in disputes with headmen of non-Christian villages in 1881 and obtained, through the mediation of the missionaries, support from the Sultan of Zanzibar entailing the despatch of a police contingent and a requirement that his enemies pay him compensation.[46]

By 1893, Hilalio was a troublemaker targeted for German official discipline. He had seceded from the mission, founded his own separate village and had been excommunicated, yet managed to befriend the District Commissioner and escape punishment because his African accusers failed to appear against him. Three years later, he was an officially designated headman, or *jumbe*, able to receive the District Commissioner in an extremely tidy village, a model in colonial terms, where he had a special building for office work. In the evening, he entertained his guests with a dance performed by his numerous 'wives'.[47] The cause of his removal from Nguru to the position of Akida in Kungulio/Kibambawe was an escalating feud with the Holy Ghost missionaries at Mhonda, who antagonized the German authorities by complaining of him as now a Muslim whose misdeeds were covered by the 'pro-Muslim' policy in recruiting African administrators. Indeed, he had been the forerunner of a pattern of conversion by Christian village heads to Islam, once they received official appointments as *jumbes*. Two of his missionary adversaries were deported from German East Africa.[48]

There is no information available directly linking Hilalio with the Bokero cult leadership in the critical years 1904 and 1905. The conditions that had contributed to his career of opposition, aggrandizement and manipulation of power and legitimacy were nevertheless at play among the host of converging anxieties and antagonisms which made for the moral fusion of an anti-colonial struggle.

Elsewhere in Africa, where religious mobilization and armed conflict occurred, there was a similar unevenness of impact as contending ideological ingredients, ambitious accumulators, and colonial harassment came together. We have already drawn attention to Walter Rodney's suggestion that Maji Maji can be compared with the Bailundu war of 1902, the Natal rebellion of 1906 and the 1912 Nyabingi resistance movement in Rwanda and Uganda.[49] Incipient class interests energized leaders who projected a spiritual order accessible to all who believed and participated. Later, in a more mature colonial situation, class was still to be ambiguous: 'conflicts over class rarely assume the simple adversial form we have been taught to expect', as Lonsdale has put it.[50]

At the turn of the century, leadership was equivocal. If the prophetic moment is fraught with internal tensions as well as foreign oppression, its leadership must be precarious, without long-term roots of legitimacy and particularly in need of a commissioning ideology and sanctification. To gain from comparison, it is necessary to be as clear as possible about continuities and discontinuities in light of cultural, social and economic conditions unfolding several decades before a prophetic moment and extending equally after it.

Were this a book-length discussion of Maji Maji, a chapter of comparisons featuring the outbreak in terms of the issues of structure would certainly be necessary. Here it must suffice to prepare for comparison by recapitulating certain corrections that must be introduced into the historiography of Maji Maji itself. The relationship of the people and the rebel leadership to the colonial economy was not one of resistance to commodity relations. Rodney was misled by the post-independence narrative in asserting that while in West Africa, Africans took the initiative in engaging in export-oriented activities, in German East Africa it was done only under the lash. The crunch of a recession in the price of rubber in 1902 played a part in the disappointment of some African traders and contributed to their anti-foreign ardour. The diminishing returns on forced communal cotton growing put pressure on *jumbes*, but their sponsorship of spirit mediums took place in Rufiji where there was no forced cotton growing. In the Rufiji valley and delta, the continued existence of slavery and pressure of the administration in the months before July 1905 for the unemployed to take waged work combined with the independency of the mountain people in a passionate rhetoric of slavery versus freedom. In the background, therefore, was not only the Matumbi war of 1898, but a half century of heightened tension between 'Arabs' and Muslims of freeborn status, to which ex-slaves could aspire.[51] Islam in itself was a neutral religious element in the rising.

Another point of difficulty in early analyses was where to place witchcraft eradication. Before Larsen worked through the ways in which rubber wealth bred suspicions, Ranger had projected witchcraft eradication backward, suggesting that eradicators had established the far-flung lines of communication over which the *hongos* of Maji Maji then moved.[52] The eradicators who followed Kinjikitile and his generation established a pattern, but the lines of movement between Kilwa and Lake Nyasa were not pioneered by religious agents but by caravans of increasing frequency, putting diverse people in touch and carrying information and rumour from place to place.

Within the Rufiji and Kilwa Districts, at the heart of the rising, it is important to draw also from Stollowsky's account a sense of how comprehensive a movement it was. The female presence among ritual agents, as uprooters of cotton, and as a substantial, integrated element among those swelling the throng procuring medicine, was more than symbolic or subordinate. Such women's activism is yet another aspect of the build-up to the Maji Maji rebellion that deserves close attention.

By way of conclusion, a perspective upon Kinjikitile's career may be proffered. At the time of his birth, roughly in 1870, Zanzibar was just losing its independence, but the apparatus of 'the new Sultanate' under British tutelage was strengthened.[53] The subsequent years saw the continuing subordination of the indigenous Swahili elite to immigrant Arabs and a separation of wealthier 'legitimate' traders from the 'illegitimate' traders and those using Muslim brotherhoods to mobilize their following. The anti-slavery activities of the Holy Ghost Fathers in Bagamoyo and its hinterland aligned them *de facto* with the legitimate upper stratum and against the socially ambiguous smaller traders. The ingredients of an anti-foreign polarization therefore existed along the coast and the caravan routes to the interior. The more indigenous Swahili operators were displaced from the central routes and became redeployed with the opening up of the Kilwa and Lindi hinderland in the early German period. Rubber gave the incentive for increasing traffic to Liwale and Mahenge in the 1890s. The tax receipts in 1898 in the Kilwa District, which still included the future Rufiji District, were almost all in cash. Kinjikitile, at the turn of the century, probably paid his tax in coin. The medicine he later dispensed carried a fee in the same currency.

Maji Maji

Kinjikitile's induction as a spirit medium in 1902 took place as the colonial situation approached one of its sinister conjunctures. The lowering of rubber prices internationally in 1902 had immediate reverberations along the nerve-lines of credit. At the same time, in parts of the Kilwa District, *jumbes* were required to convey the directive to grow cotton on communal plots. The following year, a drought reduced the harvest of crops and vine rubber, cotton had to be be replanted, and delegations of pilgrims went to the Bokero cult centre at Kibesa on the Rufiji to request intercession to bring rain. In 1904, the Bokero cult system gained increasing influence through the activities of Kinjikitile at Ngarambe, where a sub-shrine had meanwhile been established. In 1905 the rubber prices were up, but the returns on communal cotton had shrunk from negligible to nothing. Tax collection was more intense and reached district borderlands as never before, putting *jumbes* as well as ordinary tax-payers under unprecedented pressure. Meanwhile, slavery remained a legal status in German East Africa and was a feature of social and productive relations in the Kilwa and Rufiji Districts, where it gave a meaning to freedom that supplemented the discourse of oppression heretofore identified by historians more exclusively with the independency of the Matumbi.

To separate ideological innovation, commissioning agent and prophetic moment is to give greater attention to the dynamics and interplay among the causes of a major anti-colonial rebellion. Does this mean that we must entirely abandon Kinjikitile? The answer is no, for several reasons. Whatever scholars say, he will live on in the popular mythology of Tanzania. He must also remain a central figure in an interpretive study, for even if he was not at the top of the Bokero hierarchy and his intellectual contribution to the Maji Maji ideology was probably modest, he must continue to claim attention as a key commissioning agent, whose significance was enhanced by his place at the vortex of the conditions culminating in a major prophetic moment.

Notes

1. John Iliffe, 'The organisation of the Maji Maji rebellion', *Journal of African History*, 8 (1967), p. 495.
2. Gilbert E. Gwassa, 'The outbreak and development of the Maji Maji War 1905–07' (Ph.D. thesis, University of Dar es Salaam, 1973); Lorne E. Larsen, 'A history of Mahenge (Ulanga) District, c. 1860–1957' (Ph.D. thesis, University of Dar es Salaam, 1976).
3. *Maji Maji Research Project, 1968: Collected Papers* (Dar es Salaam, 1969); G. E. Gwassa and J. Iliffe (eds), *The Records of the Maji Maji, Part 1* (Nairobi, 1968); O. B. Mapunda and G. P. Mpangara, *The Maji Maji War in Ungoni* (Nairobi, 1969).

4. Address by Julius Nyerere to the United Nations, quoted in Gwassa and Iliffe, *Records*, p. 29.
5. But see Donald Denoon and Adam Kuper, 'The "New Historiography" in Dar es Salaam', *African Affairs*, 69 (1970), and T. O. Ranger, 'The "New Historiography" in Dar es Salaam: an answer', *African Affairs*, 70 (1971).
6. An example of biting political commentary is given in *Maji Maji*, no. 12, September 1973 (a publication of the University Branch of the TANU Youth League):

Maji Maji 1973, by Pheroze Nowroejee

Once before
In 1904
We believed
And believed it was enough
To believe.
Believed in the water.
Believed it was weapon enough,
That it was shield and sword,
God and hongo.*
That anointment made sterile the colonial infantrymen
And flying metal was impotence, flourished.

And we died
And we failed.
Now again we believe
And again believe
That it is enough
To believe.
Now we believe in Azimio†,
Believe again that it is weapon enough,
That it is
God and alchemy.
That utterance alone
Castrates the imperialist
And his metal is impotence, flourished.

Not so, not so.
Do not die.
Do not fail.

* hongo = messenger
† Azimio = resolutions, ideological formulations, for example, the Arusha Declaration of 1967.

7. Lorne E. Larsen, 'Problems in the study of witchcraft eradication movements in southern Tanzania', *Ufahamu*, 6, no. 3 (1976), p. 88. A scholar who had to rely entirely on documents because of the closure of the region to researchers was Patrick Redmond, whose discussion is nevertheless worth noting: 'Maji Maji in Ungoni: a reappraisal of existing historiography', *International Journal of African Historical Studies*, 8 (1975).
8. A. A. Boahen (ed.), *UNESCO General History of Africa, Volume 7: Africa under Colonial Domination, 1880–1935* (Berkeley and London, 1985).
9. Walter Rodney, 'The colonial economy', in Boahen (ed.), *UNESCO History*, Volume 7, p. 332.
10. Ibid., p. 338.
11. John Iliffe, *A Modern History of Tanganyika* (Cambridge, 1979), p. 130.
12. K. A. Opoku. 'Religion in Africa during the colonial era', in Boahen (ed.), *UNESCO History, Volume 7*, p. 516.

13. See, Allison Des Forges, 'The drum is greater than the shout: the 1912 rebellion in northern Rwanda', in Donald Crummey (ed.). *Banditry, Rebellion and Social Protest in Africa* (Portsmouth, NH, 1986). See also, Iris Berger and Holger Bernt Hansen, in this volume.

14. Michael Adas, *Prophets of Rebellion: Millenarian Protest Movements against the European Colonial Order* (Chapel Hill, NC, 1979).

15. Ibid., p. 183.

16. Kinjikitile's apotheosis was accomplished through the work of Gilbert Gwassa. See especially, 'Kinjikitile and the ideology of Maji Maji', in T. O. Ranger and I. N. Kimambo (eds), *The Historical Study of African Religion* (London, 1972). Kinjikitile is also the hero of a popular modern play in Swahili.

17. Gwassa, 'Kinjikitile' p. 204.

18. Ibid., p. 215. Gwassa's thesis has not been generally available. I am grateful to John Iliffe for sharing his notes on the work.

19. This general shift was signalled by T. O. Ranger, 'The people in African resistance', *Journal of Southern African Studies*, 4, no. 1 (1977).

20. Before the appearance of the document, discussed at length below, I had become painfully aware of the tenuousness of the case for Kinjikitile as the omnibus prophet, although attempting to save appearances. See Marcia Wright, 'Kinjikitile', *Encyclopedia of Religion* (New York, 1986).

21. The ramifications of complex commodity relations were first discussed in my paper, 'Rubber and the Kilwa hinterland, 1878-1906', Historical Association of Tanzania conference paper, 1974.

22. T. O. Ranger, 'African initiatives and resistance in East Africa, 1880-1914', in Boahen (ed.), *UNESCO History, Volume 7*, p. 52.

23. Otto Stollowsky, 'On the background to the rebellion in German East Africa in 1905-06', translated by John W. East, *International Journal of African Historical Studies*, 21 (1988).

24. John Iliffe, 'The effects of the Maji Maji rebellion of 1905-06 on German occupation policy in East Africa', in Prosser Gifford and Wm. Roger Louis (eds), *Britain and Germany in Africa: Imperial Rivalry and Colonial Rule* (New Haven, 1967), p. 561; Graf Adolph von Goetzen, *Deutsch Ostafrika im Aufstand* (Berlin, 1909).

25. Stollowsky, 'Background to rebellion', p. 681.

26. Ibid., p. 688.

27. Ibid., p. 686.

28. 'Bokero' was also called Kologelo, perhaps Kolelo, another manifestation or variant name of the Bokero deity. His real name, according to Gwassa, may have been Ngamea or Ngameya. No scholar has attempted to retrieve details of this medium's career and family. The Maji Maji research project and Gwassa's own research concentrated on Ngarambe, Kinjikitile and the Matumbi people.

29. Stollowsky, 'Background to rebellion', p. 687.

30. Ibid., p. 691.

31. Ibid., p. 692.

32. Ibid.

33. Ibid., pp. 692-3.

34. Ibid., p. 693.

35. Ibid., pp. 683-4.

36. A.R.W. Crosse-Upcott, 'The social structures of the Ngindo-speaking people' (Ph.D. thesis, University of Cape Town, 1956). All scholars who have studied the social history of this area have noted the interrelatedness and similarities between groups of different names. A longer-term history of the lower Rufiji river would show continuous dispersals and resettlements owing to flood and other locally variable conditions.

37. Larsen, 'History of Mahenge', p. 77.

38. Ibid., pp. 81–2. For the Donde–Ngindo area, see Crosse-Upcott, 'Social structures', and Wright, 'Rubber and Kilwa hinterland'.
39. For the outline of this argument, see Marcia Wright, 'East Africa, 1870–1905', in R. Oliver (ed.), *Cambridge History of Africa, Volume 6* (Cambridge, 1981).
40. Larsen, 'History of Mahenge', p. 127.
41. Ibid., p. 90.
42. Stollowsky, 'Background to rebellion', p. 694.
43. Hongo here refers to an exaction or toll to gain passage, not a messenger of the gods.
44. Stollowsky, 'Background to rebellion', p. 695.
45. See Crummey (ed.), *Banditry*, intro., and D. N. Beach, 'From heroism to history: Mapondera and the northern Zimbabwean plateau, 1840-1904', *History in Africa*, 15 (1988).
46. J. P. Kiernan, 'The Holy Ghost Fathers in East Africa, 1863–1914' (Ph.D. thesis, University of London, 1966), pp. 211, 244.
47. A. Leue, 'Nguru', *Deutsche Kolonialzeitung*, 28, 32, 34 and 37 (1906), pp. 333, 362. I am grateful to John East for drawing attention to this valuable memoir of a colonial official.
48. Kiernan, 'Holy Ghost Fathers', pp. 317–8.
49. Rodney, 'Colonial economy', p. 332. For recent discussion of Natal and Nyabingi, see chapters by Marks and Des Forges in Crummey (ed.), *Banditry*.
50. John Lonsdale, 'Wealth, poverty and civic virtue in Kikuyu political thought', in Bruce Berman and John Lonsdale, *Unhappy Valley*, Volume 2 (London, 1992), p. 352.
51. See August Nimtz, *Islam and Politics in East Africa: The Sufi Order in Tanzania* (Minneapolis, 1980).
52. T. O. Ranger, 'Connections between "primary resistance" movements and modern mass nationalism in East and Central Africa', *Journal of African History*, 9 (1968), p. 450; Larsen, 'Problems of witchcraft eradication movements'; Lorne E. Larsen. 'Witchcraft eradication sequences among the people of Mahenge (Ulanga) District, Tanzania'. The latter paper was completed in 1974, but has never been published.
53. Abdul Sheriff, *Slaves, Spices and Ivory in Zanzibar: Integration of an East African Commercial Empire into the World Economy, 1770-1873* (London, 1987), esp. ch. 6.

Seven

The Colonial Control
of Spirit Cults
in Uganda

HOLGER BERNT HANSEN

Among the anti-colonial movements to emerge in Uganda, the Nyabingi
spirit cult is perhaps the best known. The Nyabingi spirit cult first came
to the attention of colonial officials in the Kiga region of southwest
Uganda immediately prior to the First World War. For the next three
decades the followers of Nyabingi were the focal point of the most serious
and sustained challenge to the authority of European colonial power in
the territories of Uganda. Nyabingi was hardly less of a threat to the
British in Uganda than the Maji Maji rebellion of 1905 was to the
Germans in Tanganyika, not least when the strategic importance of
the Kigezi District, where Nyabingi activities remained concentrated, is
taken into account. Yet the Nyabingi movement has never achieved
prominence in a nationalist historiography.[1] One reason for the low
profile of the Nyabingi cult must be its confinement to the Kiga area. But
it is also important to note the dominating influence of the Protestant and
Roman Catholic churches on both the political and social history of this,
and many other parts of Uganda. The Christian churches, with their
ultimate monopoly of intellectual and religious life in colonial Uganda,
pushed African religions to the margins. The language of colonial
officials echoed this, tending to label the followers of African religions
as 'traditionalists' or people 'without any religion'.[2] And traditional
religion in general was held in low esteem. For some colonial officials,
even Islam was considered to be far preferable to 'paganism' as a transi-
tional stage towards the acceptance of Christian faith.[3]

Map 4   Southwestern Uganda

While the Nyabingi cult has been analysed in its religious and political contexts, little is known of how its adversaries, the colonial government in general and its local agents in particular, perceived the movement. On what grounds did the colonial state adopt a policy towards Nyabingi? How did they seek to control the forces that gave Nyabingi its impetus? How did they distinguish such religious expression and anti-colonial behaviour from other, more familiar and more 'established' religious activities? And, perhaps most importantly for the historical interpretation of Nyabingi, to what extent did the value system imposed by colonial officials influence the legacy of the Nyabingi movement? Historians and anthropologists who have studied Nyabingi, and other similar cults in Uganda, have not focused upon such questions, tending instead to present them as archetypical prophetic, millenarian movements.[4] Such an interpretation has the advantage of placing Nyabingi more easily into a larger and comparative frame of reference, yet it gives insufficient emphasis to the fact that the colonial authorities' vigorous suppression of the cult was based upon an understanding that categorized it as a subversive witchcraft movement.

The Colonial Control of Spirit Cults in Uganda

Difficulty with the categories of analysis deployed by colonial observers of Nyabingi has been a common theme in the literature on the cult. Following May Edel's initial research, both Denoon and Brazier have argued that colonial officials did not distinguish between the Nyabingi cult and other traditional religious practices, which meant that they tried to indiscriminately suppress all expressions of indigenous religion.[5] In her detailed study of the Nyabingi as a political force, Elizabeth Hopkins is also inclined to characterize the colonial officials as ignorant and uninterested:

> Given their simple rubrics in dealing with traditional supernatural categories, the British officials may well have failed to appreciate the cult's position within the indigenous religious structure.[6]

In the most recent and most extensive study of the religious content of the Nyabingi cult, Freedman undermines even further the idea that the colonial officials had any sense of the religious values inherent in traditional religion:

> . . . the British sought to abolish, by threat of punishment, any exhibition of traditional religious activity whether Nyabingi-related or not . . . There should be no surprise therefore at the poverty of British documentation. Nyabingi practice customarily proceeded by offerings and private consultations, hardly very visible transactions. The British made it even less visible. With deliberate repression they drove it even further from view.[7]

Freedman goes on to dismiss the one government official who actually studied the phenomenon of Nyabingi, J. E. T. Philipps, as having almost turned a blind eye to the cult, limiting himself to 'personal surmisings on the seditious threat to British colonial authority by the remnants of the Nyabingi practitioners'.[8]

The existing literature has therefore stigmatized the approach of colonial officials to traditional religion in two respects. In the first place, it is asserted that they lacked knowledge of the phenomenon and so left no reliable documentation. It is true that the officials involved lacked professional expertise in anthropology and in religious matters. All the same, it is surely essential to clarify as precisely as possible the standards by which colonial 'knowledge' of Nyabingi was assembled and documented in order to ascertain its historical value. This brings us to the second point. It is claimed that the lack of proper categories employed by colonial officials, 'their simple rubrics' in Hopkins' terms, helps to explain why they failed to appreciate the wider social and religious context of the Nyabingi phenomenon. In the 'pre-Evans-Pritchard era' all colonial officials evidently lacked the most elementary conceptual tools that their successors were later able to employ, yet their own analytical approach, however unsystematic it may appear, should still be examined closely for the evidence it may offer.

This chapter will therefore return to some of the written sources on Nyabingi, to examine the way in which the colonial perception of the cult developed. By adopting a historiographical approach to establish the terms upon which contemporary commentators treated the movement, we will then be better placed to ask whether an understanding of Nyabingi is really enhanced by the use of 'prophetic' and 'millenial' concepts. In order to place the colonial view in a broader context, I will begin with a brief account of the Nyabingi cult, based on recently published research.

A profile of the Nyabingi cult

The cult first appeared among the Bakiga, north of the kingdom of Rwanda, in the late eighteenth century. Its main manifestation was the worship of the goddess Nyabingi, said to be the spirit of a queen with some connections to the Tutsi rulers in Rwanda. Since Nyabingi was murdered by her husband, who was of alien origin, her spirit became associated with resistance to foreign intrusion and dominance.

This association was strengthened in the Kiga region in the nineteenth century by the desire of the predominantly agricultural Bakiga to withstand the cultural incursions of neighbouring pastoralists, and more generally by their efforts to resist the dominating influence of the two centralized polities which bordered their lands, the Tutsi kingdom of Rwanda to the south and the Ankole kingdom to the east. Hence, a political dimension was attached to the Nyabingi cult from an early stage, and the preservation of Kiga autonomy and the acephalous character of Kiga society were major functions entrusted to Nyabingi. Her spirit was invoked and her priests and priestesses called upon whenever assistance was needed against external threats. Internally, Nyabingi also served as a protector against the usurpation of the ancestors.

In an era of social disruption throughout the interlacustrine region in the second half of the nineteenth century, with famine and epidemic causing movements of peoples and areas such as Kiga experiencing increasing population pressures, it appears that the previously distinct divine powers of the Nyabingi and the secular powers of the elders or clan heads came to overlap.[9] This strengthening of the political capacity of Nyabingi proved crucial when external threats to the Bakiga increased in the final two decades of the century, first from the Tutsi kingdom and soon afterwards from the colonial scramble for the inter-lacustrine area, with the Bakiga finding themselves at the centre of the territorial rivalries of Germany, Belgium and Britain. The region was finally placed under British authority and, from 1909 onwards, British administration began to be established in the new Kigezi District. The British recruited Baganda agents as assistants to staff their new administration and were soon imposing poll taxes and labour duties.[10]

With these developments, the merger of the political and religious powers proved decisive as it helped to 'transform Nyabingi worship from an ideology of local clan authority to a millenarian challenge to external domination'.[11] Nyabingi became the embodiment of the ideal of Kiga autonomy and served as the major vehicle for anti-colonial agitation and the expression of anti-European sentiments. The Nyabingi priests were the first people with 'supra-lineage authority', and it was thereby the Nyabingi cult that brought about an enlargement of the political scale among the Bakiga in response to colonial rule.[12]

It is important to emphasize that neither the latter development nor the origin of the Nyabingi cult can be ascribed to the advance of the colonial frontier. Colonial penetration helped to define new goals and influenced modes of expression and behaviour, but the defensive attitude towards external threats and 'the ideology of protest' were long-established elements of the cult. According to Elizabeth Hopkins, what is most characteristic of the development of the Nyabingi movement is the interplay between shifting situational factors and features inherent to the cult, which explains both the tenacity of the movement and its periodic resurgence.[13]

Over the two decades from 1910 to 1930 the clashes between the followers of Nyabingi and the colonial government have been fairly well documented, and can be briefly outlined here. Immediately after the establishment of the first rudimentary administration, and while a boundary commission with members from the three colonial powers involved was still at work, a woman named Muhumusa took refuge in the Kiga area after an attempt to accede to the Rwandan throne. Muhumusa proclaimed herself to be the personification of the Nyabingi and made an attempt to rally support among the Bakiga against the ruling Batutsi in Rwanda. Although her activity was not directed primarily against the newly established British administration, but against alien intrusion in general, the British quickly came to view Muhumusa as a potentially hostile force, especially after she organized several raids against those Bakiga who co-operated with the British administration. In September 1911 the British authorities took military action against her. In spite of Muhumusa's claim 'that the bullets of the *Wazungu* (Europeans) would turn to water against her' she was defeated and captured, while more than forty of her followers were killed.[14] Muhumusa was deported from the district and remained under detention in Kampala until her death in 1945 – testimony to the seriousness with which the British treated her and the Nyabingi cult in general.

In the years immediately before the First World War, Muhumusa's followers continued to create occasional disorder among the Bakiga, 'owing to the anti-European preaching' and the demand 'not to obey the English'.[15] The war presented further opportunities for resurgence in the activities of Nyabingi. There was an attack on an Anglo-Belgian border post in early 1915, on which occasion Nyabingi's 'sacred white sheep' escaped unharmed by the bullets.[16] Much more serious was the Nyakishenyi rebellion in 1917, when the headquarters of a Baganda agent was attacked by a force of 1,400 men. The agent escaped, but 63 of his followers were massacred, half of them Baganda, and the courthouse, the Anglican church and the mosque, all symbols of foreign influence, were destroyed.[17] The number of people involved shows the capacity of the movement to rally people to its anti-European ideology, and suggests that the Nyabingi cult was perceived as an appropriate instrument for maintaining Kiga autonomy against foreign influence and control.

To restore control and prestige, the British took stern measures. Two of the minor chiefs involved with the cult were publicly executed, and a number of people were tried under the Witchcraft Ordinance and either imprisoned or deported.[18] This did not prevent new leaders of the Nyabingi movement from mobilizing once again in 1919, directly prompted this time by the alien innovations of the colonial administration, not least by the increased presence of the Baganda agents. The plan to attack the district headquarters in Kabale was thwarted when the British struck first in a surprise attack, killing the Nyabingi leaders and capturing the movement's sacred white sheep, which were later burnt publicly. The head of the defeated Nyabingi leader was sent to the British Museum in London.[19]

After a few skirmishes in 1920, which kept the British sensitivity to the movement alive, the subsequent years have been termed 'years of accommodation and alienation'.[20] Baganda agents were gradually replaced with Kiga chiefs, starting from the lowest level with the *Muluka* chiefs.[21] There was even a softening of attitude, with some officials arguing that there was no cause for undue alarm and that the importance of the Nyabingi movement should not be exaggerated.[22] Yet there were still searches for 'Nabingi articles', and prosecutions of people suspected of 'practising Nabingi rituals' continued.[23]

Those who had imagined that the movement was on the wane were surprised when the Nyabingi cult reappeared on a large scale in 1928, once again acting as the focus for anti-European resistance by claiming 'that "Nyabingi" was more powerful than the government, that no work should be done on Mondays in the shambas, that no taxes should be paid, and that Europeans should be driven out'. The plan of the Nyabingi followers on this occasion was to overrun the district and Anglican mission headquarters in Kabale; again it was believed that bullets from the Europeans could be rendered harmless by the Nyabingi leader.[24] While the defeat of the Nyabingi forces in 1928 represented the last major outburst of the cult, the British still considered it to be a potential threat over the next few years. Although the number of cases prosecuted steadily dropped, the colonial administration remained alert to the emergence of new leaders, not least in view of the continued activity of the cult across the colonial boundary in Rwanda. It was even rumoured that people from Rwanda visited Muhumusa in Kampala, 'to be initiated in the Nyabingi rites'.[25] So, almost symbolically, events came full circle, as the same so-called 'prophetess' who first confronted the British with the Nyabingi movement in 1911 was still seen as an active medium for the Nyabingi spirit as late as 1939.

But by the 1930s the threat posed by Nyabingi in Kigezi was more imagined than real. Even before 1928 the position of the Nyabingi cult and its appeal to the Bakiga had probably started to decline. This can largely be explained by the changes in British policy, most especially the withdrawal of Baganda agents from Kigezi. The activity of the Baganda agents and their policy of 'Gandaization' in language and administration were felt at the local level by the smallest unit, the lineage, and had become the major butt of Bakiga hostility. With the adoption of the *Muluka* system, and the appointment of chiefs at parish level, only local Bakiga were recruited to the posts.[26] The *Muluka* system was quickly established as a training ground for the higher-level chieftainships, *Gombolola* (sub-county) and *Saza* (county), and within only five to seven years the 'Kigaization' of these higher offices was already underway.[27] Although the policy of withdrawing Baganda agents started later in Kigezi than elsewhere in the Protectorate, it served similar purposes and had similar effects. For the Bakiga it meant integration into the colonial system without coercion and without alienation, because it was largely done on their own terms, or, to be more precise, through their own 'agents'. While Nyabingi had nourished the customary opposition to foreign intrusion and helped to identify the culprits, it was the Baganda agents who served as scapegoats for the new kind of authority brought by the colonial intrusion. In this respect, the colonial penetration of Kigezi followed a pattern typical of other parts of Uganda.

In another sense, too, a more general pattern prevailed in Kigezi, strengthening the integrative forces of the new colonial order and counter-balancing the appeal of the Nyabingi cult. Denoon's analysis of the first generation of *Muluka* chiefs in the early 1920s shows that they were fairly young and mostly Christian, often trained by Baganda catechists. Later in the 1920s, when some of them were promoted to *Gombolola* and later *Saza* chiefs, they were Christians, except for a few Muslims.[28] Denominational rivalry quickly became a major issue among this group, since religious adherence was the main criterion in the recruitment of chiefs. Consequently, the Protestant and Roman Catholic missions, which had so far been represented only by catechists, now sent European missionaries to Kigezi, one of whose priorities was to start schools in which to train suitable candidates for the chiefly posts.

During the 1920s Kigezi therefore experienced the same so-called 'Christian revolution' as had happened in other districts of Uganda.[29] Hopkins has argued that disillusionment with the Nyabingi movement would seem to have 'caused mass production of Christians'.[30] On the other hand, Captain Philipps singled out government policy, and not least people's perception of that policy, as the primary explanatory factor:

> People believed that the Government had ordered that animists who did not adopt 'the Government religion' (Protestantism) within six months would be (considered as Nabingists and) imprisoned.[31]

These two conflicting interpretations of the developments of the 1920s raise the question of the real impact of the Nyabingi movement and its role in influencing government policy. It also raises the question of whether there was a causal relationship between the discrediting of the Nyabingi cult and the widespread conversion to Christianity. Did the Bakiga react to their disillusionment with Nyabingi and turn to the now more moderate government policy, which was both accommodating towards their grievances and offered them a religious alternative by way of Christianity and its means of adapting to all the changes? Or was it rather the government that held the initiative, using another religion in its efforts to control or even eliminate the Nyabingi cult as a political force, and bringing about a Christian revolution in the process?

These questions may not necessarily represent mutually exclusive alternatives, even if Brazier is inclined to argue that Christianity succeeded where the Nyabingi cult failed in breaking down the old barriers in Kiga society and enlarging the political scale.[32] The answer must depend upon the colonial officers' whole perception of the Nyabingi cult, their understanding of its relationship to other religious phenomena, and the role they attributed to it in the policy-making processes.

The colonial perception of the Nyabingi cult

It was the massacre at Nyakishenyi in 1917 that first stimulated colonial officials to look for causes of Nyabingi beyond a simple and under-standable will to resist European conquest. The District Commissioner speculated upon the powers of witchcraft and superstition:

> As might be expected among unsophisticated savages the powers of super-stition are enormous. This explains the influence of the local witchdoctors, who initially combine their claims to supernatural powers with promises of liberation of the natives from European rule and restoration to their former condition . . .[33]

The next District Commissioner to come to Kigezi, Captain J. E. T. Philipps, who served there from 1918 to 1920, and survived the 1919 Nyabingi plot to attack the district headquarters, gave the matter deeper study. In spite of his short term of service, Philipps took an active interest in the Nyabingi cult and collected, through a network of informants, much information on the cult and its appearances among the Bakiga. Apart from his official correspondence, he drew up a detailed report, entitled 'The Nabingi. An anti-European secret society in Africa', completed just after the 1919 battle.[34] After his return to Britain he infringed conventional decorum by sending a copy directly to the Colonial Office,[35] and it was only just before the resurgence of Nyabingi in 1928, that he had the same report printed in an international journal.[36]

We have already noted Freedman's dismissal of Philipps' whole approach as too narrow because of his emphasis on the anti-colonial and anti-British aspects of Nyabingi. Such an interpretation is unacceptable. Philipps' report remains a major contemporary source, in fact the only one available. In spite of his closeness to the events and the very short time at his disposal, his account is impressively detailed and comprehensive in scope: and there can be no doubt that his expressed views influenced both colonial policy at the time and the interpretations of later analysts.

It is, of course, not surprising that Philipps should have placed great emphasis on the political dimension of the Nyabingi movement; after all, by 'preaching an anti-European crusade under Nabingi direction' British colonial rule, and thereby Philipps' own authority, was being directly challenged.[37] But Philipps widened the political dimension by recognizing the importance of the origins of Nyabingi in the kingdom of Rwanda and the fundamental anti-Tutsi attitude ingrained in the cult. He clearly linked it to the Hutu–Tutsi cleavage in Rwandan society, characterizing it as 'the champion of the numerically superior "labouring" classes against the aristocratic Batussi'. More than simply an anti-colonial movement, Philipps saw Nyabingi as anarchic and 'subversive of any ordered form of government'.[38]

As described by Philipps, the Nyabingi movement had a very simple organization with all its actions surrounded by 'supernatural significance'. Whenever a leader was deported, another person, usually a woman, was possessed by the Nyabingi spirit. So-called 'ordained' apostles with the white sheep as their emblem were sent out to initiate followers and collect tithes; they worked by a mixture of healing and curses, and were also active in remedying sterility. All in all, the cult had everywhere proved 'revolutionary in method and anarchic in effect',[39] while at the same time engaging in terrorism and suffering from 'the same dangerous and illogical problem of religious fanaticism world over'.[40]

Given his negative assessment of the Nyabingi cult, it is significant that Philipps did *not* consider it to be a true expression of African traditional religion. On the contrary, he saw it as 'opposed to the established native "religion"', by which he meant the *Kubandwa* religion (now called *emandwa*), which he identified with Rwanda.[41] He went on to make a careful comparison between Nyabingi and *Kubandwa*, whose ritual

> shows curious elements of hypnotic suggestion and witchcraft, contains much that appears ridiculous, but more that borders the sublime [p. 312] . . . The whole aspect of Nabingi is of a fanatic anarchic sect as opposed to the liberal and religious principles of the indigenous Kubandwa cult.[42]

The principal difference which Philipps saw between Nyabingi and

Kubandwa was that the latter was 'an established monotheistic faith traditionally allied with the native Government'.[43] To emphasize this, he described the Rwandan situation by employing European church-state categories. The king (*Mwami*) of Rwanda can be seen as the personification of the deity (*Imama*). No intermediary stood between the Supreme God and the king, according to Philipps, and the Banyarwanda practised 'an organised and comparatively pure form of monotheism', a kind of state religion where the kings act as 'Defenders of the Faith'.[44] The activities of the Nyabingi cult, not least the tithe collections and the intrusion into royal privileges, were therefore seen by Philipps as 'non-conformist' and a threat to the 'established church' – even more so when the movement made appeals to the Bahutu against the government.[45] Going on to describe how the monotheistic faith was first allied with and co-operated with the government, Philipps uses terms similar to those used in any situation where an established church exists. The state religion helps to unite the country and instills loyalty in the people; it clearly has a supportive function for the state; it also has an instrumental value for the government; and it provides a means of control and promotes morality in society.

With his emphasis on the instrumental value of 'the established Kubandwa cult' in mind, Philipps suggested that this 'traditional' religion should be used in combating the Nyabingi movement.[46] Pointing to the repeated failure of military measures to fully suppress Nyabingi, he offered a completely new policy. While arguing that education and civilization may work in the longer term, he recommended as immediate action the 'increased tolerance of the Ruanda Imandwa (anti-Nabingi institution)'. In practice this was to be achieved by withdrawing the Baganda agents, who were a focal point for Nyabingi hostility, and starting a process of localizing the chieftaincies, not least in those parts of Kigezi where the Banyarwanda/Batutsi lived. The latter were the hereditary rulers of this particular area, Philipps contended, and by drawing on people's loyalty to the traditional religion these chiefs could be instrumental in stemming the tide of Nyabingi progress.[47]

Philipps' suggestions were speedily adopted as colonial policy. The colonial reaction to Nyabingi was thus derived not from wilful ignorance of African practice and belief, as others have argued, but from an attempt to harness a European understanding of 'traditional' African practices to deal with the situation. However, in view of the strong ethnic divisions in the region and the antagonisms between the Batutsi and the Bahutu/Bakiga, it must be doubted whether the appeal to traditional religion can explain the apparent tranquility of the early 1920s, or whether the capacity ascribed to the traditional religious system had any real effect. The removal of the Baganda agents and the relaxation in the enforcement of tax collections and labour duties had a more palpable impact, and accounted for the subsequent reaction of Philipps' superiors, some of whom thought that he had tended to exaggerate the importance of the Nyabingi revolt.[48]

Philipps' analysis also had important implications for colonial attitudes to and understanding of witchcraft. By stressing the fanatical traits of Nyabingi, its use of prophecies and the tendency to call upon supernatural forces, the cult was portrayed as representing the 'black arts'. Philipps' identification of Nyabingi with witchcraft was explicit:

> By means of an unusually developed form of Witchcraft, in which hypnotic suggestion plays a leading part, the country within the sphere of its operations is completely terrorised.[49]

Reinforced by these remarks, which only reiterated already widely held European views, the earlier practice of prosecuting under the Witchcraft Ordinance of 1912 escalated after the 1919 events, the Ordinance even being amended to more easily accommodate prosecution of the numerous Nyabingi cases.[50] Thus, while Philipps' careful analysis of the Nyabingi cult had clearly separated it from other forms of African religion and belief, his report also made it easier for the government to neglect the political ideology of the Nyabingi movement and simply regard it as a witchcraft movement.[51]

Faced with the unexpected outburst of Nyabingi activity in 1928, the District Commissioner expressed his conviction that any show of leniency would be regarded 'as evidence of omnipotence by the indestructible Nyabingi spirit', and that stern government action was required against the cult.[52] The District Commissioner expressed the opinion that Nyabingi witchcraft differed from the ordinary witchcraft practised elsewhere because it was basically anti-government.[53] In this the Provincial Commissioner concurred, even considering it misleading to describe the movement as witchcraft; it should rather be connected with 'the pagan Imandwa secret rites'.[54] But this point was disputed by the District Commissioner who argued, echoing Captain Philipps' report from 1919, that 'Imandwa is of much more personal a nature – and infinitely less harmful – than Nyabingi'; while Nyabingi was opposed to any form of government, *Imandwa* was not anti-government.[55] It is apparent that the administration was once again uncertain about the nature of the forces they were up against.

In the discussions of 1928 it is surprising that no reference was made to Captain Philipps' 1919 report. Apparently ignorant even of its existence, the Chief Secretary in Kampala asked the local administration in April 1928 to have a report prepared on the whole Nyabingi question, its origin and history as well as its aims and objectives, since little information was available at the Secretariat. A month later the Chief Secretary had unearthed the Philipps report, sending it to the Provincial Commissioner. But meanwhile a Roman Catholic priest in Kigezi, Fr. Lacourisière, had already been invited to provide information on the Nyabingi.[56] This incident serves as a warning against expecting too much consistency within the colonial administration. With the changing personnel, the memory span of the colonial service was evidently short, and policy as a consequence often appeared random.[57]

It is clear from this discussion that Philipps' study of Nyabingi is an important historical source on the movement and colonial reactions to its activities. Why, then, have other scholars tended to dismiss his contribution? Three substantive comments may be offered in response to this question. Firstly, while some Bakiga may have understood Philipps's policy toward Nyabingi as being an assault on all forms of traditional religious activity,[58] this is simply an incorrect reading of the officials' attitudes and intentions. Philipps and a number of his colleagues drew a clear distinction between Nyabingi, which they categorized as a kind of witchcraft, and *emandwa* which they considered to be part of the Bakiga's religious heritage. Of course, this is not to say that Philipps' analysis of the place of Nyabingi in African belief and practice was entirely satisfactory. For example, May Edel, researching in Kigezi during the 1930s, contradicted an important element of Philipps's report when she emphasized the close connection of Nyabingi with the *emandwa* tradition, and it is apparent that the relationship between the two was more complex than Philipps appreciated. Iris Berger makes the same point in her contribution to this volume.

Secondly, Philipps has been accused of having pursued a policy of 'Tutsi-ization' in order to exploit the Batutsi's anti-Nyabingi bias. But Denoon surely overinterprets Philipps's remarks on 'increasing toleration of the Rwanda imandwa' and 'employment of Tutsi', when he implies that Philipps tried to introduce the Rwanda religion and a Tutsi administration into Kigezi. Elizabeth Hopkins has already pointed out that what he meant, and what he in fact put into practice, was that Batutsi hereditary rulers should fill the chiefly posts vacated by the Baganda agents *only* in those parts of Kigezi inhabited by

Banyarwanda: in all other parts of the district he pursued a policy of localization by appointing mainly Bakiga.[59] After all, Philipps was not so obsessed with his anti-Nyabingi drive that he would have overlooked the fact that the introduction of Tutsi rulers would have stirred up support for Nyabingi in its campaign against foreign intrusion, rather than neutralizing its appeal. The withdrawal of Baganda agents and the localization of the chiefly office was part of a general Protectorate policy, and this serves to remind us that the Nyabingi cult, though important, was not the only factor in policy formation in Kigezi district, even for Captain Philipps.

Thirdly, Brazier also points to Philipps' 'Tutsiphile' inclination by implying that he wanted to introduce the ideally-functioning *emandwa* 'church-state system' from Rwanda into Kigezi. Brazier even alleges that Philipps held an Erastian view of the relations between church and state. This was put into practice in Rwanda, where *Kubandwa* was an arm of the state, whereas the Nyabingi cult was theocratic – much to the dislike of Philipps.[60] But just as he did not want to impose Tutsi chiefs on the Bakiga, nor did he favour imposing a *Kubandwa* religious superstructure on an acephalous society like that of the Bakiga. What he asked was only whether 'some sympathetic use can be made of the liberal and religious principles of the indigenous Kubandwa cult by white administrations in combating the Nabingi where military measures have so repeatedly failed'.[61] Hence, Philipps did not pursue an Erastian view, but limited himself to pointing out the assets and potential of the *emandwa* cult in the Kigezi situation, where in his opinion there was a need to strengthen the traditional lines of authority and exploit the concept of authority and government found in the *emandwa* tradition. This whole approach also had some bearing on Philipps' and other officials' attitudes to Christianity and its role in neutralizing the Nyabingi phenomenon.

Did Christianity succeed in providing an acceptable alternative to the Nyabingi cult, as some researchers have argued?[62] Philipps addressed himself to this problem when he returned briefly as District Commissioner of Kigezi and acting Provincial Commissioner of the Western Province in the late 1920s. His attitude was cautious. There was a danger of alienating and politicizing followers of the traditional religion, he argued, if the expansion of Christianity used aggressive methods. This might create a feeling of persecution and antagonism against Christianity and Europeans in general. Philipps was especially critical of 'Dr. Sharp's Mission', the local station of the low-church, almost fundamentalist Rwanda Mission, whose activities had already caused problems for the colonial administration in the 1920s, and which in the 1930s was to spark off the East African revival movement, the Balokole.[63] Besides the Rwanda Mission's active policy to 'combat catholicism', Philipps saw other difficulties:

> one of the dangers of these illegal aggressions by native proselytisers, mistaught by Europeans ignorant of the nature of the religions or cults which they are endeavouring to destroy and replace, is not only the creation in Africa of a feeling of persecution and antagonism against (such) Christianity (if not against Europeans in general) . . . [they are also] known to trespass on private residences of Africans, chiefs and peasants, to destroy or molest their shrines.[64]

Philipps called such actions a violation of religious liberty, and his immediate successor as District Commissioner added 'that "Nyabingi" will in the course of time fade into insignificance as compared with the dangers of religious intolerance, as thus displayed'.[65] Going on to explain what the cult of the ancestral spirit – which, like modern researchers, Philipps termed *Mandwa* – meant to people in terms of deliverance from evil, he concluded by offering a profoundly sympathetic view of African traditional religion, surely rare among European officials at this time:

> Animists in Africa are set down contemptuously as 'heathen'. A sense of both History and the realities of the world, as well as perspective, seem still to be relatively rare.[66]

The influx into the Christian churches that occured in Kigezi in the late 1920s was neither a function of disillusionment with Nyabingi, as Elizabeth Hopkins has argued, nor a result of the colonial officials' deliberate employment of missionary Christianity to stem the Nyabingi tide. Philipps's criticism of the missionary aggressiveness serves as a warning against such an assumption in two respects. In the first place, while colonial officials were of course aware of the wider instrumental value of Christianity as something which initiated people into a common culture and furthered the concept of loyalty and respect for government,[67] the 'Christian revolution' was seen as part of a general trend and gradual process, not as a means of combating Nyabingi and actively furthering the interests of Christianity at the expense of traditional religion. Secondly, colonial officials did not necessarily conceive of Nyabingi and Christianity as alternative categories; nor did they see the immediate need for a replacement of the traditional religion with Christianity. The colonial adminstration in general, and not just Philipps in particular, attached some positive value to the traditional religion, not least to the social institutions it guaranteed. Even more importantly, for the sake of tranquility and good order, a gradual process of change was preferable (in the religious as well as the secular field) to a revolutionary change which could easily cause turmoil and disruption, irrespective of whether the driving force was Nyabingi or missionary Christianity.[68]

Colonial policy, spirit cults & 'established' religion

Spirit cults were not intrinsically threatening to colonial rule and there is little evidence to support a view that colonial policies deliberately obstructed their expressions of African belief. The key factor was not religion or belief, but the maintenance of colonial order. In his survey of religion and protest in East Africa, F. B. Welbourn found in Uganda only movements which he classified as 'independent churches', offshoots of Christianity and mission churches rather than primarily related to African traditional religion.[69] The same distinction was drawn in a colonial memorandum on Ethiopianism in Uganda, submitted towards the end of the First World War, just after the Nyabingi-inspired Nyakishenyi rebellion in 1917. 'Ethiopianism and the gospel "Africa for the Africans" is a purely Christian development', it was asserted, 'which, if left to itself, may even do a certain amount of good'. On the other hand, 'Outbreaks of fanaticism may and have occurred, but these are purely local and can be dealt with by sympathetic and firm but just treatment'.[70] Such outbreaks were rare and localized in scale, and were not primarily to be identified with the independent churches, but implicitly with local movements springing from traditional religious beliefs.

Accordingly, colonial policy in Uganda treated such 'outbreaks' in a localized manner. At the same time as Captain Philipps submitted his recommendations for the handling of the Nyabingi phenomenon in 1919–20, the government was experiencing similar clashes with the Yakan cult, at the time better known as the Allah Water Cult. This cult appeared in the northern corner of the Protectorate, in the new district of West Nile, and on a smaller scale than Nyabingi. After the first serious outbreak it was considered to be of hardly any political significance, although officials recognized that it could not simply be reduced to a witchcraft phenomenon. Officials would appear to have seen no parallel between Nyabingi and Yakan, and no mention of the former phenomenon exists in the documentation dealing with the Yakan cult.[71] The colonial government judged such movements as purely local phenomena with no potential for expansion to neighbouring areas.

Even if the traditional religion had little potential for enlarging its scale, it could not just be dispensed with in the local context in favour of the advancement of Christianity. As we have seen, some colonial officials even argued for the need to distinguish between proper traditional religious behaviour on the one hand and witchcraft on the other. We have also seen that they did not mindlessly prosecute charges of witchcraft under the Witchcraft Ordinance, and that they did reflect on what should be covered by the term 'witchcraft'. The more differentiated concept of witchcraft employed in connection with the Nyabingi cult should be linked with the contemporary discussion of an amendment of the Witchcraft Ordinance in 1917. The District Commissioner in Lango, J. H. Driberg, who two years later became actively involved in handling the Allah Water Cult, and who some ten years later was to become a Cambridge anthropologist, commented on the advancement of witchcraft among the Langi and argued strongly for the necessity of a distinction between witchcraft and religion:

> I must here differentiate witchcraft which is either malevolent or predatory, from the other manifestations of native religious life, which exhibit themselves in a veneration for fetishes, in exorcism and in all the multifarious ceremonials, which for lack of a better title I will designate as religion.[72]

One way of distinguishing traditional religion from witchcraft, and implicitly from a spirit cult like Nyabingi, is to adopt the concept of 'establishment' which Philipps himself introduced when he spoke of 'the established Kubandwa cult'. Established forms of traditional religion are those which are organized, controllable and supportive of political authority, in contrast to the unruly or unpredictable behaviour characterized in movements such as Nyabingi. Here we can draw on I. M. Lewis who, in his initial paper on spirit possession and deprivation cults, spoke of thoroughly established religions where the spirits represent man's experience of order and disorder in his universe. Although 'such religions are still permeated by the notion of spirit', they have become established in the sense that religion is so assimilated in social life that its main function is to sustain moral order and create order in the universe.[73] In the case of Kigezi District, whereas *emandwa* was supportive of the political and moral order, Nyabingi could be interpreted as a reforming religion with revolutionary potential.[74] It is then necessary to investigate just what Nyabingi was intent on reforming. Here perhaps we will ultimately find that there is more to 'millennialism' than reform or revolution, and the fact that Nyabingi was identified as subversive of established order by colonial officials is insufficient justification for categorizing it with other 'millennial' resistance movements in colonial Africa.

The perception of traditional religion which prevailed among colonial officials was basically functional, with great emphasis on instrumental aspects such as sanction and control. This point of view was reflected in colonial legislation. When the introduction of a 'Native Land and Customs Ordinance' was under discussion in 1914, it was pointed out that it should be remembered that 'the vast majority of the peasants are pagans, while the chiefs are in most cases "Christians" '.[75] It was therefore important . . .

> that native councils smitten with zeal for 'progress' or a desire to meet the views of missionaries or officials should not be allowed to proclaim the abolition of or alteration in 'heathen customs' which still retain their force with the bulk of the people.[76]

And it was especially important to protect social institutions like marriage and inheritance, in view of the danger of disruption by the over-zealous approach of some Christian missions. A number of colonial officials appreciated the value of African institutions in maintaining social order and tried to protect them, while they worked for a gradual process of change.[77]

As regards spirit cults like Nyabingi, we may then conclude that control, tranquility and security were key words in policy-making. The colonial state's basic approach to the traditional religion and its offshoots, the spirit movements, was primarily guided by one main criterion – whether any instrumental value could be ascribed to such religious phenomena. Did they in any sense serve the purposes of the state, or did they represent a risk of outbreaks of fanaticism? Colonial perception of traditional religious phenomena was not therefore based on an entirely negative attitude. Provided that their followers did not violate the functional criteria laid down by the state, there was room for them within the fabric of colonial society.

Notes

1. See, for example, the brief discussion of Nyabingi in T. O. Ranger, 'Connections between "primary resistance" movements and modern mass nationalism in East and Central Africa', *Journal of African History*, 9 (1968), pp. 437–53, 631–41. For the most recent discussion of the historiography of prophetic religions like Maji Maji and Nyabingi, see Marcia Wright's contribution to this volume.

The Colonial Control of Spirit Cults in Uganda

2. H. B. Hansen, *Mission, Church and State in a Colonial Setting: Uganda 1890–1925* (London, 1984), p. 226.
3. Colonial Office (CO) minutes, February 1906, CO 536/3–5447/1905–06, Public Record Office, London (PRO).
4. Elizabeth Hopkins, 'The Nyabingi cult of southwestern Uganda', in Robert I. Rotberg and Ali A. Mazrui (eds), *Protest and Power in Black Africa* (New York, 1970); John Middleton, 'The Yakan or Allah Water Cult among the Lugbara', *Journal of the Royal Anthropological Institute*, 93 (1961).
5. May Edel, *The Chiga of Western Uganda* (New York, 1957); D. J. W. Denoon, 'Agents of colonial rule, Kigezi 1908–30', East African Institute of Social Research conference (Kampala, January 1968), p. 17; F. S. Brazier, 'The Nyabingi cult: religion and political scale in Kigezi 1900–30', East African Institute of Social Research conference (Kampala, January 1968), p. 11.
6. Hopkins, 'The Nyabingi cult', p. 297.
7. James Freedman, *Nyabingi: The Social History of an African Divinity* (Tervuren, 1984), p. 40.
8. Ibid., p. 40.
9. Freedman, *Nyabingi*, p. 83ff.; D. J. W. Denoon (ed.), *A History of Kigezi* (Kampala, 1972), p. 212ff. See also Iris Berger's account of the Nyabingi cult in her contribution to this volume.
10. Denoon, 'Agents', p. 6; Denoon, *A History*, p. 216ff. See also Elizabeth Hopkins, 'Partition in practice: African politics and European rivalry in Bufumbira', in S. Förster, W. J. Mommsen and R. Robinson (eds), *Bismarck, Europe and Africa. The Berlin Africa Conference 1884–85 and the Onset of Partition* (London, 1988).
11. Freedman, *Nyabingi*, p. 20; Edel, *The Chiga*, p. 156.
12. Cf. Paul Baxter's review of May Edel, *The Chiga*, in *Uganda Journal*, 22, 2 (1958), p. 193–6.
13. Hopkins, 'The Nyabingi Cult', p. 331ff. Cf. also Iris Berger in this volume.
14. Hopkins, 'The Nyabingi cult', p. 271ff.; Denoon, 'Agents', p. 4ff.; M. J. Bessell, 'Nyabingi', *Uganda Journal*, 6, 2 (1938), p. 79ff.
15. Affidavits by Asst District Commissioner (DC) McCombie and Chief Ruagalla, 8 April and 25 March 1913, Minute Paper (MP) 146 A, Provincial Headquarters Western Province, now in the Uganda National Archive, Entebbe (EBB).
16. Bessell, 'Nyabingi', p. 82.
17. F. S. Brazier, 'The incident at Nyakishenyi, 1917', *Uganda Journal*, 32, 1 (1968). Cf. also Bessell, 'Nyabingi', p. 82, and Hopkins, 'The Nyabingi cult', p. 289ff.
18. The latter was the case of the female 'witch-doctor' Ninabatwa, who, after spending one year in prison was banned from returning to Kigezi for a six-year period. During her deportation she stayed with Muhumusa in Mengo. Minutes 1919–23 in SMP 5571, EBB.
19. Bessell, 'Nyabingi', p. 83f.; Hopkins, 'The Nyabingi cult', p. 300ff.
20. Hopkins, 'The Nyabingi cult', p. 307.
21. Denoon, 'Agents'. p. 14ff; Denoon, *A History*, p. 222ff.
22. See various correspondence in MP 146 A, EBB.
23. Ag. DC Kigezi to PC Western Province (WP) 23 April and 13 August 1923, MP 146 A.
24. Ag. PC to Chief Secretary, 29 March 1928, SMP 3173, EBB. Cf. Hopkins, 'The Nyabingi cult', p. 314ff.
25. Resident Buganda to Chief Secretary, 14 April 1939, MP 146 B, EBB.
26. The policy of replacing Baganda agents was first initiated in the sub-district Rukiga in 1914, when Ag. DC Sullivan expressed his dislike for the Agent System and proclaimed that 'the present gang of Baganda sycophants' should not be allowed to hold any official position: 'Scheme for the organization of Rukiga', March 1914, in SMP 3851, EBB.

27. Re. replacement of Baganda agents with locally recruited chiefs see B. Turyahikayo-Rugyema, 'The British imposition of colonial rule on Uganda: the Baganda agents in Kigezi (1908–1930)', *Transafrican Journal of History*, 5, 1 (1976), p. 111–33. For the development of chieftainship among the Bakiga see Paul Baxter, 'The Kiga', in Audrey I. Richards, *East African Chiefs* (London, 1960), ch. 12.

28. Denoon, 'Agents', p. 14ff.

29. Hansen, *Mission, Church, State*, pp. 325–44, 445–59.

30. Hopkins, 'The Nyabingi cult', p. 318.

31. Note by J. E. T. Philipps from 1929, File 131: CMS 1914–61, Provincial Headquarters Western Province, now in EBB.

32. Brazier, 'The Nyabingi cult', p. 14f.

33. DC to PC, 14 September 1917, quoted from Hopkins, 'The Nyabingi cult', p. 291.

34. A copy is enclosed in MP 146 A, EBB.

35. Colonial Office (Winston Churchill) to Governor, 31 October 1921, MP 146 A, EBB.

36. J. E. T. Philipps, 'The Nabingi. An anti-European secret society in Africa, in British Ruanda, Ndorwa and the Congo (Kivu)', *Congo* 1 (Bruxelles, January 1928).

37. References are made to the printed article from 1928 which is identical with the 1919 report. Quotation from Philipps, 'The Nabingi', p. 318.

38. Ibid., pp. 314–7.

39. Ibid.

40. DC Philipps to PC WP, 26 June 1919, MP 146 A, EBB.

41. Op.cit. For a general account of the *emandwa* cult in the area and also among the Bakiga, see May Edel, *The Chiga*, ch. 7, and Iris Berger in this volume.

42. Philipps, 'The Nabingi', p. 317.

43. Ibid., p. 316.

44. 'State of Rebellion', September and the first weeks of October 1920, by Captain Philipps, MP 146 A.

45. Philipps, 'The Nabingi', p. 312ff.

46. Ibid., p. 317. See also Excerpt from PC's Report on the Western Province for the month of June 1919, MP 146 A, EBB.

47. Philipps' policy proposal is enclosed in PC WP to Chief Secretary, 13 November 1920, MP 146 A, EBB. For a leading Baganda agent's reaction against Philipps' new policy in 1920 see Denoon, *A History*, p. 195f.

48. See note 22.

49. DC Philipps to PC WP, 26 June 1919, MP 146 A, EBB.

50. Minutes in SMP 2156, EBB; cf. Hansen, *Mission, Church, State*, p. 282.

51. This is confirmed by Governor Coryndon's dispatch to CO, 23 April 1921, CO 536/110-25298/21.

52. DC Kigezi to PC WP, 12 May 1928; PC to DC, 23 May 1928, MP 146 B, EBB.

53. DC to PC, 12 May 1928, MP 146 B, EBB.

54. PC to DC, 23 May 1928, MP 146 B, EBB.

55. DC to PC, 2 June 1928, MP 146 B, EBB.

56. Chief Secretary Rankine to PC WP, 16 April and 10 May 1928; PC to Fr. Lacourisière, 20 April 1928, all in MP 146 B, EBB.

57. Captain Philipps returned to Kigezi as DC in the last part of 1928, and he commented on the unexpected release of a Nyabingi detainee in the following words: 'Wonderful people, the English – even Kipling noticed the peculiar-ity!' Note to a colleague 5 June 1930, MP 146 B, EBB.

58. Based on her experiences from field work in the early 1930s, May Edel has strongly emphasized that the suppression of all traditional religious practices was in fact the consequence of the government's policy. Edel, *The Chiga*, p. 157ff.

59. That Philipps' policy was highly appreciated and he himself popular among the Bakiga is confirmed by the autobiography of one of the early appointed Kiga chiefs, P. Ngologoza, *Kigezi and its People* (Dar es Salaam, Nairobi, Kampala, 1969), p. 75f.

60. Brazier, 'The Nyabingi cult', p. 14.
61. Philipps, 'The Nabingi', p. 317.
62. Brazier, 'The Nyabingi cult', p. 14f.; Hopkins, 'The Nyabingi cult', p. 318ff.
63. Kevin Ward, 'Uganda: The Mukono crisis of 1941', *Journal of Religion in Africa*, 19, 3 (1989).
64. Philipps to Chief Secretary, 15 October 1930 with encl. memo of 1 October 1930, SMP C. 1605 A, EBB.
65. DC to PC, 21 August 1931, file no. S. 61, EBB.
66. Philipps to CS, 15 October 1930, SMP C. 1605 A, EBB.
67. See Hansen, *Mission, Church, State*, pp. 453ff., 465-471, 475.
68. Cf. Hansen, *Mission, Church, State*, pp. 277f., 465ff.
69. F. B. Welbourn: *East African Rebels: A Study of Some Independent Churches* (London, 1961).
70. 'Memorandum on the Subject of Mohammedanism and Ethiopianism in Relation to Future Administration in East and Central Africa', encl. in Ag. Governor Wallis to Secr. of State, 30 October 1917 (marked secret), CO 536/86-2457/1917-18.
71. See the minutes from 1919-20 in SMP 6354, EBB. For a recent discussion of the Yakan cult and for further references see Tim Allen, 'Understanding Alice: Uganda's Holy Spirit Movement in context', *Africa*, 61, 3 (1991).
72. Driberg to PC EP, 5 October 1917, MP 53/1917, Eastern Province Provincial Headquarters, now in EBB. Apart from Driberg who became a full-time anthropologist and author of a number of books on the Langi, it was not uncommon in the early colonial period that administrators took a special interest in the people among whom they were posted and undertook special surveys which sometimes appeared in academic journals. We have already met J. E. T. Philipps, and another example is the PC of the Northern Province, A. H. Haddon, who in 1920 produced a substantial report on the Allah Water Cult (in SMP 6354). As was the case with J. E. T. Philipps, the value of such early anthropological writings by administrators has often been questioned as they are considered to be biased in favour of the government's policy and thereby tending to distort reality. For a critical examination of this kind of ethnographic writing see Douglas H. Johnson, 'C. A. Willis and the "Cult of Deng": a falsification of the ethnographic record', *History in Africa*, 12 (1985), pp. 131-150.
73. I. M. Lewis, 'Spirit possession and deprivation cults', *Man*, 1, 3, ns, (1966), p. 323.
74. See D. J. N. Denoon's and B. J. Turyahikayo-Rugyema's introduction to Ngologoza, *Kigezi and its People* (Dar es Salaam, Nairobi, Kampala, 1969).
75. DC Busoga to PC, EP 2 May 1914, MP 111/1913, Provincial Headquarters Eastern Province, now in EBB.
76. Minute 28 June 1915, MP 111/1913, EBB.
77. Hansen, *Mission, Church, State*, pp. 275, 302, 433.

Eight

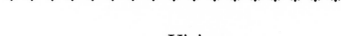

Visions
of the Vanquished

Prophets & Colonialism
in Kenya's Western Highlands

DAVID M. ANDERSON

The stories of the colonial conquest of Kenya tell of many prophets. Some foresaw the coming of the white man and predicted the disasters that would follow, but their prophecies were seldom heeded until all was lost. Others emerged as 'prophets of rebellion', leaders of armed resistance to the invading Europeans. Mbatian, Moraa, Mekatilile, Mugo wa Kibiro and Koitalel offer examples of those who now feature in the writing of Kenya's modern history as heroic prophets, commonly portrayed in word and deed as defenders of African cultures against the incursions of colonialism.[1] Their power as historical actors stems not just from the model of resistance they may offer, but also from their visions of the future: the attribution to them of predictions about the colonial world, about the subjugation of Africans to the wills and ways of the European. The prophets *knew* what the future held, and even if they were criticized or ignored in their own times, history has vindicated those to whom accurate predictions are now attributed. The historical significance of many of the African prophets of the period of colonial conquest in eastern Africa has thus grown with the passage of time.

This chapter will examine one group of 'prophets' whose historical prominence has endured over the past century, the *orkoiik* (sing. *orkoiyot*). *Orkoiyot* is the Nandi term for a particular type of ritual practitioner, or mantic, found among the Kalenjin peoples of Kenya's Western Highlands. Colonial ethnography described the group now referred to as Kalenjin by the name 'Nandi-speaking peoples', this comprising several different 'peoples', each speaking dialects within the same language family and each displaying similar cultural traits. Among this group the Nandi and Kipsigis (Lumbwa) were the most prominent, the other Western Highlands Kalenjin being Elgeyo (Keyo), Marakwet, Tugen (Kamasia) and Pokot (Suk).[2] All the groups among the Kalenjin recognized a range of mantics, each placed in separate categories and each with distinctive functions; but those given the title *orkoiyot* were distinguished by being thought to be the most powerful of all practitioners. The most gifted of their number were believed capable of prophecy and foresight as well as being skilled in several arts of divination. The abilities of the *orkoiyot* could not be learned, but were invariably hereditary, existing among Nandi and Kipsigis only within the lineages of specific clans. The extent of the powers inherited by a single *orkoiyot* varied, as did the ability of any individual to utilize those powers. Thus, whilst all *orkoiik* theoretically held the potential to act as prophets, relatively few were actually recognized and attributed with powers of prophecy.[3]

Our understanding of the historical significance of the *orkoiik* has been made more difficult by their role in the dynamic changes experienced by Nandi during the nineteenth century. Nandi oral histories, recounted in a range of sources spanning the early 1900s to the 1970s, share an insistence upon the important influence of the Kapuso family of Uas Nkishu *loibonok*, who are said to have settled among the Nandi in the 1860s following the dispersal of the Uas Nkishu after defeats by other Maasai sections.[4] Such intrusions of 'alien' mantics are not unusual in the histories of eastern African peoples,[5] but among Nandi this has become integral to a wider historical reconstruction of political, economic and social change in the second half of the nineteenth century. In this period Nandi expanded their territory of settlement, as they spread north and north-eastwards into the lands affected by the internecine struggles of the Maa-speakers. Access to greater areas of good pastureland allowed an increased dependence upon livestock husbandry, and there is also evidence of increased militarism in the organization and control of age-sets. In this last element, it is generally accepted that the *orkoiik* came to play a central role, acting as a focus of political authority in the organization of war-bands and cattle raids. Before the 1860s, the influence of Nandi *orkoiik* of the Kopokoi and Kipsogon lineages, both within the Talai clan, was confined to relatively small territorial constituencies. By contrast, the 'immigrant' *orkoiik* descended from Kapuso, who had been 'adopted' by the Talai clan, drew a wider following after the 1860s, their successes in the sponsoring

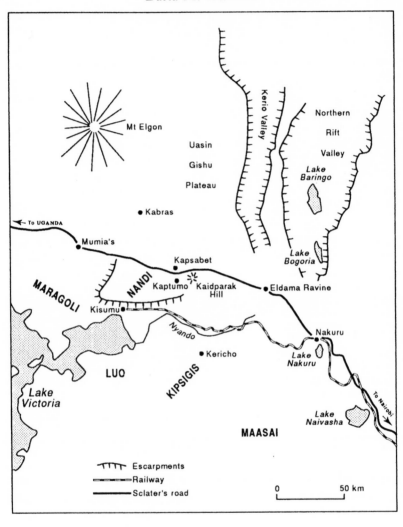

Map 5   Western Kenya, circa 1905

of raids bringing them great wealth in cattle. By the end of the century, the Kapuso *orkoiik* were dominant among Nandi mantics, and held unprecedented economic and political power.[6]

The encounter between the *orkoiik* and the forces of colonialism was notable. The *orkoiyot* Koitalel led the armed resistance of the Nandi people against colonial conquest from the late 1890s to 1905. After Koitalel's defeat, other *orkoiik* continued to take a leading role in protest against colonial rule, culminating in 1923, and again in 1957, in acts of open rebellion.[7] As symbols of early resistance to colonialism, the *orkoiik* were reified in the nationalist historiography that emerged in the late 1960s and 1970s. Here was a heroic history *par excellence*, in which the stories of the *orkoiik* were set within a nationalist frame and retold to express the continuities of African struggles against colonialism.[8] Like the 'prophets of rebellion' described by Michael Adas, and in close parallel with analyses of leadership in the Maji Maji rising and the Nyabingi movement, the combination of spiritual and political authority in the person of the *orkoiyot* has been stressed in literature on Kalenjin history.[9]

The emphasis of this essentially nationalist historiography reflects the early colonial view of the *orkoiik* to a surprising extent. Up to 1910, the British were convinced that Koitalel had represented the 'paramount' political and religious leader of Nandi, and that his role, and the apparent superior political status of the *orkoiik* clan, was a legitimate expression of a recognized indigenous system of government. But, after 1910, colonial administrators increasingly reported that many Nandi and Kipsigis elders presented the *orkoiik* not as their legitimate political representatives, but as a subversive and unwelcome influence. From having initially sought to utilize the *orkoiik* as agents of colonial government, by the early 1920s the British had come to perceive them as dangerous miscreants, posing a potentially serious threat to law and order.[10]

This chapter examines these changing colonial perceptions of the *orkoiik*, focusing especially upon the construction of colonial knowledge between the 1890s and 1935. The opening section will describe the process by which information about the *orkoiik* was gathered up to 1910, when a partial, even distorted picture of their role took shape. The second section moves on to consider the alternative account of the *orkoiik* that emerged by the 1930s, rooted in the views expressed by elders whose authority clashed with that of the *orkoiik*. In both these sections the emphasis is upon colonial sources, that is, the writings of colonial officials, ethnographers and anthropologists. In the final section the broader historiographical implications of this analysis will be discussed.

David M. Anderson

Prophetic encounters with colonialism, 1890s–1910

In the period of colonial conquest, the British encountered four prominent *orkoiik*, each of whom formed a link between the pre-colonial past
and the colonial future of the Western Highlands. The first, Kimnyole,
was by then already dead, but his memory – and the recounting of
his prophecies – reverberated through the years of colonialism. The
other three, Koitalel, Kipeles and Kipchomber arap Koileke, were very
much alive when the British arrived, although each was to endure a
rather different fate at the hands of their conquerors; the first was to
be killed during the suppression of Nandi resistance; the second was
to die 'in office', as colonial 'Paramount Chief' of Nandi; and the last
was to be deported from the Kipsigis area by the British on charges
of subversion, to die in exile far from home. We must consider the
colonial encounter with each in turn.

Kimnyole is the earliest *orkoiyot* for whom we have any biographical
information, and he is remarkable for being one of the few *orkoiik* to
whom prophecies are directly attributed. Kimnyole lived in Samitui,
where he provided his services for Nandi of the southwestern locations,
especially the Kaptumoiis *pororosiek*.[11] He was stoned (or clubbed) to
death by the Kaptumoiis Nandi at Samitui in 1889 (or 1890), and his
hut and property burned.[12] The fact of his death, and that it was at the
hands of the Nandi themselves is undisputed. But the motive for his
killing has been variously attributed to the defeat of the Nandi warriors
in an attack sponsored by the *orkoiyot*; the return of stock carrying
rinderpest to the Nandi herds from a raid sanctioned by Kimnyole;
and the combined impact of disease and drought in the later 1890s,
for which the *orkoiyot* was held accountable.[13] Whatever the reason,
Kimnyole's murder subsequently took on greater symbolic significance,
when prophecies attributed to the *orkoiyot* appeared to be fulfilled after
his death:

> Before he was put to death, Kimnyole is said to have prophesied that white
> people would come who would wage war with the Nandi, kill their sons, seize
> their cattle, and drive them out of their homes, and that they would bring
> with them a strange being like a serpent that would crawl along the ground,
> shriek and puff smoke. He advised all those who could do so to go to live
> in the heavens as the earth would no longer be a proper place to live in.
> All the misfortunes which have befallen the Nandi are attributed to their hav-
> ing murdered their orkoiyot.[14]

The principal misfortune which had befallen the Nandi was their defeat
at the hands of the British, in a bloody and protracted conflict that

had ended in 1906 with sections of the Nandi being forcibly driven from their lands and resettled in a newly created 'Reserve', more distant from the Uganda railway. In the process they had lost much of their wealth in livestock – the British expeditionary force of 1905–6 admitted to the seizure of 16,213 head of cattle and 36,205 sheep and goats – and more than 1,400 Nandi men had been killed, among them the *orkoiyot* Koitalel, who, by some accounts, was Kimnyole's son.[15]

Between 1895 and 1905 Koitalel emerged as the most prominent *orkoiyot* among Nandi. Nandi oral histories have described the years following Kimnyole's death as a period in which no single *orkoiyot* held a dominant position among the Nandi, but that Koitalel's determination to oppose the British gradually brought him to pre-eminence, and that he thereby eclipsed the other leading *orkoiik* of the time, Kipchomber arap Koileke and Kipeles.[16] While the same oral sources indicate that many Nandi did not share this perception of Koitalel's predominance in the early 1900s, it is apparent that both Nandi and colonial views of the *orkoiik* came to be dominated by the apocalyptic events surrounding the British conquest of Nandi in 1905–6, events in which Koitalel played a central role.

The most important primary source on these events, and on the agency of the *orkoiik* in this crucial period, is the diary of Koitalel's assassin, Richard Meinertzhagen, then a captain in the 3rd Battalion of the King's African Rifles.[17] Meinertzhagen was first sent to the Nandi area in April 1904, when he spent only three months in the district.[18] By then Nandi had earned a considerable reputation among the British for 'truculence'. Nandi attacks upon traders' and government caravans moving up the Sclater's Road were frequent from 1894 onwards, necessitating that escorts be provided for travellers between the government posts at Eldama Ravine and Mumia's. The construction of the Uganda railway along the Nyando Valley, on the southern edge of Nandi territory, intensified British anxieties about the threat posed by the Nandi and gave rise to the opinion that they should be 'moved back' from the line of rail. Acts of 'hostility' perpetrated by Nandi led to the first British military campaign against them in November 1895. Further campaigns were mounted in June 1897, July 1900 and March 1903. As well as these large military expeditions, each of which lasted one to three months, other smaller punitive patrols, organized by the district administrator, were sent against the Nandi in November 1899, January 1900, May 1900 and November 1902. The fifth military expedition, which began in October 1905, was by far the largest and was intended to finally deal with 'the Nandi problem'.[19]

David M. Anderson

From his arrival for his second term of duty in Nandi in April 1905, Meinertzhagen was aware that a major campaign against the Nandi was likely, and much of his time was spent in collecting information that might be useful to a military expedition. He came to be especially concerned about the activities of the Nandi *orkoiyot* Koitalel, whom he already had reason to identify as the leader of Nandi resistance to British authority. Koitalel was but one of several *orkoiik* in Nandi. Although all members of the same clan, and often close relatives of one another, *orkoiik* were rivals, each cultivating clients for the services they could offer. Where Kimnyole had worked his arts amongst the Kaptumoiis and Kakipoch *pororosiek* in the southwest parts of Nandi, Koitalel's main following was amongst the Kapchepkendi and Kipkaptalam *pororosiek* of the eastern and southeastern marches of Nandi territory. Success in divination, and especially in the direction of war parties and cattle raiders, increased the reputation of an *orkoiyot*, and by this means Koitalel had widened his authority from the late 1890s. In such turbulent times *orkoiik* enjoyed greater opportunities in offering guidance to raiding parties, and Koitalel became particularly identified with his opposition to colonial incursions.[20]

By mid-June 1905, Meinertzhagen was convinced of Koitalel's centrality to Nandi politics:

> I hear that the Laibon, the chief medicine man of all the Nandi, is busy making medicine against the Government and that various meetings take place regularly among the elders to discuss a means by which they can rid themselves of British rule . . . There is little doubt that the Nandi are brewing up for trouble and are daily becoming more daring.[21]

Over the following weeks Meinertzhagen assembled a 'portrait' of Koitalel; 'a man of 40 or so', who he described as 'the spiritual head of the Nandi, or supreme witch-doctor . . .' '[H]e is rapidly assuming political power and becoming a dictator in the worst sense,' wrote Meinertzhagen, 'for he will weld the Nandi into a formidable fighting force which in a few years might challenge our position in East Africa and constitute a deplorable example to other tribes.'[22]

By late September, with the military expedition against the Nandi imminent, Meinertzhagen increasingly focused upon the role of Koitalel:

> I received news today that the Laibon has just convened a large representative meeting of the whole Nandi tribe, at which it was decided that the British Government was afraid of the Nandi, that no expedition would take place, and that therefore the Nandi must renew their aggressive tactics and drive all Government officials and troops from the district. Uproarious

scenes took place, and it was further decided that both Isaac and I must be murdered.[23]

In October, Meinertzhagen recorded in his diary that Koitalel wished to place his head on a stake outside his hut, alongside that of a policeman murdered by Nandi a few weeks earlier.[24] Threats to Isaac, as the senior British civilian official in Nandi, and Meinertzhagen, as senior military officer, were not surprising, but reports of this sort contributed significantly to the British 'demonizing' of Koitalel. The struggle with Koitalel came to be seen increasingly in personal terms by Meinertzhagen, and perhaps not without reason. Nandi warriors twice attempted to ambush him, in July and August 1905, and an attempt was made to poison him with the 'gift' of a pot of tainted honey. The hand of the *orkoiyot* was seen to be behind all of these incidents.[25]

For Meinertzhagen, and by extension for the British in general, it was the person of Koitalel, rather than the 'office' of *orkoiyot*, that came to be seen to represent all that was evil among the otherwise 'peaceable' Nandi.[26] At a meeting of Nandi 'chiefs' held in July 1905, Meinertzhagen reported that:

> . . . [t]he chiefs complained that they could not control the young hotheads in their tribes who were clamouring for war, also that the *Laibon* or chief medicine man was preaching war against the Government and teaching his people all sorts of nonsense, persuading them that our bullets turn to water when fired at Nandi, that we are not to fight them, etc.[27]

In the same month, news was received that Kimokon, another Nandi *orkoiyot* living in Bushiri, had been murdered at Koitalel's instigation for offering to assist the British in recovering stolen firearms and arresting a suspected murderer. Here, in the British interpretation, was evidence that Koitalel was actively preventing others from working to restore law and order to Nandi. The removal of Koitalel's 'evil influence' thus came to be seen as crucial to the success of the British campaign against Nandi, and Meinertzhagen began to plot ways of capturing or killing the *orkoiyot*.[28]

That opportunity came when Koitalel and Meinertzhagen finally met, face to face, on the morning of 19 October 1905, in a forest clearing on Kaidparak Hill. The meeting, arranged at Meinertzhagen's request ostensibly to discuss terms for peace, quickly broke up in chaos amid hand-to-hand fighting when (according to Meinertzhagen) the Nandi took up their weapons. Twenty-five Nandi were killed in the melee, including Koitalel, who was shot at close range by Capt. Meinertzhagen.[29] While the British officer made no mention of any prophecies of Koitalel in his report upon this incident, he did provide his own epithet for the deceased:

> The Nandi Laibon deserves some obituary notice, as he was a man of some consequence. He was both spiritual and temporal chief of all the Nandi, his office being hereditary. As both he and all his successors male were gathered today, I much regret that the dynasty must stop from today.[30]

This statement, though misleading in several respects, reflected the view then prevalent among the British, that Koitalel had been the unchallenged political head of the Nandi people. It was a view furnished in no small part by Meinertzhagen's own 'intelligence gathering'.

The opinions Meinertzhagen had formed of the activities of the *orkoiyot* and of the politics of the Nandi during 1905 were drawn from a narrow and quite particular range of sources. Only one month after arriving in Nandi, Meinertzhagen 'established an intelligence service to find out exactly where the *Laibon* Koitalel lives, what are his intentions, and what might be his plans if the Government launched an expedition.'[31] In September he gave a fuller account of his 'intelligence system':

> . . . The men I have employed are taken from a small colony of Uasin Gishu Masai who live not far from my house. They hate the Nandi but can pass to and fro unmolested. I have them scattered about the country, a few living in some capacity with the *Laibon* and most of the larger chiefs. By this means I hear about everything which is going on in the district.[32]

It is notable that Meinertzhagen describes Koitalel by the Maasai term *laibon*, and not the Nandi term *orkoiyot*. This reflected the perspective of his informants, the Uas Nkishu Maasai agents who provided him with virtually all the intelligence he received about Koitalel between May and October 1905. Thus, Meinertzhagen's view was essentially a Maasai view, tending to attribute the *orkoiyot* with all the characteristics of a Maasai *laibon*; he saw Nandi through Maasai eyes.

After the killing of Koitalel, Capt. Meinertzhagen was to have one further encounter with an *orkoiyot*. On 22 December 1905, whilst employed surveying the eastern boundary of what was to be the new Nandi Reserve, Meinertzhagen was visited in his camp by one 'Kabellas'.[33] Meinertzhagen treated his visitor with courtesy:

> I asked him to come into my tent and he sat down. He was silent for a long time, just staring at me. Then he asked me if I was the person who shot Koitalel. I told him I was. Another long silence. He then said that Koitalel was a bad man and he was pleased I had shot him.[34]

'Kabellas' was none other than Kipeles, an *orkoiyot* and a Talai clansman of Koitalel. Although Meinertzhagen seems not to have understood Kipeles' apparent pleasure at the death of Koitalel, the *orkoiyot's* attitude was not surprising. The two *orkoiik* had been rivals, Kipeles opposing the confrontational tactics advocated by Koitalel against the British. Although Kipeles had himself resisted any co-operation with the British – fleeing to Kabras at the height of the military operations, and losing much of his personal wealth in cattle as a consequence – in December he had finally presented himself to the British, in the company of several elders, to sue for peace. Paradoxically, with the British victory Kipeles had the opportunity to benefit very directly, his own reputation enhanced by Koitalel's failure. Although he was no more a 'chief' than had been Koitalel, the British were (by 1905) convinced that the *orkoiik* clan were a 'ruling dynasty': Kipeles, the most prominent of the remaining *orkoiik* in Nandi, was taken up as Koitalel's successor. One week before the encounter between Kipeles and Meinertzhagen, the victorious British had held a meeting with prominent Nandi elders, to lay down the terms for peace, including the forced removal of Nandi into a Reserve away from the line of rail. At this gathering the British had formally declared 'Kabellas' the new 'chief' of Nandi, to replace Koitalel.[35] Later, in March 1909, they went so far as to officially confirm Kipeles as Paramount Chief of all Nandi.[36]

The circumstances of the British struggle to conquer Nandi can therefore be seen to have influenced the colonial understanding of the *orkoiik* in profoundly important ways. Maasai informers gathered the intelligence upon which the British military acted and upon which decisions about future civil administration were made; Maasai warriors assisted as auxiliaries in British attacks on Nandi;[37] and many British officials, both military and civil, brought with them to Nandi a prior awareness of the role of *laibons* among Maasai.[38] But if the British were too ready to accept a Maasai view of Nandi, it must also be realized that there were some among Nandi who actively fostered a similar interpretation. Among the *orkoiik*, in particular, there were those who stood to benefit considerably from British promotion of their clan as a 'ruling dynasty'. We can gain an insight on this by examining the earliest ethnographic accounts of Nandi.

The only substantive early ethnography of any of the peoples of Kenya's Western Highlands, *The Nandi: Their Language and Folk-lore*, was researched and written by a colonial officer, A. C. Hollis, between 1905 and 1908, and published in 1909.[39] Hollis had previously published a book on Maasai culture and language, and it is very apparent that his interpretation of Nandi society was often highly derivative of his knowledge of Maasai.[40] But for the details of his Nandi ethnography, Hollis relied upon a fascinatingly narrow range of principal informants. Firstly, in learning the rudiments of the Nandi language, Hollis obtained the services of 'two small boys, named Oriare and Matang'.[41] Oriare he describes as 'a Masai-speaking Nandi', and Matang as 'a Swahili-speaking Kipsikis or Lumbwa'. It is reasonable to assume that both had some prior contact with the British administration, and it is quite likely that Matang's Swahili derived from colonial rather than coastal contacts. We know nothing further of Oriare, but it seems probable that he was from one of the Uas Nkishu Maasai families who settled among Nandi in the latter part of the nineteenth century. In the neighbouring area around Eldama Ravine, and within Nandi itself, the early British administration relied heavily upon information on local conditions provided by 'friendly' Uas Nkishu Maasai settled close to the government posts and, as we have seen, there was one such settlement close to the British fort at Kaptumo.[42] To a large extent, therefore, Hollis drew upon the same community as had Meinertzhagen.

Secondly, and more interesting still, are the direct sources of Hollis's information on Nandi ethnography; this was provided, in the main, by three Nandi who had fought against and been defeated and captured by the British. Two of these informants were political prisoners. The first, arap Sirtoi, was a prominent elder of the Nandi Kapchepkendi *pororosiek*.[43] He had been imprisoned at Mombasa, where Hollis was stationed from August to December 1905. In Hollis's own words, arap Sirtoi 'gladly relieved the monotony of his existence by spending a few hours with me two or three times a week talking to me of his country and describing the customs and folk-lore of his people'.[44] The second prisoner was named arap Kuna. He was interned at Machakos, where Hollis encountered him during 1906 or 1907. Arap Kuna is described as a 'chief' of the eastern section of the Kapkiptalam *pororosiek*.[45]

Those *pororosiek* on the eastern and southeastern edge of Nandi, including Kapchepkendi and Kapkiptalam, along with Kamelilo to the south, had been most directly affected by early colonial penetration. This part of Nandi was then utilized predominantly as grazing land, with the Kapchepkendi and their herds occupying the area immediately to the south of the Sclater's Road – the main British artery of communication between the coast and Lake Nyanza prior to the construction of the railway – and the Kapkiptalam being resident immediately to the north. As we have already noted, it was from these eastern and southeastern *pororosiek* that the *orkoiyot* Koitalel drew the bulk of his support in the struggles against the British.[46]

Hollis' third informant was a Nandi warrior named arap Chepsiet, who had been wounded in the fighting of 1905–6. While we know nothing of arap Chepsiet's background, the concentration of the British forces in those areas that had supported Koitalel suggests that he was also from the Kapkiptalam, Kapchepkendi, Kamelilo or Tuken *pororosiek* of the east and southeast of Nandi territory. These were the sections that were 'driven' northwest, into the new Nandi Reserve, between January and March 1906.[47] Arap Chepsiet was in Hollis' service from April 1906 until the latter's departure from East Africa on leave in April 1908.[48]

In addition to his lengthy interviews with these three individuals, Hollis made two visits to Nandi. The first followed the Nandi expedition of 1905–6, and the second visit was in February 1908. On this occasion Hollis 'had the advantage of meeting influential men and women of all the clans' on his journey through the Nandi Reserve from Kapwaren to Kaptumo.[49] But later the same month Hollis encountered his most distinguished and, by the author's own description, his most authoritative informant:

> I was also able in February last [1908] to go through some of my notes with the chief medicine man of Lumbwa [Kipsigis], Ar-ap Koileke, who is probably better acquainted with the folk-lore of the Nandi and Lumbwa than any one living.[50]

Kipchomber arap Koileke was one of a group of *orkoiik* who left the Nandi area to move south into the lands of the Kipsigis following the death of Kimnyole, sometime during the early 1890s. In many accounts he is presented as the brother of Koitalel, and the elder son of Kimnyole, his departure from Nandi being attributed to rivalry between the two brothers. While the precise relationships set out in these accounts must be treated cautiously, it is evident that both Koitalel and Kipchomber arap Koileke were leading members of the same lineage of *orkoiik*.[51] By 1908, when he was visited by Hollis, Kipchomber was established as the most prominent *orkoiyot* among Kipsigis, and was also recognized by the colonial administration as the senior chief of the district, for which he received an annual salary of 600 rupees.[52] At this time, and up to his deportation from Kipsigis in January 1914, Kipchomber arap Koileke was also frequently consulted by Nandi. After the death of Koitalel some Nandi *pororosiek*, notably those who had supported Koitalel, appear to have recognized the superiority of Kipchomber in preference to other *orkoiik* resident in Nandi, regularly petitioning for his advice and assistance. The prestige of Kipchomber among some sections of the Nandi was vividly demonstrated in December 1909, when a group of 14 Nandi political prisoners, held in Mombasa jail for their part in the Nandi resistance of 1905–6, petitioned Kipchomber arap Koileke, rather than their own 'Paramount Chief', the *orkoiyot* Kipeles, to intervene with the government to effect their release.[53]

The views Hollis formed on Nandi society and on the role of the *orkoiik* were thus derived from the most prominent surviving *orkoiik*, and brother of Koitalel, Kipchomber arap Koileke, and from two British-styled 'chiefs' arap Sirtoi and arap Kuna, senior elders of *pororosiek* who had supported Koitalel and who had been most recalcitrant in their opposition to the British. Kipchomber arap Koileke proclaimed the same authority over Kipsigis as had Koitalel over Nandi, and asserted this unequivocally to Hollis. The *pororosiek* to which arap Sirtoi and arap Kuna belonged, along with the Kamelilo, had thrown in their lot with Koitalel, and their success in accumulating the livestock necessary to exploit pastures of eastern Nandi had depended upon his rising star. If Hollis appears to have followed earlier European writers, notably Hobley and Meinertzhagen, in likening the authority of the *orkoiyot* to that of the Maasai *laibon*, this may therefore have had as much to do with how his informants *wanted* matters to be perceived as with the undoubted hegemonic influences of Maasai culture on British thinking prior to 1914. Hollis, like Meinertzhagen, was utterly convinced of the political authority of a single, dominant *orkoiyot*, writing that:

> The Orkoiyot, or principal medicine man holds precisely the same position as the Masai Ol-oiboni, that is to say he is supreme chief of the whole race.[54]

This represented as profound a misunderstanding of the historical circumstances of the Maasai *loibonok* as it did of the Nandi *orkoiik*, yet recent events among both peoples had seen these mantics take increasingly political roles, first in dealing with the regional political developments of the mid-nineteenth century, then in dealing with ecological disasters, and finally in confronting colonialism. It is hardly surprising that the *orkoiik* and their supporters should have sought to entrench themselves in the position of enhanced influence into which these events had tended to promote them.

While Hollis's views on the political power of the *orkoiyot* should therefore be treated with caution, his intimacy with arap Koileke contributed to a fuller (though admittedly somewhat partisan) picture of the functions of the *orkoiyot*. In describing what the *orkoiyot* actually does, Hollis provides surprising detail:

> He is a diviner, and foretells the future by such methods as casting stones, inspecting entrails, interpreting dreams, and prophesying under the influence of intoxicants. He is also skilled in the interpretation of omens and in the averting of ill-luck. When foretelling the future by casting stones (*parparek*), he uses a box called a *ketet*, or a piece of bamboo stalk called *soiyet*, and he throws the stones on to a fur *kaross*; when making amulets or medicine (*pusaruk* or *kerichek*), he uses an ox-horn and pours the ingredients into the person's hands . . .
>
> . . . They [the Nandi] look to him for instruction when to commence planting their crops; he obtains rain for them, either direct or through the rainmakers, in times of drought; he makes women and cattle fruitful; and no war party can expect to meet with success unless he has approved of the expedition.[55]

This largely technical, functional and essentially positive description of the *orkoiik* can be contrasted with that written by another colonial official, C. W. Hobley, in 1902:

> The Nandi are firm believers in their *laibons* or witch doctors, and these individuals exercise a great influence over them, and very often for evil, as was clearly demonstrated by the recent Nandi rising. They are in great fear of the *laibons*, because it is believed that they kill many people by witchcraft; they are supposed to be able to kill people at a distance of many miles.[56]

It is notable that where Hollis is careful to make it clear that the *orkoiik* were not witches [*ponik*], a category for which he provides quite separate ethnographic information,[57] Hobley makes no such distinction. It may be the case that Hobley, in ignorance of Nandi language, has used the term 'witchcraft' carelessly; but it nonetheless remains apparent that his statement about public fear of the '*laibons*' differs sharply from that presented by Hollis. Hobley gives a picture of the *orkoiik* that is derived from outside the circle of the *orkoiik* and their immediate followers, it would seem, in contrast to the 'insider's' view provided by Hollis. In this respect, it is also significant that Hobley does not confuse Nandi 'chiefs' with the '*laibons*', listing the former in considerable detail, by location, and giving a separate list of the latter – 'Kibeles, Koitalel, Kipchumber' being the three mentioned as the most important.[58] In sharp contrast with Hollis and Meinertzhagen, Hobley does not invest the *orkoiik* with any political authority, although he acknowledges their ritual importance and their involvement in cattle-raiding by Nandi warriors. Indeed, where Meinertzhagen and Hollis place great emphasis upon the authority of an *individual*, Hobley writes of the *orkoiik* collectively – as a group who provide a number of services, rather than as a person holding the authority of an 'office'.

In the wake of the Nandi campaign of 1905, Hobley's dissenting voice was no longer heard. The British administration did not question the legitimacy of *orkoiik* political authority. Koitalel was demonized as an 'evil' influence, but the office of the *orkoiyot* was upheld as the traditional seat of authority among Nandi. Accordingly, the British sought to turn it to their own uses, appointing *orkoiik* as colonial chiefs over both Nandi and Kipsigis: the 'ruling dynasty' was imposed.

Changing Visions, 1910–1935

As the framework of colonial administration was constructed in the Western Highlands, and colonial officials made greater efforts to comprehend the nature of Nandi and Kipsigis society, an alternative and altogether more sinister picture of the *orkoiik* began to take shape. In the process, the certainties of colonial knowledge about the *orkoiik*, as these had been assembled up to 1910, crumbled away. There were three closely linked elements to this: firstly, having believèd that the *orkoiik* held traditional and legitimate political authority, the British came to realize that any such claim was hotly contested, and to believe that those *orkoiik* who held any sway at all over Nandi and Kipsigis achieved this only through fear and threat; secondly, where it had been supposed there was a well-established dynastic line among the *orkoiik*, the British became aware of intense rivalries between factions within the Talai clan who were in competition with one another; and thirdly, that where it had been thought that the *orkoiik* held a monopoly of ritual authority and mystic power, it was realized that other categories of mantic overlapped with their functions. Each of these elements of changing colonial perception will now be considered in turn.

Kipeles and Kipchomber arap Koileke were appointed as Paramount Chiefs over Nandi and Kipsigis respectively. Neither proved a success. After a visit to Kipsigis as Provincial Commissioner in 1907, John Ainsworth had recommended Kipchomber's employment in government service, extolling his virtues and claiming that he wielded 'supreme influence' over the people.[59] By 1911, Kipchomber's reputation was tarnished by the suggestion that he was directly involved in many cases of cattle theft committed by Kipsigis. Evidence of this accumulated over the following months, and in August 1913 it was further revealed that Kipchomber was receiving regular 'tribute' from sections of the Kipsigis and Nandi, in the form of foodstuffs and livestock. It was also rumoured that the *orkoiyot* intended to 'make medicine and drive the Europeans out'.[60] Among those who gave information against Kipchomber were arap Kitchwen, a young government headman, and arap Brogochut, one of the few Kipsigis to accept mission education in the early years of colonial rule. As a result of their statements, and those of several other Kipsigis, Kipchomber and two fellow *orkoiik* were arrested and deported from Kipsigis in January 1914.[61] Kipchomber died in 1916, still exiled from his adopted homeland.

Having concluded that Kipchomber ruled by fear and extortion, British administrators were at the same time forced to admit that, while many Kipsigis welcomed the removal of the *orkoiyot*, many others feared the consequences of the deportation. In April 1915, Kipsigis women attacked the hut of one of the mission converts who had given information against Kipchomber. A plague of locusts which followed, and the delayed onset of the rains, were widely attributed to Kipchomber's powers, and rumours abounded that these misfortunes had been predicted by the *orkoiyot*. Again, in the drought of 1918–19, many Kipsigis elders set up a clamour for the return of the *orkoiyot*. When the outbreak of Spanish influenza struck Kipsigis later in 1919, the son of Kipchomber, Kenduiwa, was reported to have returned to the district and was capitalizing upon the combination of drought and illness among the people to enhance his own standing.[62] The *orkoiik* had been removed from the role of government agents, but their influence as mantics remained strong. Kipsigis might not like living with the *orkoiik*, but it seemed that some could not live without them.[63]

The same was true in Nandi, but here it was not the chosen Paramount Chief, Kipeles, who held the respect and fear of the people, but other members of the Talai clan. After the death of Koitalel, Kipeles was never able to cultivate a large following among Nandi, and his association with government in his role as Paramount Chief did little good to his reputation. Colonial officials regularly lamented his ineffectiveness, openly admitting that he possessed 'little or no authority'.[64] Where Kipchomber had come to be seen as a tyrant, Kipeles was nothing more than a figure-head, unable to control other Talai, whose activities frequently brought them into conflict with Nandi elders. It seemed that the British had backed the wrong man.

By 1918 it was admitted that they not only had the wrong man, but they had seriously misunderstood both the nature of Nandi government and the role of the *orkoiik*. Confronted by the failure of attempts to govern Nandi through the agency of the *orkoiyot*, the then District Commissioner, C. S. Hemsted, began to investigate the *orkoiik* more closely. He came to the conclusion that any tribal authority held by such individuals lay in the area of military organization and not in government per se.[65] This was an astute observation, to be reaffirmed in subsequent anthropological research conducted by Huntingford and others.[66] It was through links with the *murran*, the younger, unmarried men of the junior age-grades, that an *orkoiyot* derived political power and economic gain. The *orkoiik* in fact operated in conjunction with the nominated representatives of the *murran* age-grade in each *pororosiek*, and therefore had no direct dealings with the elders. *Murran* stood to benefit by the livestock they accumulated from raids sanctioned or blessed by the *orkoiyot*, and in any military operation it was the *orkoiyot*, not the elders, who held sway. The power and authority of any *orkoiyot* was thus expressed through the strength of their attachment to the younger age-grades, and this tended to draw them into conflict with the elders over questions relating to the discipline and control of younger males. Far from ruling over the elders, the *orkoiik* were consequently deliberately kept at a distance from the daily affairs of Nandi communities. Describing any successful *orkoiyot* as a sort of 'religious recluse', who would not willingly participate in government, Hemsted concluded that no such person could be successfully employed in an 'executive capacity'.[67]

As a first step to achieving control over the *orkoiik*, Hemsted adopted a policy of containment. He set about creating a separate administrative location for the Talai clan, where they could be closely supervised by government, and could to some extent police themselves through nominating their own chief and headmen. The creation of the new location was agreed at a large public meeting, attended by more than 500 Nandi, including a dozen of the most prominent *orkoiik*, as well as representatives of all other Nandi clans, government chiefs and headmen. By June 1920, some 120 Talai men and their immediate families had moved into Location 26, having nominated arap Kinegat as president of their own Local Native Council, with Kimoson arap Kepterer (alias arap Kipeles, brother of the late Paramount Chief) as vice-president, and arap Kiptoi as headman.[68] This marked an important watershed in colonial policy toward the Nandi *orkoiik*, although it was by no means a wholly successful measure. The *orkoiik* would continue to practise their arts from Location 26 and elsewhere, but their brief reign of colonial political authority over Nandi had come to an end. Containment had been achieved, if only in part; control would prove move difficult.

Amongst the *orkoiik* themselves the status of individuals was a matter of dispute. Growing British awareness of this marked the second element in their changing vision of the *orkoiik*. As we have seen, there had been evidence of internal squabbles among the Nandi Talai during the period of British conquest, but this became more overt after Koitalel's death and was exacerbated by British attempts to establish the *orkoiik* as a 'ruling dynasty' of chiefs. Upon Kipeles' death in September 1911, the British continued to pursue the notion of a 'Paramount' *orkoiyot*, appointing Lelimo as his successor.[69] Lelimo was reckoned to be a son of Koitalel, and in so far as colonial officials were able to comprehend a genealogy for the Talai, this relationship appeared to offer substantial legitimacy. Other reasons for the selection of Lelimo are not clear, but it is possible that he was the only member of Koitalel's close lineage who was prepared to accept the post. In fact, the British soon came to realize that Lelimo enjoyed less respect among Nandi than had Kipeles. The new 'Paramount' was openly disobeyed. In January 1915, for example, government pressure upon Lelimo to cajole younger Nandi out to work on the European farms resulted in violent threats against the *orkoiyot*, who quickly retreated from the fray.[70] Lelimo drew his government salary, but he had no influence or authority over his fellow clansmen, let alone over Nandi more generally.

Whoever the administration may have wished to promote as 'official' *orkoiyot*, recognition among Talai, and especially public acclaim, determined which *orkoiyot* really carried the greatest influence.[71] Such powers could not be conferred by government, and nor could it be assumed they would follow in a direct family line. From 1911 to 1918, arap Kinegat was the most influential *orkoiyot*; but he was a member of the Kipsokon lineage of Talai, not the lineage from which Koitalel was descended. Upon arap Kinegat's death, toward the end of 1918, the young Barserion arap Kimanye, another son of Koitalel, emerged with the widest following.[72] Where arap Kinegat had been much involved in thefts of cattle from European farms, Barserion's opposition to colonial authority became more overt. He had never moved into Location 26, instead remaining resident as a squatter on a European owned farm on the border of the Nandi Reserve, beyond the scrutiny of the administration in Nandi. In 1923 Barserion was arrested by the British for his part in the organization of a planned rising by Nandi against Europeans on the Uasin Gishu Plateau.[73] He was deported from the Western Highlands, and remained in exile for seven years.

During his absence, the government recognised Kimoson arap Kepterer as head of the Talai, but officials openly admitted that the Nandi public acclaimed the powers of one Koine arap Samwei, who was said to be the chosen 'deputy' of Barserion. In 1921 it was reported that Kimoson was 'gradually becoming *passé*', the Talai under his charge 'continually leaving' Location 26 to settle elsewhere.[74] By 1924, District Commissioner Castle-Smith described Kimoson as a 'delightful' old man, but admitted that he only had influence over 'petty matters': 'You must look to the Koitalel family for the Chief Orkoiyot of the Nandi, and in any case never a government man', wrote Castle-Smith.[75]

Kimoson resigned as chief in 1927 due to poor health, by then an 'old and somewhat infirm' man, and Kirongor arap Lein was appointed as the next 'government man'.[76] Arap Lein, like Kimoson, stood in small local repute, his powers thought to be limited and insignificant by comparison with others; 'he is not the real power in the Talai clan, but only a figure-head', reported District Commissioner Hislop in 1934.[77] 'He seems not to have any miraculous gifts, and as Headman gives much assistance in controlling those who do', wrote another official.[78] The 'real power' remained with Barserion arap Kimanye, who had been brought back from exile in 1930, an occurrence which it was said he had predicted. It was hardly coincidental that requests for his return should have come from some members of the Talai only a few months after the death of his 'deputy', Koine, in October 1929.[79]

The division between the 'official' Talai chiefs (appointed by government) and the 'unofficial' leaders of the *orkoiik* (acknowledged by repute) can be interpreted as reflecting a dynastic dispute within the Talai clan. This is certainly the impression given by G. W. B. Huntingford, who went so far as to employ the unfortunate term 'Kings of the Nandi' in his 1935 article on *orkoiik* genealogy.[80] The dynastic parallel this suggested implies a principle of succession for which we have no direct evidence; but, on the other hand, it does appear that the traumatic events of the conquest had polarized politics among Talai, and that for three decades and more thereafter the immediate family of Koitalel held significant power within the clan while enjoying considerable support among several *pororosiek*. But if the claims of Koitalel's kin were strong, they were also contested by other Talai. To some extent, these struggles fell out along lineages, as each sought to demonstrate the inherited powers that lay within the family. For many Talai, however, it seems likely that intra-clan quarrelling had less to do with grand dynastic struggle than with the more mundane matter of earning a daily living as a diviner.

Colonial officials who began to perceive the disputes among Talai also became increasingly aware of the existence of other categories of mantic who sold their services among Nandi and Kipsigis. This, the third element in changing colonial perceptions, again began to emerge with Hemsted's investigations on 1918, when he compiled information about mantics who apparently operated in competition with the *orkoiik*.[81] From the late 1920s, colonial understanding of this was developed further in the ethnographic writings of Huntingford, who identified five types of mantic among Nandi, each of whom specialized in differing forms of divination, sometimes combined with other skills or powers.[82]

In Huntingford's estimation, the most common practitioners of *ngorset* (divination) among Nandi were known as *kipsakeiyot*. Like the *orkoiik*, a *kipsakeiyot* was, by definition, a member of the Talai clan. Their powers were wide-ranging and their methods varied, but they were essentially concerned with detection of and protection from witchcraft, although some were also believed to cast spells and to bewitch. Like their clansmen the *orkoiik*, then, they were capable of good or evil actions. The *kipsakeiyot* did not have powers relating to the spirits, and so could not communicate with the ancestors, nor 'see' the future.[83] These two particular powers, relating to the world of spirits and to foresight, marked the distinction of the *orkoiik*. Expressed in simple terms, the most gifted Talai held the powers of *orkoiik*, whilst lesser individuals might only operate as a *kipsakeiyot*.

Amongst clans other than Talai were found two further types of diviner, the *kipsachit* and the *sakeyout*. Both these categories of mantic used water as a medium for divination. The *kipsachit*, according to Huntingford, divined by beating upon or shaking a gourd filled with water or beans, to raise the spirits of ancestors to speak from the gourd.[84] He gives less information regarding the methods of a *sakeyout*, who are described as using 'smell' and a gourd of water to contact spirits. They also gave charms and protections against evil, and acted as witch-finders.[85] Although Huntingford does not speculate as to the relationship between the *kipsakeiyot* of Talai and the non-Talai *sakeyout*, it seems that clan affiliation was more important in differentiating between them than was actual practice, precisely because practice varied from one practitioner to another. Furthermore, where the successful *kipsakeiyot* might achieve recognition as an *orkoiyot*, no such transformation was possible for the non-Talai *sakeyout*. It is also notable that these non-Talai practitioners were associated only with the *detection* of evil, and not with the *practice* of evil.

David M. Anderson

The importance of clan affiliation appears less significant among Kipsigis, a suggestion which is reinforced to some extent by the limited information provided by Orchardson on Kipsigis divination. Orchardson has described a category of women diviners among Kipsigis, termed *chebsageyot*.[86] Unlike the Nandi *sakeyout*, the *chebsageyot* was attributed with the power of visions, or 'dreams', the best of which occurred in a waking trance and not in sleep. These practitioners therefore combined powers of 'sight' associated with the *orkoiik*, with a mechanical, if somewhat unusual, divining technique:

'. . . the *Chebsageyot* . . . pours out onto a skin mat a small basketful of eleusine grain (about two pounds), which has been brought by the client. A cowrie shell from which the top has been cut is placed on the heap of grain. The *Chebsageyot* takes the mat in both hands and throws the grain in the air with rapid dexterous movements similar to those used when winnowing. When the shell comes to rest again on the grain, she examines the position and notes the amount of grain (if any) lodged in the cavity. From these indications the *Chebsageyot* is supposed to read the case. . . .'[87]

The fifth category of diviner described by Huntingford, and also noted by Hemsted in 1918, was the *kipungut*. These practitioners were not of Nandi origin, but from Maragoli, although they were regularly consulted by Nandi to detect the source of witchcraft. They could also assist in identifying criminals, and in providing charms and protections against evil.[88]

The existence of other mantic categories demonstrates the wide range of specializations and combinations of techniques available, and suggests that flexibility and innovation were very much part of the service provided by individual practitioners. However, while various types of mantic might co-exist, this did not undermine the recognition that the most respected *orkoiik* held powers of insight and divinatory revelation that far out-weighed those of other, lesser, practitioners; and only the most gifted *orkoiik* might give prophecies affecting the wider community. While colonial officials were aware, by the 1920s, of the variety of mantics practising among Nandi, there is little evidence to suggest that they were able to easily distinguish one from the other. In the case of the Talai clan, officials found it convenient to refer to all males as *orkoiik*, and ignore the category of *kipsakeiyot*. It is probable, therefore, that many of those Talai described in colonial reports as 'lesser' *orkoiik*, were in fact *kipsakeiyot*. Distinctions within Talai were blurred in colonial eyes, but those between Talai and non-Talai tended to be sharpened. By the 1930s, colonial officials readily accepted a generalization which identified all Talai practitioners as evil (or potentially so) and all others as benign. This was a gross simplification, but it made it easier to implement a policy of control and containment solely against the Talai clan.

The British view of the *orkoiik* hardened along these lines in the 1930s. Attempts to confine the Talai to particular locations and to place them under closer government supervision proved only partially successful. Prominent and lesser *orkoiik* alike were continually implicated in investigations of cattle thefts, and in the early 1930s raids on European farms by Nandi and (especially) Kipsigis increased sharply. Burglaries and the theft of firearms also became more common throughout the Western Highlands at this time, and evidence was gathered which closely connected *orkoiik* with many of these offences. In 1933 and 1934, eight prominent Kipsigis Talai were convicted in connection with a variety of stock thefts and burglaries, and dozens of others faced criminal charges for related offences. The colonial authorities claimed to have uncovered a sophisticated network of organized crime headed by the *orkoiik*, who, it was claimed, had the ultimate intention of gathering sufficient resources to stage a full rebellion in the Western Highlands. Some said the rebellion had been prophesied by Kipchomber, who foretold there would first be a great war (1914–18); then a drought (1919); then an earthquake (January 1928); and that following these events the people should prepare to remove the Europeans.[89]

These startling revelations reinforced the, by then, prevailing view of the Talai as an 'evil' clan, who had turned ever more towards witchcraft. As a consequence, the colonial government took the unprecedented step, in 1935, of passing an ordinance which gave authority to remove the entire Kipsigis Talai clan, and all their possessions, from the Kipsigis Reserve, to be resettled at Gwassi, in Kenya's Nyanza Province, close to the shores of Lake Victoria. In this inhospitable land, hemmed in by tsetse fly and distant from other Kipsigis clans, they would be supervised by a District Officer, and not permitted to return to the Western Highlands.[90] The Nandi Talai, who were less deeply implicated in organized crime but were none the less suspected of involvement in cattle thefts, were to be permitted to remain in their own location in the Nandi Reserve, where they would also be placed under ever closer government scrutiny.[91] From being hailed as the 'rulers' of Nandi and Kipsigis in the immediate wake of British conquest, by 1935 colonial perceptions of the *orkoiik* had transformed them into a caste of criminal outlaws, whose behaviour threatened social order and who were seen to have no legitimate authority in African society.

This view of the *orkoiik* also dominated anthropological accounts of Nandi and Kipsigis from the 1930s, most notably the writings of Huntingford and Peristiany. As the owner of a farm close to the Nandi Reserve, and then as an instructor at the government school in Nandi, Huntingford had a close association with the district and its people from 1920 until the 1940s. As is apparent from his regular correspondence with colonial officials in Nandi, as well as from his published writings, Huntingford saw the *orkoiik* as the prime source of discontent among Nandi, and was keen to offer his advice to government on matters of social control. It is undoubtedly the case that Huntingford's opinions contributed something to the evolving colonial view of the *orkoiik* well in advance of the publication of his two major works on Nandi, in 1950 and 1953, although it is not possible to say to what extent his 'local expertise' had a direct impact upon official policy.[92] Peristiany's familiarity with Kipsigis was altogether slighter. He arrived in 1937, without having been able to acquire even the rudiments of the language, and remained in the district for only nine months. By that time, the last of the Talai clan had already been removed from the district, and so he had no direct experience of the *orkoiik* and appears to have more or less eliminated them from his enquiry, not even offering any discussion of the impact of their departure. He was content merely to record that they had been 'hated and feared by the people', and that the government had been wise to eject them.[93] This was surely an opinion shared by some, though by no means all Kipsigis.

Prior to 1910, as we have seen, the early ethnographic 'construction' of colonial knowledge about the *orkoiik* was closely bound up with the process of conquest; likewise, after 1910, it is difficult to separate the experience of colonial administration in the Western Highlands from the emergence of an anthropology of the region's peoples. The academic insights of ethnographers and anthropologists and the administrative probing and planning of colonial officials may appear as separate pillars of knowledge, but they were assembled in close proximity and were linked by the arch of a dominant paradigm; all were part of the same colonial structure.

History, genealogy, prophecy

Colonial observers evidently had difficulty in placing mantics, perhaps especially the *orkoiik*, into appropriate categories. Some, like Hemsted and Dobbs, took the trouble to try to find out more, but others seemed not even to bother with whatever information may have been logged in the district record book by their predecessors. It is a mistake, therefore, to assume that the learning curve of colonial knowledge was continuously accumulative. An official's local knowledge was usually severely limited, and their comprehension of the societies in their charge was often seriously hampered as a result. These shortcomings were reflected in the confusions and contradictions of colonial terminology. *Orkoiik* were variously described in the writings of administrators and soldiers as 'kings', 'supreme chiefs', 'ritual leaders', 'medicine-men' and 'spiritual heads', but also as 'witches', 'witch-doctors' and 'witch-doctor-rulers'. In their efforts to draw out comparisons that might strike a cord with readers, anthropologists such as Huntingford could be equally guilty of an imprecise and confusing use of language.[94]

The vaguenesses of colonial terminologies and categories present obvious difficulties for historical reconstructions, but we should resist the temptation to project any understanding of mantic categories and practice from the ethnographic present back into the past. The activities of the *orkoiik* underwent change over time, and even indigenous definitions of mantic categories were not constant or fixed. Colonial officials in the Western Highlands may have misunderstood a great deal about *orkoiik* and other mantics, but some of their uncertainties surely arose from the very ambiguities cultivated by the mantics themselves and reflected in the meanings attached to their actions by their African followers.

This point may be illustrated by considering the difficulties presented in employing *orkoiik* genealogies in historical reconstructions. It can be argued that the colonial innovation of seeking to recognize a 'chief' among the Talai has had an impact upon the presentation of genealogy, feeding back into the oral histories of the *orkoiik*, so that attempts are made to construct lists of those who 'ruled'. Genealogical claims are easily opened to manipulation, and there is much evidence to suggest that relative mantic status has been the defining basis of the genealogies contructed for the Talai, rather than actual biological relationships.[95] Read in this way, *orkoiik* genealogy is about power not kinship.

But such fictive genealogies of *orkoiik* cannot be entirely dismissed as a creation of the colonial encounter. Because of the importance of the inheritance of supernatural powers, genealogy is one of the crucial markers in claims for status and authority among *orkoiik*. Prominent *orkoiik* are known to nominate favoured successors from their own immediate family, and although this is often not the eldest son, and may even be a nephew or younger cousin of the *orkoiyot*, anyone publicly acknowledged in such a manner has a considerable advantage in gathering a following. Thus, it has always been in the interests of *orkoiik* to 'construct' genealogies as a means of establishing their credentials.

The colonial encounter intensified this by giving a new prominence to genealogy in the establishment of political authority, firstly in seeking to create the *orkoiik* as chiefs over others, and then in trying to select an 'official' senior *orkoiyot* from among their number as clan 'chief'. In this process, questions of genealogy became more politicised. Here, again, the problem was not simply made by colonial rule. At the time of conquest, for example, Koitalel had been opposed by some *orkoiik*, and there was evidently debate among Nandi after their military defeat in 1905 as to whether they had fared better or worse as result of Koitalel's actions. His prophecy that bullets would turn to water had not been accurate; indeed, it was Kimnyole, not Koitalel, who appeared as the true prophet. Koitalel's failure merely confirmed the powers of Kimnyole, and re-emphasized the error of those *pororosiek* of the southwest who had put him to death. But, of course, those were not the same *pororosiek* who had suffered so severely in the military conquest. There were those, after 1905, who wished to vindicate Koitalel, just as there were those, like Kipeles, who had opposed Koitalel and who stood to benefit from his demise. Politics among the *orkoiik* was part and parcel of their own rivalries, and these were an inevitable consequence of competition between them to establish a reputation and a following. Any *orkoiyot* might thus have strong motives in promoting a particular version of the history of Talai and of the place of their own lineage in that history.

This is vividly revealed by the fact that at least three alternative (and conflicting) genealogies of the *orkoiik* have been recorded which take the lineage back into the nineteenth century. These can be distinguished in general terms. The first proposes a simple dominant familial line from a single Uas Nkishu *laibon* refugee – usually called Kapuso – down to Koitalel and his children. This account tends to pull all *orkoiik* within its orbit, assigning each a position appropriate to their alleged status as mantics. It is a composite picture, stressing the dominant hegemony of Maasai influences and giving an appearance of unity among the *orkoiik* from the 1860s. This, in turn, vindicates Koitalel's role by confirming the legitimacy of his paramount status, while at the same time retaining a clear sense of the essentially alien status – Maasai, not Nandi – of those who opposed colonial intrusions.[96] The second version suggests that two rival *orkoiik* lineages emerged headed by Kopokoi and Kipsokon, the two sons of the immigrant Kapuso. The families of Kopokoi and Kipsokon are said to have vied for ascendancy between the 1870s and 1900s, with the Kopokoi emerging as the more powerful. This account has the advantage of providing a historical root for the many recorded rivalries among *orkoiik* throughout the colonial period, and in explaining why many Nandi failed to support Koitalel in his struggles against the British, and why some *orkoiik* appear to have opposed him.[97] The third reconstruction conflates the first two, by placing the line of Kapuso alongside those of Kopokoi and Kipsokon (which are here taken to be Talai lineages which pre-date Uas Nkishu incursions), thus creating a tripartite division. In this account the Maasai element is kept discrete, either as a quite separate lineage or (more commonly) as an 'adopted' element within the Kapokoi lineage. This version, already recounted in the introduction to this chapter, allows more subtle interpretations: it accommodates *orkoiik* rivalry while confirming Koitalel's legitimacy, though necessarily within a narrower domain, and thereby facilitates the argument that Koitalel and his followers subverted 'traditional' (Nandi) practice in favour of external (Maasai) influences.[98]

None of these genealogies represents a verifiable account of *orkoiik* history, and each ultimately has more to do with explaining events in the twentieth century than with recording the history of the nineteenth century. Faced with contradictory genealogical accounts, interested Europeans such as Hemsted and Huntingford tended either to assume that one was right and the others wrong, and so sought to privilege one version, or tried to reconcile the contradictions between the genealogies into what seemed the most plausible, unitary historical reconstruction.[99] However, if the different versions are accepted as discrete histories of the same events, then they can be read most meaningfully as highlighting disputes of interpretation among Nandi about Koitalel's political legitimacy amid the traumas and consequences of colonial conquest, about the wider position of the *orkoiik* within Nandi society, and about the subsequent reaction of members of the Talai clan to the impositions of colonial rule. Above all, these histories reveal a discourse about power and authority in colonial times that operated at two levels; an internal discourse *between okoiik*; and a broader discourse between groups of *orkoiik* and their wider community. The conflicts prompted by colonial incursions have therefore reworked the histories of pre-colonial transformations, giving new justifications and new motives for the rationalization of the past.

Finally, there is the matter of prophecy itself. There may be good reason for doubting whether the *orkoiik* of the Western Highlands merit the distinction of being remembered as 'prophets' at all. Certainly, not all Talai were *orkoiik*, and not all *orkoiik* were attributed with powers of prophecy. Few prophecies are directly attributable to any of the leading *orkoiik*, and what words are attached to them seem to have been ascribed retrospectively. But this points to the enduring importance of the most prominent *orkoiik* in moral discourse about the future of African society, and about the political choices people have made in the past and will make in the future. To invoke the names of the *orkoiik* as prophets of that future, even by putting words in their mouths, is to call up powerful symbols of dissent. Koitalel, Kipchomber, Kipeles and Barserion arap Kimanye *were* directly involved in a moral discourse during their own lifetimes, and although their visions of the future may have proved to be false, this does not invalidate their role as important historical actors, whose past memory can be called upon, reworked and adapted, to speak to the problems of the present and give meaning to recent events. The *orkoiik* prophets may have been vanquished by the forces of colonialism, but their visions have remained a powerful historical symbol of the choices in the present and the possibility of alternative futures.

Notes

1. For Mbatian: John L. Berntsen, 'Pastoralism, raiding and prophets: Maasailand in the nineteenth century' (Ph.D., University of Wisconsin-Madison, 1979). For the prophetess Moraa wa Ngiti: Bethwell A. Ogot and William Ochieng', 'Mumboism: an anti-colonial movement', in B. A. Ogot (ed.), *War and Society in Africa: Ten Studies* (London, 1972), pp. 149–72. For Mekatilile: Cynthia Brantley, *The Giriama and Colonial Resistance in Kenya, 1800–1920* (Berkeley, 1981); 'Mekatilile and the role of women in Giriama resistance', in Donald Crummey (ed.), *Banditry, Rebellion and Social Protest in Africa* (London & Portsmouth, NH, 1986), pp. 333–50; A. J. Temu, 'The Giriama War 1914–15', in B. A. Ogot (ed.), *War and Society*, pp. 215–36; Rebeka Njua and Gideon Mulaki, *Kenya Women Heroes and Their Mystical Power* (Nairobi, 1984); For Mugo wa Kibiro (also known as Chege wa Kibiro): B. A. Ogot, 'Politics, culture and music in central Kenya: a study of Mau Mau hymns, 1951–1956', *Kenya Historical Review*, 5 (1977), p. 281; Jomo Kenyatta, *Facing Mount Kenya: The Traditional Life of the Gikuyu*, (London, 1938), pp. 41–44; and John Lonsdale, Chapter 11, below. A full discussion of Koitalel follows.
2. The essential ethnographies are far from adequate, but the most important are: G. W. B. Huntingford, *Ethnographic Survey of Africa: East Central Africa, Part VIII The Southern Nilo-Hamites* (London, 1953); *idem, Nandi Work and Culture* (Colonial Research Studies No. 4, HMSO, London, 1950); *idem, The Nandi of Kenya: Tribal Control in a Pastoral Society* (London, 1953); C. W. Hobley, *Eastern Uganda: An Ethnological Survey* (Anthropological Institute, Occasional Paper No. 1: London, 1902); A. C. Hollis, *The Nandi: Their Language and Folklore* (Oxford, 1909); J. G. Peristiany, *The Social Institutions of the Kipsigis* (London, 1939); Ian Q. Orchardson, *The Kipsigis* (abridged by A. T. Matson: Nairobi, 1961).
3. The only ethnographic account of any detail is Huntingford, *The Nandi of Kenya*,

pp. 38-52. See also, J. G. Peristiany, 'The ideal and the actual: the role of prophets in the Pokot social system', in J. H. M. Beattie and R. G. Lienhardt (eds), *Studies in Social Anthropology* (Oxford, 1975), pp. 188-212.

4. P. K. arap Magut, 'The rise and fall of the Nandi orkoiyot c. 1850-1957', in B. G. McIntosh (ed.), *Ngano: Studies in Traditional and Modern East African History* (Nairobi 1969), pp. 97-100; A. T. Matson, *Nandi Resistance to British Rule 1890-1906* (Nairobi, 1972), pp. 28-32; Alice Gold, 'The Nandi in transition: background to Nandi resistance to the British, 1895-1906', *Kenya Historical Review*, 6 (1978), pp. 91-3; Henry A. Mwanzi, 'Koitalel arap Samoei and Kipchomber arap Koilege: southern Kalenjin rulers and their encounters with British imperialism', in B. E. Kipkorir (ed.), *Imperialism and Collaboration in Colonial Kenya* (Nairobi, 1980), pp. 18-22; Hollis, *The Nandi*, pp. 49-50; Huntingford, *Nandi Work and Culture*, pp. 12-3;

5. See Waller, Chapter 2, this volume.

6. Gold, 'Nandi in transition', pp. 93-6; Magut, 'Rise and fall', pp. 97-102; J. E. G. Sutton, 'The Kalenjin', in B. A. Ogot (ed.), *Kenya Before 1900* (Nairobi, 1976), pp. 43-7; W. R. Ochieng', *An Outline History of the Rift Valley of Kenya up to 1900* (Nairobi, Kampala and Dar es Salaam, 1975), pp. 77-108; B. J. Walter, *The Territorial Expansion of the Nandi of Kenya* (Athens, Ohio, 1970).

7. For a recent survey, see David M. Anderson, 'Black mischief: crime, protest and resistance in Kenya's Western Highlands', *Historical Journal*, 36, iv (1993), pp. 851-77.

8. This characterizes the writings of Mwanzi, Magut and Ochieng', cited above, and also Samuel K. arap Ng'eny, 'Nandi resistance to the establishment of British administration 1893-1906', in B. A. Ogot (ed.), *Hadith 2* (Nairobi, 1970), pp. 104-26; but it has found its most populist expression in the literary works of Ngugi wa Thiong'o. For all the relevant references, see Carol Sicherman, *Ngugi wa Thiong'o: The Making of a Rebel. A Source Book in Kenyan Literature and Resistance* (London, Munich and New York, 1990).

9. Michael Adas, *Prophets of Rebellion: Millenarian Protest Movements against European Colonial Order* (Cambridge, 1987 [1979]); and in this volume, Hansen, Chapter 6, for Nyabingi, and Wright, Chapter 7, for Maji Maji.

10. Anderson, 'Black mischief', *passim*.

11. The *pororosiek* were territorial divisions, representing the most important level of political authority among Nandi. Elders councils (*kokwet*) were organized within *pororosiek*, and warriors were mobilized and deployed on the basis of the *pororosiek*. Huntingford, *The Nandi of Kenya*, pp. 8-15; *idem*, 'The Nandi pororiet', *Journal of the Royal Anthropological Institute*, 65 (1934).

12. Matson Papers, 'Nandi Laibons: some comments', p. 1, Rhodes House, Oxford, [RH] MSS.Afr.s.1792.

13. Magut, 'Rise and fall', pp. 100-2; Gold, 'Nandi in transition', pp. 94-6; Matson, *Nandi Resistance*, pp. 31-2.

14. Hollis, *The Nandi*, p. 50.

15. A. T. Matson, *The Nandi Campaign Against the British 1895-1906* (Nairobi, 1974), remains the only summary of the military conquest.

16. Matson, *Nandi Resistance*, pp. 31-2; Gold, 'Nandi in transition', pp. 95-6.

17. Richard Meinertzhagen, *Kenya Diary, 1902-1906* (Edinburgh and London, 1957). The originals of the diaries are held at Rhodes House, Oxford, under restricted access.

18. Ibid, pp. 157-69, 194-6.

19. This summary is drawn from Matson, *Nandi Resistance* and *The Nandi Campaign*.

20. Gold, 'Nandi in transition', pp. 95-100; Ng'eny, 'Nandi resistance', pp. 108-110; B. J. Walter, 'The Territorial Expansion and Organisation of the Nandi, 1850-1905', (MA dissertation, University of Wisconsin-Madison, 1969), pp. 144-59. Koitalel first came to the attention of the British during the military expedition against Nandi

in 1900, when the remains of the murdered trader, West, were found in the *orkoiyot's* hut; 'Political history of the Nandi Reserve', p. 4, Nandi District Political Record Book [PRB], vol. 1, Kenya National Archives microfilms [KNA(mf)] NAN/5, Seeley Library, Cambridge.

21. Meinertzhagen, *Kenya Diary*, pp. 202-3.
22. Ibid, p. 211.
23. Ibid, p. 221.
24. Ibid, p. 230.
25. Ibid, pp. 207, 213, 230. For an alternative interpretation, see Ng'eny, 'Nandi resistance', *passim*.
26. Meinertzhagen, *Kenya Diary*, pp. 222-3.
27. Ibid, p. 216.
28. 'Political history of Nandi Reserve', p. 9, Nandi District PRB, vol. 1, KNA(mf) NAN/5; Isaac to Sub-Commissioner, 27 July 1905, Matson Papers, RH MSS.Afr.s.1792/3/20-27.
29. For discussion of differing views on the event, see Ng'eny, 'Nandi resistance', pp. 118-21. For Meinertzhagen's own account, *Kenya Diary*, pp. 233-8. For oral accounts of Uas Nkishu Maasai, numbers of whom accompanied Meinertzhagen's column, see 'Maasai oral sources on Nandi campaigns', collected by R. D. Waller, Matson Papers, RH MSS.Afr.s.1792/5/22.
30. Meinertzhagen, *Kenya Diary* p. 234.
31. Ibid, p. 197.
32. Ibid, p. 221, also pp. 203-4, 216.
33. Ibid, p. 267.
34. Ibid, p. 266. The photograph of Kipeles appears at p. 269 of *Kenya Diary*.
35. Ibid, pp. 264-5; Nandi Field Force Intelligence Diary, IV Column, 10 November 1905 and 13 December for comments on Kipeles, and 19 November 1905 for the *orkoiyot's* arrival at the British fort; all in Matson Papers, RH MSS.Afr.s.1792; 'Political history of Nandi Reserve', p. 14, Nandi District PRB, vol. 1, KNA(mf) NAN/5, for meeting with 'Nandi chiefs' and the terms set by the British.
36. 'Political history of Nandi Reserve', p. 13, Nandi District PRB, KNA(mf) NAN/5.
37. Matson, *Nandi Campaign*, pp. 18-19.
38. Richard D. Waller, 'The Maasai and the British 1895-1905: the origins of an alliance', *Journal of African History*, 17 (1976), pp. 540-51, *idem*, Chapter 2, this volume.
39. A. C. Hollis, *The Nandi: Their Language and Folk-lore* (Oxford, 1909; reprinted Oxford, 1969, with a new introduction by G. W. B. Huntingford). The reprint omits the introduction to the first edition by Sir Charles Eliot.
40. A. C. Hollis. *The Masai: Their Language and Folklore* (Oxford, 1905).
41. Hollis, *The Nandi*, p. iv.
42. On the wider history of Uas Nkishu, see Richard D. Waller, 'Interaction and identity on the periphery: the Trans-Mara Maasai', *International Journal of African Historical Studies*, 17 (1984).
43. Hobley, *Eastern Uganda*, p. 58.
44. Hollis, *The Nandi*, p. iv.
45. Hobley, *Eastern Uganda*, p. 58.
46. Matson, *Nandi Resistance, passim*, for colonial penetration up to 1899; Gold, 'Nandi in transition', p. 95.
47. 'Political history of Nandi Reserve', pp. 11-14, Nandi District PRB, vol. 1, KNA(mf) NAN/5; Gold, 'Nandi in transition', pp. 96-8.
48. Hollis, *The Nandi*, p. iv. Arap Chepsiet continued to work for the British subsequently, and was well known by Huntingford in the 1920s. See Huntingford's introduction to the reprint of Hollis, p. xi.

49. Hollis, *The Nandi*, p. v; 'Political history of Nandi Reserve', p. 17, Nandi District PRB, vol. 1, KNA(mf) NAN/5.
50. Hollis, *The Nandi*, p. v.
51. G. W. B. Huntingford, 'Genealogy of the Orkoiik of Nandi', *Man*, 35 (1935). This will be discussed in greater detail below.
52. C. M. Dobbs, 'Memorandum on the Lumbwa Laibons', 12 May 1930, Public Records Office [PRO] CO 533/441/1; Lumbwa Annual Report 1906/07, KNA(mf) PC/NZA.1/1 (AR 1231).
53. Dobbs, 'Lumbwa Laibons', p. 4, PRO CO 533/441/1.
54. Hollis, *The Nandi*, p. 49.
55. Ibid, p. 9.
56. Hobley, *Eastern Uganda*, p. 40.
57. Hollis, *The Nandi*, p. 51.
58. Hobley, *Eastern Uganda*, p. 59.
59. Lumbwa Annual Report 1906/07, KNA(mf) PC/NZA.1/1 (AR 1231).
60. Dobbs, 'Lumbwa laibons', p. 10, PRO CO 533/441/1.
61. Ibid, pp. 12-14.
62. Ibid, pp. 14-18.
63. I borrow this insight from Paul Spencer, 'The Loonkidongi prophets and the Maasai: protection racket or insipient state?', *Africa*, 61 (1991).
64. 'Special Report, 31 December 1909', by C. S. Hemsted, KNA(mf) NAN/1 (AR1106); 'Memo on future of Nandi & Kipsigis Reserves', 4 May 1911, from notes of Nandi District Records in Matson Papers, RH MSS.Afr.s.1792/3/20-27.
65. 'Scheme for Native Administration', by C. S. Hemsted, 27 June 1918, Nandi District PRB, Section IV, Part A, KNA(mf) NAN/5.
66. Huntingford, *The Nandi of Kenya*, pp. 76-98; *idem*, *Southern Nilo-Hamites*, pp. 32-7.
67. 'Scheme for Native Administration', by C. S. Hemsted, 27 June 1918, Nandi District PRB, Section IV, Part A, KNA(mf) NAN/5.
68. 'Removal of Ngetunda (Wizards) clan to Location 26', C. S. Hemsted, 8 November 1919, Nandi District PRB, vol. 1, Section I, Parts F & G, KNA(mf) NAN/5.
69. Nandi District Quarterly Reports, September 1911 and December 1911, both KNA(mf) NAN/1 (AR 1108 & 1109); 'Political history of Nandi Reserve', pp. 25, 27, Nandi District PRB, vol. 1, KNA(mf) NAN/5.
70. 'Political history of Nandi Reserve', p. 32, Nandi District PRB, vol. 1, KNA(mf) NAN/5.
71. This had been observed as early as 1909 by C. S. Hemsted, then in his first tour as District Commissioner for Nandi. Nandi District 'Special Report, 31 December 1909', KNA(mf) NAN/1 (AR 1106).
72. In 1911, at the time of Kipeles' death, Barserion was still a boy, and was reported to be under the care of 'three experienced headmen' of Talai, who were schooling him in the arts of the *orkoiik*. Nandi District Quarterly Report, December 1911, KNA(mf) NAN/1 (AR 1109).
73. Diane Ellis, 'The Nandi protest of 1923 in the context of African resistance to colonial rule in Kenya', *Journal of African History*, 27 (1976), pp. 555-76. See also, Anderson, 'Black mischief'.
74. Nandi District Annual Report, 1921, KNA(mf) NAN/3 (AR 1134).
75. Nandi District PRB, vol. 1, Section III, 'Notes on Headmen', 13 November 1924, KNA(mf) NAN/5.
76. Huntingford, 'Genealogy'; Kimoson died in October 1929, after a long illness. See Nandi District PRB, Section I, Parts F & G, 'Genealogical tables', by C. Tomkinson, 1930.
77. Nandi District Annual Report 1934, KNA(mf) PC/RVP.2/6/1 (AR 1149). Arap Lein was twice assaulted by *murran* when drunk, and in 1935 was finally deposed as chief

for his repeated drunkenness. Nandi District Annual Report 1935, KNA(mf) PC/RVP.2/6/1 (AR 1150).

78. Nandi District PRB, vol. 1, Section I, Part H, entry by B. W. Bond, 1926, KNA(mf) NAN/5.
79. Anderson, 'Black mischief'.
80. Huntingford, 'Genealogy'.
81. Nandi District PRB, vol. 1, Section I, Parts F & G, 'Diviners', by C. S. Hemsted, 1920, KNA(mf) NAN/5.
82. Huntingford, *The Nandi of Kenya*, pp. 46, 108, 110, 115, 141; idem, *Southern Nilo-Hamites*, p. 38; Nandi District PRB, vol. 1, Section I, Parts F & G, 'Ngorset', by G. W. B. Huntingford [c. 1927], KNA(mf) NAN/5.
83. Huntingford, *The Nandi of Kenya*, pp. 46, 108.
84. *Idem*, pp. 141-2.
85. *Idem*, pp. 46, 108, 141.
86. This may correspond to the *chepsargaiot* mentioned by Hemsted (see note 81), but he does not provide a sufficient description for proper comparison. Nor does Huntingford offer any comparison with the *kipsakeiyot*.
87. Orchardson, *The Kipsigis*, pp. 121-2.
88. Huntingford, *The Nandi of Kenya*, pp. 46, 108, 110, 115. For Hemsted's comments, see note 81.
89. Dobbs, 'Lumbwa laibons', PRO CO 533/441/1.
90. For a full account, see Anderson, 'Black mischief'.
91. Ibid. See also, David M. Anderson, 'Stock theft a moral economy in colonial Kenya', *Africa*, 56 (1986), pp. 399-416.
92. Note the many contributions made by Huntingford to the Nandi PRB, cited variously above. His major published work, *The Nandi of Kenya*, carries the revealing sub-title *Tribal Control in a Pastoral Society*, accurately reflecting the emphasis adopted by the author. Also, *Nandi Work and Culture* has a long closing section dealing with proposals for the most effective methods of tribal control for modernization.
93. Peristiany, *Social Institutions*, p. 3 and p. 225 for a version of the Kapuso story.
94. Compare, for example, the language of Huntingford's 'Genealogy' with his later publications, especially *Southern Nilo-Hamites*.
95. Huntingford, 'Genealogy'. See also, for example, the various attempts by administrators to reconstruct genealogical tables for the Talai: Nandi District PRB, vol. 1, Section 1, Parts F & G, 'Table of the Chief Orkoiyots or Laibons', C. S. Hemsted, 3 June 1918 and 'Genealogical tables', C. Tomkinson, 1930, KNA(mf) NAN/5.
96. Magut, 'Rise and Fall', especially pp. 97-100, 104-7.
97. This is emphasized in early ethnography, and thus appears to have substantive authenticity. See Hollis, *The Nandi*, pp. 49-50, and Huntingford, 'Genealogy'.
98. For evidence supporting this intepretation, see Nandi District PRB, vol. 1, Section 1, Parts F & G, 'Table of the Chief Orkoiyots or Laibons', C. S. Hemsted, 3 June 1918 and 'Genealogical tables', C. Tomkinson, 1930, KNA(mf) NAN/5.
99. Nandi District PRB, vol. 1, Section 1, Parts F & G, 'Table of the Chief Orkoiyots or Laibons', C. S. Hemsted, 3 June 1918. For Huntingford, see the unpublished genealogical tables gathered in connection with his research in the late 1920s, Huntingford Papers, School of Oriental and African Studies Archive, University of London.

Part Three

Prophetic
Histories

Nine

The Prophet Ngundeng
& the Battle of Pading

Prophecy, Symbolism
& Historical Evidence

DOUGLAS H. JOHNSON

What can we really know about what a prophet said, or did, or intended to do in his life, when a prophet's reputation so often grows in the re-telling? How far can historians use the reported stories and words of a prophet to reconstruct the past? How are we to approach the tales of mystical and miraculous happenings which so often accumulate around a prophet's name? Are prophets merely to be treated in the same way as legendary figures in foundation myths whose life stories can be taken to represent distilled experiences of history but cannot be reliably accepted as referring to actual, dateable events?

The battle of Pading (1878) was a formative event in the early career of the Lou Nuer prophet, Ngundeng Bong. An account of it reproduced in the 1930s was used by the anthropologist Evans-Pritchard as evidence of Ngundeng's central role in organizing the Nuer for war. Nuer informants in the 1970s who recounted it to me understood the significance of the battle quite differently, and presented it as the beginning of Ngundeng's career, not as a warrior, but as a peace maker. Such radically different interpretations might suggest that recollections of the battle must be unreliable as evidence for the reconstruction of actions and sayings during the prophet's life; that in regard to this crucial event, at the very least, oral testimony can provide us with evidence for use only in analysing indigenous historiography. Yet a comparison of different versions collected from various Nuer and Dinka sources between 1905 and 1982 reveals, on the contrary, important evidence of the past, as well as important developments in the understanding of a common past. In the accounts of the battle of Pading presented below we will observe how the Nuer and Dinka are both engaged in a continuing process of historical interpretation, but also how some of their own religious symbolism and expression are derived from or reinforced by historical experience.

The two decades immediately preceding the battle of Pading saw the occupation of large tracts of Dinka land east of the Bahr el-Jebel by the Lou and Gaawar Nuer. The Dinka were not entirely expelled from their former homes, and large numbers were adopted by Nuer families. Intermarriage between Nuer and Dinka and the expansion of kinship ties between the two peoples inhibited the continuation of violence on the scale which preceded Nuer settlement. A Nuer–Dinka society began to replace a Nuer and a Dinka society.[1] The importance of this development is illustrated in the four most important leaders of Lou and Gaawar society in the 1860s and 1870s, all of whom played some part in the events leading up to and after Pading. Among the Lou the most influential earth-master, Yuot Nyakong, was a Dinka, and Ngundeng Bong represented himself as seized by the Dinka divinity, DENG. Among the Gaawar another earth-master, Nuaar Mer, was also an adopted Dinka, and his main rival and nemesis, the prophet Deng Laka, was another adopted Dinka.

Both Yuot Nyakong and Nuaar Mer became associated with the Egyptian trading companies who established their outposts in the area in the 1860s. Yuot is still remembered by the Lou as a man of great sanctity, and he may have directed the traders' slave-raiding activities away from the Lou and towards the Nyareweng, Padang and Ngok Dinka. Nuaar Mer was an active ally of the slavers and used them in raids against the Luac, Rut and Thoi Dinka in particular, as well as against other sections of Gaawar Nuer. The slavers departed in 1874, depriving Nuaar Mer of his main external support and perhaps exposing Yuot Nyakong to revenge by former Dinka victims of the merchants. By the end of 1878 Yuot Nyakong had been killed by the Nyareweng Dinka; Ngundeng Bong, the prophet of DENG, had taken his place as leader among the Lou and had achieved a decisive victory over the Dinka at Pading; and Deng Laka, the prophet of DIU among the Gaawar, was poised to defeat and kill Nuaar Mer at the battle of Mogogh early in 1879. The death of Yuot and the battles of Pading and Mogogh were a combination of events which together had a decisive influence on the internal development of Gaawar and Lou Nuer societies, as well as on external relations between the Nuer and Dinka of the region.[2]

Douglas H. Johnson

The following accounts of the battle of Pading come from a variety of sources: contemporaries of Ngundeng, one of his sons, and a succession of younger Nuer and Dinka men, three or four generations removed from the battle and its participants. They are here given in the order of the age of the informants, as this allows us to judge to a certain extent their sources of information. The style of narrative varies with the age and experience of the teller. The earliest accounts, told to employees of the Anglo-Egyptian government, include a political moral about the government's perceived alliance with the Dinka which has since dropped out of the story. The oldest man I interviewed spoke without embellishment, leaving explicit interpretation to others. The younger men gave more fluent accounts, even in the most abbreviated versions, as if relating a well-known story. None but the last narration is likely to be a full account, since the conditions of interviewing varied, and the topic of the battle came up in different ways.[3] For this reason we cannot attach too much significance to the absence in some versions of elements found in others, but even in the process of summarizing for the sake of brevity, we see how the most important elements are selected and emphasized. Pading is not just part of the remembered past; it has now become part of the Nuer historical interpretation of their own society, revealing their interest in the intervention of Divinity in their history.

Nuer versions of Pading

The first account of the battle of Pading was printed in 1905 and comes, surprisingly, not from a Lou Nuer but from the Gaawar prophet, Deng Laka. It relates the death of Yuot Nyakong, an ally of the previous Egyptian government about whom the newly arrived British administrators had already heard.[4] When the administrator H. H. Wilson first contacted the Gaawar prophet Deng Laka (here referred to by the name of his divinity, DIU) in March 1905, he reported an important discovery about the origins of the Nuer–Dinka conflict which then so concerned the government:

> I . . . went down with Shawish Said Ahmed, a Nuer policeman, and talked to Diu for about two hours, after which he retired with his people for a time, and then came up into the camp, where we discussed the whole of the Dinka and Nuer situation. At his request the Dinka sheikhs (guides) were present. So far we have only heard the Dinka side of the story, so it is interesting to note the Nuer version even at some length. The Dinkas complained of the Nuer as horrible monsters, who have turned them out of their country,

seized all their cattle, and carried off their women and children. Diu's version is this, which the Dinka sheikhs, confronted by him, were unable to deny. Some 18 years ago the Dinkas occupying the districts of Lauch [Luac], Rich, Tei [Thoi], Nyarweng, &c., enticed the head Nuer sheikh, Ewot Nyakong, into their country on pretext of asking him to lay a ghost that had appeared in their midst, and kept him a prisoner demanding an enormous ransom in cattle, which was paid. The Dinkas then murdered Ewot and tried to make off to the Sobat, but Diu stopped them at Fadding, and collecting all the Nuers wiped them out, as he put it 'mara wahid' [Arab. – 'in one go']. Having kept the Dinka sheikhs as prisoners for some time, he offered them the chance of going back and running their old districts, taking with them their people and cattle, but the Dinkas left the country and went down to the mouth of the Filus [Fulluth], where they are now, and from where, themselves secure under Government protection, they keep up a kind of guerrilla warfare against the Nuers.[5]

Deng Laka appears to be claiming the credit for both the battle of Pading and avenging Yuot's death. We cannot be certain that this was his intention. This full, and probably at times heated, discussion between several parties was relayed to Wilson through the medium of army Arabic, and there was room for misunderstanding. Yet, given the fact that today both the Gaawar and the Dinka recognize the importance of the outcome of Pading to Deng Laka's own rise to power, we should not be surprised if Deng Laka himself acknowledged the same significance. What is important to note for the time being is that the story of Pading was used by Deng Laka to gain government sympathy for the Nuer against the Dinka, and that for government officials it helped to explain the opposition that existed between the Nuer and Dinka communities.

The next version of the battle was recorded by Evans-Pritchard in about 1930 from a veteran of the battle.[6] Evans-Pritchard included it as part of a continuous narrative about the rise of Ngundeng, and it is related in conjunction with an account of the death of Yuot Nyakong (whom Evans-Pritchard calls 'Yoal') at the hands of 'a neighbouring Dinka prophet, called Deng'. Yuot went among the Dinka, though Ngundeng warned him he would die if he went. The Dinka seized Yuot and held him for ransom. When the ransom was paid they killed him anyway. Before he was murdered Yuot uttered the following curse, which is significant given the fact that he was both a Dinka and the greatest living earth-master among the Lou at that time: 'Kill me. It is nothing. Never shall your women give birth to children on my earth; let them deliver in the tree tops. You may kill me but I have children and when the rains come again their footsteps shall mingle with yours in the mud.' After a description of Yuot's death, Evans-Pritchard continues the story:

It seems that for some time after Yoal's death the Nuer were seriously discomforted by Dinka raids, their cattle carried off and their huts and byres burnt. Ngundeng would not sanction any counter raiding till one day he secretly gathered around him a small but picked band of youths and went as though to pasture his cattle on the confines of Dinka country. He gave orders that if any Dinka were found and captured he was to be brought in uninjured. The man who told me this story captured a Dinka and brought him to Ngundeng who allowed him to see the herds, how numerous they were and how ill-protected. He gave the captive the best milk to drink and before sending him back to his people made him presents of a new spear and club. On his return he told the Dinka, as Ngundeng had foreseen, how fine were the herds he had seen and how easy to take, and they gathered together near Fading [Pading] a large force recruited from four or five Dinka tribes and aided by a contingent of Gaawär Nuer. Ngundeng went out against them as though, unaware of their presence, he was quietly pasturing his herds. But when the Dinka began to attack he rushed to meet them with a crocodile-marked bullock and sacrificed it before the advancing enemy calling on the God Deng to help his people. Meanwhile the Dinka prophet, Deng, had run out to meet his rival wishing to strike Ngundeng's bullock before it fell to the ground pierced by his spear, but a Nuer intercepted the Dinka prophet before he could reach the crocodile-marked bullock and killed him so that he and the bullock fell to the ground simultaneously. The God Deng, my informant pointed out, refused the prayers of the Dinka on account of his rejection by the Dinka when he had come among them on his descent to earth and to dwell among the children of men, and he accepted the sacrifice of the Nuer who received him when he left the inhospitable Dinka and entered into their country.

The two forces met in the marshes and the Dinka were overcome with great slaughter since their fight was impeded by the sticky mud of the swamp in which they laboured and by Ngundeng's ritual which made their feet heavy. But whilst the Dinka fell in great numbers to Nuer spears the Nuer are said not to have suffered a single casualty. And so it came to pass as Yoal foretold that the footsteps of his captors would mingle with the footsteps of his sons in the mud. This story is often told together with the one describing how the Dinka deceived God and stole the Nuers' calf to account for their ceaseless feud.

Evans-Pritchard cites the battle as an example of the continuous strain of Nuer–Dinka hostility. But there is much more in this story told to an Englishman by a Nuer who had lived through the events of the late nineteenth century only to see his people conquered by the new government (Ngundeng's son, Guek, had been killed by the government in 1929). The two points that receive most emphasis in his account are Ngundeng's spiritual succession from Yuot, and his successful claim to being the sole prophet of DENG.

Yuot Nyakong was the main representative of Divinity acknowledged by all Lou, and it is important from the point of view of internal Lou politics that Ngundeng, who was both an earth-master (from a different lineage) and a prophet, should claim spiritual succession from Yuot. In the reciprocal prophecies uttered concerning Yuot's death and Ngundeng's vengeance, Ngundeng's equality with Yuot is established. Yuot had also been the main Lou contact with the nineteenth-century predecessors of the Anglo-Egyptian government. The irony of the Lou position in the early twentieth century was that many of the Dinka responsible for Yuot's death were allied with the new government and had been instrumental in persuading that government to attack Ngundeng in 1902, and his son Guek in 1927. By aligning Ngundeng with Yuot, and both against these Dinka, the Lou informant seems to have been trying to illustrate to Evans-Pritchard (whom the Nuer associated with government) the false premises of official hostility to the Lou. He stressed the past treachery of the government's current allies, at the same time that he established Ngundeng's position as the natural successor to an old friend of the former regime. This was precisely the way Deng Laka had told the story to Wilson 25 years earlier, and to greater effect. The new government had already heard of Yuot as the old government's ally and main representative among the Nuer. This man had been treacherously killed by the Dinka, the government's current allies. The Nuer had taken the government's revenge for them. Both in 1905 and 1930 the story of Pading was told to make a political point to a person assumed to represent government.

The way in which the spiritual rivalry between the Nuer and Dinka prophets is expressed is of particular interest. The divinity DENG is said to have come among the Dinka first and was rejected by them before coming to the Lou and Ngundeng. This parallels the Dinka Aiwel myth, where Aiwel Longar came into Dinka society as an orphan and was treated very badly until he revealed himself as the offspring of a Power.[7] Ngundeng consciously patterned himself after Aiwel, as will be seen in some of the following narratives. Ngundeng combined attributes of Aiwel and the Dinka divinity DENG to establish his claim to being a man of Divinity. This is not just a claim of Nuer superiority over the Dinka. It is Ngundeng's specific claim to represent Divinity to both the Nuer and the Dinka.

The next version was related to me by Garang Ngundeng shortly before his death in 1976.[8] He was the oldest living child of the prophet Ngundeng at the time. While he was born after Pading, he had clear memories of his father's final years. His information about Pading, then, was derived from participants, including his father. He told the story as an example of the things Ngundeng did which proved his

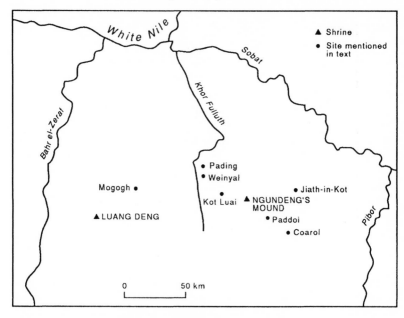

Map 6   Pading and adjacent area

seizure by DENG. It followed an account of the 1902 government patrol against his father.[9]

When Divinity came, all the Dinka were eager to destroy him. When he [Ngundeng] realized this, he fled and went to Coarol, in that direction [east]. [He then turned back] Kor Ruac said, 'Brothers, Divinity has turned back. Let us fight.' Kor said [to Ngundeng] 'Why did you want to take people to Jikany [in the first place]?' When they reached Paddoi, Ngundeng tried to talk to him, but Kor slapped him. He slapped him on the cheek, slapping Ngundeng. Ngundeng said 'EE!' People were about to spring up. Ngundeng said, 'No. Do not defend Divinity. That [pointing to Kor] is a child of Divinity. Let us go to the river. It will appear in the river.'

So he went to Pading. He said, 'Let the village be built here in Dinka country.' When the village was built and the work was finished, he made the Dinka come. The prophet of DHOL [Ngundeng's disciple] was at the lower end of the river at Pul Cieni. The prophet DHOL was there with his brother the prophet of GUIC-GUIC. When the battle was brought, it faced them first. The prophet [Ngundeng] took the crocodile-marked ox to meet the Dinka. The Dinka said, 'They are spoiling it.' He speared its body, and it fell, its horn boring deep into the ground. Ngundeng said, 'Kill the rest of them. Do not touch any of the Dinka that live in Mogogh, The Gaawar will kill them soon. After you are finished come back.' Some of the Dinka were chased into the river and were fished out with fishing spears. They were fished out for two days. That was finished. That was one thing.

This is the most matter-of-fact version of all those collected in 1975–6, and it certainly is much abbreviated, as those Lou who listened to Garang later commented. Despite that it contains the main elements of the story which are found in nearly all the following versions. It mentions the threat of Dinka raids which Ngundeng tried to avoid by moving the Lou herds to the east. His return to Pading confused his followers and created opposition, but fighting was prevented, and therefore division avoided, by reference to Divinity. The sacrifice of the crocodile-marked ox is mentioned, and its result is implied rather than stated, that because of it the Dinka were defeated. Ngundeng was selective in his targets. He urged the Lou not to attack the Dinka living at Mogogh – Nuaar Mer and his followers – reserving them for the other Gaawar to deal with.

To this extent Garang's account is very much like Evans-Pritchard's, even including an oblique reference to the Gaawar. But it connects Ngundeng with the Gaawar prophet Deng Laka in a way that Evans-Pritchard does not. Ngundeng is represented as foretelling, though indirectly, Deng Laka's victory at Mogogh, and in foretelling it, bringing it about.

The Aiwel symbolism emerges even more strongly here with the description of the Lou fishing the Dinka out of the river with their fishing spears. An episode in the Aiwel myth, where Aiwel stood on a river bank spearing with his fishing spear those persons who followed him across the river, is here applied to an event in Ngundeng's own life. The image of spiritual superiority in both tales is clear. But there is one other message from Divinity in Garang's story which does not appear in Evans-Pritchard's, though we cannot know if he heard it and omitted it as unimportant. This is the opposition of Kor Ruac who strikes Ngundeng. Ngundeng prevents his people from retaliating by saying 'Do not defend Divinity', an injunction that both he and his son repeated over and over during their careers. He reminded the Lou that despite his violent action, Kor Ruac was created by Divinity, too. The message here is implicit, and it is made explicit in later accounts: children of Divinity should not fight one another; leave all thoughts of retribution to Divinity.

The next version was told by Macar Ngundeng, a posthumous son of the prophet.[10] Macar was uninitiated at the time of his brother Guek's death in 1929. He could have heard accounts of Pading from eye-witnesses, but by the early 1930s very few veterans were still alive. It seems likely, then, that he would have heard a number of accounts from secondary sources, from men like his half-brother Garang who had learned of the battle from veterans. This version, more than Garang's, stresses Ngundeng's doctrine of peace as it was then understood, as well as the spiritual power that helped him defeat his enemies:

When Divinity became a Divinity, Nuaar Mer was the first to doubt him. Nuaar Mer had destroyed all the lands. The Dinka said, 'We will bring the spear to the Lou. The Lou have uncountable cattle; we shall bring a spear [raid] and capture them from Pading.' Ngundeng fled from Pading. He told the Nuer that they should flee. They fled. He passed through his own country until he reached Paddoi. He went as far as Jiath-in-Kot. As he approached Jiath-in-Kot during midday, there was a white bull. He used to say that there was a white bull that Divinity had seized. It came to the cattle camp in midday. It was shaking. The bull came and stood in the middle of the camp facing them. Then it turned around [facing Pading]. When they tried to call him back, he would not listen, but went steadily on towards Pading. Ngundeng told the Nuer, 'Go and bring the calves and the cattle from the pasture. We are going back, we go back to Pading.' The Nuer went back. They slept at Paddoi, then they left Paddoi and slept in Kot Luai. Then people left and slept at Weinyal. Finally they slept at Pading. His people reached Pading. He camped. The prophet of DHOL's band also camped.

The Dinka came by the camp, coming to spy. The Nuer were hungry. They were very thin. They used to rub themselves with ashes, turning their bodies white. In the morning the Nuer brushed their teeth with cow-dung ashes [and spat out the ashes]. The Dinka said, 'The Lou have a disease which is killing them. We will collect their cattle without opposition.' Ngundeng told the Nuer, 'Dinka will be coming. If the Dinka come tomorrow, when people go after cattle they will find two Dinka.' The Nuer went after cattle and two Dinka were found. They were picked up sitting under a tree, but one Dinka escaped and the other was brought to the camp. Ngundeng asked him, 'What do you want?' The Dinka said, 'We are coming to spy on you. You will be captured.' Ngundeng asked, 'We will be captured?' The Dinka said, 'Yes.' Ngundeng told him, 'Go back, but do not come along with the Dinka. If it is cattle, you will be given cattle captured by them.'

The Dinka came soon afterward. They first hit DHOL's camp, and his people were wounded and fled. Then they came to Ngundeng's camp, running out and spearing wildly.

There was a crocodile-marked ox which used to repel all the other disciples. Ngundeng told the people, 'I have reserved the crocodile-marked ox for something which will come. It will be defeated by the crocodile-marked ox only, the crocodile-marked ox with overhanging horns.' It was said that everyone who pretended to be a prophet was told to spear this ox, and when they tried it, the spear bent or bounced back.

When Ngundeng took the crocodile-marked ox by himself, he led it towards the Dinka, then he reversed it, killing the Dinka. He was walking without a weapon. His weapon was revealed to him by Divinity. It was said to be the root of an *inderab* [*kot*] tree. 'Dig it out,' [Divinity said]. 'This will be your defence in the world.' The root of the *kot* tree was dug up. It was bent like a bow and it was covered by metal rings of many colours. That was his weapon.

When the ox fell the Dinka were scattered completely. He took only the baton and held it up. It struck. When it struck, all the people [*naath*] lay down on their stomachs. It thundered and the Dinka were killed. When he killed the Dinka, they died in the river Pading.

Their cattle were left by themselves in their place. The Lou said, 'We must go to their cattle.' Ngundeng said, 'You Lou, do not go to the cattle. The Gaawar have been spoiled by the Dinka.' They lived on lotus found in the river. That lotus was what they lived on. They possessed nothing else but that lotus. 'It will be replaced by those cattle. Those cattle shall replace that lotus for the Gaawar.' Those cattle were forbidden to the Lou. They were later seized by the Gaawar. Ngundeng did not know which battle [they were taken in]. He was not aware of it. All his things are revelations.

In this version two themes are developed: Ngundeng's military preparations for battle, and his attempts to avoid fighting. His military strategy of luring the Dinka into an ambush is essentially that mentioned by Evans-Pritchard. But Ngundeng first tried to avoid war by fleeing. It is only at a signal from Divinity that he returns and makes his preparations. It is not just the sacrifice of the ox that achieves the victory, it is also the use of his baton, the *dang*. A *dang* is a small decorated stick that the Nuer sometimes carry instead of a spear. At negotiations for marriages it is used to emphasize the speaker's words, just as a spear is used at a sacrifice. Ngundeng's baton was made out of the wood of a *kot* tree, a tree with strong associations with Divinity. Here it is used instead of a spear to emphasize Divinity's words as spoken through Ngundeng. The baton replaces the spear, so that Ngundeng advances without a weapon. The baton kills the Dinka, *without the Lou having to fight them.* Not only is Divinity seen here as protecting the Nuer from an unprovoked attack, but the idea of divinely sanctioned peace is given a bold illustration: Divinity strikes down those who dare to break the peace, and in doing so saves those who keep the peace, preventing even the necessity of fighting in self-defence.

The next narrator, Bil Peat, was of the same age-set as Macar Ngundeng, and was also not yet initiated at the time of Guek's death.[11] His family is closely connected to Ngundeng's, his father having been a singer for the prophet, and his brother having been killed with Guek in the battle at Ngundeng's Mound in 1929. His version, like Macar Ngundeng's was probably derived as much from secondary sources as from eye-witnesses:

> When they were observing the Nuer, the Luac Dinka wanted to come and kill him [Ngundeng] and take his cattle. He fled and went up to a village called Kerial and went to stay there. By night he was told by Divinity, 'Go to Pading.' He said, 'What about those people who want me?' He was told by Divinity, 'I will help you.' He left and went to Pading. All the people gathered there, even the cattle camp of DHOL, who was a prophet.
>
> When he arrived at Pading, he was visited by the Dinka, and they found him. He told the Nuer, 'There will be a Dinka who will come, and you will catch him in the woods. But don't kill him, just bring him.' That Dinka was caught the following day. The Dinka came and slept with him at his camp fire. People were brushing their teeth with ashes, and putting their fingers down their throats to vomit and clear their throats in the morning. The Dinka asked, 'Why do people vomit by night?' The Dinka was told that these people were dying, there was a disease killing them. He said, 'Are they dying?' Ngundeng said, 'Yes.' The Dinka said, 'We will want to come.' Ngundeng said to him, 'If you come for these cattle, you will collect them freely. This is how they [the Lou] die.' Ngundeng gave him milk. The Dinka told him, 'So, we will bring you a battle.' He was told by Ngundeng, 'You bring the battle, but don't you return with the other Dinka.'
>
> [The Dinka returned to his land] People [*naath*] were told, 'The cattle there cannot be counted. The people [*nei*] looking after the cattle are dying.' The Dinka brought the battle to Pading.
>
> When the battle was brought Ngundeng led a crocodile-marked ox towards them. It was an ox of his family, an ox of the divinity called BIEL. The Dinka and the Nuer lined up opposite each other. The ox was tethered between them. Ngundeng speared it, and the ox broke its rope and fell among the Dinka. There was lightning and thunder from the sky. The Dinka and Nuer were thrown down. Ngundeng took his sheepskin sleeping mat [*dual*] and hit one person. All his own people got up. Then he killed the Dinka. He went on killing the Dinka until they reached the Dinka cattle camp. The Nuer were about to take the cattle of the Dinka, but Divinity refused and said, 'They will replace the lotus of the Gaawar. The Gaawar are suffering from hunger. These will cure their hunger.' There were some persons who wanted to increase their own strength and they did not listen to him. When a man disobeyed, his legs split open in ulcers until he changed his mind, then he healed.
>
> When all the Lou heard that the Dinka had been struck down by thunder, the Nuer said, 'It has become a divinity.' Those who had rejected him before now came. He was accepted [*ngäth*].

Here again is a detailed description of Ngundeng's preparations for the battle which agrees in all essentials with previous accounts. Ngundeng first avoided battle; he then prepared an ambush for the Dinka and deceived their spies. When the Dinka attacked he sacrificed an ox, but Divinity intervenes even more strongly in this account; for all the combatants are struck down by Divinity's thunder indiscriminately. It is only through Ngundeng that the Lou are revived, using a sheepskin in the way also used to cure sick persons.[12]

Other elements emphasize that this was a battle in self-defence, not a raid for plunder. Ngundeng spares the Dinka spy's life by warning him not to join the raiders. This is consistent with Ngundeng's teachings as they are now understood, that his divinity punished only those who actively opposed him. Ngundeng is portrayed as offering a potential enemy the choice not to oppose Divinity. The gift of life this represents is symbolized in the gift of milk, a detail also mentioned by Evans-Pritchard. In that version the additional gifts of a club and a spear seem to represent the choice he gave the Dinka: peace or war, life or death.

Finally, there is mention of the Gaawar suffering from famine, as in Macar's story. Ngundeng is seen as conferring upon the Gaawar, who need sustenance the most, the gift of life through the gift of the cattle they would take when they overthrew Nuaar Mer. In all respects, then, this battle is different from a cattle raid, for the victors did not undertake it for their own gain. Bil Peat's assertion that the Lou fought all the way to the Dinka cattle camp, and *then* gave up the cattle, seems to be an extrapolation of the earlier versions' claim that Ngundeng reserved the Dinka cattle for the Gaawar. The Dinka cattle would not have been near Pading as no raiding party would have brought its cattle along before a raid. The Gaawar had to be closer to the cattle left behind than the Lou. Yet, it must be remembered that Bil Peat came of that generation who had very little direct experience of cattle-raiding. What would have been implicitly understood by older informants would not necessarily have been appreciated by his generation.

The next version was told by a much younger man than the previous informants. Cuol Puyu was a Mor Lou born after the death of Guek, whom his father knew personally. Cuol's own sources, then, were entirely secondary, and perhaps even tertiary; for he was of a generation whose information about Ngundeng came increasingly from persons who had only known persons who had known Ngundeng. Cuol was a particularly well-known singer of Ngundeng songs, having learned them from older renowned singers, including one of Ngundeng's sons. This account was offered as an explanation to a reference contained in one of Ngundeng's songs:[13]

> When people were at a camp called Pading, which is between Dinka and Nuer, he [Ngundeng] said, 'When you go hunting, if you find a Dinka, do not kill him.' A Luac Dinka was found hiding in the bushes. Some persons

said, 'Kill him.' Some persons said, 'We were told by Nyayiel's son that if a person is found, do not kill him.' He was caught and brought to the camp fire. Ngundeng was told by those who went after cattle, 'We got that man.' He asked them, 'Did anybody touch him?' They said 'No.' He said, 'Give him milk.' He was given milk. He was unable to drink it. They made some porridge. It was given to him. After three days he was able to drink cow's milk. After four days milk was added to his porridge. After five days he was fully recovered.

When ten days had passed he said to Nyayiel's son, 'I have to leave.' Nyayiel's son asked him, 'Do you know the way to your village?' He said, 'I know it.' He used to look at people brushing their teeth in the morning. Cow dung ashes were used for brushing, ashes that were red like the soil during the beginning of the dry season. Nyayiel's son said, 'Let him go.' When he went he told his people [*nei*], 'The Nuer will not be found [if we delay]. They will be captured by other people. They are dying of a cough, a cough which catches them in the morning. They vomit blood in the morning.'

The Dinka came. When they came by night, they surrounded Pading. All the people were asleep, even the children. Nyayiel's son was awake smoking his pipe. They left the river behind them. They went and lay down where they thought they would chase people. A woman got up. She wanted to go out by night [to relieve herself]. She found them smoking tobacco. She came and woke her husband. 'We have a war.' Her husband came to Nyayiel's son bringing the news. Nyayiel's son said, 'Sleep.'

When the dawn broke, at the time of the cock's crow, Nyayiel's son told people, 'Do not fear and do not run away.' When the day broke, Nyayiel's son got up. He took his baton and his pipe. The baton was in his right hand, and the pipe was in his left hand. The Luac met him. He told the Nuer, 'Do not start.' He went towards the Dinka and frightened them with his baton. The baton thundered and was broken. The rest of the people [*naath*] died on land, but some died in the river. The remainder were killed by those who had spears at hand. When they finished they returned to camp. Of his own people [*nei*], not one died. He said, 'Collect all the spears of those Dinka who died on land, and those who died in the river, and those who were killed by hand.' He said, 'Gather them down here, but don't take any of them. Those people in the river, fish them out.' There were fish in the river, but the battle drove them away. When someone hid in the river, he was found, and he was killed. Some persons would find spears that they liked, and kept them aside. But Divinity was observing them.

Here the elements found in the other versions are further transformed. Ngundeng does not deliberately deceive a Dinka spy; instead a Dinka whom he rescued from starvation treacherously leads his fellows back to attack. The steps Ngundeng takes to deceive his enemies in other stories are represented here as an accidental misunderstanding which induces the Dinka to attack. Ngundeng's military preparations, detailed in all other versions, are here totally removed. The only concession to tactical considerations given is the remark that the Dinka faced the Lou with their backs to the river, which accounted, in part, for the high casualties they suffered. With all the preparations for self-defence removed, Divinity's intervention is heightened. Not only do the Nuer not fight, they do not even prepare to fight. Their efforts are not aided by the sacrifice of an ox before battle, but Divinity's power is directed entirely through Ngundeng and his baton. The image of Divinity's power is reinforced by the repetition of the Aiwel motif, of the Dinka being fished out of the river for days after the battle. And while there is no mention of the Gaawar and the reservation of Dinka cattle for them, Ngundeng's prohibition against collecting Dinka spears for individual use again established that this was not a battle fought for gain. In yet another way Cuol Puyu's version is different from others. His image of Ngundeng is of the prophet in later life, armed with the special brass pipe he had made at the turn of the century, not in the 1870s.

Our final Nuer version comes from a grandson of Ngundeng, Dhieyier Bol Ngundeng, who was about the same age as Cuol Puyu.[14] It has the flavour of an 'official history'. Dhieyier was presented to me as the foremost family authority on Ngundeng's life. He was carefully instructed by various sons of Ngundeng, and though he admitted that he knew a number of stories about the prophet told by others, he confined his own account to stories he had heard from his paternal uncles.

Unlike all the other versions given here, this story was told within the chronological framework of Ngundeng's life. All others were told incidentally, either in response to a direct question as an example of the proof of Ngundeng's seizure by DENG, or as an illustration of Ngundeng's refusal to fight either Dinka or 'Turuk'. In Dhieyier Bol's narrative the battle of Pading was placed in sequence with other events in Ngundeng's life leading up to his final acceptance as a prophet by the Lou. It was in turn followed by the story of the building of the Mound, and the events that took place around the Mound up through Ngundeng's death and the death of his son, Guek.

After Ngundeng revealed to his immediate section that he was seized by DENG, he spent the dry season with most of the other Lou at Pading. There he began teaching the Lou the songs composed by his divinity, and while the Lou were interested, they did not understand the meaning very well. Then came the threats of raids.

There was a Dinka named Nuaar Mer. He was a strong man. He walked as one with the *ansar* (i.e. slavers), and he had a divinity, too. He captured everyone, including Gaawar. He lived in Mogogh. When Ngundeng was going to Pading these Dinka said, 'Let us capture [them]. We have captured everyone. Can we just leave these many cattle?' They discussed it with their leader, Nuaar Mer.

Ngundeng told the Nuer, 'The Dinka want to capture us, we must leave,' he said. The Nuer said, 'We cannot leave.' He said, 'We must go.' The Nuer left. The Nuer passed through Gun, and passed Paddoi. They came to Jiath-in-Kot. They camped there. After making camp, they slept two days, sleeping there. They were expecting to go to the river [Pibor]. One of their cattle was a white bull . This beast began to lead the herd past the camp. They were going to bring them back, but Ngundeng said, 'Don't bring them back. Bring their calves. Let us return to Pading, the white bull has decided it.' They collected the calves of the cattle, they untied the ropes. They collected the cattle-ropes and gradually overtook the cattle. They put the ropes on them.

There were men of his age-set, and they said, 'Ngundeng is taking people away to a place of death. Why did we Nuer run away from the Dinka in the first place? We must kill Ngundeng.' They said, 'If we are going to kill him, who will go first?' One man named Kor Ruac said, 'I will be the first, if you are afraid of Ngundeng.' They said, 'Right.' The Nuer were walking single file along a path, and Kor Ruac was behind Ngundeng. He tried to beat Ngundeng with a wide-headed stick. [People shouted] 'Ngundeng is being killed!' People wanted to rush to fight Kor Ruac. Ngundeng said, 'Sons of my maternal uncles, do not defend Divinity. This stick which was taken from his hand, was it taken by you? Let us continue. That is finished, let us not fight.'

So they went to their camp at Pading. They went and made camp. When they camped he said, 'You, Dinka are coming tomorrow. Those who will be looking after cattle, they will find two Dinka. One will have one eye, the other will have two eyes. The man with two eyes will escape. He will not be caught. The one-eyed man will be caught. You bring him to my camp fire.' The Dinka were found when the cattle were grazing. The man with two eyes escaped. The man with one eye was caught. They brought him to Ngundeng. They told Ngundeng, 'We found two people,' one man said. Ngundeng said, 'That is very good. It is good that you brought him. Man! Where do you come from?' 'I come from Dinka.' 'Why?' 'We are coming to spy on you.' 'Why? 'We wanted to capture you.' 'Right. You take some milk. Tomorrow you will return to your people. Let them come, but do not come back yourself. If this camp is captured, then you will get cattle from your people. Don't you come with them.' He let that man drink from his milk. In the morning he had a cow milked and the Dinka drank the milk. He was told, 'Go, but do not come back.'

This man went to his own camp. He told them, 'The Nuer are there, certainly, but what they will do, I do not know.' They asked him, 'What could they do, the Nuer? We are going to capture them.' He said, 'I will go with you together, and I will remain behind. I will not be in the front.'

The Dinka spent three days in their camp. On the third day they went to war, thinking that they would capture Ngundeng's camp. Ngundeng said, 'Dinka are coming tomorrow to come and capture your camp, but do not fear this.' Some people said, 'You, Ngundeng, if you say people should not fear these Dinka, have they finished capturing all the people? Are we to escape? What strength do we have if all the people have failed?' He told them, 'Don't worry, my mother's brother's sons.' The Dinka came early in the morning at dawn. They reached the first camp, and as they reached it the people of the camp fled, crying 'The Dinka have come.' Ngundeng told the Nuer, 'You, get up and go to war.' Some of them ran away, some others went ahead. They were afraid because the Dinka killed people. He called back those who ran away. He told them. 'Return to war, people.' He remained in the camp with the dogs, and with his two small prophets. When people went ahead he told his prophet, 'You, get up and take the crocodile-marked ox.'

He had the root of a tree which he had dug up before his divinity was accepted [*ngäth*]. This root had been smoothed, it had copper and aluminum rings wound around it. That was his gun. He took his baton and his spear. This baton is the root of a *kot* tree. The crocodile-marked ox with white spots on its side was taken. His people and the Dinka had not yet met. He went and passed through the Nuer. He went between them. He speared the ox and the ox ran away. It fell with its head to the Dinka on the riverside. He took that stick which is the baton and lifted it up. There was lightning like the lightning of rain. When it thundered all the Dinka fell down. The people brought the war, they were killed by the Nuer. They were not killed by those in battle, it was because they were felled by the thunder of the baton.

Ngundeng was accepted [*ngäth*] here. From there they decided to capture the Dinka cattle. He refused. He said, 'This war was not brought by me. No people [*nei*] who are called children of one man, who are born of Divinity, should fight. I am defending myself because I am being killed. Those cattle are to be taken by those whose cattle have been captured. Their weapons, which are their spears,' he said, 'put them together in one place. No one is allowed to take any. That is not my fault [*duer*], it is their fault, those people who brought me war. He who takes a spear as his own, will get his thing [will be punished].' People were afraid.

Dhieyier Bol's account is by far the most elaborated of all the versions we have. It relates in detail what many give in abbreviation. It contains elements found in all the other versions, though it does not contain everything that is found in them. In this story the Dinka under Nuaar Mer decide to raid Ngundeng. He flees to safety but returns to Pading, a return signalled by the white bull. He meets some opposition and Kor Ruac tries to kill him. Unlike Garang Ngundeng's version, Kor is prevented by the intervention of Divinity, who takes the stick out of his hand. When Ngundeng's friends try to retaliate, Ngundeng stops them, as he does in Garang's story, by uttering the injunction against defending Divinity, as represented by himself. Divinity's power to prevent a fight among the Nuer presages the dramatic intervention at the battle of Pading.

Some attention is paid to Ngundeng's strategy, his deception of the

Dinka spy and his learning of the Dinka plans. Here again he offers the captured Dinka the option not to fight Divinity, which this time is accepted. But here again the power of Divinity aids the Nuer in battle, and the sacrifice of the ox and the use of the baton kill the Dinka without the Nuer having to fight. At the end of the battle Ngundeng announces even more clearly than in the other versions his abhorrence of war and refuses to allow the Lou to turn a battle in self-defence into a campaign of retaliation. Again, since the Gaawar had suffered most from Nuaar Mer, it was they who should benefit from the defeat of his followers.

Dinka versions of Pading

Many of the versions cited above identify the force who attacked the Lou as 'Nuaar Mer's Dinka', a reference to the Gaawar Nuer leader and his mixed following. Modern Gaawar and Dinka sources agree that the bulk of the raiding party at Pading came from Mogogh, but they also deny that Nuaar Mer was directly involved in the planning of the raid. There is even some doubt whether many Gaawar went along.[15] From the Lou perspective these distinctions are unimportant; the raiders clearly came from Mogogh.

The Lou sometimes assume that other Dinka, frequently mentioned in Ngundeng's songs, were also present at Pading. Ayong Yor, a Luac Dinka leader who was an early ally of the Anglo-Egyptian government and who accompanied the 1902 patrol, is commonly thought to have been involved, but it seems clear from Dinka accounts that he was not at Pading. This leaves us with no clear idea from modern Lou testimony just who organized the Dinka raid. Evans-Pritchard's cryptic reference to a Dinka 'prophet' named Deng is neither repeated nor elucidated by the Lou versions given here, and I met with no success with direct questions about him and his identity. It is only in modern Dinka accounts, recorded in 1982, that this man re-enters the story.

The end of the 1870s was a time when the Egyptian government was actively campaigning against the merchant companies in the Southern Sudan, and the merchants' armies of irregular slave-soldiers were being disbanded and transferred to government service. A number of these former slave-soldiers took this chance to return to their home areas. After the armed camps on the Zeraf were closed a stranger, a Dinka calling himself Deng Cier (DENG Star) appeared to the Rut, Thoi and Luac. No one knew where he came from, but he was circumcised, and many assumed that he was one of the soldiers from the White Nile. He claimed to be seized by DENG; thus the celestial name. He behaved in a strange way and composed songs of equal peculiarity. The Gaawar, too, remember Deng Cier, even identifying him as a circumcised Atuot. Nuaar Mer feared the Divinity he claimed to have and could not openly oppose him, and some members of Nuaar's Teny section did accompany Deng Cier when he led his raiders out in the early dry-season (September–December) of 1878.[16]

There were some among the Dinka who actively opposed Deng Cier. The Rut Dinka of the old shrine at Luang Deng refused to acknowledge Deng Cier's claim to seizure by DENG. So, it is said, did Ayong Yor. They apparently dismissed him as a madman who came from an unknown place. Many of the Rut, Thoi and Luac Dinka living at Mogogh, however, did join Deng Cier, while the Nyareweng did not.[17] The following Dinka version is a composite account, taken from several Luac and Thoi informants. First is a statement by Thuar D'jok, a Thoi chief, and Cuol Yoal Abiel, a Luac:[18]

> A person from an unknown place came. He was called Deng Cier. Deng Cier came. He had a free-divinity [*yath*]. His divinity told him that there were Nuer cattle at Pading, and he wanted these cows to be taken by the Dinka. Then the people (that is Rut and Luac) said, 'Yes, but where did this man come from?' and he was circumcised, that Deng Cier. They were wondering where he came from because he was not one of them.

Ayong Yor's son, Lueth Ayong Yor, recalled:[19]

> Deng Cier was a Dinka. Deng Cier came from Rut, he came together with Rut and Luac. They came to Pagak. My father was there. They asked my father to go with them. He refused. The Rut wanted to fight my father. The Luac said, 'Well, leave him.' Four men from my father's section came along in support of Deng Cier.

Thuar D'jok and Cuol Yoal continue:

> It was that Deng Cier who led the Dinka to Pading to fight Ngundeng. Deng Cier himself went to find out about the Nuer that were sick. He found the people in the morning washing their mouths with ashes, clearing their throats. He thought it was a disease, people dying from a disease. So he brought back information that the Nuer were suffering, dying, and the Dinka would find it easy to collect the cattle and kill the sick people.

Another Luac chief, Malok Lam, stated:[20]

> Deng Cier organized the Dinka to go and fight the Nuer at Pading. First he sent his spies. His spies came with information that all the Nuer were sick. You could hear the noise of them cleaning their teeth and clearing

their throats, and that was taken by the spies to mean the sound of sickness and death. So, he ordered his people to head on. When they arrived at Pading, Deng Kur [Ngundeng] said, 'These people are coming to attack us.' They asked him, 'Why are they attacking us?' So Ngundeng just fired his baton, and it was as if they were stunned, they just died. They were eating grass, the Dinka. It was DENG who sent his strength against them, and then they died.

A Thoi elder, Thon Marol, gave a more matter-of-fact account of the Dinka defeat:[21]

> In Pading itself a hippo came out. Some people said the hippo should not be killed. Some said it should be killed, so the hippo was killed. Then Deng Cier came with a torch [Arab. = *batteria*][22] and a short sword. He used to gather people and tell them they were going to fight the Nuer. The people of Luang Deng refused to join the fight. So when they were crossing Pading the Nuer came upon them while they were inside the stream. So they were crossing Pading and it was deep, some people nearly drowned. They [the Lou] were using harpoons [*yuai*].

Deng Cier's precise fate is uncertain. Malok Lam recounted:

> As soon as Deng Cier learned that the Nuer defeated the Dinka, he began to say, 'I regret now that I brought myself and my people just to die. I regret, I regret.'

Others claim that Deng Cier's body was never found, that either he was killed or he just disappeared.[23] One effect of the aftermath of Pading is as clear to the modern Dinka as it is to the modern Gaawar: if the battle of Pading had never taken place, the Dinka would not have been defeated by Deng Laka at Mogogh shortly after.

These Dinka accounts of Pading show considerable agreement with the main outlines of the Nuer versions: in the Dinka miscalculation of Lou strength based on a misunderstanding by the spies; in Ngundeng's use of the baton, directing DENG's power to kill the Dinka, overwhelming them like so many grazing cattle; and in the image of the Dinka being stabbed in the river, in this case by harpoons (*yuai*) rather than fishing-spears (*bith*), their fate being presaged by their own harpooning of a hippo in the river.

This basic agreement should not be taken as independent corroboration. All the Dinka informants interviewed here were bilingual in Nuer and Dinka. They, and their people, have a long history of a variety of contacts with the Lou and Gaawar. The grandfathers and fathers of these men corroborated Deng Laka's version of events, our first account of Pading, as early as 1905. Their apparent corroboration of Nuer accounts indicates the extent to which the modern Nuer–Dinka community has a common interpretation of events in their shared past. It is to this common interpretation of the past, and to our own reconstruction of that past, that we now turn.

Historical reconstruction & symbolic acts

We have seen in the preceding accounts not so much the structuring of myth as the development of historical interpretation. We are able, with care, to base an historical reconstruction on this interpretation, as follows.

In the mid-1870s, despite the earlier Nuer incursions and the brief appearance of the slavers, there was still a vigorous Dinka community in the Zaraf valley. Not only were they not dispersed and dominated by the Nuer at this time, they still were able to pose a threat to the Nuer. Another threat the Nuer faced, which these accounts indicate the Dinka wished to exploit, was hunger. The statement contained in both Nuer and Dinka accounts that the Dinka mistook the sight of the Lou cleaning their teeth with ashes and clearing their throats as a sign that they were ill and dying is extraordinary; for the Dinka, too, clean their teeth with ashes. But we do know from environmental studies that the end of the 1860s was a period of recurring weak Nile floods; that in late 1870s there were floods, local famines and outbreaks of cattle disease; and that in the early 1870s smallpox was spread into the Zaraf valley through the slavers' camps.[24] We know from Lou and Gaawar accounts that at this time, for various reasons, Nuaar Mer's raids among them, the Gaawar herds were much reduced and people were going hungry. The unusually extensive flood of 1878 (one of the highest ever recorded) destroyed many cultivations. If this hardship was widespread at the time, then the Dinka may have expected that the Lou would be suffering as much as the Gaawar. The Dinka at Mogogh, in the meantime, were living off the cattle of Nuaar Mer's raids.

Faced with a specific threat, Ngundeng tried first to avoid an unequal fight, and then to trap the Dinka in an ambush. Whether he deceived them or they miscalculated, they did fall into this trap. The Dinka first attacked some outlying camps, and this gave Ngundeng's main force additional warning. Ngundeng used the geography of the marshy ground around Pading (where the river was unseasonably high, due to the flood that year) and pushed the Dinka back into the river, killing them by the score. This massive defeat of the Dinka force enabled Deng

Laka later to disperse their remnant at Mogogh. Two prophets thus established themselves on the outcome of this battle.

Such is the historical reconstruction. The indigenous interpretation of these events involves a spiritual succession not only within Lou society, but within the broader Nuer–Dinka community. There are three elements here: Ngundeng's succession from Yuot Nyakong, Ngundeng's competition with a Dinka rival, and Ngundeng's use of his victory to promote a philosophy of peace.

It is important to note that the only versions where Yuot Nyakong's death was spontaneously linked to the battle of Pading were recorded during the colonial period when Nuer were speaking to men they associated with the government. In recent years Yuot has dropped out of the narrative. It was only through direct questioning that I was able to get even one of my informants to agree that Yuot's death was avenged at Pading. The linking of Yuot to Pading has always been awkward: it was the Nyareweng Dinka who killed Yuot, but the Nyareweng were not at Pading. Two reasons have already been given for his inclusion in stories told earlier this century, which relate to the political relations between the Nuer and the new government, and the importance of establishing the succession of spiritual power within Lou society. At the beginning of this century Yuot was still part of Lou living memory, and direct comparisons between him and Ngundeng could still be made. Now, however, Ngundeng's spiritual strength and the truth of his words are acknowledged over a wide area beyond Lou society. Yuot has ceased to be an important spiritual or historical link in Ngundeng's career. Ngundeng is known beyond the Lou; it is now important to those who believe in him to establish his spiritual primacy within a wider community. That is what the modern accounts of Pading, including the Dinka versions, do establish.

In these modern versions Ngundeng's main spiritual rivals come from outside Nuer society and are located among the Dinka. DENG, after all, is a Dinka divinity, and the main shrine to DENG, at Luang Deng in Gaawar country, is still run by Rut Dinka.[25] The Lou today are unspecific as to who was Ngundeng's main spiritual rival, indicating, perhaps, that the claims of a proven imposter are no longer important to remember. The modern Dinka versions recall the conflict that was still known among the Lou in Evans-Pritchard's day: a conflict between Ngundeng and a Dinka prophet of DENG. This is direct rivalry between a Nuer and a Dinka for the same divinity. In this respect it is significant that the modern Dinka stress the rejection of Deng Cier's claims by his contemporaries, especially the caretaker of Luang Deng.

Had Deng Cier been successful against the Lou not only would his prestige have eclipsed all other Dinka leaders, it could have enabled him to co-opt the shrine and force the caretaker into the background. Instead, as the Dinka acknowledge, the divinity DENG destroyed Deng Cier at Pading, using Ngundeng's baton as the instrument of destruction. The Luang Deng shrine was then able to establish a *modus vivendi* with the Nuer victor of Pading, just as it later did with the Nuer victor of Mogogh.

We have already noted some of the ways in which all accounts of Pading express elements of those teachings of peace for which Ngundeng later became famous. The most important points are those, present even in Evans-Pritchard's version, which reinforce the ideas of peace in the midst of war. It is acknowledged by all that this was a battle fought in self-defence. What is more important, it was a battle that was supposed to demonstrate Divinity's prohibition against fighting. This is demonstrated by the story of Kor Ruac's attempt to strike Ngundeng, the use of the baton to destroy the Dinka without the Lou having to fight, and Ngundeng's injunction to leave the rest of the Dinka to the Gaawar to deal with. The historical evidence that Ngundeng refused to allow his victory at Pading to become the start of a war of retribution against the Dinka is strong. This does not seem to be a later embellishment. His speech recorded at the end of Dhieyier Bol's account may express the more fully formulated philosophy of his final years, but we do know from Dinka as well as Nuer sources that Ngundeng sanctioned no subsequent raids after Pading.

Of equal symbolic importance in most of these versions is the echo of the Aiwel myth. Ngundeng's victory at Pading invites direct comparison with Aiwel, particularly as Ngundeng himself invited such a comparison throughout much of his life. In Ngundeng's life story the battle of Pading parallels the episode of Aiwel spearing the people in the river. It demonstrated Ngundeng's spiritual strength and marked a break between his early troubled life and his later career as a prophet. The parallel is so strong that we might be tempted to regard Pading as yet another borrowed element from the Aiwel myth. However, we do know the battle took place. We do know more or less what happened there. If Ngundeng subsequently modelled himself after Aiwel and recast his life story to follow the myth, he did so because in some ways the events at Pading bade him do so.

Pading is an important historical event to the Lou, and one to which they have referred at other crucial times in their past. In 1902, when the Anglo-Egyptian government and its Dinka allies raided Ngundeng and destroyed the village around the Mound, his followers expected him to raise his baton, as he did at Pading, to destroy the invaders. Ngundeng raised the baton, declared that Divinity was absent, and disbanded his force.[26] Ngundeng's son, Guek, faced similar expectations when the government was preparing to attack him. His age-mates rebuked him, saying, 'Ngundeng was able to kill people with his baton, we will kill them as we did the Dinka.' For some time Guek refused, saying 'Divinity did not show me this.'[27] Finally, the government did attack, and in 1929 Guek and a few followers were cornered at his father's Mound. Guek went to meet the Anglo-Egyptian forces, driving an ox before him, and, like his father at Pading, tried to sacrifice it before the battle began. According to one eyewitness, Guek's divinity abandoned him on the morning of the battle. He was unable to spear the ox before he was shot and killed.[28]

History did not repeat itself in 1902 or 1929. Those later experiences perhaps helped to shape the interpretation of Pading now put forward by the Lou. The three very different results of these encounters have been given a consistent interpretation. All three serve to illustrate, by reference to historical experience, Divinity's prohibition against fighting. A true man of Divinity, a true prophet like Ngundeng, keeps to Divinity's words and directs Divinity's power through himself. Those who ignore Divinity's directions, as it is implied Guek did by standing and fighting, and those who misrepresent Divinity's words, as Deng Cier did, find themselves abandoned in the end.

The central historical question the Nuer are trying to answer is not so much what did Ngundeng and Guek do, but what did Divinity do, and why? Divinity is the real subject of these stories. The mystery to be explained is contained in the different outcomes of the battles. It is perhaps because of this that the historical details concerning the prophets' actions are consistently recalled. Divinity's intentions can be inferred mainly from the prophets' actions. With agreement about what Ngundeng and those around him did comes agreement about what Divinity intended. It is Divinity who is being made to appear consistent despite the contradictory resolutions of the events. The modern interpretation of Divinity's acts rests on the acknowledgement that sacrifice and the use of Ngundeng's baton did not always achieve the same results. There is a core of historical detail which must be adhered to if one is to understand the divine will, but the interpretation of the past is conveyed through symbolic emphasis.

The symbolic acts are themselves part of the historical detail which enables us to reconstruct the event. Specific incidents in the recent historical experience of the Nuer – the gift of milk as a life-giving symbol, sacrificing an ox before battle, raising the baton, spearing the enemy in the river – draw on an existing set of Nilotic symbols. In this case symbolism is reinforced, even refashioned out of experience, an experience which is an echo of the Aiwel myth but which itself is deliberately re-echoed in the events of 1902 and 1929. Historians and Nuer herdsmen alike might be more certain of what Ngundeng *did* at Pading than what he *said*. It is through his acts, rather than through speeches which may have been placed retroactively in his mouth, that we have a few clues of what he thought at the time. For this reason we must pay attention to the symbolic imagery in the accounts of Pading. This imagery has so far enabled the Nuer to offer a consistent interpretation of a series of crucial events in their past, without forgetting the distinctive character and different outcome of each event, and without imposing a stereotypic formula on the events described.

Notes

1. D. H. Johnson, 'Tribal boundaries and border wars: Nuer-Dinka relations in the Sobat and Zaraf valleys, *c.* 1860–1976', *Journal of African History*, 23, ii (1982), pp. 189–91.
2. For a more detailed account of this period see D. H. Johnson, *Nuer Prophets: A History of Prophecy from the Upper Nile in the Nineteenth and Twentieth Centuries* (Oxford, 1994), chapters 3 & 4.
3. These extracts were transcribed by Gabriel Gai Riam and Simon Kuny Puoc, and translated by Gabriel Gai Riam, Timothy Tap, and myself. The reference numbers to the interviews are those used in *Nuer Prophets*, and can be found there under the list of sources.
4. *Sudan Intelligence Report* 113 (December 1903) p. 2.
5. 'Report by El Kaimakam Wilson Bey on march from the Sobat (mouth of the Filus) to Bor', *Sudan Intelligence Report* 128 (March 1905), Appendix A, p. 7.
6. E. E. Evans-Pritchard, 'The Nuer: tribe and clan', *Sudan Notes and Records*, 18, i (1935), pp. 57–9.
7. R. G. Lienhardt, *Divinity and Experience. The Religion of the Dinka* (Oxford, 1961), chapter 5.
8. Garang Ngundeng, L1.2.
9. D. H. Johnson, 'Ngundeng and the "Turuk": two narratives compared', *History in Africa*, 9 (1982), pp. 128–9.
10. Macar Ngundeng, L2.
11. Biel Peat, L12.1.
12. J. Kiggen, *Nuer-English Dictionary* (London, 1948), p. 84.
13. Cuol Puyu, L22.2.
14. Dhieyier Bol Ngundeng, L6.1.
15. Ruot Diu (son of Deng Laka), G10.3. Rut, Thoi, Luac Dinka elders, EHJP-1. Provisional translations of all Dinka interviews were made by Philip Diu Deng.
16. Ruot Diu, EHJP-5.
17. EHJP-1.

Douglas H. Johnson

18. Ibid.
19. Lueth Ayong Yor, EHJP-2.
20. Ibid.
21. EHJP-1.
22. The anomaly of the electric torch can be understood through its association with the educated sector, especially government employees who were the first to own such implements (see F. M. Deng, *The Dinka and their Songs* [Oxford, 1973], p. 174). Deng Cier, a nineteenth-century soldier, is here described with the accoutrements (torch and bayonet) of a twentieth-century policeman.
23. EHJP-1.
24. D. H. Johnson, 'Reconstructing a history of local floods in the Upper Nile region of the Sudan', *International Journal of African Historical Studies*, 25, iii (1992), pp. 618-20, 635-7. E. Marno, *Reisen im Gebiete des Blauen und Weissen Nil, im Egyptischen Sudan, 1869-1873* (Vienna, 1874), pp. 339, 404.
25. D. H. Johnson, 'Fixed shrines and spiritual centres in the Upper Nile', *Azania*, 25 (1990).
26. Johnson, 'Ngundeng and the "Turuk"', p. 129.
27. Dhieyier Bol Ngundeng, L6.2.
28. Deng Bor Ngundeng, L5.1.

Ten

'What is the World Going to Come to?'

Prophecy & Colonialism
in Central Kenya

CHARLES AMBLER

> Ireri called all Embu and told them, 'Now I'm going to tell you what the
> world is going to come to.' Then he said, 'You will all be defeated with
> something with a metal nose that will be so wide it will be touching both
> Kirimiri and Karue at the same time.' So he predicted after the appearance
> of that metal nose there would come a generation that would dance with their
> backs to one another. And that pointed nose was the airplane . . . And then
> the generation which was predicted to dance with their backs to each other
> started appearing. A great example of this is the current youth.[1]

In the oral records of the Mount Kenya society of Embu, Ireri wa Irugi
surfaces repeatedly as a seer who foretold the arrival of European
invaders, the defeat of Embu and the changes that would occur as a
consequence of British colonial domination. His predictions, and those
attributed to one or two contemporaries in Embu, told of the arrival
from the west of invaders who would bring 'an animal . . . from the
sky with an iron mouth. It will destroy the land.'[2] In some versions the
invaders were red men or animals who could eat fire and would carry
powerful staffs; they would overwhelm the Embu defenders and this
defeat would usher in a generation of men who would wear rings in their
ears, and an era in which children would disobey their parents and
youths would dance shamelessly with their elders. The traditions of
neighbouring communities in Meru include similar predictions of a
conquest by 'red strangers' with fur on their faces, who blew smoke,
rode on huge dogs and wore women's clothing. In the aftermath of this

conquest raiding would end but warriors would be reduced to 'digging dirt with their hands . . . as if they were women.'[3]

Many of the same elements appear in the numerous traditions of seers in the neighbouring Bantu-speaking, agricultural societies of the central Kenya highlands. The oral records of Kikuyuland describe seers who predicted the arrival from the 'big water' of strangers the colour of small white frogs. In some cases they would have fire in their mouths, wear clothes like butterfly wings and carry sticks that spit fire. They would bring with them an iron snake that belched fire, and later they would fly like butterflies.[4]

Such traditions have been especially prevalent among Kamba-speakers.[5] For example, the celebrated female seer, Syokimau, is said to have predicted that a long narrow snake would move from the coast toward the setting sun, bringing people who would possess a kind of fire that would be produced on demand. A time would then come when people would begin to speak like birds. In the repetition of these accounts the 'iron snake' is explicitly identified as the railroad, sticks that spew fire are guns and speech reminiscent of the sound of birds is said to represent local people's initial reaction to the sound of European languages.[6]

Despite the ubiquity of the prophetic traditions in central Kenya and their explicitly historical qualities, historians have paid them little serious attention. Oral testimonies and popular histories often incorporate such traditions as literal records of events, but scholars have only rarely followed that example. In his study of Meru society at the time of the European conquest, Jeffrey Fadiman asserts without qualification that the arrival of whites there 'had been predicted for three generations' and goes on to connect particular seers with precise predictions and to claim a well-defined role for these predictions in the Meru response to the British invaders.[7] Most historians, however, have either ignored or skirted the question of the historicity of prophetic traditions, preferring to read such traditions in metaphorical terms. The traditions of the rise in prophetic activity in the interior of Kenya in the nineteenth century thus emerge as a symptom and emblem of economic upheaval and social discontent in the early period of imperial expansion or a product of the tensions of the era – the colonial period – in which they were collected.[8] In other instances the seer traditions became literary devices that lend drama and emphasis to accounts of the traumatic events surrounding the imposition of colonial rule in central Kenya.[9]

None of these views conveys the complexity of prophetic traditions or their significance, or provides insight into the traditional place of seers and prophecy in the societies of central Kenya. Although popular historians might be naive in their literal reading of the lives of seers and the impact of their predictions, scholars have been equally naive in their failure to locate seers and the traditions associated with them in the contexts in which they lived, were initially constructed and have subsequently been preserved. Certainly, professional historians have made little effort to understand seers and prophets as leaders or to comprehend prophetic texts as expressions of an indigenous world view and theory of history.[10] Not only were these oral accounts of seers and their visions of the future the products of tumultuous times, they form part too of a tradition of prophecy in these societies – a tradition that has continued to find expression in the decades since the imposition of colonial rule. Unfortunately, any attempt to examine prophecy in these terms faces two immediate obstacles. First, the accounts of nineteenth-century seers were all collected after the events they were said to have predicted, and generally many decades after. Second, while there are many accounts which describe the particular events predicted by certain seers, few prophetic texts survive. This makes it difficult to trace histories of the prophetic traditions them-selves, and the processes through which they may have been developed (or invented), reconstructed (or invested with new meaning), or carefully preserved over time.[11]

Prediction & prophecy in central Kenya

In an extended memorandum dating from the 1920s on 'Witchcraft' in Embu District a British official noted that 'magic figures . . . in almost every transaction.'[12] This is an obvious point, but nevertheless worth emphasizing. In the nineteenth and early twentieth centuries the peoples of central Kenya conceived a universe governed by supernatural forces. Thus, when the District Commissioner in Meru noted in 1923 that he had 'come to the conclusion that natives here are sunk in super-stition', his analysis was as correct as his terminology was misguided.[13] Interaction with the spirit world was an essential element of life, and it was through such interaction – whether direct or indirect – that people sought to comprehend and influence events, and to predict them.

Every community in central Kenya was drawn into an active eco-nomy of magic. Local practitioners served neighbours; some who devel-oped wider reputations attracted people from considerable distances or travelled to sell their services. The settlement of specialists at Uvariri in Mbeere in present-day Embu District was known across the entire central Kenya region for the potency of the powers dispensed there.[14] Local specialists, known as *andu ago* (sing., *mundu mugo*; in the Kamba language, *mundu mue/andu awe*) grew up in the practice or were called to it. They provided remedies for various afflictions or difficulties, prepared protective charms, and in some cases cast curses against the enemies or rivals of their clients. Most also engaged in some form of divination, generally accomplished by 'reading' the entrails of a slaughtered animal or the contents of a special gourd. Although a great deal of the practice of divination aimed at the determination of the causes of particular conditions or circumstances, much of the work done by diviners involved, at least implicitly, powers of prediction.[15] People rarely made significant changes in their lives without consulting specialists for advice on the wisdom of such actions. Certainly, warriors never went out on raids without first asking a well-respected diviner or seer to predict the outcome. If problems were foreseen, plans might be changed or aborted, or rituals performed to counter the promised ill-fortune.[16]

These specialists defy easy categorization. The roles of various traditional practitioners varied among areas and over time. Moreover, individuals commonly crossed back and forth over the boundaries among specialties. But a useful distinction can be made between those specialists who dealt with specific concerns for a clientele consisting of individuals or small groups of people, and those who spoke more metaphorically and whose knowledge benefited a broader community.[17] While *andu ago* with some talent for divining future events in the lives of individuals or families are relatively commonplace figures on the central Kenya landscape, very much rarer were those women or men – prophets or seers – whose visions came to be more widely known and accepted.[18] John Middleton points to this element of prophecy when he notes, in reference to rainmaker-prophets among the Lugbara people of Uganda, that 'the notion here is that in ordinary situations men do not think or speak the absolute truth – they are ignorant of it and can see their society only in sectional terms. Rainmakers, on the other hand, know the absolute truth; they are concerned with the eternal perpetuity of . . . Lugbara society.'[19] In central Kenya, as well, men and women who rose to positions of leadership often claimed – or were assigned – prophetic powers.[20]

In the early written accounts of central Kenya societies, such individuals rarely appear. G. St. J. Orde Browne, who researched a book on the Mount Kenya societies while assigned there for several years before the First World War, makes no mention of seers. Yet the author had a deep interest in traditional history and included a chapter devoted to 'Magic and Religion'.[21] Likewise, Gerhard Lindblom's meticulously detailed and knowledgeable account of Kamba society, based on information collected around 1910, contains nothing on seers and prophecy.[22] This silence lends some credence to Kennell Jackson's suggestion that, during the colonial period, traditions were embellished to exaggerate the incidence of prophecy; yet prophetic traditions were clearly more than the inventions of colonized peoples.[23] In his 1913 study of Kitui, Charles Dundas noted the existence of active seers as well as of traditions of earlier prophecies of European expansion into Kenya.[24] Around 1911 C. W. Hobley interviewed a man he described as a 'Kikuyu oracle', who was 'credited with the extraordinary power of being the recipient of messages from the Supreme Being and in consequence the gift of prophecy' and who was still issuing predictions of harvests and outbreaks of disease.[25] Despite the fact that the news that such men or women brought – of coming epidemics, famines, invasions and social disorder – was often bad, communities held seers in high regard.[26]

The early accounts consistently draw attention to the direct divine inspiration implicit in prophecy. One Embu elder recalled in the early 1960s that people believed that Ireri wa Irugi had gone beneath the earth to receive his visions direct from God.[27] E. May Crawford, a missionary who lived in Embu between 1908 and 1910, noted that a prophet 'is called to his vocation by God, who appears to him in a dream, or vision, and tells him he must become a medicine man. This call he proclaims to the people of his village.'[28] Seers in Kikuyuland were believed to have been carried away into the sky and then sent back to earth.[29] In some cases God spoke to these prophets in violent dreams.[30] Describing the Meru political and religious leader, the *Mugwe*, one Meru elder recalled, 'He was a dreamer . . . When he had a dream he was able to say what would happen in the future . . . He was cared for by God.'[31] A seer interviewed in southern Kikuyuland in 1911 described how twice a year he fell into a deep trance-like sleep and felt himself removed from bed and then heard God's voice speaking to him. As this happened, his house appeared illuminated.[32] In an account by Jomo Kenyatta, a Kikuyu prophet described how God invaded his sleep and he awoke trembling, bruised and in such a state of hysteria that he was unable to speak until elders had gathered and offered sacrifices.[33]

The notion of prophecy in the societies of central Kenya apparently encompassed much the same ambiguity that the English-language term embraces.[34] Prophets were individuals who could predict future events; yet they were also women or men who possessed a vision of how communities should face those events and thus shape the future. In both circumstances, these were individuals in direct contact with God. In Embu and Meru traditions prophets were 'men of wonders' who acted at God's direction and in the knowledge of future events to lead their followers to new areas of settlement or to protect them from disaster.[35] Likewise, Mbeere traditions tell of a time of crisis when God directed particular elders to inform the people 'that everyone should marry'. Whatever actual circumstances this tradition may refer to, its preservation conveys very directly the belief that at critical moments in history God does speak or act directly to and through certain men or women.[36] This notion of divine intervention in the comprehension of and response to crisis is apparent in the ways that central Kenya communities defined and reacted to the strangers that arrived in the region during the second half of the nineteenth century.[37] It is evident also in the fact that the oral traditions of prophetic warnings of these strangers' arrival have not been surrendered as irrational anachronisms, but continue to be regarded as legitimate subjects of analysis and debate. Thus, a resident of Embu District interviewed in the 1960s argued that certain elements of these prophecies had yet to be fulfilled.[38] Likewise, in his book on Kamba society, Joseph Muthiani has noted in reference to the predictions of the prophet Syokimau that 'all the other characteristics she described were and still are witnessed'.[39]

Prophets of invasion

Ireri wa Irugi was famous as a seer. He predicted that the Europeans would come but he wasn't believed.[40]

It would have been surprising if nineteenth-century seers had not made predictions of the coming of strangers. The evidence, while fragmentary, suggests that some prophecies of the coming of whites were widely known and discussed in central Kenya during the decades that culminated in the British conquest of the region. Moreover, there is every reason to believe that communities would have considered the words of these prophecies – as they were then interpreted – very seriously indeed. After all, the Europeans who advanced on central

Kenya in the late 1800s did not fall out of the sky. Without disregarding the miraculous in explaining nineteenth-century prophecies of European conquest, it should be recalled that at the time these prophecies were made, central Kenya was by no means isolated from contact with foreigners.[41]

Relatively few people in the region would have had any direct knowledge of Europeans, but many were aware that a new category of foreigners had established a foothold on the East African coast during the nineteenth century. Through the nineteenth century people living in most sections of central Kenya probably comprehended the bits and pieces of gossip and information that they acquired about light-skinned and strangely attired foreigners through stories like that of Mukona Uko, the mythical coastal merchant who had, it was said, been pushed into the ocean by powerful newcomers.[42] Beginning in the late 1700s caravans from Kitui traversed the route to the coastal trading entrepôts, and gradually people from elsewhere in the region became directly or indirectly involved in the trade. Residents of areas, such as northern Kikuyuland and Mount Kenya, that were away from the major commercial routes came into contact with Kamba-speaking traders who had made the trip or with other travellers who had come in contact with them – and with the goods that they carried back to central Kenya.

During his second visit to Kitui in 1851, the coast-based missionary, Rev. J. Krapf, was introduced by his local host to a visiting trader from Embu, a man who was clearly not only familiar with the geography of central Kenya but with the nature of trade between the region and the coast. Such traders apparently visited Kitui regularly.[43] If meeting a European was then a rare or even unique event, encounters with coastal merchants would have been, by the 1850s, much more common. By that time increasing numbers of Arab and Swahili traders from the coast had begun to travel into the interior, into areas of central Kenya and beyond that had not previously been directly involved in the long-distance commerce.[44] With the expansion of trade, a growing volume of information – and misinformation – conveyed through contacts with the outside and outsiders flowed into the region. Mbeere traditions hold, for example, that God spoke to their elders through a Kamba-speaking trader who had travelled to the Indian Ocean coast.[45] Before the very end of the nineteenth century, most people in the region probably made little distinction between Europeans on the one hand and Arab and Swahili traders from the coast on the other. As late as 1898, a British traveller noted that Embu and Meru people 'do not discriminate between one safari and another, whether it is European, Arab, or Swahili'.[46]

Given the growing awareness of foreigners within communities in central Kenya, it is hardly surprising that people were anxious to learn what impact the 'red strangers' were going to have on their lives. Indeed, people would have demanded that seers speak to this issue. There is evidence that at least some of the prominent seers had travelled considerable distances from their home areas, and perhaps in some cases to the coast. Such experience would certainly have contributed to their reputations.[47] Some Embu traditions suggest that it was the actual establishment of a British foothold on the southern margins of the region beginning in the 1880s that triggered prophecies in Embu – or perhaps the reconsideration of existing prophetic traditions.[48] The language of such traditions was after all metaphorical, and thus subject to diverse interpretation.

In recitation, however, prophetic traditions observe a rhetorical formula in which the content of the prediction is accompanied by a specific explanation of meaning and an assertion of accuracy.[49] Thus, in the 1970s when an elder recalled an Embu tradition of a seer having predicted that 'you will all be defeated with something with a metal nose', he immediately added, 'and that pointed nose was the airplane'.[50] One Embu woman closed her recitation of the prophecy of Ireri wa Irugi with the words, 'Of course this has been fulfilled.'[51] Muthiani's description of the content of the prophecy of Syokimau follows the same form:

> I see men coming on the water. They will land at Kisuani (now called Mombasa), then they will start laying a long snake (railroad) across the country. I see a big millipede (train) moving on the long snake carrying people and heavy loads. These are strange people, they are so white that one can almost see their intestines, and they go around carrying fire in their pockets (matches). When they settle in our country they will spoil it by first forcing us to divide it up among ourselves.[52]

This form assigns a precision and accuracy to these prophecies that they do not entirely deserve. In the absence of original texts of these traditions, it is nevertheless clear that prophecies were conveyed in language that was not straightforward, perhaps even in a form like that of the obscure riddles that are a common element in central Kenya popular cultures.[53] Even the received traditions of these predictions are far more ambiguous than those who repeat them admit. A number of seers apparently predicted the arrival of men dressed like women, but it is by no means clear whether this should be taken to refer to Muslim traders or Europeans. The Meru tradition quoted earlier that anticipates that young men would be forced into the women's task of 'digging dirt with their hands' is generally taken to foretell the introduction of migrant agricultural labour, it might as well relate to the gender reversal implied in the prediction of the arrival of men in women's garb.[54] A number of traditions contain predictions that newcomers would bring sticks that contain fire. In the telling these are at times confidently described as matches and in other cases guns. They could as easily denote flashlights or cigarettes.

Much therefore depends on how the texts of these traditions are read. For example, many of the traditions include references to a huge snake or serpent with a metal mouth or breathing fire. Such images have typically been understood to foretell the construction of railroads and the arrival of trains or buses, or in some cases the advent of airplanes. In fact, large serpents were a stock feature of folk tales in central Kenya societies, and their appearance in the prophecies may have had a more literal implication than the interpretations of subsequent readers of the traditions would suggest.[55] Indeed, in the late 1960s one Embu elder asserted that predictions of the appearance of a snake that would 'swallow all the people' were in fact yet to be fulfilled.[56]

Explaining colonialism

Prophetic traditions of the coming of the Europeans repeatedly make the point that invasion and subjugation were inevitable and that resistance was therefore pointless.[57] Such traditions might be dismissed as later rationalizations of defeat were it not for their consistency and for the hints that the existence of prophetic warnings against resistance influenced the response of some local populations to the expansion of British power. For the people of the Mount Kenya societies, a steady expansion of alien involvement in the area culminated in the decade after 1900 in a series of armed expeditions that established British authority. Having asserted some degree of authority over the southern sections of the region in the 1890s, the British set up a permanent post at Kitui in 1898 and Murang'a (Fort Hall) in 1900. From that base, they launched assaults on northern Kitui, northern Kikuyuland, and on the country around Mount Kenya – thus fulfilling an Embu prophecy that invasion would come from the west. The British attacked Embu in 1906, meeting a fierce resistance with a dramatic show of destructive force. In the months that followed, they extended their authority over the neighbouring societies of Mbeere and Chuka, and in 1908 brought Meru under colonial control. During the next several years British rule was extended into the outlying reaches of districts across the region.

The apparent sharp distinction between the communities, like Embu, that resisted vigorously, and those that sought accommodation in fact obscures the fact that most communities were divided between those who advocated resistance and those who saw it as futile. Typically, the lines were drawn along generational lines, with the warriors pushing for armed defence and the elders and leaders arguing against it. For the elders, predictions that emphasized the pointlessness of opposing the British and the necessity of co-operation reinforced their appreciation of the power that these strangers possessed and provided ammunition for their arguments against resistance. For the youths, these predictions provided information, such as the direction of attack, that was commonly sought from seers in advance of conflict.[58]

During the decades in which British power gradually advanced toward Mount Kenya this debate apparently intensified.[59] A number of the earliest written accounts of these societies dating from the 1890s, point both to the tensions between generations and to the role that seers may have played in shaping reactions to outsiders. In his description of his visit to Meru in the early 1890s, the adventurer, W. A. Chanler, took note of these tensions. His informants told him that in many areas warriors were anxious to use violence against all foreign intruders, but that in most cases cooler heads had prevailed because the elders had been able to 'convince the young men that in the heads of the sages alone rest the fate and fortune of warriors in battle'.[60] Several years later, large numbers of armed warriors confronted Alfred Arkell-Hardwick's party when it travelled through Embu. According to Arkell-Hardwick, no attack occurred because the 'old men did not want to fight'.[61] Arkell-Hardwick attributed his luck and that of his two white colleagues to 'the prestige of the white man', but there are hints that more than prestige was involved in his comment that 'our forty men did not count for much in the eyes of the Wa'm'bu [Embu], as they knew them to be natives like themselves, and comparatively easily disposed of in spite of their guns'.[62] Chanler noted much clearer indications in Meru that prophetic warnings might have influenced local responses to European visitors:

> On the borders of the Janji country, there lived a mighty wizard . . . He was said to be an old man stricken in years, but one whose skill and ability were such that he had never been known to given any but the very best advice in all matters connected with either business or war . . . I was told

that upon the occasion of our visit . . . he . . . sent word to those people
to treat us well in order that they might be treated well by us in turn.[63]

Even if predictions of the coming of the Europeans circulated widely,
they were not necessarily accepted without debate. If in 1898 Embu
elders were able to restrain warriors from attacking Arkell-Hardwick's
party, within five years Embu policy had shifted toward outright
resistance. Embu leaders had apparently succumbed to pressures from
the warrior class and decided that it would be possible to influence the
outcome of the coming confrontations with the whites and tilt the
balance in favor of Embu forces.[64] Instead of accepting the prophetic
call for accommodation, Embu war leaders organized to defend against
predicted attacks from the west.[65] When the British sent out feelers,
Embu leaders rejected them out of hand, provoking an attack that
resulted in a devastating defeat for the Embu people. Yet at the same
time that Embu defied the invaders, communities in the adjacent
Mbeere area not only rejected resistance but collaborated in the
extension of British power.[66] Traditional accounts trace this divergence
in policy between two societies that were culturally and linguistically
closely allied to the fact that Mbeere elders were sufficiently persuaded
of the power of the Europeans and the inevitability of conquest that they
were able to restrain the warriors. It is clear from these traditional
accounts, that the source of this persuasion was less an objective assessment of British power than it was a sense that particularly respected,
and divinely inspired, local leaders argued against resistance.[67]

Colonialism & prophecy

Just as late nineteenth-century prophecies apparently played a significant role in shaping the response of some communities to the intrusion
of Europeans and other foreigners, the transmission of traditions of
those prophecies provided those same communities a means to account
for the experience of conquest and subjugation.[68] In this process, the
recollections of various predictions fused in stereotyped traditions
focused on a single exemplary seer – for example, in Kikuyuland,
Mugo (or Cege) wa Kibiru, and among Kamba-speakers, Syokimau.[69]
At the same time, the accounts of these seers and their visions were often
incorporated, as climactic events, in popular traditions of the origins
and migration of what under colonialism came to be called tribes.[70]
Such traditions drew recent events within an interpretive framework
that admitted the miraculous and did not conceive history within

a rigidly linear pattern.[71] In his novel, *Weep Not Child*, Ngugi wa Thiong'o has one of the characters recount to his sons the history of the Kikuyu including a description of the nineteenth-century seer, Mugo wa Kibiru. When his narrative reaches the advent of colonialism he notes, 'Then came the white man as had long been prophesied by Mugo wa Kibiru . . . Mugo had told the people of the coming of the white man. He had warned the tribe. So the white man came and took the land. But at first not the whole of it.'[72]

The interpretation of the imposition of foreign rule in terms of prophecies that emphasized the inevitability of conquest and the futility of opposition explained the failure of communities to challenge European invaders and, in cases where communities did resist, the failure of that resistance. Jomo Kenyatta's account from the 1930s also explicity places Mugo wa Kibiru and his predicitons in the framework of a larger Kikuyu history. It was Mugo's 'national duty' Kenyatta asserts, 'to foretell future events and to advise the nation how to prepare for what was in store'.[73] At the same time the account represents an effort to explain the supposed ease of imperial conquest:

> Mogo wa Kebiro [sic] urged the people not to take arms against the coming strangers, that the result of such actions would be annihilation of the tribe, because the strangers would be able to kill the people from a far distance with their magical sticks which spit deadly fires . . . The great seer . . . told the warriors that the best thing would be to establish friendly relations with the coming strangers . . . When the people heard what Mogo wa Kebiro had predicted they were very disturbed and did not know what to do except wait and face the coming danger.[74]

As Godfrey Muriuki has pointed out, Kenyatta's account was very much the product of a time when it was asserted that communities in Kikuyuland had not resisted the British – an assertion that Muriuki himself has shown to be false.[75]

In their descriptions of the society that would be ushered in by foreign invasion, the seer traditions also addressed directly the circumstances of the people who speak and hear them. According to Kennell Jackson, these traditions not only 'foretell the misfortunes of the time', but 'simultaneously point to the correct behavior and communal remedies'.[76] Many of the oral accounts of the seers contain social commentary in the form of predictions of the developments that will come in the wake of foreign invasion. One Embu elder repeated a local prediction that held that 'when those will be born, they will be dancing shamelessly; children mixed with grown-ups, in-laws, and all types of shameless mixtures; those will be the ones who will never obey. That time, the land will belong to women and moles.'[77] Much the same language occurs in similar traditions collected in Kikuyuland in the 1920s and 1930s.[78]

The oral accounts of Kamba seers collected by Kennell Jackson also included bitter critiques of European rule.[79] Similarly, Kenyatta's version of the prophecy of Mugo wa Kibiru acknowledges that the 'warriors' attempt to fight the strangers and their snake would be futile', but goes on to characterize the British as men 'full of evil deeds' who would attempt to seize Kikuyu lands. In Kenyatta's account, the strangers were to be treated with suspicion and kept at arm's length.[80] Not surprisingly, Louis Leakey's description of the same prophecy, collected about the same time, contains no such warnings. Leakey claims that the seer 'told the people that when they eventually saw this great snake they were not to flee from the land, for as the result of its coming there would be new wealth'.[81] Although this version might be explained as the distortion of a colonial apologist, Leakey's informants were very likely men who, like him, saw colonialism in opportunistic terms. Both variants remind us, however, that the seer traditions were not only analytical texts but active vectors of prophecy. In his book on the Mau Mau insurrection, W. A. Wachanga writes that the same tradition recounted by Kenyatta and Leakey also contained a prediction that the Europeans would leave Kikuyuland when the buildings of the independent school at Githunguri were completed. Because in Wachanga's view, 'all Gikuyus knew this prophecy', and the colonial government was aware of this, the authorities were forced to demolish the school.[82] The Mau Mau guerilla leaders and fighters seem to have drawn on prophetic traditions to sustain their resistance in the forest.[83] In *Weep Not Child* prophecy sustains a faith among ordinary farmers that the Europeans will one day leave Kikuyuland.[84]

The continuing power of prophetic traditions is a plain sign of the persistence of prophecy itself in central Kenya societies during the twentieth century. Certainly, specialists carried on the practice of divining and advising individuals regarding their personal futures, the likelihood of good rainfall and during Mau Mau the likely success of military operations.[85] During the 1960s a great many seers were active in Nairobi, and some from Embu and Meru gained considerable reputations for their skill in predicting the outcomes of football matches.[86] Yet there are few examples of prominent seers – or seer traditions – emerging in connection with the traumatic communal experiences that marked the colonial era in Kenya. A number of seers were apparently active during the first decades of this century and there is evidence that prophecy played a role in the development of Mau Mau.[87] However, I have encountered no traditions of women or men who are claimed to have foretold, for example, the forced labour, famine and disease that accompanied the First World War, the cultural dislocation associated with the controversy over female initiation, or even Mau Mau itself.

In the absence of dramatic predictions, however, the prophetic tradition retained its fundamental basis – the notion that at times of need God guides a community by speaking directly to particular women or men. In areas of Meru, the *Mugwe* leader continued to derive his authority from the general belief that his speech was at times divinely inspired.[88] Although elsewhere in the region prophecy was not connected to formal office, the idea of divinely motivated moral leadership was widespread. As one Embu elder put it, 'God speaks to someone in the form of dreams.'[89]

During the early years of colonial rule in the Kamba-speaking districts of Kitui and Machakos a series of spirit-possession movements provided the opportunity for religious leaders to preach prophetic messages.[90] During the 1890s a movement called *Kitombo* briefly flourished and was succeeded in the early 1900s by *Kyesu* (the local term for Jesus). In 1910–1922 a third movement, *Kathambi*, attracted large numbers of people to the ritual dances that were characteristic of all three. Spirits would sometimes take possession of the dancers and transmit messages that often had millennial qualities. One of the *Kyesu* songs prophesied God's coming to earth 'to purify mankind'.[91] Another echoed the seer traditions with these words: 'I tell you a dream that you may tell the Kamba. Kamba of the Europeans, you are being sorely oppressed.'[92] Likewise, a song of the *Kathambi* movement collected in 1910 included a bold threat: 'The Europeans have gone into our country to harm us . . . We will not put up with this.'[93] In actions that echoed, on a small scale, the experience of the Xhosa cattle-killing, two *Kathambi* leaders declared the imminence of the millennium and instructed people to leave their crops in the fields and to remain in their homes.[94] Momentarily, the colonial order collapsed. People refused to pay taxes, elders declined to meet colonial officials, and many men withdrew from paid employment. Repression quickly stamped out the *Kathambi* movement, but the prophetic legacy persisted.

In 1922 in southern Machakos District a man named Ndonye wa Kauti proclaimed himself a prophet and deliberately sought a following beyond his locality. His message attracted attention among people dislocated by epidemic, hunger, economic recession, and the burdens of colonial domination.[95] He explicitly claimed the role of traditional specialist, but the message that he declared he had received from God in a dream proposed a radical solution for the crisis at hand. His followers were to destroy the sacred groves and to reject traditional beliefs, but these actions would usher in a new age in which the earth would be 'good as it was before'.[96] The new society would be free of state domination, but would utilize some foreign technology. Briefly, his message swept across the district; once he had been arrested and deported, the movement collapsed. On the one hand, Ndonye's prophecy appears to belong to a category of responses to colonialism that stretches from the cattle-killing, to the Ghost Dance in America, to the Pacific cargo cults. On the other, there is precedent for such dramatic action in the indigenous prophetic tradition. Ndonye's was a radical vision, but so too was that of the Mbeere leaders who called for 'everyone to marry' even if it meant violating the fundamental strictures against marriage within clans. Moreover, if Ndonye's message was radical its source was conventional – the voice of God that came to him in a dream.

The religious groups known as *Arathi* ('prophets') that sprang up during the 1920s and 1930s across Kikuyuland and around Mount Kenya differed substantially from the spirit-possession cults and from Ndonye's movement, but the *Arathi* leaders claimed a similar divine inspiration. Although most people rejected and even despised *Arathi* teachings, the use of the term in itself suggests that they were placed within the prophetic heritage.[97] The visions of these prophets offended many, but their experience of communion with God contained the same elements of deep sleep and removal associated with the nineteenth-century seers.[98]

Prophecy & politics

In *Weep Not, Child*, Ngugi wa Thiong'o effectively juxtaposes the traditions of the prophecy of Mugo wa Kibiru with the traditions of a new prophet, Jomo Kenyatta. When Ngotho describes the imposition of British rule to the novel's main character, his son Njoroge, he does so in the context of the tradition of Mugo wa Kibiru; later at a political rally Ngotho hears a speaker describe Kenyatta as 'the Black moses empowered by God to tell the white Pharaoh "Let my people go!"' [99] Thus, in this and other novels Ngugi subtly conveys both the continuing power of prophetic expression in the lives of rural communities in

Kikuyuland and also the ways in which nationalist politics was conducted within a prophetic idiom that merged indigenous and Christian traditions.[100] What this suggests is that the moral authority and broad legitimacy that were elements of customary prophetic vision had been incorporated in a new theory of leadership.

As the example of Ndonye wa Kauti indicates, prophecy has been no stranger to politics in Kenya. Local leaders across the region often sought out the prophet's mantle, even in circumstances that were more plainly secular. In 1930, for example, a head of the branch of the Kikuyu Central Association in Embu District, having been told in a dream to abandon European clothing, began to go barefoot and to seek out the power of local diviners in his campaign for political support.[101] Although politicians both sincere and cynical identified with the prophetic tradition, even more important to the persistence of the prophetic legacy in politics has probably been the process through which people have defined or reconstructed their leaders in prophetic terms – made their leaders prophets.[102] This phenomenon – so evident in the assemblage of fragments of legend in the local knowledge of leaders like Harry Thuku, or Muindi Mbing'u in Machakos, or Kenyatta – perpetuated a vital prophetic tradition: of divinely inspired women and men addressing the needs of communities in crisis.

Notes

Grants from the American Council of Learned Societies and the University of Texas at El Paso supported the preparation of this paper.

1. Interview: Muruakori wa Gacewa, Kagaari Location, Embu District. Unless indicated, all interviews were conducted by the author during 1977-8.
2. H. S. K Mwaniki, *Embu Historical Texts* (Nairobi, 1974), p. 32, also pp. 84, 197-8; and idem, *The Living History of Embu and Mbeere* (Nairobi, 1973), pp. 154-8; Anon. *Historia ya Utamaduni a Embu* (Teachers Advisory Centre, Kigari, Embu, 1976), 19; Satish Saberwal, *Embu of Kenya*, vol. 2 (New Haven, Conn., 1972), pp. 350-1; and Interview, Ngari wa Matha, Mbeere, Embu District.
3. J. Fadiman, *The Moment of Conquest: Meru, Kenya, 1907* (Athens, Ohio, 1979), pp. 13-14; and B. Bernardi, *The Mugwe: A Failing Prophet* (London, 1959), p. 34.
4. Jomo Kenyatta, *Facing Mount Kenya* (New York, 1965 ed.), p. 43; L. S. B. Leakey, *The Southern Kikuyu Before 1903*, Volume 3 (London, 1977), p. 1151; Godfrey Muriuki, *A History of the Kikuyu, 1500-1900* (Nairobi, 1974), p. 137; and C. W. Hobley, 'Further researches in Kikuyu and Kamba religious beliefs and customs', *J. Royal Anth. Inst.*, 41 (1911), p. 438.
5. Kennell Jackson has identified at least thirteen Kamba seers who lived during the latter part of the nineteenth century: 'An ethnohistorical study of the oral traditions of the Akamba of Kenya' (Ph.D. thesis, UCLA, 1972), p. 321, 332, also 302. See also, Joseph Muthiani, *Akamba From Within: Egalitarianism in Social Relations* (New York, 1973), p. 111; J. Forbes Munro, *Colonial Rule and the Kamba:*

Social Change in the Kenya Highlands, 1889-1939 (Oxford, 1975), p. 27; and interviews.

6. Jackson, 'Traditions of the Akamba,' p. 321.

7. Fadiman, *Moment of Conquest*, pp. 12-16; and Mwaniki, *Embu Texts* and *Living History*.

8. Thomas Spear, *Kenya's Past: An Introduction to Historical Method in Africa* (London, 1981), p. 129; and Kennell Jackson, 'The dimensions of Kamba pre-colonial history', in B. A. Ogot (ed.), *Kenya Before 1900* (Nairobi, 1976), p. 237.

9. Charles Ambler, *Kenyan Communities in the Age of Imperialism: The Central Region in the Late Nineteenth Century* (New Haven, Conn., 1988), p. 95; and Robert Edgerton, *Mau Mau: An African Crucible* (New York, 1989), p. 3.

10. An important exception is John Lonsdale's on-going exploration of Kikuyu political thought. See, for example, 'La pensée politique Kikuyu et les ideologies du mouvement Mau-Mau', *Cahiers d'études africaines*, 27 (1987), pp. 329-57; and his contribution to this volume.

11. See Douglas Johnson, 'Foretelling peace and war: modern interpretations of Ndundeng's prophecies in the Southern Sudan', in M. W. Daly (ed.), *Modernization in the Sudan* (New York, 1985), pp. 121-36.

12. Kenya National Archives (KNA), Embu District Political Record Book, EBU/45A (ii).

13. KNA, Meru District, Annual Report, 1923, MRU/1. Also, Charles Dundas, 'History of Kitui', *J. of the Royal Anth. Inst.*, 43 (1913), pp. 532, 538.

14. Ambler, *Kenyan Communities*, pp. 92-4.

15. W. S. Routledge and K. Routledge, *With a Prehistoric People: The Akikuyu of British East Africa* (London, 1910), pp. 249-50; G. St. J. Orde-Browne, *The Vanishing Tribes of Kenya* (Westport, Conn., 1970 [London, 1925]), pp. 185-8; and W. A. Chanler, *Through Jungle and Desert: Travels in Eastern Africa*, (New York, 1896), pp. 228-9.

16. Munro, *Colonial Rule and the Kamba*, p. 27; J. Fadiman, *Mountain Warriors: The Pre-Colonial Meru of Mt Kenya* (Athens, Ohio, 1976), p. 26; Chanler, *Jungle and Desert*, p. 247; and H. S. K. Mwaniki, 'A political history of the Embu, c. AD 1500-1906', (M.A. thesis, Univ. of Nairobi, 1973), pp. 270-3.

17. Jackson, 'Traditions of the Akamba', p. 315; Kenyatta, *Facing Mount Kenya*, p. 41; and Chanler, *Jungle and Desert*, p. 248.

18. J. Fadiman, 'Mountain witchcraft: supernatural practices and practitioners among the Meru of Mount Kenya', *African Studies Review*, 20 (1977), pp. 92, 95; Hobley, 'Kikuyu and Kamba religious beliefs', p. 439; Jackson, 'Traditions of the Akamba', p. 315; and Leakey, *Southern Kikuyu*, Volume 3, p. 1150.

19. John Middleton, 'Prophets and rainmakers: the agents of social change among the Lugbara', in Beidelman (ed.), *The Translation of Culture: Essays to E. E. Evans-Pritchard* (London, 1971), p. 197.

20. Munro, *Colonial Rule and the Kamba*, pp. 27-8; and Orde-Browne, *Vanishing Tribes of Kenya*, p. 54.

21. *Vanishing Tribes of Kenya*. He does include considerable information on divination, however. See pp. 185-8, and a photo of a diviner at work, following p. 209.

22. G. Lindblom, *The Akamba of British East Africa* (Uppsala, 1920).

23. Jackson, 'Kamba pre-colonial history', p. 237.

24. Dundas, 'History of Kitui', p. 530.

25. Hobley, 'Kikuyu and Kamba religious beliefs', pp. 437-9. Also, Routledge, *Prehistoric People*, p. 255.

26. Jackson, 'Traditions of the Akamba', p. 316.

27. Saberwal, *Embu of Kenya*, Volume 2, pp. 350-1.

28. E. May Crawford, *By the Equator's Snowy Peaks* (London, 1913), p. 59.

29. Routledge, *Prehistoric People*, p. 255; and Leakey, *Southern Kikuyu*, Volume 3, p. 1152.

30. Interviews: Ezekiel Njiru, Kagaari, Embu District; and Mull wa Ndulwa, Migwani, Kitui District.

31. Bernardi, *Mugwe*, p. 131.

32. Hobley, 'Kikuyu and Kamba religious beliefs', p. 437.
33. Kenyatta, *Facing Mount Kenya*, pp. 41-2.
34. Bernardi, *Mugwe*, p. ix. H. E. Lambert objected to the translation of *mugwe* as prophet because of the term's religious connotations, but he was defining religion too narrowly. 'The social and political institutions of the tribes of the Kikuyu Land Unit of Kenya', (unpublished manuscript, Univ. of Nairobi Library, 1945), p. 157.
35. Bernardi, *Mugwe*, p. 63 , also, 52-4. Bernardi's strict categorization obscures considerable overlapping in roles and defining terminology.
36. Interview: Sarimu Njavari, Mbeere, Embu District.
37. See, e.g., Chanler, *Jungle and Desert*, pp. 228-9.
38. Mwaniki, *Embu Texts*, pp. 198-9.
39. Muthiani, *Akamba From Within*, p. 111. For a similar perspective, see K. Ndeti, *Elements of Akamba Life* (Nairobi, 1972), p. 120.
40. Interview: Gaukyia Mwoca, Kan'ethia, Embu District, by Salesio Njiru.
41. Muriuki, *History of Kikuyu*, p. 137.
42. Jackson, 'Traditions of the Akamba', pp. 265-6.
43. J. L. Krapf, Journal, 5 August 1895, Church Missionary Society Archives, Birmingham University, CA5/16.
44. Ambler, *Kenyan Communities*, pp. 100-5.
45. Interview: Sarimu Njavari, Mbeere, Embu District.
46. Alfred Arkell-Hardwick, *An Ivory Trader in North Kenia*, (London, 1903), p. 92.
47. Muriuki, *History of the Kikuyu*, p. 137; and Fadiman, *Moment of Conquest*, p. 14.
48. Mwaniki, *Embu Historical Texts*. p. 197.
49. See Jackson, 'Traditions of the Akamba', pp. 302-27.
50. Interview: Muruakori wa Gacewa, Kagaari, Embu District.
51. Mwaniki, *Embu Historical Texts*, p. 24. See also Mwaniki's early paper, "The Impact of British Rule in Embu, 1906-1923," History Dept., Univ. of Nairobi, 1968.
52. Muthiani, *Akamba from Within*, p. 111.
53. Jackson, 'Traditions of the Akamba', p. 321.
54. Mwaniki, *Embu Historical Texts*, p. 24; Fadiman, *Moment of Conquest*, p. 13; and Bernardi, *Mugwe*, p. 34.
55. Ambler, *Kenyan Communities*, pp. 79-80.
56. Mwaniki, *Embu Texts*, pp. 198-9.
57. Interview: Muruakori wa Gacewa, Kagaari, Embu District; Mwaniki, *Living History*, p. 156; Fadiman, *Moment of Conquest*, pp. 13-14; Bernardi, *Mugwe*, p. 34; Leakey, *Southern Kikuyu*, Volume 3, p. 1151; and Kenyatta, *Facing Mount Kenya*, p. 43.
58. Interview: Gaukyia Mwoca, Kan'ethia, Embu District, by Salesio Njiru; Mwaniki, *Embu Historical Texts*, p. 197; idem, *Living History*, p. 156; and Fadiman, *Moment of Conquest*, p. 15.
59. Fadiman, *Moment of Conquest*, p. 16.
60. Chanler, *Jungle and Desert*, p. 248.
61. Arkell-Hardwick, *Ivory Trader*, p. 69.
62. Ibid., pp. 72-3.
63. Chanler, *Jungle and Desert*, p. 248.
64. Interview: Gaukyia wa Mwoca, Kan'ethia, Embu District, by Salesio Njiru; Mwaniki, *Embu Historical Texts*, p. 198; and Fadiman, *Moment of Conquest*, p. 15.
65. Mwaniki, *Living History*, p. 156, note 63.
66. Interviews: Gatema Muyovi, Mbeere, Embu District; Maringa wa Maunge, Mbeere, Embu District; and Manunga wa Gatumbi, Mbeere, Embu District.
67. Interview, Gatema Muyovi, Mbeere, Embu District. See also Ambler, *Kenyan Communities*, p. 148.
68. Jackson, 'Traditions of the Akamba', pp. 303, 317-9. However, Jackson's assertion that prophetic traditions were 'the conscious tool of community political judgment' seems too strong.

69. Ibid., pp. 304–5.
70. Ibid., pp. 317–19; Bernardi, *Mugwe*, pp. 52–4, 63, 186–7; and Interview: Muruakori wa Gacewa, Kagaari, Embu District.
71. See, for example, Ndeti, *Elements of Akamba Life*, p. 120; Mwaniki, *Living History*.
72. Ngugi wa Thiong'o, *Weep Not Child*, rev. ed. (Oxford, 1987 [1964]), p. 25.
73. Kenyatta, *Facing Mount Kenya*, p. 41.
74. Ibid., p. 43. See Leakey, *Southern Kikuyu*, Volume 3, p. 1151 for an account of the same prophecy.
75. Muriuki, *History of the Kikuyu*, pp. 138.
76. Jackson, 'Traditions of the Akamba', p. 302.
77. Mwaniki, *Embu Historical Texts*, pp. 24, 84.
78. Kenyatta, *Facing Mount Kenya*, p. 43.
79. Jackson, 'Traditions of the Akamba', p. 305.
80. Kenyatta, *Facing Mount Kenya*, p. 43.
81. Leakey, *Southern Kikuyu*, Volume 3, p. 1151.
82. H. K. Wachanga, *Swords of Kirinyaga: The Fight for Land and Freedom* (Nairobi, 1975), pp. 20–1.
83. Ibid., Editorial Introduction by Robert Whittier; and Edgerton, *Mau Mau*, pp. 121–2.
84. Ngugi, *Weep Not, Child*, pp. 31–2.
85. See, for example, Dundas, 'History of Kitui', p. 530; and Edgerton, *Mau Mau*, pp. 121–2.
86. Andrew Hake, *African Metropolis: Nairobi's Self-Help City* (Nairobi, 1977), pp. 217–24.
87. Wachanga, *Swords of Kirinyaga*, pp. 43–4; Hobley, 'Kikuyu and Kamba religious beliefs', pp. 437–9; and Dundas, 'History of Kitui', p. 530.
88. Bernardi, *Mugwe*, p. 60.
89. Interview: Ezekiel Njiru, Kagaari, Embu District.
90. This discussion is drawn from Munro, *Colonial Rule and the Kamba*, pp. 111–17.
91. Quoted in Ibid., p. 115. Collected originally by G. Lindblom about 1910.
92. Ibid., p. 115.
93. Quoted in ibid., p. 115.
94. Ibid., p. 115. For the history of the cattle-killing, see J. B. Peires, *The Dead Will Arise: Nongqawuse and the Great Xhosa Cattle-Killing Movement of 1856-7* (Berkeley and London, 1989).
95. See Munro, *Colonial Rule and the Kamba*, pp. 118–20; and Robert Tignor, *The Colonial Transformation of Kenya: The Kamba, Kikuyu, and Maasai from 1900 to 1939* (Princeton, 1976), pp. 334–6.
96. Quoted in Munro, *Colonial Rule and the Kamba*, p. 119.
97. David P. Sandgren, *Christianity and the Kikuyu: Religious Divisions and Social Conflict* (New York, 1989), pp. 84, 121–36; KNA, Embu District, Annual Reports, 1930, 1931, 1932; Meru District, Annual Report, 1941; Central Province, Annual Report, 1930.
98. Sandgren cites the example of a traditional seer, who was hostile to educated people but somewhat more sympathetic to the Arathi. *Christianity and the Kikuyu*, p. 84, n. 25. A comparison of Sandgren's description of Arathi prophetic experiences with those that Kenyatta describes for traditionalists reveals clear similarities. see also KNA, Embu District, Annual Report, 1931.
99. Ngugi, *Weep Not Child*, p. 58, also p. 38.
100. See Lonsdale, 'La pensée politique Kikuyu', esp. p. 245.
101. KNA, Embu District, Annual Report, 1930.
102. See the discussion by Tim Allen of the appeal of Alice Lakwena and the Holy Spirit movement in Uganda. 'Understanding Alice: Uganda's Holy Spirit Movement in context', *Africa*, 61, 3 (1991).

Eleven

The Prayers
of Waiyaki

Political Uses
of the Kikuyu Past[1]

JOHN LONSDALE

Waiyaki & Mugo

This is a study in the changing uses of a heroic past and the continuity of a prophetic tradition.[2] It is a story of two stories, each with a Kikuyu hero. One, Waiyaki wa – or son of – Hinga, was born in the 1840s and died in 1892, in British custody but before colonial rule, to be buried far from home. The other, Cege wa Kibiru, nicknamed Mugo or man of power, was born about 1850. He may have died in 1908, six years after his district had come under British control. Some say he could not be buried: he had gone up to heaven, leaving not even flattened grass to mark his parting.[3] Memories of Waiyaki and Mugo then became a medium wherein men who are themselves now dead imagined a world in which they exercised moral agency and over which they wielded some control. For their stories provoked argument; the dilemmas of the present demanded guidance from the past. Outcomes became precedents; precedents imparted precepts. In this way historical speculation often becomes a source of political theory.

The story of the stories falls into four overlapping parts. Each added its own store of historical allusion to the general vocabulary of political debate. Three episodes entered Kikuyu public discourse between the wars. The first explored issues of political and military honour, the second the question of landed property and the third the conflicts of clan and generation. Of the three chapters the first two focused on Waiyaki alone; the third paired him with Mugo, reaching a grisly finale in the 1950s. All the many references to Waiyaki and, less frequently, to Mugo helped men to clarify the nature of power and subjection, invent a Kikuyu tribe and then to argue about how to fight the British. In an unfinished fourth chapter Waiyaki's memory is now helping to make modern Kenya.

The power of these tales about the past came from belief that Waiyaki's deeds and Mugo's words taught one how to face the future. Waiyaki had no spiritual authority in life. Of disputed ancestry – as most Kikuyu heroes must be, given the immigrant origin and trans-ethnic marriage alliances of their forebears – in youth he was a great warrior and in his prime a wealthy spokesman, a *muthamaki*, for his subclan or *mbari*. His *mbari* land, on the southern Kikuyu border, lay on what is now the western edge of Kenya's capital city, Nairobi. Kikuyu debate focused on his last years, from October 1890 to August 1892. At first their spokesmen represented this as a time when the British betrayed his artless friendship; only later did some openly recall a widespread private opinion that Waiyaki had resisted this foul play with force. Mugo was quite different, a diviner, *mundo mugo*, and a seer, *murathi*; both an expert and a man of God. Kikuyu healers were often such general practitioners but, as in western medicine, specialists charged higher fees.[4] He was also a prophet, not merely a seer of the future but a medium of God's warnings, obedience to which would save posterity. A foundling of the wild, his parents were unknown; his foster-father Kibiru lived 40 miles north of Waiyaki's place. Mugo the diviner was consulted by the afflicted and by men about to go to war but is best remembered for his prophetic dreams. He did not normally question their revelations. But then God forewarned him of red strangers with peeled, frog-like skins, dressed like butterflies and carrying deadly firesticks. Their monstrous snake would stretch from sea to sea, vomiting forth people and wealth as it went. Unusually, Mugo wrestled with God at this ominous news. On waking, he warned Kikuyu to keep aloof; they must neither resist nor welcome the strangers but learn from them. Their advent would be a moral test. They would bring social decay; but if Kikuyu renewed themselves and learned the secret of the invaders' power the latter would in the end depart.[5]

A contrast between their two stories may help us to understand how popular history is made. For Waiyaki's deeds were reinterpreted over time and their lessons changed; Mugo's words were not, and their changeless meaning came to monopolize the prophetic voice. In the 1930s people remembered three former seers of red strangers; twenty

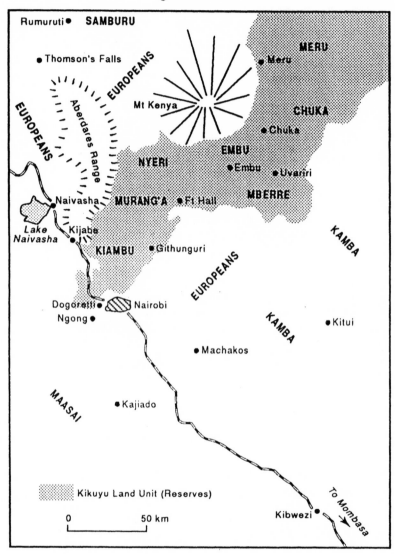

Map 7   Central Kenya

years later they appear to have recalled Mugo alone.[6] But while they took his prophecy as fixed, a subject people facing the rival demands of reform and resistance simply had to debate their past and search it for new precedents. There were three good reasons why they should do so by reconsidering the myth of Waiyaki rather than that of Mugo. First, the initial public version of Waiyaki's story deliberately suppressed divisive memories of conquest that could always be revived; Mugo's enigmatic words on the other hand could authorize almost any peaceful political initiative. Second, as will be explained in the third chapter of his story, Waiyaki was situated in linear or progressive historical time while Mugo was associated with recursive, regenerative or redemptive time, with moral renewal rather than political change. And their stories were, finally, subject to different rules of evidence. True, the sources for both were mostly oral, able to meet the changing needs of successive prophetic moments.[7] But literate Kikuyu had written texts as well and these contrasted with each other. For while British memoirs disagreed about Waiyaki, Mugo became assimilated to biblical tradition. This gave him a timeless antiquity; possibly some biographical detail, by analogy with the herdboy-dreamer Joseph; and a textual stability.[8] How Kikuyu searched their past for inspiration was thus governed by a triple tension, between the living claims of endurance and struggle, between linear and recursive ideas of time, and between the mutability of heroic reputation and the fixity of prophetic text.

Scholars have told Waiyaki and Mugo's stories,[9] but not the story of how their stories were told.[10] They have hitherto been seen as timeless calls to ethnic virtue, inspiring to all Kikuyu. But they are not as simple as that, for four reasons. Kikuyu leaders doubted prophets, questioned the claims of ethnicity, disputed political choice and managed to suppress internal – but not external – dissident editions of myth until political frustration unlocked their secret knowledge in the 1940s. The first complication, Kikuyu scepticism, is a necessary introduction to the argument; the others are part of the story.

Kikuyu, like other people, feared the future, paid for its divination and yet mistrusted their diviners; they thought them, rather like professors, to be mere slaves to fashionable theory.[11] Since they believed their intellectuals were likely to be anti-social, their calling had to be expensively trained and constantly proven.[12] Diviners were subject to scrutiny, their expertise more public than secret. Clients shared in the divining process and could challenge its findings.[13] Prophets were divisive; early in this century two reportedly founded short-lived cults, which suggests that their zealots faced general indifference or hostility. Popular opinion charged one of them with malice.[14] We may then reasonably assume that Mugo's word was not unquestioned in life; nor was it, at the time, the only word.[15]

Nor, to raise the second complication, did Kikuyu have one identity in Mugo's day; their myriad petty leaders had no unified power or loyalty. Both British and Kikuyu later invented such 'tribal' identity in order to account for alien rule. The former saw their conquest as necessary and its bloodshed therefore without guilt. For that they blamed an ethnic stereotype, a treacherous tribe; but they also left evidence of an earlier, more favourable view. Kikuyu, needing to explain subjection without despair, attributed it to white deceit rather than British superiority, and went on to debate what sort of subject people they could honourably be. All used the past to create ethnic character and political theory; the story of the stories tells how cultural craftsmen moulded popular minds. One of these belonged to a colonial ruling class, the other to leaders of a subject tribe.[16] To the British, Waiyaki's story proved their right to rule. For Kikuyu, Mugo and Waiyaki personified a past that promised collective power rather than fratricidal faction; they made struggle against the British imaginable. Internal disputes nonetheless made the struggle bloody. In the Mau Mau war Kikuyu divided against each other under different prophetic traditions. From this division they learned in 1954, possibly for the first time, how Waiyaki had been buried. Hitherto his chroniclers, white and black, had focused on his exile. All agreed that it had been caused by bad faith. The question was, whose?

Patrons & clients

Leaders deploy the wordy medium of power in political theatre. That is why my story of the stories starts with the official drama intended, above all others, to reconcile Kenya Africans to British rule. In 1932 London appointed a Land Commission to calm Kenya's constant quarrels by drawing up an agreed boundary between 'white highlands' and African reserves. The commissioners set out on a mobile enquiry into oral history. Thousands observed the itinerant drama of imperial solicitude. The chairman, Judge Morris Carter, ensured a due formality, but the majesty of the process and the weight of its 3,500 printed pages of evidence failed in their dramatic purpose. Africans refused to accept white settler rights; some Kikuyu farmers rejected Carter's recommendations.[17] Their spokesmen had already drawn a distinction between land and legitimacy. For the lesson that Kikuyu drew from the first, public version of Waiyaki's story was that white settlement called in question British honour and with it their right to rule.

The commissioners met Waiyaki's ghost soon enough. Forty years after his death, in November 1932, they opened their second day of Kikuyu hearings at Kiambu, the southernmost district centre of Kikuyuland. Waiganjo wa Ndotono, a former headman and returned political detainee,[18] rose to speak. Through Dr Louis Leakey, the locally born interpreter,[19] he opened with a history that condemned the present.

> I want to speak first about Wayaki. Once we had an elder named Wayaki. When the Europeans first came they asked Wayaki for permission to build in his area, and he gave them permission to build right near his village. Having built on his land they then . . . moved him right away. They deported him and he died in a strange land. My impression is that he was moved because he objected to his land being taken.

Waiganjo understood political theatre; so did Judge Carter. He had been a magistrate in Kenya 30 years earlier, for only a year. He had since served in Uganda but remembered enough of the British myth of Kenya's origin to confute Waiganjo. To this end he brought another hero on stage, white this time, an early British official. Surely, he suggested, 'Wayaki was deported because he tried to kill Mr Purkiss at the time the Kikuyu attacked Dagoretti Fort.' Waiganjo thought that proved his point. Why else would the British take the rest of Waiyaki's land after they deported him? They were clearly angry that he had refused to allow them more control over his land than had previously been agreed. In a popular parable Waiganjo likened government to the parasitic fig tree that grew fatter and stronger by suffocating the smaller trees which first gave it life.[20]

This first argument about Waiyaki went to the heart of Kenya's racial conflict. Kikuyu witnesses insisted that the landlord Waiyaki had befriended vagrant whites; his was the civilizing mission, not theirs. Other landowners also welcomed early settlers as clients-in-friendship, *ahoi*, whose occupation rights never amounted to property. Further, Waiyaki's patronage of the first white official, Captain Lugard, in 1890 had made the Kikuyu Britain's allies; they were not a conquered people. Queen Victoria was their witness. Lugard, an officer of her Imperial British East Africa Company (IBEAC) was Waiyaki's blood-brother. But Kikuyu generosity had been abused; the Kenya government had broken faith with both Waiyaki and the Queen, after she too had died, by taking land for white settlers. It was up to Carter's royal commission to repair British honour by restoring Kikuyu land.[21]

The myth of the just Queen was no naive delusion; Kikuyu knew their legal history. No IBEAC treaty had conveyed title to land. Its successor, the East Africa Protectorate (EAP) took such powers only in 1902, the year of Victoria's death and a decade after Waiyaki's. British dominion over African land grew again when the EAP became Kenya Colony in 1920. Government had taken 120 square miles (or six per cent) of Kikuyuland for whites to buy or lease between 1902 and 1907.[22] To believe, with Carter, that this alienation came too late to have anything to do with Waiyaki was to miss the two main points of Waiganjo's story.[23] First, Kikuyu householders were proprietors; it had been by private right that Waiyaki loaned Lugard land. Secondly, the Anglo-Kikuyu balance of power had been upset by his exile. In speaking of Waiyaki, therefore, Kikuyu both invoked the rights of property against state-sponsored white settlement and demanded a return to the past that Waiyaki had known, a colonial order that gave such rights their due.

In this first chapter of his story Kikuyu took Waiyaki's proprietorship for granted and, in two polemical contexts, focused on his power. In the 1920s their politicians, some of them official chiefs, attacked colonial oppression and, secondly, quarrelled with the missionary suppliers of their educational demand. Waiyaki's story answered both concerns with a dynastic theory of political legitimacy. First, it revealed how colonial treachery had undone the old Anglo-Kikuyu alliance. This past equality had depended on the patronage of lineage heads; today's oppression rested on the servility of client chiefs. British deceit had facilitated this Kikuyu disloyalty. Once the whites had deposed Waiyaki they could replace dynastic allies with pliant puppets, men of no pedigree who owed all to white favour. The British coup of 1892 that converted their clientage into control had been abetted by one Kinyanjui, who had died in 1929 as paramount chief – a British title – of southern Kikuyu. Some said that he had been Waiyaki's servant; that he was therefore another asset, like land, which the latter had loaned to the British. These had then rewarded Kinyanjui's service to them, first as porter and then as military scout against other Kikuyu, by making him chief in his master's stead. People also accused him of using his office as a property agency, selling other men's land to his Kikuyu allies as much as to whites. In reality his rise owed more to British weakness and his own fortitude in sustaining clients through the dreadful famine of the late 1890s but, to his enemies, he epitomized all chiefs who 'sold land for office'.[24] Perhaps Kenyatta had Kinyanjui in mind when he quoted *Lamentations* in his newspaper *Muigwithania*, 'The Reconciler': 'Servants have ruled over us: there is none to deliver us out of their hand', a use of the Bible that so incensed the governor that he wanted the paper banned.[25] Waiyaki, by contrast, had given whites land in friendship, redeemable on demand. Being of high Kikuyu status he had no need of British office; needing him, whites had been unable to take Kikuyu land.[26] If Waiyaki's story was a plea to the commission it was also a reproach to chiefs.

By 1930 many Kikuyu also opposed their missionaries, the Church of Scotland Mission (CSM) especially, on the issue of female circumcision, clitoridectomy.[27] The CSM had called on church members to renounce what whites saw as a cruel, degrading rite. Kikuyu Christians disagreed between themselves. Opponents of the ban saw circumcision as the key to female discipline and male authority. What brought Waiyaki into the quarrel was a general belief that white intransigence was embittering a domestic Kikuyu debate whose natural instinct was for compromise.[28] Only the removal of external pressure would permit proper discussion of so intimate an issue. To regain this freedom of decision Kikuyu set out to give dramatic force to the tacit legal position, which was that missionaries were clients of each *mbari* on their 'outschool' properties. Clients could not dictate terms to patrons. On both sides Kikuyu thus extended dynastic theory to church history. Both the Kikuyu Central Association (KCA), opposed to the mission ban, and the Kikuyu Loyal Patriots, an association of chiefs who accepted it, reminded Judge Carter that Waiyaki's son Munyua had replicated his father's generosity to the state in his own dealings with the Scottish mission. He had sold and granted them over 70 acres of *mbari* land. His brother, Benjamin Githeiya, was one of the first Kikuyu Presbyterian ministers, ordained in 1926.[29] Kikuyu surely ought to have more say in the colonial and missionary enterprise.

Missionaries themselves showed how dynastic property right had once been upheld and could again be restored. In 1898 the CSM had had to respect Munyua's refusal to sell a further 30 acres. Nonetheless, the Scots had got 3,000 acres without Kikuyu assent in 1905, under the new Crown Lands Ordinance. This estate, part leased, part bought from government, had never prospered. Now, in response to popular resentment and the arguments of Waiyaki's Presbyterian grandsons, the CSM wished to return most of the land to its former owners. Carter approved. He disarmed settler criticism of this reversion of 'white' land to Africans, first by arguing that the mission estate was an anomaly and then by preventing its return from setting a precedent. He noted that under the ordinance existing African residents could live undisturbed within white farm boundaries on those parts of the land they continued to cultivate. While white farmers had normally bought out these rights, the CSM had not. A reversion of title was thus within the unintended spirit of the law. More generally – for reasons to be found in the second part of Waiyaki's story – he recommended that all other such residual black rights to white land be extinguished, subject to the provision of alternative land elsewhere. The mbari ya Hinga, named after Waiyaki's father, was the chief beneficiary of Carter's approval of the CSM's wishes; many lesser lineages suffered from the state's acceptance of his wider solution.

The story of the mission land, alienated without consent and now restored to Waiyaki's line, confirmed the dynastic theory that the politics of influence could revive past alliance. Attractive to the big men of propertied *mbari*, it was irrelevant to those whose rights on white farmland were extinguished. And dynastic politics became actively hostile towards the many more households whose client tenures within Kikuyu began to be repudiated by *mbari* patrons anxious to plough up more acres for private profit. The mbari ya Hinga's tenants, who far outnumbered the right-holders, were most reluctant to exchange an absentee landlord, the mission, for an all too active one, Waiyaki's corporate heirs.[30] Twenty years later many more questioned dynastic theory. However heroic past leaders may have been, their *mbari* rights, abused by the British and then exploited by their descendants, could no longer protect the majority. These, expropriated right-holders on white farms or dispossessed domestic *ahoi*, had to look to another past for hope.

Waiyaki & Purkiss

In telling this first part of Waiyaki's story, no Kikuyu between the wars publicly admitted what they privately knew and Carter insisted, that their hero had, when drunk, drawn his sword on a white official. Kikuyu almost silenced their memory of British conquest as a whole, too, with its long lists of dead, captured cattle and burnt-out villages. Their myth of subjection acknowledged neither Waiyaki's violence against his white clients nor these heavy Kikuyu defeats; both memories might risk loss of rights. White treachery must be allowed no justification. The British, moralizing the existing order rather than imagining one that might have been, had no qualms about the minor 'punitive expeditions' that had, as they saw it, skirmished with the Kikuyu.[31] Their own myth of conquest – and Carter's instant recall all those years later confirms its mythical status – told them that the fickle Kikuyu had had to be taught a lesson. But they had once disagreed as to that. They left three firsthand accounts of Waiyaki's last years. Kikuyu always quoted the then Captain Lugard, who had not witnessed the final act. As a young man he had admired Waiyaki and the Kikuyu for their friendly intelligence and industry; by 1930 he had become an imperial elder statesman whose goodwill might matter.[32] The British who now ruled Kenya quoted Captain Macdonald, a critic of both Lugard and the Kikuyu, or the later memories of his lieutenant, Herbert Austin. Tribal and colonial political theory thus took their origin in the self-justifications of personal rivalry.

Lugard and Macdonald each used their campaign memoirs to explain why he was not to blame for the collapse of the 1890 Anglo-Kikuyu alliance. Both wrote to impress a British public; Kikuyu were their supporting players, a role that Kikuyu accounts later reversed. Lugard published first. His seeming respect for the Kikuyu was in reality condescension; he saw them as dependent creatures of British wills. He himself was a man of his word; Waiyaki showed his mettle by recognizing this and acting accordingly; he too kept his word. Both had sworn a treaty of blood-brotherhood that permitted Lugard to build a fort at Dagoretti, on Waiyaki's land. This being so, the later hostilities must be the fault not of Lugard's Kikuyu allies but of those of his British successors who lacked the manly qualities that enabled someone like him to bring peace beyond the frontier. They knew neither how to treat with 'savage tribes' nor when to stand firm; they also failed to control their African subordinates who, drunk and disorderly, raped and pillaged friendly Kikuyu. 'Vacillation and indecision' caused vastly more bloodshed than 'the strong hand and the personality which commands obedience'. Kikuyu had burned and looted Dagoretti in 1891. Even had Waiyaki led them in this venture, Lugard refused to hold his ally responsible: his treaty commitment had clearly been undermined by British weakness and stupidity. Lugard scorned one successor in particular, Purkiss, who by 1892 was in charge of the new company base, Fort Smith, built nearer to Waiyaki's village than Dagoretti had been. Kikuyu never knew his mind; they became 'hopelessly disaffected' when dealing with men without 'decision and character'.[33]

Macdonald had more respect for the Kikuyu; they were savages with minds of their own. Writing three years later and, as it happened, after 'poor Purkiss' had died, he defended his young protégé's reputation by attacking both Lugard's judgement and Waiyaki's honour. Lugard had clearly been duped by that 'amiable old scoundrel'; there never was an Anglo-Kikuyu understanding. He had also shown a poor eye for ground in siting his Dagoretti fort, impossible to supply with food or water without risking ambush; and had there left his lieutenant, George Wilson, with too weak a garrison. These unsoldierly errors had tempted the Kikuyu to revert to treacherous type as soon as Lugard had marched on to Uganda. They had twice forced Wilson to abandon Dagoretti. With this record of misdeeds behind him it was equally clear that the wily Waiyaki, not that 'capital fellow' Purkiss, was responsible for their fatal fight on 14 August 1892.

Macdonald's case against Waiyaki opened with the presumption, unconfirmed in the oral record, that he was related by marriage to the Waguruguru, 'the westerners'. These had killed Purkiss's righthand man, his Swahili sergeant Makhtub, when out, Macdonald reported, on a food-buying mission. The leading 'friendly', Kinyanjui, urged Purkiss to punish the murderers before Kikuyu were tempted into a 'general rising'. At this moment Macdonald arrived, en route from Uganda down to the Indian Ocean port of Mombasa in the ill-tempered company of his senior, Lugard. The latter was in a hurry to get home, to rebut criticism of his conduct in the recent Buganda civil war, and would not wait. Macdonald therefore took command of the expedition to avenge Purkiss on the Waguruguru. Guided by Kinyanjui, the British-led column of Indian and African troops killed many people and burned villages but captured almost no cattle, the Kikuyu store of wealth. Purkiss suspected Waiyaki of warning his in-laws, who had hidden their stock in the forest accordingly. The old rogue came to the fort, Macdonald said, to taunt Purkiss on his failure when the latter returned, frustrated and footsore, from harrying the Waguruguru. They quarrelled. Purkiss first punched Waiyaki or Waiyaki first drew his sword. Purkiss seized the weapon and caught its owner a glancing blow on the head. The other British officers subdued Waiyaki, who spent a cold and humiliating night chained to the flagpole. Next day Macdonald charged him with attempted murder. Waiyaki's only reported defence was drink. British accounts differ on whether he was sentenced to exile or remanded for trial in Mombasa; either way, Kikuyu were dumbfounded by such leniency. Refusing the ransom offered by Waiyaki's family, the British marched their ally, now their prisoner, away. Warriors gathered as if to dispute the escort's passage, hesitated and withdrew. Waiyaki died several days' march later, probably of his wound, at Kibwezi, half way to the coast and the site of the first Scottish mission, soon to be abandoned in favour of Kikuyu. Two years later almost to the day, in a symmetry noted by both British and Kikuyu, Purkiss also died at Kibwezi, of blackwater fever. Perhaps Waiyaki's spirit had called him home; they were buried close enough together.[34]

Both Kikuyu dynastic and British colonial theories had to explain this crisis of conquest. Each papered over their own side's differences and blamed the other. Kikuyu had more divisions to hide. Waiyaki's own *mbari* was split; it had hostile neighbours; and seniors and juniors generally, household heads and warriors, took opposite views on external trade. By the 1930s some Kikuyu had imagined a generous and peaceable Waiyaki, untroubled by such conflict, as the best external defence against the British. Probably much earlier – but I cannot date this domestic Kikuyu negotiation – others had constructed the same beneficent patron to camouflage internal divisions that, if publicly aired, would have embarrassed the mbari ya Hinga in its clannish efforts to use colonial power. Kikuyu called such suppressed knowledge *kirira*; it was part of the common currency of social control. Collusion between elders to conceal conflict prevented it from getting out of hand.[35]

In reality, Kikuyu differed on their British problem. First, Waiyaki's hospitality was disputed within his *mbari*, mainly on the question of land. The terms on which he allowed the British to build their two successive forts are unclear; they seem to have been controversial from the start. The written evidence is no better than the oral. On 11 October 1890, Lugard recorded in his diary the purchase of Dagoretti for goods to the value of 14 goats. Waiyaki made his 'sole property' over to the IBEAC as its 'entire property for ever . . ., to build on or cultivate or otherwise as they see fit'. But back in England Lugard became uncharacteristically vague, writing in his memoir only of 'a present' given for 'ground'.[36] Perhaps he remembered that the Company had only doubtful right to land in the East African interior. No record survives of the negotiations for Fort Smith; by Macdonald's account they were pretty brisk. If Lugard became studiedly imprecise, Waiyaki almost certainly thought his two deals with Lugard and Smith unfinished, whatever their legal status. For while Kikuyu recognized property they saw it as a social rather than market relation. Sales followed an evasive etiquette in which purchaser entertained vendor over a pot of beer. Lugard, who thought a fondness for drink the sole Kikuyu weakness, would not have indulged Waiyaki thus – or made no mention of it. Forty years on, Kenyatta was as vague as

Lugard; Waiyaki might have granted *muhoi* right to cultivate or perhaps *muthami* right to build. But again, either prospective dependant ought to brew sugar-cane beer for his patron, and to the British beer spelt trouble.[37] Nor do the goods given to Waiyaki disclose the nature of the deal; they could as well have opened relations as closed a bargain.[38]

Waiyaki had good cause to present the British as clients rather than land-purchasers; his kin had still more reason after his death. For the second site, Fort Smith, was not unequivocally his to sell. It was later claimed by another *mbari*; or it may have been the local dance-ground.[39] And, whatever the truth of that, Kikuyu deplored the British cultivation of the fort's land. Passing officials marvelled at the variety of vegetables that Purkiss served at table.[40] None of them considered the view of the Kikuyu, who later recalled the fort's kitchen garden with anger. It had deprived them of a market and flouted what Waiyaki had apparently given out as the terms of the British tenancy, which were to build, not plant.[41] Then in 1899, seven years after his death, famine carried off large numbers of Kikuyu. Many blamed the huge food purchases made by the fort to supply the railway construction labour, in the midst of drought; it was *ng'aragu ya ruraya*, the famine of Europe. Waiyaki's heirs would scarcely have admitted that the calamity stemmed from a rash sale of land on his part. Some did indeed call Waiyaki *ngamini*, over-generous, but his own *mbari* would have protested to the contrary, that it was the British who had overstepped the bounds of clientship.[42]

Labour, secondly, was as contentious an issue as land, and involved Waiyaki's neighbours. The British came up from the coast with Swahili soldiers and porters but also needed Kikuyu builders and porters, both locally and to fetch supplies from Mombasa. Kikuyu later had two contrary traditions about this work. Dynastic history held that Waiyaki had, as was his right, offered his clients' labour to the British in the spirit of alliance. The dissident view was apparently excluded from public discussion for 70 years, until after Kenya's independence. This recalled British demands for forced labour, *kiaro*, to which Kikuyu reacted first by flight and then by armed resistance, led in the end by Waiyaki himself. Lugard could have been cited in support of either view since, by his account, his immediate successor Wilson had both 'compelled' 300 men to rebuild Dagoretti after its sack and 'enlisted' 200 Kikuyu porters, apparently voluntarily. The ambiguity is most plausibly resolved by Kikuyu division. The British garrison was small, varying between 50 and 150 men; it is not unlikely that the freely enlisted Kikuyu, who as warriors used to keep public order by vigorous

means,[43] compelled the labour of others. There are indirect suggestions of this in the oral record. It looks as if Waiyaki used his clients
to make weaker neighbours meet the demands of his British friendship.
His heirs cultivated a different memory. This was that Kinyanjui,
the first Kikuyu head porter in British employ, had gone out in
client-service to Waiyaki and had thereby prospered, as clients of a
good patron should – and remember him accordingly. Dynastic labour
theory thus reminded the British that they owed their main instrument
of rule, Kinyanjui, to Waiyaki's patronage; and chiefs, that government
was not their only master. Both purposes required Waiyaki to be a
generous man of peace.[44]

Dynastic history had, nonetheless, much fighting to forget; one loses
count of the skirmishes. The British were forgetful too; it was easier to
blame Kikuyu treachery than to examine Lugard's argument that they
had failed to control their own men. But why did Kikuyu not simply
reverse Lugard's view and publicly justify Waiyaki as a defender of
his people? One reason must be that in recalling resistance to whites
it was difficult to forget violence between Kikuyu. That judgement
raises a third issue, that of Waiyaki's power and self-interest. He was
not, as whites supposed, a chief. Kikuyu had no chiefs, nobody with
the political or military power to impose wide obedience or general
policy. Their political culture was intensely opportunist, not least on the
southern frontier which expanded by inter-*mbari* competition for client
workers and warriors. Waiyaki is said to have increased his following
by giving asylum to famine refugees. In the 1880s up to 5,000 people
may have trusted in his protection; he in turn felt able to grant safe
passage over a radius of some ten miles.[45] But that made him only one
rich elder among many. If he had many client spearmen so did others.
His authority rested neither on deference nor on unchallenged force
but on negotiation, whether with other Hinga elders or, through his
age-set and marriage connections, with the big men of nearby *mbari*,
or even with his clients.

Informed Kikuyu explanation of colonial warfare could not avoid
exposing these political weaknesses, just as Lugard blamed British
failures in control. And Waiyaki's weakness could be all too clearly
measured against his self-interest. For while Kikuyu hated British
brutality they competed to use white power. Waiyaki had tried to retain
his early monopoly on gun imports and the export of food,[46] but failed.
The British struck terms with other *mbari* leaders for food supply; still
others learned to use white – that is, Swahili – guns in local quarrels.
Sergeant Makhtub, whose death led to Waiyaki's, had gone out not to

buy British rations but to help a Kikuyu friend recover his dowry after his wife had left him.[47] Perhaps Kikuyu suppressed Waiyaki's fight with Purkiss mainly because, as if to crown Waiyaki's failures, both guides on the foray to punish Makhtub's Waguruguru killers were deserters from his cause. One, Kinyanjui, had (perhaps) been his client; more agonisingly, the other, Muiruri, was an age-mate from another *mbari*. He and Waiyaki were once so close that Lugard thought them brothers.[48] If Kikuyu betrayal helped whites to kill Kikuyu then resistance to the British was better not talked about. It became *kirira*. Yet without the Waguruguru affray there was no obvious motive for the battle between Waiyaki and Purkiss. In the public edition of his story therefore, Waiyaki did not fight.

Privately, Kikuyu knew they had resisted; they also told themselves that Waiyaki had forbidden his warriors to make any foolhardy rescue bid as he was marched away into exile; he had even threatened to curse them. Here was the final issue of conquest. Waiyaki was an elder; warriors were juniors. Lying at the heart of Kikuyu society, generation conflict became a persuasive explanation of subjection. Elders had the first say in the matter. Parents in the 1930s – who resented the new insubordinations that literacy and migrant labour made available to their young – thought that impatient warriors of 40 years earlier must have been the main threat to Waiyaki's and other elders' good relations with the British. Kinyanjui had not been the only warrior to lead the British out against rival *mbari*, and some youths had become bandits, possibly nicknamed *mau mau*, the greedy eaters, during the great hunger of the late 1890s.[49] Nor were these memories merely a projection of the elders' self-interest. Waiyaki's men had indeed protected travellers against other Kikuyu; he had pointedly returned property which the Company had left in his safe keeping during its retreat from Dagoretti; and had arranged a frightful display of white firepower against Kikuyu shields.[50] Waiyaki, it is clear from both the contemporary white record and later Kikuyu memory, was one, perhaps the strongest, among many frontier elders who had a commercial interest in peace with the red strangers. Facing competition from other *mbari* to trade grain and vegetables in return for Anglo-Swahili power, he was also plagued by bachelor warriors for whom the newcomers were merely a sport or temptation. Perhaps it was simply as a land-colonizing elder that Waiyaki was most convincingly and necessarily a man of peace.[51]

Both Kikuyu and British polished up their myths of Waiyaki. Pointing out the moral of dynastic history to a British audience in 1938,

Kenyatta adroitly avoided all mention of Kikuyu resistance by quoting Lugard's condemnation of British pillage. His one reference to Waiyaki made none to Purkiss, leaving British behaviour quite inexplicable: 'The chief, Waiyaki, who had entered into a treaty of friendship with the strangers, was afterwards deported and died on his way to the coast.' The Kikuyu, noble but naive, lost 'most of their lands through their magnanimity, . . . [and] through the insidious trickery of hypocritical treaties.'[52] But privately Kikuyu did blame Purkiss, *Mbaya*, the wicked one.[53] Waiyaki never went to crow over him. Indeed, Purkiss had had to summon Waiyaki no less than three times before the latter had left a beer-drink to come to the fort, there to face unequal combat. As in the British accounts, so for the Kikuyu the 'other' was a foil to their own hero. For Waiyaki, generous to the end, had offered his treacherous captor a goat of reconciliation, to show that he and his people bore no grudge.[54]

As the British worked over their own myth of Waiyaki, so he became more wicked and whites more upright. Thirty years on, Austin, Macdonald's lieutenant in 1892, turned an old soldier's memory into a stirring 'Boy's Own' tale that said more about building English character than British empire. Waiyaki was now not merely devious; he was also ungrateful. 'The white man's fearless guidance' had emboldened his warriors to rout Maasai raiders early in 1892, yet a victory that should have earned Purkiss Waiyaki's 'unswerving loyalty' only encouraged that 'scheming rogue' to get rid of his protector. Austin was in the fort's messroom with other officers, taking tea (so he said) after the sally against the Waguruguru, when Waiyaki passed down the veranda to Purkiss's room, if not with murder then at least with insolence in mind. But white manliness triumphed over black treachery. Purkiss, seeing Waiyaki draw his sword, 'dealt him a right-hander under his chin'. Captain Pringle was then on to Waiyaki 'in two bounds' and 'hung on like a bulldog'; English fair play then protected the defeated Waiyaki from the Swahili garrison's anger. Kikuyu weakness of will, on the other hand, was confirmed next morning when the nineteen 'lesser chiefs' who witnessed his trial professed indifference to his fate. The British were free to shoot Waiyaki or deport him as they chose and then to appoint a successor – an open admission of Kikuyu incapacity to rule themselves.[55]

This first episode in the story of Waiyaki's story, which reached its climax before Judge Carter, was, at bottom, about the political implications of a competition in military honour. Heroes proved, traitors and weaklings forfeited, the right to self-mastery or alien overrule. On either side heroic virtue rested on the obedience of clients and followers. Successful command conferred the right to dispose of landed resources, by patronage or ordinance. Both sides suppressed any dissident voices that questioned heroic virtue from within. Kikuyu spokesmen were unanimous that Waiyaki's hospitality was unprotestingly abused; among the British only Lugard thought that Purkiss had been in the wrong. In the next episode of Waiyaki's story, which dealt with the rights of property rather than the rituals of war, this control of shameful, damaging, knowledge was much less complete. The British discovered a weak – but not unguarded – Kikuyu flank that, for the time being at least, threatened the authority of the whole dynastic position.

Farmers & hunters

The doubt against which Kikuyu seemed anxious to guard was how they had got their land. Their dynastic theory paired martial honour with the civilizing virtue of cultivation. In the first chapter of his story their Waiyaki was an upright man whom whites betrayed, in the second an improving landowner whose generosity was rewarded with theft. The British had long justified their rule by denying Waiyaki's probity, symptomatic of much else that Africans lacked. The question now was whether that guilty verdict would sway the state's decision on Kikuyu property. After all, Carter had been commissioned to examine the justice not of conquest but of white settlement. His reply to Waiganjo at Kiambu had shown where his sympathies lay in the first, political, version of the story: Waiyaki was a twister to whose memory the British owed nothing. But that did not necessarily prejudge the issue of tenure. One of the stoutest white supporters of Kikuyu proprietorship, the Anglican missionary Harry Leakey, nonetheless conceded that Waiyaki had 'failed to keep his pledged word'.[56] Since the legality of British land seizure and the extent, if any, of the restitution now due rested on the substantiality of Kikuyu title, Carter had to hear the history of their land settlement. But the boundaries of his enquiry were unclear; the heroic-mythical manner in which both British and Africans imagined their history meant that Waiyaki the patron and Waiyaki the landholder were not easy to separate. The commission's witnesses told his story in both chapters, political and legal, at once. Not that property ever is a purely legal issue. In the Kikuyu case it was argued between coalitions of white and African interests on either side, each of them a triple alliance.

The Prayers of Waiyaki

The three groups for whom Waiyaki was a cultivating, civilizing, landowner are already to some extent familiar. To Kikuyu spokesmen his property was the economic basis of the old Anglo-Kikuyu alliance. Lugard's apparent purchase of Dagoretti, secondly, set a precedent for one strand of a divided British official opinion. And the Presbyterians were not the only missionaries to accept the proprietorial force of Waiyaki's story.

Of Waiyaki's Kikuyu advocates the single most eloquent was Koinange, head of the chiefs' party, the Kikuyu Loyal Patriots and patron to the Anglican Church Missionary Society (CMS), rather as Waiyaki's son Munyua had sponsored the CSM. Waiyaki's memory proved to him three key points of dynastic theory. The first two were commonplace. First, Munyua's land sale to the CSM showed that Kikuyu had private property. Next, the British must remember that they owed all to Kikuyu friendship. Wilson, Lugard's deputy, had relied on Waiyaki for porters: 'Is that not a marvellous thing', Koinange asked Carter, 'for only one European with a lot of natives who did not kill him?' But finally, and with the originality that marked him out for leadership, Koinange used Waiyaki's private wealth to public advantage, to prove Kikuyu land claims in general. In a spirited exchange with a settler witness he insisted that Kikuyu cattle paths had once crossed what was now white farmland. Whites, forgetting the Waguruguru column's frustration, did not believe that Kikuyu had ever owned cattle. Koinange refuted them by naming past tycoons, Waiyaki among them, whose large herds had naturally needed salt. And the only salt licks in the area had since been enclosed by white farms.[57]

Koinange used Waiyaki to correct whites on points of detail but he had a larger purpose. All Kikuyu witnesses, similarly, had a specific demand which they set in historical perspective. What they wanted was legal paper from the state, title deeds with which to defend *mbari* land against further white settlement; but such instruments would also, they argued, crown their culture. For the needs of the present had driven them to quarry their past; and there they had found a community sustained by the twin disciplines of moral economy, generous wealth and ambitious labour. They then deployed the virtuous 'tribal' character thus revealed beneath the intrigues of clannish history in two arguments that flattered colonizer and colonized with their mutual likenesses. First, as Koinange's Loyal Patriots put it, a British grant of title deeds would simply recognize their 'old custom . . . From the beginning we were buyers and sellers.'[58] And, no less importantly, Kikuyu sweat deserved this British tribute. For Kikuyu had cleared untamed forest and farmed it. They had civilized nature at least as heroically as the white settlers who, as Kikuyu well knew, based their moral title to idle African land on the superior productivity, the civilizing mission, of commercial farming.

Koinange's opponents in the KCA best produced this admirable past. In a wonderful illustration of how printed language can create national history,[59] they had distributed hundreds of printed claim forms on which all aggrieved *mbari* could list, in the same order, the livestock, honey barrels, tools, weapons and branding irons that their ancestors had paid to the Ndorobo hunters of the primeval forest in one distant past, 'many centuries ago'. Heading more than 400 plaintiff *mbari*, the mbari ya Hinga testified that Waiyaki and his brother Githeiya alone had paid 3,000 sheep and goats for their forest land.[60] Other southern Kikuyu immigrants had, it seemed, paid over one quarter of a million smallstock, 3,000 cattle, 2,000 barrels of honey and as many assorted pieces of ironmongery.[61] And this huge investment was but a fraction of the total, since most *mbari*, untouched as they were by land alienation, had no need to disclose their payments. Nonetheless, as the KCA impressed on Judge Carter, Kikuyu land title did not rest on purchase alone. By contrast with the uncivilized, because game-eating, Ndorobo, Kikuyu 'actually occupied and cultivated' the land they bought. An 'eye witness of no less importance than Lord Lugard' had seen their whole country 'under tillage'. True, Kikuyu energies were later sapped by the 'famine of Europe'. But if officials 30 years ago had thought the transfer of Kikuyu fallows to immigrant settlers warranted by the lack of beneficial occupation, the KCA thought the same principle ought now to secure the reversion to Africans of the 90 per cent of alienated land that whites had yet to plough.[62] Kikuyu had a keen eye for the propaganda of production; from his home address, the blandiloquently named 'Kiyambaa *Estate*', chief Koinange complained that settlers were busy ploughing up more acres in order to preempt Judge Carter's findings.[63]

Some British officials accepted Kikuyu claims to private tenure, but by 1930 they were not the most influential. Lugard and the first few settlers had dealt with Waiyaki and others on a freehold basis. But the official view had divided as the century turned. Senior men and government lawyers held that any Kikuyu idea of individual tenure must have been recently borrowed from whites. Like all other Bantu the Kikuyu must naturally see land not as a market commodity but as a common good over which their traditional authorities stood as trustee for the ancestors. While the state had a duty to see that native cultivators evicted from new white farms were compensated for their labour, the question of buying out property did not arise. Africans had no title to a specific acreage; alienation caused them disturbance, not loss. Kikuyu occupation rights were derived from tribal membership. Any family disturbed by white settlement could always, in the absence of any general land shortage, reclaim them from the tribe – or so this side of the argument went.

District officials and their provincial commissioners, on the other hand, who learned their Kikuyu land law 'in the field', stuck obstinately to the Lugardian view. By 1914 they were convinced that evicted Kikuyu were owed compensation for real loss rather than mere disturbance. Since they had been landowners with private or lineage (*mbari*) title within fixed boundaries they could not expect to be accommodated by neighbours lucky enough to be left outside the white farm boundary. The state had expropriated them and the state must pay.[64] The preoccupations of war and fresh white settlement thereafter meant that the issue remained unresolved in the official mind. That was why, in 1933, Carter had still to decide.

British protestant missionaries were dynastic theory's third set of supporters. Products of traditional society themselves, they constructed traditionality in Kikuyu. The CSM had acknowledged Waiyaki's property right by offering to reinstate his heirs on their lost acres. His Anglican partisans emerged from a quasi-dynastic alliance between Chief Koinange, their local patron, and Canon Harry Leakey, for 30 years head of the CMS Kabete mission, barely five miles from Waiyaki's. Leakey, the bearded one, *Giteru*, needed the chief's patronage; in return, he had encouraged chiefs to form a political association; and his exhumation of Koinange's grandfather's bones from under a white coffee estate was the climax to Carter's Kikuyu history lesson. *Giteru*'s more famous son Louis was in Koinange's debt for sponsoring his entry both into a Kikuyu age-set and, by certifying a competence in the Kikuyu language, to Cambridge University and the start of a promising career.[65]

The Leakeys urged three points in 60 pages of evidence to Judge Carter. First, Kikuyu had occupied their southern frontier for at least a century, perhaps three, without once relaxing their civilizing grip; Louis had the archaeological evidence. And their pioneers had bought out Ndorobo, since only willing sales would keep ancestral souls at peace. Finally, government ought to recompense dispossessed Kikuyu by making over to them those white farms that, in the middle of a depression, their owners had vacated.[66] They could almost have been members of the opposition KCA.

Like many others Harry Leakey, but not yet his son, called on Waiyaki to support this Kikuyu case. Oral Kikuyu and literate British knowledge both contributed to his version of the story. For Koinange was almost certainly the source of his belief that Lugard had bought Dagoretti from Waiyaki, as the CMS had paid Chege wa Muthemba for Kabete – in two white endorsements of Kikuyu property. Koinange himself probably reached this controversial conclusion when as a youth he had cooked for the CSM missionary who had bought from Waiyaki's son Munyua. Such was the Leakeys' association of Koinange with Lugard that young Louis wrongly thought of them as fictive blood relatives.[67] Conversely, Kikuyu may well have been alerted to Lugard's value as witness to their agrarian virtue by the canon's use of his memoirs to disprove white accusations of native idleness.[68] At all events, the first point that Waiyaki's story helped *Giteru* to illustrate was the beneficial nature of Kikuyu property. Secondly, he argued that since Waiyaki's had been one of many large frontier fortresses it was vain for white farmers in that area to claim that they had made fruitful an empty land grazed only by nomad Maasai. And, finally, Waiyaki was a 'great hereditary chief'.[69] Leakey was wrong in that but his error reminds us of the imaginative power of dynastic theory. Waiyaki the hereditary farmer-chief gave anonymous tribal history a name and life to political theory; to the Kikuyu demand for their stolen lands he was the irrefutable hero.

But not to everybody. Not to many of the Ndorobo forest hunters from whom Kikuyu said they had bought their land. Nor to Sidney Fazan, district commissioner (DC) of Kiambu and, more powerfully, secretary to the Land Commission, who differed with Louis Leakey on future Kikuyu land policy. Nor to disbelieving settlers. Together, but not in collusion, these formed the anti-dynastic triple alliance.

Some Ndorobo spokesmen characterized Kikuyu property as theft. Their most hostile witness had ingeniously anglicized his name as Lewis Kaberere wa Hunter. His evidence devastated dynastic theory. He accused the mbari ya Hinga – and the name means 'dissembler' – of treachery more vile than any Carter remembered. Their elders had adopted his grandfather Bera in order to buy his land, only to turn on him and kill him. And Waiyaki himself, when he 'had power from the white man' – as Lugard's client therefore rather than his patron – had beaten up his people a second time. 'The Mbari ya Hinga claim that the land is theirs. That is not true.'[70] While some Ndorobo also complained that Kikuyu sorcery had frightened them into selling, others conceded that they had willingly sold land.[71] Since several of these last were now 'adopted Kikuyu', Fazan discounted their support for dynastic theory. And in his view Kikuyu ruined their own case by the fabricated uniformity of their claims, by the 'fantastic and ridiculous' numbers of livestock involved, by disputing whose ancestors had paid whom and, finally, by conflict between the printed avowal of land purchase 'many centuries ago' and oral evidence that Ndorobo sellers were often the fathers of men still living.[72] Soured Ndorobo and over-anxious Kikuyu thus allowed Judge Carter to dismiss the historical defence of property; he concluded that Kikuyu had acquired it only partly by legal means and largely by 'force and chicanery',[73] the very crimes that later obliged the British to conquer them. Kikuyu probity and property did indeed stand or fall together.

The past raised other objections to the restoration of *mbari* land. The strongest was the most recent. Alarmed by his first day of expectant Kikuyu evidence, Carter warned that he 'had to take facts as they are'; and the fact was that he could not return white farmland to Africans. He could award any compensation he thought was due only in empty – and thus inferior – areas elsewhere.[74] He later asserted that the politically impossible was in any case undesirable. For should he advise the restitution of supposed Kikuyu land, inter-*mbari* wrangles would first need to be adjudicated at tedious length; claims would have to be expensively surveyed; and there would be Ndorobo counter-claims. Since no Kikuyu (or Ndorobo) could say, unchallenged, who had what rights on which farm it would, he argued, be more equitable to extinguish all residual African rights to white land and compensate Kikuyu as a whole, not each aggrieved *mbari*.[75] In rejecting the guidance of Kikuyu history the commission accepted, gratefully, we may think, an Ndorobo version of the past. Carter allowed the Scottish mission to restore property to the mbari ya Hinga as an exception. He refused to follow Waiyaki's supporters in treating him as heroic champion of a general principle. Moreover, one had to think of the future.

For the second element in the anti-dynastic alliance was the new cast of the official mind. The 1930s depression had woken government to the need to help black as well as white farming. If one man personified the new thinking it was Fazan. Intellectually the most gifted DC of his generation, with a keen sense of the state's self-interested duty to reform social ills before popular anger became obstructive, his four years in Kikuyu districts had given him sternly enlightened views on land policy. Kikuyu needed better farming, not more land. And now as the Land Commission's secretary he could get his own visions of the future, sketched out when DC, adopted as influentially recommended solutions to Kikuyu grievance.[76] Not that Fazan was impressed by dynastic theory, far from it. He saw *mbari* seniors as trustees of merely 'sectional interests', those 'fortunate families' who were descended from big hunters, not of Kikuyu in general.[77] The dynastic grip of their *mbari* tenure had to be prised open, to encourage private investment by improving farmers – whether *mbari* 'right-holders' or their tenants was immaterial. Only then might agricultural growth win the race with rising population. This utilitarian attack on dynastic theory was the more damaging for owing nothing to the rights and wrongs of colonial history. Fazan had already clashed with Louis Leakey's romantic conservatism on this score.[78] Leakey's friends the Kiambu chiefs accused their old DC, in turn, of a 'Russian' desire to redistribute 'the things which belong to a rich man or the property of a hard worker',[79] who were one and the same in Kikuyu social theory. But Fazan's thinking carried the day. If settlers would not, the Kikuyu future could not permit *mbari* to recover their lands as *mbari*. The state's public duty to black posterity underpinned private white interest. Any resettlement of Kikuyu farmers must be planned under statutory smallholder regulations, not left to *mbari* suzerainty. In short, if not in so many words, not only was Waiyaki's title to property dubious, his private wealth was not to Kikuyu public advantage.

White settlers concluded the case against Kikuyu landlords by implying that they were hiding a guilty secret – or practising *kirira*, had they known the term. All settler witnesses swore to the former emptiness of their farms. Koinange, who seems scarcely to have let Carter out of his sight, forced some to retract this claim. Settlers then countered by arguing that if the land had belonged to anyone it was to the Ndorobo and they of course were only hunters, not improvers.[80] And one settler, Tait, reckoned that Kikuyu had taken steps to suppress this Ndorobo story. Supporting his case that the latter had 'been diddled out of their land by the wily Kikuyu', he asked why else chief Kinyanjui had kept the Ndorobo elder Thindi in preventive detention, allegedly by threats of witchcraft. And why had Koinange become Thindi's warder on Kinyanjui's death?[81] He received no answer. Tait's insinuation was a product of the settler desire to justify their civilizing mission by its contrast with harsh African history. White land had in their view been justifiably alienated from recent Kikuyu immigrants who were not only guiltily uncertain of their rights but who had been dying off when the British first arrived. Twenty years later, when Mau Mau insurgency seemed to reconfirm the Kikuyu reputation for treachery, two settlers repeated Tait's question, one in a critical review of Louis Leakey's *Mau Mau and the Kikuyu*.[82] Many settlers saw in Mau Mau a frenzied reversion to ancient savagery that proved the continuing need for white supremacy over blacks incapable of self-rule. Leakey angered them by arguing, to the contrary, that Kikuyu had once been admirably civilized; they were not a criminal tribe. Wicked modern men like Kenyatta had been able to build an evil movement only because unattended grievance and social change had weakened the elders' beneficial authority.[83]

Leakey was here restating dynastic theory. It was not his first attempt. Carter had accepted that Ndorobo charges of Kikuyu banditry discredited such dynastic claims. But Kikuyu notables did not abandon a dynastic view of history. Indeed, dismayed by white refusal to make amends for Waiyaki's betrayal, they were all the more anxious to secure their title against fellow Kikuyu. The 1930s saw a scramble for land in which the successful litigants were those who could prove the strongest lineage tie with the soil.[84] Dynastic history was more than ever in demand. It was in this urgent atmosphere that Leakey had vied with Kenyatta to restore dynastic authority by literary means. Both resurrected Waiyaki. Kenyatta's hero was an unconvincing paragon of simple virtue. By using both white memoirs and private Kikuyu memory – and perhaps his own recollection of conveying Waiganjo's wigging to Carter – Leakey showed, more plausibly, why Waiyaki had opposed Purkiss. He also set out better than Kenyatta the legal basis for the second, proprietorial, chapter of Waiyaki's story; Kikuyu cosmology, especially the fear of ancestors, had in his view guaranteed that full payment was made to willing Ndorobo land sellers.[85] Leakey had enjoyed Koinange's hospitality while working on his book; and the chief's political self-interest is plain to see throughout *The Southern Kikuyu*, the posthumously published, 1,400 page apotheosis of Kikuyu dynastic theory.[86] But while Leakey was staying as his guest Koinange's thoughts were not entirely taken up with the deeds of Waiyaki; in his search for political effectiveness he was almost certainly turning to the words of Mugo wa Kibiru as well.

Structure & agency

Disillusion with the Land Commission's findings, as has long been known, drove Koinange and other chiefs to conciliate their critics, the teachers and traders in the KCA.[87] The alliance was always uneasy, thanks to a less well understood tension in Kikuyu ideology, personified by Waiyaki and Mugo. By 1930 chiefs could represent themselves as dynastic heirs rather than the upstart puppets caricatured by the KCA; many were senior members of their *mbari*, one of three intermixed Kikuyu structures of power that were as much ideal concepts of society as tangible organizations. Their rivals used a second concept, that of generation conflict and succession, as a vehicle of dissent. They saw themselves as one of the alternate generations (*riika*) that regularly exchanged ritual authority, at least in the mind's eye, within and between *mbari*. Kikuyu thought they had formerly enacted such successions at festivals called *ituika*, perhaps every three decades or so, most probably when driven by the need to cleanse the land from the fear of sorcery that polluted personal relations during a severe famine. Half a dozen ceremonial *ituika* zones imaginatively linked Kikuyu who were otherwise divided by hundreds of jealously propertied *mbari*. This tension between subclan *mbari* and generation *riika* underlay that between chiefs and KCA.[88]

Waiyaki was a model for *mbari* spokesmen, Mugo a prophet in the revivalist cause of *riika* solidarity. The third chapter of Waiyaki's story now examines the friction between their prophetic traditions, to explain why Kikuyu differed on how to use their ideal social structures as real political agencies within and then against the colonial regime. Debate came to blows by 1952. *Mbari* elders then competed with a candidate *riika* – that is, with the collective identity of half their number – for the allegiance of juniors of warrior age. These were the youngest recruits to a third social structure, the chronologically graded ladder of seniority that was annually renewed by adolescent initiation into age sets, also called *riika*. Ideally these were all-inclusive, in reality very fragmented. The political movement called Mau Mau divided over the question of how far juniors were subject to seniors' authority, an issue that the myths of Waiyaki and Mugo helped all to debate.

This third chapter also takes us deepest into the question of how Kikuyu saw history. When not trying to impress strangers with their past they argued it out between themselves. Like many people – such as Marxists and Christians, Jews and Muslims – they saw time in two dimensions, linear or progressive and yet also cyclical or recursive. The first past told of material and moral advance, the other of cycles of social decay and moral renewal; the notion of 'recursion' or 'regeneration' perhaps better expresses the Kikuyu – possibly universal – hope that history's cycle will spiral to some higher, redemptive plane.[89]

Kikuyu used progressive history to advise Judge Carter that their agriculture had civilized Ndorobo forests, a moral as much as a material claim. A good life, similarly, was at once a material wealth-creating, fee-paying progress and a struggle for virtue. But their moral time was regenerative too. Individual accumulation incurred collective costs; it could go on to finance collective gains. Pondering the human tragedy of unachieved community, Kikuyu use the rueful proverb 'birds which land together fly up separately' to mean that young men seek their fortune in moral company with their age-mates and then produce wealth, a household virtue, within their *mbari*.[90] But rich elders who had successfully cultivated nature by the same means accumulated enough wealth to assuage the sorcerous envy of the unsuccessful that periodically made all vulnerable to famine or other disaster. They could come together again, no longer as age-mates circumcized in the same year but as a generation two or more decades deep, to win civic virtue at *ituika* by sacrificing their private wealth to public well-being.

Linear time was incorporated in *mbari* genealogies and in the annual age-set *riika* whose names, never repeated, were taken from current events. Generation *riika* were cyclical, alternating under the names *Mwangi* and *Maina*, whose members were believed to be reincarnated in their grandchildren. Generations were also regenerations; their repeated renewals of the social order were associated with new achievements that earned them specific names as well. Kikuyu thus spoke of the *Ndemi* or 'cutters' who had cleared the forest; *Mathathi*, the ochre-painted warriors who defended their predecessors' gains; and *Iregi*, the 'refusers' who destroyed the consequent royal despotism and instituted property-owning democracy. That authors differed in their generation sequences and there never was a tyrant king simply shows history's polemical potential, especially when linear and recursive time are entwined.[91] Kikuyu brought both theories of history to bear on the problem of what to do about the British.

Waiyaki's embodiment of *mbari* progress is patent, Mugo's links with *riika* regeneration more speculative but evident from the timing and idiom of his words. He is thought to have admonished Kikuyu prior to the great hunger of 1899, at a time when a *Maina* generation's authority must have been weakened by the recent cattle plagues of pleura-pneumonia and rinderpest, by locust infestation and smallpox, and when a candidate *Mwangi* generation was impatient for recognition.[92] Many must have seen the preparatory years of their *ituika* as a struggle against natural disaster and alien conquest. This era of moral conflict between the selfishness of survival and the generosity of leadership, we may assume, constituted a prophetic moment such as leads people to turn to dreamers, and dreamers to preach social renewal, for which the local idiom was provided by *ituika*.

Ituika rituals were *kirira*, knowledge restricted to qualified elders who paid to learn. Little therefore is known of them; they doubtless differed across Kikuyuland. But some at least ended in taming the hairy-tailed rainbow-dragon *ndamathia* that devoured life but could be persuaded to bring rain, restore fertility and yield up the dead, with their herds. Eight elders of a retiring *riika* revealed such secrets to the new while feasting at a purpose-built hut, *thingira*, to which each had his own door.[93] People later understood Mugo to have made regenerative reference to both dragon and powerhouse. The red strangers whom one should neither fight nor befriend would bring an iron snake that both consumed and created wealth; their power would fade when Kikuyu had built an eight-doored *thingira*. Mugo himself could well have seen the first railway trains, and they demanded subsidy before offering new markets for Kikuyu produce. But that is to put too literal a meaning on his words. Kikuyu naturally imagined monsters at times when power changed hands and it was logical, knowledge being power, to attribute British strength to schooling. As the *thingira* of *ituika* had housed the transfer of arcane lore, so a specific school became Mugo's *thingira* of freedom. More generally, people understood him to foretell a cycle of social decay and moral renewal. Juniors with bells in their ears would soon disobey seniors; cooked food, normally freely available to visitors, would be sold by the roadside; promiscuity and theft would flourish. The strangers would leave when Kikuyu not only learned their alien secrets but also redeemed their own society.[94]

It is difficult to date Mugo's dreams, still more so to tell when later meditation hallowed his cautious advice into prophetic wisdom. But it appears that a colonial Kikuyu discourse between redemptive faith in his timeless words and political exploitation of Waiyaki's debatable – and datable – role in colonial progress or regression went through four phases. The evidence is slender but suggestive. Hopes of *riika* regeneration seem to have preceded the *mbari* plans for progress that inspired Kikuyu evidence before the Carter commission. Then, with their progress rebuffed by the state, Kikuyu opinion divided within both historical theories of change, first in the turmoil preceding the Mau Mau war and then in its forest campaign.

Early British officials knew about Kikuyu prophecy. In 1910 senior commissioner Charles Hobley met Kichura wa Thiga, an 'oracle' who, like Mugo, found his mediumistic trances exhausting. He had long foreseen a peaceful coexistence of black and white.[95] Four years later many settlers left their farms to go to war on the German East African (now Tanzanian) border. Geoffrey Northcote, DC Kiambu and a man not easily alarmed, thought many Kikuyu looked to the early fulfilment of what he called 'the *old* prophecy' that whites would disappear. Elders, it seems, conveyed this hope in a dance connected with *ituika*, preparations for which were well advanced in Murang'a district too by the end of the war.[96] I have found no wartime discussion of Waiyaki. In these early colonial years, then, there seems to have been no dialogue between him and Mugo. Many Kikuyu wanted to be rid of the colonial state, as Mugo foretold; but clannish rivalry to enjoy its power had yet to produce a myth of Waiyaki that sanctioned a general theory of legitimate Anglo-Kikuyu authority.

The second phase of the colonial dialectic of *mbari* and *riika* was dominated by this Waiyaki, the wraith at Carter's elbow. But what Kenyatta called 'the spirit of *ituika*'[97] was also abroad between the wars. Dynastic and generational theory each had dominant and dissident forms. The literates of leading lineages used dynastic theory to try to negotiate better terms with the state. The landlord patron Waiyaki was their answer to venal chiefs, crusading missionaries and greedy settlers. His main supporters, Koinange's Loyal Patriots, larded their petition that chiefs be 'ennobled' with a catalogue of the help their predecessors had rendered. Waiyaki's assistance to George Wilson was the first; Kikuyu carrier service in the recent Great War the most sacrificial. An easy assimilation of Kikuyu and colonial ideas of progress led the Patriots to try to control Carter by giving him a chief's 'customary gift'. But neither chiefs were customary, nor was the gift, which was none other than a request that missionaries pray God to give the commission wisdom![98] If chiefs thought they had found the secret of legitimate authority, Kenyatta's KCA was their established opposition. As a candidate *riika* of *irungu* 'straighteners' it opposed both colonial oppression and, in an echo of Mugo, Kikuyu sexual indiscipline.[99] Waiyaki and Mugo thus inspired conventional rivalry between those incumbent and aspirant male elites who had each, by profiting from colonial rule and western learning, earned the right of the wealthy to control the social order.

Before the Second World War only Ndorobo voiced open African dissent from dynastic theory. Louis Leakey heard private accounts of Waiyaki's resistance and of his attempts to curb his warriors, but his disputes with other *mbari* and his coercion of *kiaro* labour remained hidden much longer.[100] Kenyatta may have hinted at such criticism when in *Facing Mount Kenya* he lamented that Waiyaki's 'natural generosity and hospitality' made him forget Mugo's advice to treat whites with watchful courtesy, and so let Lugard in.[101] Dissenting redemptive thought was more strident than this. Many KCA members obediently paid their *Mwangi* seniors the fees for learning the secrets of *ituika* and deplored loose urban living. But some looked for a more instant release than any that Mugo had promised a persevering people. In 1922 post-war troubles evoked dreams of deliverance by Moses or a Messiah; later, some thought the missionary motive for banning clitoridectomy was to prevent the birth of a Kikuyu Son of God.[102]

Dominant dynastic and generational thought were closer to each other than either were to their dissident voices. Chief Koinange brought them visibly together when in 1939 he opened his Kenya Teachers College at Githunguri, headed by his American-trained son Peter Mbiyu. The college recruited from the independent schools – boosted by the clitoridectomy crisis – that helped *mbari* to keep control of their young. Koinange got age-sets to compete in raising funds for the college at events sponsored by *mbari* elders. Some also saw in Githunguri the achievement of generational hopes; here was the eight-doored *thingira* forecast by Mugo, house of the red strangers' knowledge and portent of freedom. I do not know if Koinange drew that analogy himself; but his son later affirmed that Githunguri would fulfil 'the prophecy'.[103] Some Kikuyu seem to have unified their inspirational history accordingly. An elder recorded in 1936 thought that Waiyaki's father Hinga was Mugo's too; and a later source who equated Githunguri with Mugo's *thingira* claimed that the dying seer had entrusted his duties to Waiyaki.[104]

The opening of Githunguri marked the high point of elite historical theory, both progressive and regenerative. For if the First World War had raised hopes of Mugo, the Second dashed faith in Waiyaki. The British resettled some *mbari* on its eve, in line with Carter's boundary changes, and then banned the KCA for allegedly aiding the enemy.[105] The state seemed to respect neither dynastic right nor generational vigour. Kenyatta's strikingly altered view of Waiyaki at this time opened a third phase of Kikuyu historical discourse that lasted until 1952. In 1938, in *Facing Mount Kenya*, his Waiyaki forgot Mugo's warning to stand aloof, thanks to a trusting generosity that the British then exploited. In 1942, writing *My People of Kikuyu* for a Christian pamphlet series, Kenyatta took a similar view of Waiyaki's counterpart in northern Kikuyu, Wang'ombe. He had allowed the British to build at what became their district headquarters, Nyeri and Murang'a – a bolder assertion of dynastic rights over colonial rule than anything claimed for Waiyaki.[106] But two years later, when addressing a very different, pan-African, audience, Kenyatta changed his mind. In his pamphlet, *Kenya: the Land of Conflict*, Waiyaki heeded Mugo's warning, kept his warriors alert, and held Lugard to a strictly commercial treaty, with 'no territorial concessions of any kind'. When the British violated these terms he had 'struggled hopelessly with spears, bows and arrows against Maxim guns.' Lured into the fort by a false promise of peace, this 'powerful national ruler' was deported, to die.[107]

Why did Kenyatta overturn Waiyaki the peaceful patron of empire into its violently protesting victim? A new anti-imperial audience was not his only reason; others reversed history too but without the same stimulus. In 1946 chiefs joined KCA men to deny the very basis of dynastic theory: Africans, they told government, had never traded land with white pioneers. Carter would have been astounded to read in a petition signed by Koinange that 'this allegation on land transaction is an error from which all evil of Afro-European relationship begin.'[108] Koinange, whose father had welcomed the Hungarian traveller Teleki in 1887, was even moved to apologize to his fellow Kikuyu: 'We Kiambu people are to blame for the Europeans' entry . . . Count Teleki, we opened the way for him and lived in a friendly manner as well as with Mr Lockhart [sic].'[109] Unable to abandon heroic-mythical history, like Kenyatta he simply reversed it. Their expectations of the future had changed; so too did the lessons of the past. Judge Carter had killed hope, the post-war world induced fear. The state took ever more power over African land. Fearing the growth of landlessness, DCs favoured *ahoi* tenants against their *mbari* patrons in the courts; compulsory soil conservation labour then attacked the moral basis of ownership, which was sweated self-mastery; and all *mbari* with an independent school feared that educational reform would threaten *mbari* property.[110] It was time to deny that Kikuyu leaders had given colonial rule any, even dependent, rights in land and to remove from dynastic theory all suspicion of seeking a legitimate politics of collaboration.

Conservatives & militants

It remained to settle the nature of a legitimate politics of opposition, an issue in which history was also involved. It came to torment Mau Mau, a movement so called by its victims and enemies. To its members it was 'the community', *Gikuyu na Muumbi* the ancestral progenitors, or *ithaka na wiathi* – normally given as 'land and freedom' but really 'self-mastery through land'. But Mau Mau was not a community; it was a marriage of convenience between failed politicians. Of these, conservative elders around Kenyatta wanted back their 'stolen lands' but not at the cost of losing to juniors their inherited *mbari* power. Small traders and workers in Nairobi, by contrast, needed a new power to accumulate capital or force up wages. By 1948 both parties were discredited; each sought the other's help. Their incompatibility grew clearer as Africans became more impatient; mounting violence naturally prised power loose from elders, to be picked up by anyone bold enough to stoop. Beneath their joint desire to end British rule, therefore, Mau Mau's two wings had conflicting priorities. The conservatives wanted to regain authority, the militants to lead effective action.

The politics of the past became more strident and Waiyaki and Mugo more partisan, the former recruited by both sides. An account of how Kikuyu scanned history for guidance in this period shows, perhaps more clearly than any other form of analysis, not only how far Kenyatta differed from the militant wing of Mau Mau but also how disunited the militants were themselves. Mau Mau's strategic debate about how to get rid of the British reflected an internal Kikuyu conflict far older than that which divided them between country and town, old wealth and new ambition. Mau Mau was not class war; there were alliances of rich and poor on both sides of the civil war that the British forced on all Kikuyu as much as some Kikuyu declared it on others. No, the deepest discord, underlying the more recent ones, was the continuing tension between lineage and generation, *mbari* and *riika*, progressive property and redemptive solidarity. The moral authority earned by *mbari* elders was too parochial to be politically effective; juniors who demanded action had more easily mobilized *riika* affiliations but lacked the seal of plutocratic merit.[111]

Inventions of the past grappled with this contradiction in how to create the future. To summarize, linear, progressive history turned out to be too narrow for conservative use, recursive time too linked to peaceful renewal to unite the militant imagination. Each side had problems with history. While Waiyaki the landlord-patron still inspired rich elders, now rural capitalists, their dispossession of dependants compromised his wider appeal. Recursive hopes did at least enjoy a broader social base. In the past only the rich elders of a candidate generation could invest in the virtue of *ituika*; nowadays a growing number of literates and their kin knew something of Christian eschatology. Mugo remained a diligent – that is, wealthy – Kikuyu saviour but Waiyaki, now joining him in regenerative time, became in some respects a suffering one. The rural establishment still had a popular idiom of peaceful aspiration at its disposal. It is less easy to document the militants' view of Waiyaki and Mugo but it seems that while the former, as warrior, might sanction war as well as protest, the seer remained a man of peace. When war finally came and the British declaration of Emergency drove Mau Mau into the forest, its fighters left Mugo behind, just when they had most need of divination and prophecy. And a dreadful fate awaited Waiyaki. Some desperate forest fighters imagined for him a past that no supporter of dynastic theory, even one as disillusioned as Kenyatta, could have accepted, however much in more peaceful days Kenyatta had once inspired them.

To turn back, then, to the intellectual origins of Mau Mau, one must understand Kenyatta, a man who helped invent the myths of Waiyaki and Mugo in order to imagine the Kikuyu and then became a captive of the tradition he had created. On his return from London in 1946 he enjoyed all the attributes of leadership. He had been educated overseas; he enjoyed self-mastery on his 30-acre farm; he married well, twice over. Thanks to one father-in-law, chief Koinange, he became head of Githunguri and, with it, the age-set competition in civic virtue. He had a herald in the newspaper *Mumenyereri*, and powerful allies. These were scarcely radical. His KCA colleagues were now elders like himself. The educated young elite of other black nationalities in the Kenya African Union (KAU), of which he became president, were petitioners not protestors. His friends in Britain's Labour government wanted colonial development, not decolonization. All these considerations shaped his political calculus. He knew that young Kikuyu were impatient and the settlers obdurate; but he also feared that political violence was less likely to change colonial policy than to alienate his allies, senior Kikuyu, other Africans and British liberal opinion. But political caution only confirmed Kenyatta in a conservative social project he had long preached, which was that industrious civic virtue would both save the Kikuyu soul and earn British political respect. Pursuing this populist extension of dynastic theory he now tried to revive – and in a pan-Kikuyu sense, to create – annual age-sets as vehicles of self-esteem, led by successful *mbari* elders and thus under his control. He damned theft and thuggery, modern expressions of the peasant sin of idleness, and praised self-help. Protest by the deserving would reinforce, undisciplined violence weaken, political demands. Not that he had any innocent faith in gradualism, far from it. He fully expected the British to lose their nerve, arrest him and perhaps fire on his followers. But if Britain were to be shamed into political reform then it was essential that his supporters' restraint, like Waiyaki's friendship, should give British repression no shred of justification.[112]

History encouraged Kenyatta. By 1944, in *Kenya: The Land of Conflict*, he had decided, in an account that contrasted Waiyaki's control with British indiscipline, that Kikuyu had indeed fought, but only after the whites had broken their word. His analysis of the next clash, headed 'New Times, New Tactics', developed the theme. After the Great War Harry Thuku had led a protest movement controlled by 'leading elders', men of wealth and education. Panicky police had shot some of the orderly demonstrators who prayed, as traditionalists, Christians and Muslims, for his release. But his supporters' self-discipline saved Thuku from death, if not from detention, and won from the British a declaration that African interests in Kenya were paramount over those of white and Indian immigrants. Now, after more African sacrifice in the Second World War, it was up to the British to put policy into practice. Translated into Kikuyu, this political history lesson remained in print until 1952. It was, very explicitly, not a call to arms.[113]

That was the issue that split Mau Mau. Its two wings imparted their political education in oaths of initiation and in song. The conservatives, to turn to them first, are the easier to document since they also made more open use of print. As to their oaths, Kikuyu had always employed costly tests of loyalty to protect any joint enterprise in their fragmented society. There were *mbari* oaths, *riika* oaths, warrior oaths, as well as legal ordeals that put justice beyond the reach of human partiality. KCA leaders, Kenyatta included, had repeatedly sworn mutual loyalty, not least because as wealthy men they feared the envious canker of sorcery. The first Mau Mau oath, which demanded economic sacrifice and obedience to an ill-defined cause, grew out of theirs. Mau Mau memoirs all mention its attendant political education; few say what was taught. General China told his recruits 'history'; another forest leader, Kahinga Wachanga, called his own first oath one of understanding; it taught 'uneducated Kikuyu . . . the necessity of opposing the Europeans . . . using pacifist methods' before fighting or, if that failed, then prayer; a third, Karari Njama, heard that Kikuyu must burst British eardrums with argument before resorting to revolt; Josiah Kariuki, a small trader in the Mau Mau support network, and one of only two initiates to mention Waiyaki by name in this connection, learned that he had made blood-brotherhood with Lugard after Mugo warned that armed resistance would end in annihilation.[114] The establishment Mau Mau of the first oath then, the oath of unity, looked back to the peaceful Waiyaki of previous dynastic theory.

That conclusion stems less from the slender and pliant evidence of memory than from ampler and unchanging contemporary sources, printed in songbook and pamphlet. The political poets were establishment men. Their *nyimbo*, as they are called, naturally forecast victory over the settlers, but their martial language was figurative rather than literal; nor was it pronounced. They devoted more space to distinguishing between patriots and traitors. Here the message was clear. Those who furthered freedom were those who worked for wealth; the idle poor would get no cattle. And Waiyaki and Mugo knew whose side they were on. The Waiyaki of song urged that one could not cultivate and befriend wild animals – the British – at the same time; he loved 'progress'. But the most interesting aspect of the *nyimbo* was their effort to overcome the narrow fragmentation that was dynastic theory's chief weakness. They tried in two ways. First, just as chief Koinange had done twenty years earlier in referring to the cattle owners' need for salt-licks, they turned Waiyaki's private property to public advantage. In a fresh twist to his story they both reinforced the post-war dogma that landowners had granted the British no rights and made a breathtaking leap in Kikuyu law. For Waiyaki, it now appeared, had laid a dying curse, *kirumi*, on the land, so that none should sell it to whites. Conventionally this sworn entail was valid only among close kin and age-mates; Waiyaki had thus become the *muramati*, the sub-clan trustee, of all Kikuyu or their universal age-mate. Secondly, Mugo the prophet joined Waiyaki the cultivator, as he had never done before, to curse the barren ones who were too disobedient – with bells in their ears – to be the single-minded ploughmen of freedom.[115] But how would freedom be won? It was in the redemptive idiom of generation succession and social renewal that conservative thought was most creative.

For it was now, at this time of danger when, as he foretold, 'Conflict and hatred will increase and friendships will diminish', that Mugo was first expected to be reborn within Kikuyu, whether within people's hearts or as a living being was left to a fully Christian ambiguity. Either way, he would personally bring the freedom that he had previously warned must be earned through discipline and school. *Nyimbo* still sang of that book-learned rather than violent emancipation, clearly supportive of *mbari* elders whose school properties were the gates of knowledge. And the new biblical echoes of redemption, whether Christian or Mosaic, were equally welcome to the wealthy; for those who abused Mugo were those without livestock and land.[116] Kenyatta nursed his own regenerative hopes. On his return from England he had forecast that, since British rule began under Queen Victoria, 'we are bound to get our freedom when another lady occupies the throne as the British Queen.'[117] But it turned out to be Waiyaki, the old Queen's ally, who came most dramatically to his aid, in the protean shape of Mugo, Moses, Christ and Kenyatta himself, all brought together in the entirely Kikuyu idiom of ancestral rebirth and generation succession.

Waiyaki returned in 1952, in a remarkable pamphlet.[118] As later translated by Ngugi wa Thiong'o, Mbugua Njama's *Mahoya ma Waiyaki, The Prayers of Waiyaki* was a prophetic tract, written with an enigmatic obscurity appropriate to a time when none could be trusted, to rally a chosen but, for the moment, unworthy people. Njama urged his readers to pray for their warriors but preached against violence; liberation would come with sacrifice, prayer, learning and the patriotic use of wealth. He took his history from Kenyatta, local traditions and the Gospels. His Waiyaki had fought only when forced; he had tried to talk peace at Fort Smith where, in a perhaps embarrassing illustration of how persuasive the older, optimistic, dynastic theory could still be, 'he had given the white people a plot of land to build on'. On his capture he forbade his warriors to retaliate, 'for it is not good that you should lose your lives because of me. Let me be taken when I shall be taken. If I die, I die, so be it.' Crying with rage they obeyed, even when bees came to their aid by attacking Waiyaki's guards on the march.[119] After dying in distant Kibwezi, Waiyaki prayed at God's right hand to be resurrected so that he could visit the white men's country, learn their secrets and return to lead his people from slavery. It was in Kenyatta, of course, that he was reborn. Kikuyu must support him – as they wished the warriors had Waiyaki – while heeding his repeated lesson that 'our fight is not one of might, but is a war of right, and justice cannot be obtained unless we are united, so that we can demand our rights together . . . [T]oday the spear is the pen, the sword is the book, the shield is reason and the club is unity.'

Njama attacked two sets of people for blocking unity, like tree-stumps obstructing cultivation. The first target, not directly named, can only have been the urban workers whom Kikuyu leaders had long decried, exporters of the sweat that profited whites at Kikuyu expense.[120] They looked like adults, but how could they be, with no land to cultivate, houses like cowsheds, and miserable pay? Yet their European ambitions made them slander African leaders; a three-ton lorry could not bear the weight of their shame. At the other end of the social scale wealthy Christian revivalists scoffed at Waiyaki's curse. With good clothes and clean bodies they were rich. But they affected to despise the world.

That can only have been because they feared others would become equally rich. If, then, their Christianity was not to be mere hypocrisy they should stand aside and 'let those who are not Christians, or those who like wealth, ask for what they want'. Waiyaki had become the father of rural capitalism and its moderate politics. He had no time for morally feckless but politically militant migrant workers, nor yet for the few born-again Christians who abdicated their plutocratic responsibility for social renewal, implicit in the ever present discourse of *ituika*.

Oracular pamphlets and *nyimbo* supported Kenyatta with both dynastic and regenerative thought. In his reluctance to fight he reincarnated Waiyaki; as overseas scholar he had been more than obedient to Mugo. I do not know if Njama wrote with Kenyatta's knowledge, but had the British read the *Prayers* they might have been less surprised that Kikuyu failed to resist his arrest – and that of 180 others – on the night of 20 October 1952, the first act of the Mau Mau Emergency.[121] Nor do I know how far Kenyatta hoped his captivity would fulfil the story of Kikuyu discipline, British repression and reparation he had set out in 1944. Events may give a clue. Many Kiambu elders who had held back from what they saw as a hooligan movement, now rushed to join what his arrest reassured them was a reputable project after all and thus support its leader, as Waiyaki's *Prayers* had wished. Moreover, Mau Mau did little fighting in the next few months; while gathering their strength some militants also hoped that a favourable verdict at the end of Kenyatta's long trial would bring reform without the need to suffer.[122]

Two conclusions emerge from the slender evidence for the militant view of the past. First, many young warrior recruits were ignorant, especially squatters on white farms or Nairobi workers.[123] The historical currency of political debate did not apparently circulate beyond those who needed to know, *mbari* elders in Kikuyuland for whom a superior past was the chief legal defence of property and literate politicians anxious to prove that they shared the heritage of their unlettered kin. But there was also a regional geography of historical knowledge within Kikuyuland. Waiyaki was a hero of southern Kiambu; Murang'a's Mugo was adopted by Kiambu too, as patron saint of Githunguri. Waiyaki's fate was part of Kiambu's daily discourse; parents there warned disobedient children that they might share it.[124] In stark contrast, when Gucu Gikoyo – a decidedly delinquent child – took his first oath he and his fellow recruits had to admit that they had no idea that whites had taken their land, nor had they heard of

Waiyaki.[125] But then Gikoyo came from Murang'a district, further north. And as tenant of other *mbari* three times over, illiterate, alternately jailbird and labourer, he was a man whom the conservatives and Waiyaki, in his *Prayers*, would despise.

Secondly, the ignorance, youth and often landlessness of their recruits all allowed militant leaders to create a past that subverted elders' authority. Even the songwriters allowed insolence its voice. The refrain 'Let the elders keep silent, they let the land be taken' sometimes replaced one that enjoined solidarity between generations, perhaps consciously rebutting elders who had once blamed the warriors for angering the British.[126] Militants did not reject the invented ethnic past; they had no other. Like the elders they used it. In linear time the implications of their historical differences for Mau Mau policy are best seen in relation to the meaning of Waiyaki's alleged curse or *kirumi*. Conservatives saw it, in the *nyimbo* and the *Prayers*, as a symbolic deterrent to any further association with whites. Militants went much further; they told the ignorant Gikoyo that it would destroy all who did not fight to regain the lost land.[127] Moreover, Gikoyo was warned of this danger on taking his first oath which, unusually, required him to fight – an undertaking normally reserved to the militants' own 'platoon' or *mbatuni* oath, which originated among farm squatters or in Nairobi, not in Kenyatta's Kiambu.

Opinion also divided over the political demands of regenerative time. All but one of the generation successions of the past had consummated a peaceful process of investment in the right to replace outworn ritual elders in the task of restoring social order. Allusions to *ituika* scattered through the *nyimbo* recalled Mugo's advice to learn the strangers' secrets and abolish delinquency; Kenyatta's politics also reproduced this same conventional view of *ituika*. Militants had the exceptional *ituika* in mind in which, by Kenyatta's account in *Facing Mount Kenya*, the *Iregi* generation had violently overthrown tyranny. But Kenyatta had also argued that subsequent *ituika* honoured this origin of Kikuyu democracy by peacefully rotating power in 'constitutional revolution.'[128] Some whites believed Kenyatta devised Mau Mau as a new *iregi* revolution.[129] But then they also assumed he was the movement's sole organizer. Everything he said in public between his return in 1946 and his arrest in 1952 – even to crowds of hostile Kikuyu youth – suggests, rather, that he trusted in Mugo's prophecy of earned and disciplined change. If militants were inspired by his 1938 account, Kenyatta himself seems to have thought better of it. In any case the militants were divided. They conscripted the peaceful symbols of *ituika* for their *mbatuni* fighting oath; and those who imagined a general massacre of whites called it the 'great *ituika*',[130] a gross distortion of all that Mugo had ever been heard to say. A later, wartime, *nyimbo* also converted the thunderous rain with which the rainbow dragon supposedly rewarded *ituika* into the noise of battle.[131] But however hard the militants tried to subvert the conservatives' past it held them still in its sway, inhibiting many from acting on their own. Mau Mau fighters told elders to keep silent; yet they also called themselves *itungati*, rearguards who owed service to seniors.[132] Once Gikoyo learned of Waiyaki's curse he knew he had to fight; looking back twenty years later he still saw Mau Mau as the outcome of Waiyaki's dying commission, his 'last bitter words'.[133]

There is no proof that other guerrillas shared Gikoyo's belief since there is little evidence of any kind; casualties were high, memoirs few. What there is suggests that few did; their sense of history in this fourth, wartime, phase of political discourse was too different from that of earlier politicians. Tales of Waiyaki and Mugo had previously mediated between dynastic and regenerative pasts, Kikuyu time and Biblical history, and the hopes of the literate and the unschooled. Kenyatta and Gikoyo – once he was told – heard the same stories in different ways. But in the forest war the many insurgent rivalries came to be seen principally as a cultural clash between units that accepted the authority of literacy and those who rejected its alien tyranny. The former were subject to Dedan Kimathi and his 'Kenya Parliament'; the latter followed Stanley Mathenge, calling themselves 'Kenya *riigi*', the hut door that shut out the night.[134] Prophetic traditions that had been a means of argument were transmuted into weapons of conflict. In the process Mugo almost dropped from sight and Waiyaki's story took a strange new turn. There are three explanations for this revolution in the politics of the past, to be found in political geography, class difference and the strains of war.

The geography of Mau Mau mobilization is almost sufficient cause. Starting as a conservative movement in Kiambu, it became more militant as Nairobi's workers took their anger home to the already aroused northern districts of Murang'a and Nyeri.[135] Mugo and Waiyaki were or had become southern Kikuyu heroes; Mau Mau was largely a northern war. Most war memoirs are by men of Nyeri, furthest north, and no Nyeri fighter thought Waiyaki's curse had led to war; only one mentioned him at all.[136] While two commanders called themselves after Nyeri's Wang'ombe and one after Murang'a's equivalent patron of empire, Karuri wa Gakure, none adopted 'Waiyaki' as *nom de guerre.* Nor did Kimathi take obvious opportunities to recall Waiyaki's fate, either when offering to free African kings more recently detained, the Kabaka of Buganda and Seretse Khama – both of whom had forest leaders named after them – or when warning against British treachery during proposed peace talks. His instructive history of struggle went back no further than Thuku in 1920.[137] More surprisingly, there seems to have been little recollection of Mugo. He was a Murang'a man; it was 'common gossip' that 'the time had come for all prophecies to be fulfilled';[138] and Kimathi was fascinated by dreams. Yet he made only one reference to Mugo, in a diary entry on 'famous national seers'; and he got him wrong, thinking Chege and Mugo to be different people.[139]

But there was more to Mugo and Waiyaki's absence than geographical eccentricity; the forest fighters' sense of history·was also very one-sided. They often thought in regenerative time, quoting *riika* proverbs and naming combat units after past generations, but their linear time stopped when it started, with God's gift of Kikuyuland to Gikuyu and Muumbi.[140] Recent *mbari* history was doubtless too divisive. But one can detect a class differentiation in historical consciousness too, in a world where educational levels often reinforced differences in access to land. Few men who by reason of their age and property knew their dynastic history entered the forest. They either joined the 'loyalist' resistance to Mau Mau, whose thoughts remain yet more secret than the insurgents' own, or else, especially if better educated, were likely to be detained as the movement's most visible – and moderate – leaders. At Easter 1955, some of these latter, after hearing the parable of the Good Shepherd and deciding to educate their illiterate fellow detainees, recalled that Waiyaki had died in detention before them, 'a source of strength and some joy.'[141] Literate and unlettered prisoners developed mutual trust; at least one detention camp became a mass literacy class.[142] It was different in the forests. Few fighters were educated; the gap between them and the unschooled widened into a murderous gulf. They did not listen to the same stories. They had no dynastic heroes to share; their redemptive times could revolve in totally different worlds.

This distinction developed, thirdly, because of the nature of the war. After its fighters lost their early initiative Mau Mau had to break up into small forest bands. Facing privation and danger in isolation, these fell prey to mutual suspicion. There was widespread fear of sorcery; Kimathi and Mathenge suspected it of each other, a terrifying metaphor for the fragmented parochialism that structured Kikuyu politics but destroyed military trust. It was perhaps their fear of envious fragmentation that made Kimathi's forces so insufferably reliant on mission education and Biblical inspiration in the eyes of their *riigi* critics who forecast that literate leadership would enslave the poor. Kimathi took on a Messianic arrogance, more Moses than Christ, seeking defence from sorcerous envy in the Bible and meeting God in his dreams. Mathenge's men followed an older Kikuyu tradition of insurance and control, obeying diviners and prophets whom Kimathi's men hated and despised for their superstitious disruption of battle plans.[143] It was as if the rigours of war had taken Kikuyu back to their first conflicts of faith between Christianity and the old religion. Among the forest veterans men of Mathenge's *riigi* and unlettered men generally seem to have renewed their old Kikuyu belief in the afterlife and its potential for this-worldly rebirth. Wachanga wrote of executed fighters herding Kimathi's cattle in the underworld; Gikoyo thought he found the hill of cattle under which flocks and herds awaited rebirth.[144] But Kikuyu reincarnation, to return finally to the story of Waiyaki, depended, crucially, on a good death.

And a good death, some insurgents began to suspect as the war turned against them, was something that Waiyaki had been brutally denied. With hindsight one can suggest that these doubts had surfaced as early as June 1953 when some forest fighters, in a counter-coronation, buried over 2,000 shillings of the new Queen Elizabeth's coinage upside down, cursing them to render them worthless to any finder.[145] A more dreadful deed the following year graphically explained why the British Crown, even in the days of good Queen Victoria, should be deemed accursed. Mau Mau women prophets on Mount Kenya, led by one Mama Mwangi, also known as Mama Future, became convinced that their men would lose unless they reversed Waiyaki's fate. A white settler must be sacrificed in the same way as Waiyaki had met his death. One night, therefore, a band of forest fighters entered the unlocked farmhouse of Gray Leakey, Louis Leakey's cousin, strangled his wife and then led the old man, nicknamed *Morungaru* or 'straight', high up the mountain, there to bury him alive, head down – an act that reinforced white opinion that Mau Mau was 'lost in the haunted wilderness of superstition'.[146] Apart from the burial party the only witness was the young son of the Leakey's Kikuyu cook.[147] What was at issue was much more than the symbolic reversal of Waiyaki's supposed fate; Leakey's sacrifice also turned upside down all previous Kikuyu assumptions about Waiyaki's exemplary power.

No Kikuyu text written earlier than the late 1960s agreed with the militant women seers that the British did Waiyaki to death in a manner that magically destroyed both the power he would otherwise have exercised in the afterlife and any hope of his reincarnation.[148] He had previously been said to have died of wounds, illness or hunger. There may well have been an earlier, suppressed suspicion of British sorcery, perhaps seen in 1929 when people sang that Koinange would be buried alive because he supported the missionaries over clitoridectomy.[149] But none of the politicians who used Waiyaki's memory to press for a legitimate politics of colonial collaboration would have wanted the story of inverted burial to get about, still less Kenyatta if he thought his search for a legitimate opposition was helped by belief that he was the reborn Waiyaki. Seventy-five years on, Waiyaki's own descendants would have nothing to do with the idea, although they were aware of it.[150] It is possible – but the date of origin would have to be ascertained – that a *nyimbo* heard at the Anglican girls' school at Kahuhia, Murang'a, in 1955 – 'Waiyaki died at Kibwezi and on his grave they planted a banana tree' – was the establishment's answer to the way Leakey's death had given substance to the dreadful allegation. For the song expressed a version of myth that held that in 1892 a seer, knowing the reverse burial meant 'that the black man's power had been toppled and that the white man was on the saddle', told the elders that Africans would be slaves for ever unless they exhumed and reburied Waiyaki. On finding his 'grave of shame' the elders did as they were told and planted the banana.[151] There would otherwise have been no dynastic theory of effective pressure on the British, no reasoned defence of the Kikuyu lands before Judge Carter, no redemptive hopes of Mugo's learned liberation, no *Prayers of Waiyaki*, perhaps not even the curse that authorized Mau Mau. The women prophets of the Mount Kenya forests may have reassured desperate young forest fighters; they may have given voice to long suppressed popular suspicion; but in opening up this *kirira* or secret knowledge they also destroyed the imaginative foundations of modern Kikuyu high politics.

Ethnicity & the State Nation

By telling stories about Waiyaki and Mugo, Kikuyu leaders defined a series of political issues. They also created a knowledgeable audience. This came to see itself as Kikuyu, not only a self-conscious ethnic group but also a particular political community, one in which power remained fragmented while political imaginations enlarged. By suppressing some versions of Waiyaki's story Kikuyu spokesmen imaginatively reinforced a dynastic form of politics that kept power parochial and property secure against a tide of social change. While *mbari* seniors also evoked regenerative time in prophecies of social renewal they guarded against its subversive potential by stressing the plutocratic demands of both past *ituika* and Mugo's laborious future freedom. Mounting popular anger against the British eventually forced suppressed histories to the surface, but Kikuyu still clarified their disagreements by reference to Waiyaki and Mugo. Kikuyu, one could say, created themselves as a political community by agreeing to disagree about a common stock of stories. During their Mau Mau crisis, however, they found not only that they were bitterly divided but that, in the forest, division aroused mutual loathing. Not all Kikuyu had been listening to the same stories. How much more must that be true of the people now called Kenyan, a nation lumped together by alien conquest and, more recently, by the unequal favours of the independent state? Kenyans at Independence in 1963, like Kikuyu on the eve of conquest in 1892, had no common stock of stories. How were they to create one? This unfinished fourth chapter of Waiyaki and Mugo's story suggests two ways. One is deliberate, when stories are told for an intended political effect, either official or dissident. But their images can exclude as large an audience as they attract. The other is more spontaneous, as when private dramas arouse common reactions. A public that shares in these, however divided its opinions, is on the way to becoming a political community. Whenever Waiyaki has been used for an intended political effect he has been inescapably Kikuyu; when his name has come up more accidentally his identity has been more ambiguous, even potentially Kenyan.

Looking, then, at the contrivances of nation-building, Kenyatta put independent Kenya together by conservative alliances with 'district bosses' or ethnic 'big men'. But first he had to reassemble Kikuyu in a way that big men could control, after the Mau Mau civil war. It was to one of Waiyaki's great grandsons, another Munyua and a man clearly not bewitched, to whom he turned as his ministerial ambassador to the last remaining forest-fighters at independence.[152] There was no better dynastic authority available. Today 'Waiyaki Way' is the main highway leading west out of Nairobi. Some say that the conically roofed hall of what was intended to be the ruling party's, KANU's, headquarters, now the Kenyatta Conference Centre in Nairobi, is Mugo's *thingira* of freedom.[153] The dissident novelist, Ngugi wa Thiong'o, has matched this co-optation of ethnic heroes to state-national purposes with his own vision of Waiyaki in a pan-tribal pantheon of resisters who fought the British, a hero for political opposition today.[154] But no such contrivances can include all Kenya's nationalities; imaginatively excluded from the story their members feel politically threatened, as some Ndorobo did before Judge Carter. Modern Kenyans have protested against that disregard as strongly as Lewis Kaberere wa Hunter; many, like perhaps the elder, Thindi, have been imprisoned for their pains. The centenary of Waiyaki's arrest has provided Kenyan civil rights activists with a focus for their campaign to show how oppressive and exclusionary deliberate nation-building can be.[155]

But Kenya also provides an example of how a public can enlarge itself by responding to private tragedy and conflict. In early 1987 Waiyaki unexpectedly had a new claim to notice: his double clan and ethnic affiliation, both Muceera Kikuyu and Kaputie Maasai. That is why his father was Hinga, a dissembler. Such trans-ethnicity had been a condition of social mobility in pre-colonial times. The British, seeing 'tribal tradition' as the rock of political stability, were suspicious of it; Kikuyu spokesmen therefore made little of Waiyaki's ambiguity. But his double ancestry now makes him look like a modern Kenyan. Appropriately enough it was another death and disputed burial that aroused this reflection. Waiyaki's great-grandaughter Wambui, sister to Kenyatta's ally Munyua, married the Luo lawyer 'S.M.' Otieno in 1963, the year of Independence, and on 17 August, the anniversary of her ancestor's captivity. When Otieno died late in 1986 his Luo clansmen disputed his widow's wish to bury him at the marital home outside Nairobi, not far from Waiyaki's place. They claimed that 'S.M.' was for ever his clan's son and should thus return to Luoland, his proper 'home'. The legal case revolved around the polar opposites of modernity and tradition, Kenyanness and tribalness, Christianity and barbarity, women's rights and male authority and, therefore between the statutory law that awarded the corpse to the widow and the 'customary law' that gave it to the clansmen. Wambui argued that her late husband, a modern Kenyan, should be buried by her, an equally modern Kenyan and not according to an ethnic 'custom' – that was in any case as recently invented as Kenyanness. She used her descent to back her claim. 'S.M.' had only one clan; she had two ethnic identities behind her. Her parents were not only Christian, they were Presbyterian elders; one of Kenya's leading schools was on her family land. Her family history, in this modernized dynastic theory, was as

'Kenyan' as her husband's profession and modern style of life. When his clansmen were nonetheless given his body she saw it as a defeat for modernity, women and middle-class Kenya.[156] By no means all Kenyans who followed the 'S.M. case' were Luo or Kikuyu, but that did not exclude them from the drama. They all feared death; they had all suffered the conflicts of 'modernity' and 'tradition', each of them a new social construct; they were all men and women. They all had to work out how to be Kenyan. Here was a story to help them.

Notes

1. Many have helped me, especially my colleague Richard Waller and Thomas Colchester, lately of the Kenya government, who met the myth of Waiyaki in 1954. I also thank the editors and other contributors; members of the Overseas History seminar at Cambridge University and of the African History seminar at the University of Columbia; and the 1991 history admission candidates to Trinity College, Cambridge, who had to comment on four of my primary sources.
2. For the latter see, Charles Ambler, Chapter 10 above.
3. Charles Mucuha, 'Cege wa Kibiru' and 'Waiyaki wa Hinga' (both 1967) for biographical details: University of Nairobi, History Department Research Project Archive (hereafter: UCN/HD – RPA), deposits B/2/2 and B/2/2(1). Thanks to the then department chairman, Professor Ahmed Salim and to Dr David Sperling for access to this archive.
4. L. S. B. Leakey, *The Southern Kikuyu before 1903*, Volume 3 (London, 1977), p. 1121.
5. Shadrack Kinyanjui (aged 82), Obadia Njuguna (75), Peter Njiri (90), interviewed by Mucuha in 1967; and traditions collected by Revd W. B. Anderson: UCN/HD – RPA, B/2/2. Jomo Kenyatta, *Facing Mount Kenya* (London, 1938), pp. 41–4.
6. Kabetu Waweru 'An elder's story' in Leakey, *Southern Kikuyu*, Volume 1, p. 32; ibid. Volume 3, p. 1151.
7. For the concept, Marcia Wright, Chapter 6 above.
8. See Ngugi wa Thiong'o's early novels for timelessness: *Weep Not, Child* (London, 1964), pp. 29–30, 36, 55–6, 58, 65; *The River Between* (London, 1965), pp. 2–3, 8–9, 22–5, 44–5, 93, 100–01, 106–12, 117, 151–3, 168; *A Grain of Wheat* (London, 1967), p. 13. Compare Kinuthia Mugia, *Urathi wa Cege wa Kiburu* (Nairobi, 1979) pp. 3–4 – translation by courtesy of Revd John K. Karanja – and *Genesis* 37 for dreaming herdboys.
9. Carl Rosberg and John Nottingham, *The Myth of Mau Mau* (New York, 1966), pp. 13–14, 82, 180–1; Brian McIntosh, 'The Scottish Mission in Kenya, 1891–1923' (Ph.D. thesis, Edinburgh University, 1969), pp. 99–101; Godfrey Muriuki, *A History of the Kikuyu 1500–1900* (Nairobi, 1974), pp. 137–8, 142–52; Valeer Neckebrouck, *Le Peuple affligé: les déterminants de la fissiparité dans un nouveau mouvement religieux au Kenya central* (Immensee, 1983), pp. 10–11, 254–6; David P. Sandgren, *Christianity and the Kikuyu: Religious Divisions and Social Conflict* (New York, 1989), pp. 12–15; Marshall S. Clough, *Fighting Two Sides: Kenyan Chiefs and Politicians, 1918–1940* (Niwot, 1990), pp. 8–9; Leakey, *Southern Kikuyu*, Volume 1, pp. 26–33, 54–86.
10. But see Carol Sicherman, *Ngugi wa Thiong'o: The Making of a Rebel* (London, 1990), pp. 182–5, 349–57, for a start.

John Lonsdale

11. G. Barra (ed.), *1,000 Kikuyu Proverbs* (Nairobi [1939], 1960), nos. 249, 404, 456, 503, 504, 505. Barra, a missionary, may have censored proverbs favourable to prophets. But the other collector, Ngumbu Njururi, in his *Gikuyu Proverbs* (Nairobi, [1968], 1983), gives only one in their favour, no. 141.

12. Leakey, *Southern Kikuyu*, Volume 3, pp. 1124-44.

13. W. S. and K. Routledge, *With a Prehistoric People: The Akikuyu of British East Africa* (London, 1910), pp. 263-8; Leakey, *Southern Kikuyu*, Volume 3, pp. 1146-50.

14. Routledge, *Prehistoric People*, p. 255; C. W. Hobley, 'Further researches into Kikuyu and Kamba religious beliefs and customs', *J. Roy. Anthr. Inst.* 41 (1911), pp. 437-9: I take Routledge's Kishuro to be Hobley's Kichura.

15. Ngugi's *River Between* is a fictional account of such scepticism over Mugo.

16. For constructions of ethnicity see Leroy Vail (ed.), *The Creation of Tribalism in Southern Africa* (London, 1989); John Lonsdale, 'The moral economy of Mau Mau', in Bruce Berman and John Lonsdale, *Unhappy Valley: Conflict in Kenya and Africa*, Volume 2 (London, 1992), pp. 265-504.

17. Rita M. Breen, 'The politics of land: the Kenya Land Commission (1932-33) and its effects on land, policy in Kenya' (Ph.D. thesis, Michigan State University, 1976).

18. Kenneth King, (ed.) *Harry Thuku; An Autobiography* (Nairobi, 1970), pp. 21-36, 80; Robert L. Tignor, *The Colonial Transformation of Kenya: The Kamba, Kikuyu and Maasai from 1900 to 1939* (Princeton, 1976), pp. 48-9, 230.

19. For his role in Kikuyu politics see Bruce Berman and John Lonsdale, 'Louis Leakey's Mau Mau: a study in the politics of knowledge', *History and Anthropology* 5 (1991), pp. 143-204.

20. Government of Kenya, *Kenya Land Commission Evidence*, Volume 1 (Nairobi, 1934), p. 153; cited hereafter as *KLCE i*; the Kikuyu Central Association (KCA) had published the fig tree parable in its journal, *Muigwithania*: Grigg to Passfield, 12 October 1929, Public Record Office (PRO), CO533/392/1.

21. Andrew Gathea, chief Koinange, Kikuyu Loyal Patriots, KCA, Ndirangu wa Wang'ombe, mbari of Kiarie wa Mureithie: in *KLCE i*, pp. 165-6, 170, 171-2, 191-8, 211-2, 239-41, 322-3. For settlers as *ahoi*: Koinange, ibid., p. 129; Kenyatta, *Facing Mount Kenya*, p. 44.

22. M. P. K. Sorrenson, *Origins of European Settlement in Kenya* (Nairobi, 1968), ch. 3; John Overton, 'The origins of the Kikuyu land problem: land alienation and land use in Kiambu, Kenya, 1895-1920', *African Studies Review*, 31 (1988), pp. 109-26.

23. In any case, Carter got his facts wrong. Both main sources show that Waiyaki fought Purkiss a full year after Kikuyu attacks on Dagoretti: F. D. Lugard, *The Rise of our East African Empire*, Volume 2 (Edinburgh, 1893), pp. 535-7; J. R. L. Macdonald, *Soldiering and Surveying in British East Africa 1891-1894* (London, 1897), pp. 112-21.

24. For Kinyanjui and Waiyaki see: H. H. Austin, 'The passing of Wyaki', *The Cornhill Magazine*, ns. 54 (1923), pp. 613-22; obituary in *Muigwithania* i, 10 (Feb-March 1929), p. 3: Kenya National Archives (KNA) DC/MKS.10B/13/1; Kabetu Waweru (who exonerated Kinyanjui of collusion in Waiyaki's downfall) in Leakey, *Southern Kikuyu*, Volume 1, p. 31; testimony of Githagui, Waiyaki's son (aged 90), Tiras Waiyaki, Waiyaki's grandson (64) and ex-senior chief Josiah Njonjo (82) to Mucuha in 1967: UCN/HD - RPA: B/2/2(1); but also *KLCE i*, p. 265, where Waiyaki's heirs claimed kinship with Kinyanjui. For his 'heavily contested' land, *KLCE i*, pp. 277-86. See Muriuki, *History of Kikuyu*, pp. 93-4, 148, 152-3, 174-5 and Tignor, *Colonial Transformation*, pp. 45-57 for critical views of Kinyanjui; Rogers, 'British and Kikuyu', p. 260 for a more sympathetic one.

25. Johnstone Kenyatta, Editorial in *Muigwithania*, i 4 (Aug 1928), p. 4, quoting *Lamentations* 5.8: KNA, DC/MKS.10B/13/1; correspondence in PRO, CO533/382/6.

26. Most succinctly in Jomo Kenyatta, *Kenya: The Land of Conflict* (London, 1944), pp. 7-10.

27. Lonsdale, 'Moral Economy of Mau Mau', pp. 386-95 for a recent account.

28. A point emphasized in Henry Muoria Mwaniki's unpublished memoirs, 'The British and my Kikuyu tribe' (unpublished manuscript 1982, privately held), pp. 42-4.

29. Obituary of Munyua Waiyaki in *Muigwithania* i, 4 (August 1928): KNA, DC/MKS.10B/13/1; evidence from Kikuyu Loyal Patriots, KCA and Dr J. W. Arthur, *KLCE i*. pp. 172, 198, 457-9; R. Macpherson, *The Presbyterian Church in Kenya* (Nairobi, 1970), pp. 26-7, 39.

30. For these two paragraphs see, CSM Council, 'Memorandum on the Mission Estate at Kikuyu' and 'Further Memorandum', *KLCE i*, pp. 815-44; *Report of the Kenya Land Commission* (Cmd. 4556, 1934), pp. 122-3; McIntosh, 'Scottish Mission', pp. 148-92, 218-38; and Macpherson, *Presbyterian Church*, p. 35.

31. For Anglo-Kikuyu differences on the rules of war, see Margery Perham and Mary Bull (eds), *The Diaries of Lord Lugard*, Volume 1 (London, 1959), pp. 344-5 (31 October 1890).

32. Lugard, *Our East African Empire*, Volume 1, pp. 325-8, was a favourite Kikuyu text. See, KCA in *KLCE i*, pp. 197-8; Jomo Kenyatta, *Facing Mount Kenya* (London, 1938), pp. 45-6. Muriuki, *History of Kikuyu*, pp. 142-51, takes Lugard's view. Kenyatta, in London during the 1930s, knew of Lord Lugard's influence in imperial circles; chief Koinange met him at the parliamentary committee on Closer Union in East Africa. For his East African interest at the time see, Margery Perham, *Lugard, The Years of Authority 1898-1945* (London, 1960), pp. 673-93.

33. Lugard, *Our East African Empire*, Volume 1, pp. 323-37 and Volume 2, pp. 534-7. Kikuyu cited only this version of Lugard's story of Waiyaki; none (apart from the historian Muriuki) used his diaries, available from 1959, which differ from the memoirs in one crucial particular discussed below.

34. This British account of August 1892 is a composite of Macdonald's *Soldiering and Surveying*, pp. 111-21 and Austin's 'Passing of Wiyaki'; Muriuki, *History of Kikuyu*, pp. 142-9 has a similar account. The memory of John Ainsworth, in 1892 in charge of the next fort, two days' march away at Machakos, had become very faulty before being published in F. H. Goldsmith, *John Ainsworth: Pioneer Kenya Administrator 1864-1946* (London, 1955), pp. 17-22. I take 'Waguruguru' to be an Anglo-Swahili corruption of the Kikuyu *andu a ruguru*.

35. Greet Kershaw, 'The land is the people: a study of social organisation in historical perspective' (Ph.D. thesis, Chicago University 1972), p. 80.

36. Lugard, *Diaries*, Volume 1, pp. 318-9; idem, *Rise of our East African Empire*, Volume 1, p. 325.

37. Kenyatta, *Facing Mount Kenya*, pp. 25-40.

38. Sorrenson, *Origins of European Settlement*, pp. 176-7 cites other Kikuyu land sales to whites but not until the late 1890s, by which time prices had much increased.

39. Mbari of Kiarie wa Mureithie in *KLCE i*, p. 322; evidence of ex-chief Josiah Njonjo and Samuel K. Wenjia, August 1967: UCN/HD - RPA B/2/2(1).

40. Lugard, *Diaries*, Volume 3, p. 379; Macdonald, *Soldiering and Surveying*, p. 108; Sir Gerald Portal, *The British Mission to Uganda in 1893* (London, 1894), p. 86.

41. Leakey, *Southern Kikuyu*, p. 78, reporting the views of informants who had been young men in the 1890s.

42. For Kikuyu views on the cause of the great hunger, see Leakey, *Southern Kikuyu*, Volume 1, p. 86; Muriuki, *History of Kikuyu*, p. 155; for alternative views, Peter Rogers, 'The British and the Kikuyu, 1890-1905: a reassessment', *Journal of African History*, 20, 2 (1979), pp. 255-70, p. 264; Lonsdale, 'Moral economy of Mau Mau', p. 346. For Waiyaki's nickname, *ngamini*, see his son Githagui's reminiscence in UCN/HD - RPA B/2/2(1), echoed by Kenyatta, *Facing Mount Kenya*, pp. 44-7.

43. As witnessed in 1887 by Ludwig von Hohnel; see his *Discovery of Lakes Rudolf and Stefanie*, Volume 1 (London, 1894), pp. 293, 304, 308-10.

44. For dynastic labour theory, see Kikuyu Loyal Patriots memorandum, *KLCE i*, p. 172; the testimony of Waiyaki's descendants and others in UCN/HD - RPA B/2/2(1) is uncomfortably ambivalent; see also Lugard, *Rise of Our East African Empire*, Volume 2, p. 536.

45. Testimony of Githagui in UCN/HD RPA B/2/2(1); von Hohnel, *Lakes Rudolf and Stefanie*, Volume 2, pp. 298-317; *Report of the Kenya Land Commission*, map facing p. 46.

46. A judgment based on von Hohnel, *Lakes Rudolf and Stefanie*, Volume 1, pp. 298-317.

47. Muriuki, *History of Kikuyu*, p. 147; for another example see, A. T. Matson, 'George Wilson and Dagoretti: Kinanjui's account', *Uganda Jl*, 30, 1 (1966), pp. 91-2.

48. Lugard, *Rise of our East African Empire*, Volume 1, p. 327 (where Muiruri is Miroo); Austin, 'Passing of Wyaki', p. 617 (where he is Mlu); reminiscence of Waiyaki's son Githagui: UCN/HD - RPA B/2/2(1).

49. Leakey, *Southern Kikuyu*, Volume 1, pp. 31, 82 for 1930s reminiscence; for later memories in like vein, Church of Scotland, *Mau Mau and the Church* (Edinburgh, 1953), p. 5; Muriuki, *History of Kikuyu*, pp. 94-5; testimony of Githagui, Samuel Wenjia, (contradicted by Josiah Njonjo) in 1967: UCN/HD - RPA B/2/2(1); David Leonard, *African Successes: Four Public Administrators of Kenya's Rural Development* (Berkeley, 1991), p. 17.

50. Von Hohnel, *Rudolf and Stefanie*, Volume 1, pp. 294, 310-11; Lugard, *Rise of our East African Empire*, Volume 2, p. 536.

51. Kershaw, 'Land is people', pp. 88-90, 148, 199; Muriuki, *History of Kikuyu*, pp. 149-51. Roger, 'British and Kikuyu', p. 255-60.

52. Kenyatta, *Facing Mount Kenya*, pp. 46-7.

53. Leakey, *Southern Kikuyu*, Volume 1, pp. 30, 75.

54. Muriuki's informants in his *History of Kikuyu*, p. 149, fn 55; and testimony of Githagui and ex-chief Josiah Njonjo; for Waiyaki's forgiveness, Kibaara Kabatu, 'Account of the struggle for independence' (Kikuyu MS, nd.) also in UCN/HD - RPA B/2/2(1); Austin's 1923 account ('Passing of Wiyaki', p. 621) also portrays an unexpectedly forgiving Waiyaki. I do not know if Kabatu's tradition was influenced by Austin's text.

55. Austin, 'Passing of Wiyaki', pp. 616-21.

56. H. Leakey to *East African Standard*, 15 February 1919, reprinted in *KLCE i*, p. 855.

57. *KLCE i*, pp. 172-3, 169-70.

58. Ibid, pp. 171-2.

59. For which thesis see Benedict Anderson, *Imagined Communities: Reflections on the Origin and Spread of Nationalism* (London, 1983).

60. *KLCE i*, pp. 266-7.

61. From the summary of *mbari* claims prepared by the Land Commission's secretary S. H. Fazan: *KLCE i*, (pp. 258-375); the originals were 'far too voluminous' to print.

62. For Kikuyu aversion to Ndorobo, Leakey, *Southern Kikuyu*, Volume 1, pp. 441-2 and cf. Michael Kenny, 'Mirror in the forest: the Dorobo hunter-gatherers as an image of the Other', *Africa* 51 (1981), pp. 477-95. The KCA quoted Lugard, *Our East African Empire*, Volume 1, p. 328, in *KLCE i*, pp. 197-8; the *mbari* of Kiarie wa Mureithie, possible owners of Fort Smith, also argued (*KLCE i*, p. 324) for the return of empty white farms.

63. Koinange to Secretary of State, 7 January 1934 (emphasis added): PRO, CO533/441/9.

64. Memoranda by Commissioner for Lands and Chief Native Commissioner (July-December 1932), in *KLCE i*, pp. 28-81; also Sorrenson, *Land Reform*, ch. 2, and H. E. Lambert, *The Systems of Land Tenure in the Kikuyu Land Unit* (University of Cape Town, 1949). For Kikuyu confirmation of the field officials' view, see Luka Wakahangara (murdered 30 years later with his family, at Lari, by Mau Mau) in *KLCE i*, p. 185.

65. For these family connections see, Clough, *Fighting Two Sides*; Berman and Lonsdale, 'Louis Leakey's Mau Mau'; Lonsdale, 'Moral Economy of Mau Mau', pp. 377-8.
66. *KLCE i*, , pp. 663, 854; 662-3, 673, 680-2, 865-6, 870-1; and 658, 675, 685, 860, respectively, for expressions of these three views.
67. Evidently Leakey did not accept Lugard's 'present' as payment (*Our East African Empire*, Volume 1, p. 325) for he heard of the purchase 'on the very best authority'; this could well have been Koinange whom Leakey had known 'intimately' for nearly 20 years and 'never found . . . untruthful': *KLCE i*, pp. 866, 868. For the CMS purchase of Kabete, ibid., p. 848; Koinange as mission cook, p. 719; and Louis Leakey's admitted error, p. 665.
68. Leakey to *Leader of British East Africa*, 1 March 1919, in *KLCE i*, pp. 871-2.
69. Ibid., p. 855.
70. Lewis Kaberere wa Hunter's oral evidence, 23 January 1933: *KLCE i*, pp. 223-5.
71. For Ndorobo evidence (and Kikuyu ripostes) see *KLCE i*, pp. 221-33, 265-7, 318, 345-7, 350, 785 (in A. R. Barlow's evidence), and 1107-1111 (from official records).
72. For Fazan's criticisms, *KLCE i*, pp. 258-9, 365-70; and *Report of the Kenya Land Commission* (Cmd. 4556, 1934, cited hereafter as *KLC Report*), pp. 69, 84-93, 105, 111.
73. *KLC Report*, p. 93.
74. *KLCE i*, p. 149 (at Kiambu, 15 November 1932, a few minutes before Waiganjo spoke).
75. *KLC Report*, chapter 9.
76. For Fazan's 'Consolidation scheme' when DC Kiambu in 1930 and the conclusions of his 'Economic Survey of the Kikuyu Reserves' (1931), see *KLCE i*, pp. 25-6, 1032.
77. S. H. Fazan, 'Minority Report' in *Report of Committee on Native Land Tenure in Kikuyu Province* (Nairobi, 1929), p. 56.
78. Leakey had signed the main report of the 1929 committee without reservation; this had made a point of supporting the *mbari*: trustees: ibid., p. 40.
79. Kikuyu Loyal Patriots memorandum, *KLCE i*, p. 177.
80. For settler and official evidence critical of Kikuyu claims see *KLCE i*, pp. 397-408. 479-81, 532-45, 589-604, 615-56, 694-708, 716-54, 773-9, 880-90, 894-919, 921-35.
81. *KLCE i.*, pp. 592-3.
82. W. H. Taylor, review article in *East African Standard*, 6 March 1951; also C. T. Stoneham, *Out of Barbarism* (London, 1955), p. 112.
83. John Lonsdale, 'Mau Maus of the mind', *Jl of African History*, 31 (1990), pp. 393-421; Berman and Lonsdale, 'Louis Leakey's Mau Mau'.
84. Michael Cowen, 'Differentiation in a Kenya location' (University of East Africa conference paper, Nairobi, 1972); summarized in Lonsdale, 'Moral Economy of Mau Mau', pp. 361-2.
85. Compare Kenyatta, *Facing Mount Kenya*, pp. 44-7 and 24-8 with Leakey, *Southern Kikuyu*, Volume 1, pp. 54-86 and pp. 87-108.
86. Carolyn Clark, 'Louis Leakey as ethnographer', *Canadian Jl. of African Studies*, 23, 3 (1989); Berman and Lonsdale, 'Louis Leakey's Mau Mau', pp. 170-2.
87. Rosberg and Nottingham, *Myth of Mau Mau*, pp. 155-60.
88. For this untested interpretation of *ituika* and the KCA's self-image see Lonsdale, 'Moral economy of Mau Mau', pp. 344-6, 369-74, 449.
89. I find J. D. Y. Peel, 'Progression and recursion in African social thought', pp. 277-91 in Christopher Fyfe (ed.), *African Futures* (Centre of African Studies, Edinburgh, 1988) most helpful at this point and have adopted his novel use of the term 'recursion' equivalent to ideas of regeneration and redemption. But, as discussion with Richard Waller has helped to clarify, Kikuyu did not make the same distinction between material and moral time that underpins Peel's scheme.

John Lonsdale

90. Ngumbu Njururi, *Gikuyu Proverbs* (Nairobi [1968] 1983), p. 7; Justin Itotia with James Dougall, 'The voice of Africa: Kikuyu proverbs', *Africa*, 1 (1928), p. 486.
91. Compare Kenyatta, *Facing Mount Kenya*, pp. 85, 186–95; *idem, My People of Kikuyu* (London 1942), pp. 10–14; Parmenas Githendu Mockerie [Mukiri], *An African Speaks for his People* (London, 1934), pp. 36–42. For less speculative discussion of Kikuyu views of history: Muriuki, *History of Kikuyu*, pp. 1–24; and Kershaw, 'Land is people', pp. 112–207.
92. For Mugo as a historical figure see Muriuki, *History of Kikuyu*, pp. 137–8.
93. Kenyatta, *Facing Mount Kenya*, pp. 189–94; Leakey, *Southern Kikuyu*, Volume 3, pp. 1281–4; Hobley, 'Further researches', pp. 419–22; H. E. Lambert, *Kikuyu Social and Political Institutions* (London, 1956), p. 60.
94. Mucuha's 1967 collection of traditions in UCN/HD – RPA, B/2/2; Kenyatta, *Facing Mount Kenya*, pp. 41–4; Kinuthia Mugia, *Urathi wa Cege wa Kibiru* (Nairobi, 1979), pp. 2–7. See Rosberg and Nottingham, *Myth of Mau Mau*, p. 181 for the eight-doored *thingira*, Maina wa Kinyatti (ed.), *Thunder from the Mountains: Mau Mau Patriotic Songs* (London, 1980), pp. 16–18, 26 for moral renewal.
95. Hobley, 'Further researches', pp. 437–9.
96. Kiambu District Annual Report (1914/15), p. 1 (emphasis added) and Lawford (DC Fort Hall) to PC Nyeri, 8 April 1919: KNA, KBU/7 and PC/CP.1/7/1 respectively. I can see no sign in these nor in the 1914/15 Kenia [Central] Province Annual Report (PC/CP.4/1/1), that a Kikuyu 'saviour' was yet associated with the prophecy, as Valeer Neckebrouck infers from the last source in *Le Onzième Commandement: étiologie d'une église indépendante au pied du mont Kenya* (Immensee, 1978), pp. 106, 128.
97. Kenyatta, *Facing Mount Kenya*, p. 196.
98. Petition in *KLCE i*, pp. 171–9; p. 178 for the ennoblement of chiefs.
99. Lonsdale, 'Moral economy of Mau Mau', pp. 371–97.
100. Until the oral researches of Godfrey Muriuki and Charles Mucuha in the 1960s.
101. Kenyatta, *Facing Amount Kenya*, pp. 43–7.
102. Lonsdale, 'Moral economy of Mau Mau', p. 370; H. Virginia Blakeslee, *Beyond the Kikuyu Curtain* (Chicago, 1956), p. 187.
103. Rosberg and Nottingham (*Myth of Mau Mau*, p. 181) only learned of the analogy by interview in 1963, the year of Kenya's independence. Mbiyu Koinange's *The People of Kenya Speak for Themselves* (Detroit, 1955), written for an American liberal audience, does not speak of such matters but see, Wanjiku Mukabi Kabira and Karega wa Mutahi, *Gikuyu Oral Literature* (Nairobi, 1988), p. 151.
104. Kabetu wa Waweru (1936) in Leakey, *Southern Kikuyu*, Volume 1, 32; Gathuri Chege (1963) in Rosberg and Nottingham, *Myth of Mau Mau*, 180.
105. Berman and Lonsdale, 'Louis Leakey's Mau Mau', pp. 174–8.
106. Kenyatta, *Facing Amount Kenya*, pp. 45–7; *Idem, My People of Kikuyu*, p. 62.
107. Jomo Kenyatta, *Kenya: the Land of Conflict* (London, 1944), pp. 7–9.
108. Senior chiefs Nderi, Koinange and Wambugu, with local councillors James Beauttah, Johana Kunyiha and others, 'Memorandum on African Land Tenure . . . in Kenya', to Secretary of State (nd. but 1946): PRO, CO533/544/2 (courtesy of Joanna Lewis).
109. In *Mumenyereri* (12 July 1948): KNA, MAA.8/106 (courtesy of David Throup).
110. Berman and Lonsdale, *Unhappy Valley*, ch 10, pp. 420–1 and 446–7.
111. These two paragraphs rely on Lonsdale, 'Moral economy of Mau Mau', pp. 401–51.
112. Kenyatta's politics is discussed, with sources, in ibid., pp. 410–4, 424–5.
113. Kenyatta, *Kenya: The Land of Conflict*, pp. 7–11, 22–3; Lonsdale, 'Moral economy of Mau Mau', p. 412.
114. Waruhiu Itote, *Mau Mau General* (Nairobi, 1967), p. 283; H.K. Wachanga, *The Swords of Kirinyaga: The Fight for Land and Freedom* (Nairobi, 1975)., pp. xxxvi–vii; Donald L. Barnett and Karari Njama, *Mau Mau from Within* (London, 1966), p. 120;

The Prayers of Waiyaki

Josiah M. Kariuki, *Mau Mau Detainee* (London, 1963), p. 21: this last text does not explicitly link political history and the oath but the context does.

115. I have relied on the translations of the *nyimbo* in L. S. B. Leakey, *Defeating Mau Mau* (London, 1954), ch. 5 and Maina wa Kinyatti (ed.), *Thunder from the Mountains*; for the points made here see Kinyatti, pp. 13-15, 25, 26, 29. For previous discussion of the *nyimbo*, see Bethwell A. Ogot, 'Politics, culture and music in central Kenya: a study of Mau Mau hymns 1951-1956', *Kenya Historical Review* 5, 2 (1977), pp. 275-86 and Lonsdale, 'Moral economy of Mau Mau', pp. 439-40, 443-4. For *kirumi* see also, C. W. Hobley, *Bantu Beliefs and Magic* (London, 1922), pp. 145-53; Kenyatta, *Facing Mount Kenya*, p. 114; Leakey, *Southern Kikuyu*, Volume 1, p. 123.

116. Leakey, *Defeating Mau Mau*, p. 57; Kinyatti, *Thunder*, pp. 15, 17-18, 20-22, 27.

117. Henry Muoria Mwaniki, 'I, the Kikuyu and the White Fury' (typescript, 1986), pp. 63-4.

118. Reproduced in McIntosh, 'The Scottish Mission in Kenya', Appendix iv; also, Sicherman, *Ngugi*, pp. 350-5.

119. I have seen no earlier reference to bees helping Waiyaki. Bees did attack a British caravan 7 months after Waiyaki's deportation, wreaking a havoc among the porters that Kikuyu must have seen; see Sir Gerald Portal, *The British Mission to Uganda in 1893* (London, 1894), pp. 94-6.

120. For discussion of Kikuyu labour theory, see Lonsdale, 'Moral economy of Mau Mau', pp. 333-4, 337-8, 355-61, 365-6, 379, 381-2, 405, 410-11, 414-6, 432, 439, 441, 453, 455.

121. Governor Baring to Secretary of State Lyttelton, 10 October 1952: PRO, CO822/443; report by Commissioner of Police quoted in *Historical Survey of the Origins and Growth of Mau Mau* (Cmnd. 1030, 1960), p. 159; Kingsley Martin, 'Report on Kenya: the African point of view', *New Statesman and Nation* (London), 6 Dec 1952. The chairman of the Mau Mau central committee later recorded that Kenyatta told people to accept his arrest: Eliud Mutonyi, 'Mau Mau chairman' (typescript, nd.), p. 78.

122. Greet Kershaw's conclusions, from fieldwork done in the mid-1950s, generously shared.

123. From negative evidence in Barnett and Njama, *Mau Mau from Within*; Joram Wamweya, *Freedom Fighter* (Nairobi, 1971); Ngugi Kabiro, *Man in the Middle* (Richmond, BC, 1973); Karigo Muchai, *The Hard Core* (Richmond, BC, 1973); Mohamed Mathu, *The Urban Guerrilla* (Richmond, BC, 1974).

124. Henry Muoria Mwaniki, 'The British and my Kikuyu tribe' (typescript, 1982), p. 18.

125. Gucu Gikoyo, *We Fought for Freedom* (Nairobi, 1979), p. 35.

126. Leakey, *Defeating Mau Mau*, pp. 61, 71; Kinyatti, *Thunder*, pp. 19-20, 23-4, 27, 85, 86, 93.

127. Gikoyo, *We Fought*, pp. 35, 316-18.

128. Kenyatta, *Facing Mount Kenya*, pp. 186-97; *idem*, *My People of Kikuyu*, pp. 12-15. In fact the *iregi* got their heroic reputation from northern Kikuyu frontier wars in the early nineteenth century: Muriuki, *History of Kikuyu*, pp. 45-6, 63-5. For Mau Mau images of *iregi*, see Itote, *Mau Mau General*, p. 55; Kinyatti, *Thunder*, pp. 30, 98.

129. S. H. Fazan, '[Secret] Report on the Sociological Causes Underlying Mau Mau with some Proposals on the Means of Ending it' (21 April 1954) p. 1 and Appendix II.

130. Rob Buijtenhuijs, *Essays on Mau Mau* (Leiden, 1982), pp. 127-33; Renison Muchiri Githige, 'The religious factor in Mau Mau with particular reference to Mau Mau oaths', (MA thesis, University of Nairobi, 1978) pp. 53-6.

131. Kinyatti, *Thunder*, p. 45.

132. Lonsdale, 'Moral economy of Mau Mau', p. 450.

133. Gikoyo, *We Fought*, p. 316. For an unresolved intertextual problem here, see below, note 148.

John Lonsdale

134. The sources for the split are, on 'Parliament's' side, Barnett and Njama, *Mau Mau from Within* and Maina wa Kinyatti, (ed.) *Kenya's Freedom Movement: the Dedan Kimathi Papers* (London, 1987); on the *riigi's*, Wachanga, *Swords of Kirinyaga*; for contrasting comment see, Luise White, 'Separating the men from the boys: Constructions of gender sexuality and terrorism in central Kenya, 1939-59', *Intnl Jnl of African Historical Studies*, 23 (1990), pp. 10-15; Lonsdale, 'Moral economy of Mau Mau', pp. 456-7.

135. Rosberg and Nottingham, *Myth of Mau Mau*, pp. 262-76; elaborated on in Lonsdale, 'Moral economy of Mau Mau', pp. 423-40.

136. Wachanga, *Swords of Kirinyaga*, p. 43.

137. Ibid., pp. 182-7; Itote, *Mau Mau General*, pp. 292-4; Kinyatti, *Kenya's Freedom Movement*, pp. 18-20, 67, 114-15.

138. Barnett and Niama, *Mau Mau from Within*, p. 175 (the only Nyeri reference to Mugo other than Kimathi's, below).

139. Kinyatti, *Kenya's Freedom Movement*, pp. 82, 87, 115.

140. Barnett and Njama, *Mau Mau from Within*, pp. 79, 158, 162-3, 176, 180, 245-6, 323, 442; Githige, 'Religious Factor', appendix on *nyimbo*; Itote, *Mau Mau General*, pp. 55, 141; Kinyatti, *Thunder*, pp. 93, 98.

141. Gakaara wa Wanjau, *Mau Mau Author in Detention* (Nairobi, 1988), pp. 140-1. At about the same time villagers in Kiambu were singing, 'Our people who are in jail, detained because of freedom, do not worry, Waiyaki was also there . . .' (recorded by Greet Kershaw in 1956).

142. Wamweya, *Freedom Fighter*, p. 185; White, 'Separating the men from the boys', pp. 11-12, 21.

143. For evidence of this conflict, that culminated in the damaging split between Parliament and *riigi*, see, Barnett and Njama, *Mau Mau from Within*, pp. 180, 185, 187-8, 191, 198-206, 216, 219-20, 228, 233-5, 237-41, 244, 250, 254, 263-5, 288, 306-8, 326, 334-8, 364-5, 367-8, 380, 382, 391, 394-402, 406-7, 413-16, 423, 441-82; Kinyatti, *Thunder*, pp. 81, 88-91; idem, *Kenya's Freedom Movement*, pp. 28, 32-41, 73, 83-4, 96-8, 111-3; Wachanga, *Swords of Kirinyaga*, pp. 25-30, 80-1, 110-11, 122-3.

144. Wachanga, *Swords of Kirinyaga*, p. 65; Gikoyo, *We Fought for Freedom*, p. 184; while Gikoyo, from Murang'a rather than from Mathenge's Nyeri, does not seem to have been a *riigi* member, he shared their views.

145. Wachanga, *Swords of Kirinyaga*, p. 63.

146. *East African Standard*, Leading Article (Nairobi, 26 October 1954).

147. For different accounts see, Wachanga, *Swords*, p. 43; *East African Standard*, Report of Kaleba's Trial (12 November 1954); Special Branch Headquarters 'Flash Report - Interrogation of Kaleba' 28 October 1954: KNA, DC/NYK.3/12/34 (courtesy of Randall Heather); Thomas Colchester: 'Note on the Association between the death of Chief Waiyaki in 1893 [sic] and the Leakey Sacrifice in the Mau Mau Emergency', 16 March 1966: Rhodes House, Mss.Afr.s.742(3); Agnes Leakey Hofmeyr (Gray Leakey's daughter), *Beyond Violence* (Nairobi, 1990); Stanley Kinga, 'Why we buried Leakey alive', *Daily Nation* (Nairobi, 10 May 1991).

148. Three of the four texts I know are, Ngugi wa Thiong'o, *Grain of Wheat*, pp. 13-15. (1967); Wachanga, *Swords of Kirinyaga*, p. 43 (1975); and Gikoyo, *We Fought for Freedom*, pp. 318-9 (1979); how far the two Mau Mau memoirs picked up the story from what schoolchildren were reading in the novel is a question I cannot answer. The fourth is Kibaara Kabatu's manuscript, in note 150 below.

149. John Spencer, *James Beauttah, Freedom Fighter* (Nairobi, 1983), p. 18, footnote 4.

150. Compare all the oral testimony collected by Charles Mucuha in 1967 with the manuscript account by Kibaara Kabatu, then in the possession of Waiyaki's grandson Tiras: all in UCN/ND - RPA B/2/2(1).

151. Information from Dr Jocelyn Murray, then a teacher at CMS Kahuhia; Gikoyo, *We Fought for Freedom*, pp. 318-19.
152. David W. Throup, 'The construction and destruction of the Kenyatta state' in M. G. Schatzberg (ed.), *The Political Economy of Kenya* (New York, 1987), p. 40.
153. Henry Muoria Mwaniki, personal communication.
154. In his foreword to Kinyatti, *Kenya's Freedom Movement*, p. xiv.
155. The One Million Signature Petition Against Detention Without Trial in Kenya Committee, *Petition to Mark the Centenary of Detention Without Trial in Kenya, 14 August 1892-14 August 1992* (Nairobi, London and New York, 1991).
156. For the use of Waiyaki in the court proceedings see, Sean Egan (ed.), *S. M. Otieno: Kenya's Unique Burial Saga* (Nairobi, 1987), pp. 6, 16, 18-19. For the broader picture, see J. B. Ojwang and J. N. K. Mugambi (eds), *The S. M. Otieno Case* (Nairobi, 1989); and Atieno Odhiambo and David W. Cohen, *Burying 'S.M.'* (London, 1992).

Bibliography

Adamson, J. *The Peoples of Kenya*. (New York, 1967).

Adas, Michael. *Prophets of Rebellion: Millenarian Protest Movements against European Colonial Order*. (Cambridge, 1987 [1979]).

Albert, Ethel. 'Women of Burundi: a study of social values', in Denise Paulme (ed.), *Women of Tropical Africa*. (Berkeley, 1963).

Allen, Tim. 'Understanding Alice: Uganda's Holy Spirit Movement in context', *Africa*, 61, 3 (1991).

Almagor, Uri. 'Raiders and elders: a confrontation of generations among the Dassenetch', in Katsuyoshi Fukui and David Turton (eds), *Warfare Among East African Herders*. (Osaka, 1979).

Ambler, Charles. *Kenyan Communities in the Age of Imperialism: The Central Region in the Late Nineteenth Century*. (New Haven, Conn., 1988).

Anderson, Benedict. *Imagined Communities: Reflections on the Origin and Spread of Nationalism*. (London, 1983).

Anderson, David M. 'Black mischief: crime, protest and resistance in Kenya's Western Highlands', *Historical Journal*, 36, iv (1993).

Anderson, David M. and Douglas H. Johnson. 'Diviners, seers and spirits in Eastern Africa: towards an historical anthropology', *Africa*, 61 (1991).

Anderson, David M. 'Stock theft and moral economy in colonial Kenya', *Africa*, 56, 4 (1986).

Anon. *Historia ya Utamaduni a Embu*. (Kigari, Embu, 1976).

Arkell-Hardwick, Alfred. *An Ivory Trader in North Kenia*. (London, 1903).

Aune, D. E. *Prophecy in Early Christianity and the Ancient Mediterranean World*. (Grand Rapids, 1983).

Austin, H. H. 'The passing of Wyaki', *The Cornhill Magazine*, ns. 54 (1923).

Bagge, S. 'The circumcision ceremony among the Naivasha Masai'. *Journal of the Royal Anthropological Institute*, 34 (1904).

Barnett, Donald L. and Njama, Karari. *Mau Mau from Within*. (London, 1966).

Barra, G. (ed.), *1,000 Kikuyu Proverbs*. (Nairobi, 1960 [1939]).

Bibliography

Barton, C. Juxon T. 'Notes on the Kipsikis or Lumbwa tribe of Kenya Colony', *Journal of the Royal Anthropological Institute*, 53 (1923).

Barton, J. *Oracles of God: Perceptions of Ancient Prophecy in Israel after the Exile*. (London, 1986).

Baxter, Paul. 'The Kiga', in Audrey I. Richards (ed.), *East African Chiefs*. (London, 1960).

Beach, David N. 'From heroism to history: Mapondera and the northern Zimbabwean plateau, 1840-1904'. *History in Africa*, 15 (1988).

Beattie, J. H. M. and Middleton, John. *Spirit Mediumship and Society in Africa*. (London, 1969).

Beattie, John H. M. 'Group aspects of the Nyoro spirit mediumship cult', *Human Problems in British Central Africa*, 30 (1961).

Beidelman, T. O. 'The Baraguyu', *Tanganyika Notes and Records*, 55 (1960).

Beidelman, T. O. (ed.). *The Translation of Culture*. (London, 1971).

Berger, Iris. 'Rebels or status-seekers? Women as spirit mediums in East Africa', in Nancy J. Hafkin and Edna Bay (eds), *Women in Africa: Studies in Social and Economic Change*. (Stanford, 1976).

Berger, Iris. *Religion and Resistance: East African Kingdoms in the Precolonial Period*. (Tervuren, 1981).

Berman, Bruce and Lonsdale, John M. 'Louis Leakey's Mau Mau: a study in the politics of knowledge', *History and Anthropology*, 5 (1991).

Bernardi, B. *The Mugwe - A Blessing Prophet: A Study of a Religious and Public Dignitary of the Meru of Kenya*. (Kisumu, 1989). Originally published as *The Mugwe: A Failing Prophet* (London, 1959).

Berntsen, John L. 'Maasai age-sets and prophetic leadership, 1850-1910', *Africa*, 49, ii (1979).

Berntsen, John L. 'Pastoralism, raiding and prophets: Maasailand in the nineteenth century'. (Ph.D. thesis, University of Wisconsin at Madison, 1979).

Bessell, M. J. 'Nyabingi', *Uganda Journal*, 6, 2 (1938).

Blakeslee, H. Virginia. *Beyond the Kikuyu Curtain*. (Chicago, 1956).

Blenkinsopp, J. *A History of Prophecy in Israel*. (London, 1984).

Boahen, A. Adu (ed.). *UNESCO General History of Africa, Volume 7: Africa under Colonial Domination 1880-1935*. (Berkeley and London, 1987).

Boddy, Janice. *Wombs and Alien Spirits: Women, Men and the Zar Cult in Northern Sudan*. (Madison, 1989).

Brain, James. 'Ancestors as elders in Africa: further thoughts', *Africa*, 43, i (1973).

Brantley, Cynthia. *The Giriama and Colonial Resistance in Kenya, 1800-1920*. (Berkeley, 1981).

Brantley, Cynthia. 'Mekatilile and the role of women in Giriama resistance', in Donald Crummey (ed.), *Banditry, Rebellion and Social Protest in Africa* (London & Portsmouth, NH, 1986).

Brazier, F. S. 'The incident at Nyakishenyi, 1917', *Uganda Journal*, 32, no. 1 (1968).

Brazier, F. S. 'The Nyabingi cult: religion and political scale in Kigezi 1900-1930'. (paper presented to the East African Institute of Social Research conference, Kampala 1968).

Breen, Rita. 'The politics of land: the Kenya land Commission (1932-33) and its effects on land policy in Kenya'. (Ph.D. thesis, Michigan State University, 1976).

Browne, Edward G. *Arabian Medicine*. (Cambridge, 1921).

Buijtenhuijs , Rob. *Essays on Mau Mau*. (Leiden, 1982).

Carroll, R. P. *When Prophecy Failed: Reactions and Responses to Failure in Old Testament Prophetic Traditions*. (London, 1979).

Chadwick, Nora. *Poetry and Prophecy*. (Cambridge, 1952).

Chanler, W. A. 'Letter to the Royal Geographical Society, 20 September 1893', *Geographical Journal*, 2 (1893).

Chanler, W. A. *Through Jungle and Desert: Travels in Eastern Africa*. (London, 1896).

Bibliography

Church of Scotland. *Mau Mau and the Church*. (Edinburgh, 1953).

Clark, Carolyn. 'Louis Leakey as ethnographer', *Canadian Journal of African Studies*, 23, 3 (1989).

Clough, Marshall S. *Fighting Two Sides: Kenyan Chiefs and Politicians 1918-1940*. (Niwot, 1990).

Crawford, E. May. *By the Equator's Snowy Peaks*. (London, 1913).

Crosse-Upcott, A. R. W. 'The social structure of the Ngindo-speaking people'. (Ph.D. thesis, University of Cape Town, 1956).

Cruise O'Brien, Donal B. and Coulon, Christine (eds). *Charisma and Brotherhood in African Islam*. (Oxford, 1988).

Dampierre, E. de. *Un Ancien Royaume du Haut-Oubangui*. (Paris, 1967).

Deng, F. M. *The Dinka and their Songs*. (Oxford, 1973).

Denoon, Donald, J. W. 'Agents of colonial rule: Kigezi 1908-30'. (paper presented at the East African Institute of Social Research conference, Kampala 1968).

Denoon, Donald, J. W. (ed.). *A History of Kigezi*. (Kampala, 1972).

Denoon, Donald and Adam Kuper. 'The "New Historiography" in Dar es Salaam', *African Affairs*, 69 (1970).

Des Forges, Alison. 'The drum is greater than the shout: the 1912 rebellion in northern Rwanda', in Donald Crummey (ed.), *Banditry, Rebellion and Social Protest in Africa*. (Portsmouth, NH and London, 1986).

Dundas, Charles. 'History of Kitui', *Journal of the Royal Anthropological Institute*, 43 (1913).

Durkheim, Emile. *Les Formes élémentaires de la vie religieuse*. (4th edition, Paris, 1960).

Edel, May. *The Chiga of Western Uganda*. (New York, 1957).

Edgerton, Robert. *Mau Mau: An African Crucible*. (New York, 1989).

Egan, Sean (ed.). *S. M. Otieno: Kenya's Unique Burial Saga*. (Nairobi, 1987).

Ehret, Christopher. *Southern Nilotic History*. (Evanston, 1971).

Ellis, Diane. 'The Nandi protest of 1923 in the context of African resistance to colonial rule in Kenya', *Journal of African History*, 27, iv (1976).

Emmet, Dorothy. 'Prophets and their societies', *Journal of the Royal Anthropological Institute*, 86, i (1956).

Erhardt, J. *Vocabulary of the Enguduk Iloigob*. (Ludwigsburg, 1857).

Evans-Pritchard, E. E. *Witchcraft, Oracles and Magic among the Azande*. (Oxford, 1937).

Evans-Pritchard, E. E. *The Nuer*. (Oxford, 1940).

Evans-Pritchard, E. E. *Nuer Religion*. (Oxford, 1956).

Evans-Pritchard, E. E. 'The Nuer: tribe and clan', *Sudan Notes and Records*, 18, i (1935).

Evans-Pritchard, E. E. 'The political structure the Nandi-speaking peoples of Kenya', *Africa*, 13, iii (1949).

Evans-Pritchard, E. E. *The Sanusi of Cyrenaica*. (Oxford, 1969).

Evans-Pritchard, E. E. 'Some reminiscences and reflections on fieldwork', in *Witchcraft, Oracles and Magic among the Azande*, abridged by Eva Gillies. (Oxford, 1976).

Evans-Pritchard, E. E. 'Zande theology', *Sudan Notes and Records*, 19 (1936).

Evans-Pritchard, E. E. *The Zande Trickster*. (Oxford, 1967).

Fadiman, J. *The Moment of Conquest: Meru, Kenya 1907*. (Athens, Ohio, 1979).

Fadiman, J. *Mountain Warriors: The Pre-Colonial Meru of Mt Kenya*. (Athens, Ohio, 1976).

Fadiman, J. 'Mountain witchcraft: supernatural practices and practitioners among the Meru of Mount Kenya'. *African Studies Review*, 20 (1977).

Farler, J. P. 'Native routes in East Africa from Pangani to the Masai country and the Victoria Nyanza'. *Proceedings of the Royal Geographical Society*, 4 (1882).

Farson, N. *Last Chance in Kenya*. (London, 1949).

Fischer, G. A. 'Am Ostufer des Victoria-Njansa', *Petermann's Mitteilungen*, 41 (1895).

Fischer, G. A. *Das Massailand*. (Hamburg, 1882).

Fosbrooke, H. A. 'An administrative survey of the Masai social system', *Tanganyika Notes and Records*, 26 (1948).

Bibliography

Frankl, P. J. L. 'The word for "God" in Swahili', *Journal of Religion in Africa*, 20, iii (1990).

Fratkin, Elliot. 'A comparison of the role of prophets in Samburu and Maasai warfare', in Katsuyoshi Fukui and David Turton (eds), *Warfare Among East African Herders*. (Osaka, 1977).

Fratkin, Elliot. 'The *loibon* as sorcerer: a Samburu *loibon* among the Ariaal Rendille, 1973-87', *Africa*, 61, iii (1991).

Freedman, James. *Nyabingi: The Social History of an African Divinity*. (Tervuren, 1984).

Galaty, John G. 'Pollution and pastoral antipraxis: the issue of Maasai inequality', *American Ethnologist*, 6 (1979).

Gellner, Ernest. *Saints of the Atlas*. (London, 1969).

Gerlach, L. P. 'Some basic Digo concepts of health and disease'. (Proceedings of a symposium on 'Attitudes to health and disease among some East African tribes', Makerere College, Kampala, December 1959).

Gerth, H. H. and Wright Mills, C. *From Max Weber: Essays in Sociology*. (London, 1948).

Gikoyo, Gucu. *We Fought for Freedom*. (Nairobi, 1979).

Giorgetti, F. *La Superstizione Zande*. (Bologna, 1966).

Githige, Renison Muchiri. 'The religions factor in Mau Mau with particular reference to Mau Mau oaths'. (MA thesis, *University of Nairobi*, 1978).

Glassman, Jonathon. 'The bondsman's new clothes: the contradictory consciousness of slave resistance on the Swahili coast', *Journal of African History*, 32, ii (1991).

Gold, Alice. 'The Nandi in transition: background to Nandi resistance to the British, 1895-1906', *Kenya Historical Review*, 6 (1978).

Goldsmith, F. H. *John Ainsworth: Pioneer Kenya Administrator 1864-1946*. (London, 1955).

Gore, E. C. *Sangba Ture*. (London, 1954).

Gorju, Julien, *et al*. *Face au royaume hamite du Ruanda: le royaume frère de l'Urundi*. (Brussels, 1938).

Government of Kenya. *Kenya Land Commission (Carter): Evidence and Memoranda*, 3 volumes. (Nairobi, 1934).

Gwassa, Gilbert E. 'Kinjikitile and the ideology of Maji Maji', in T. O. Ranger and I. Kimambo (eds), *The Historical Study of African Religion*. (London, 1972).

Gwassa, Gilbert E. 'The outbreak and development of the Maji Maji War 1905-07'. (Ph.D. thesis, University of Dar es Salaam, 1973).

Gwassa, Gilbert E. and Iliffe, John (eds). *The Records of the Maji Maji*, Part 1. (Historical Association of Tanzania, Pamphlet 1; Nairobi, 1968).

Hansen, Holger Bernt. *Mission, Church and State in a Colonial Setting: Uganda 1890-1925*. (London, 1984).

Hess, Robert L. 'The poor man of God: Muhammad 'Abdullah Hassan', in N. Bennett (ed.), *Leadership in Eastern Africa: Six Political Biographies*. (Boston, 1968).

Hinde, S. L. and H. *Last of the Masai*. (London, 1901).

Hobley, C. W. *Bantu Beliefs and Magic*. (London, 1938: first edition, 1922).

Hobley, C. W. *Eastern Uganda: An Ethnological Survey*. (Anthropological Institute, Occasional paper No. 1: London, 1902).

Hobley, C. W. *Ethnology of the Akamba and Other East African Tribes*. (London, 1910).

Hobley, C. W. 'Further researches into Kikuyu and Kamba religious beliefs and customs', *Journal of the Royal Anthropological Institute*, 41 (1911).

Hofmeyr, Agnes Leakey. *Beyond Violence*. (Nairobi, 1990).

Hohnel, Ludwig, von. *Discovery of Lakes Rudolf and Stefanie*, 2 volumes. (London, 1894).

Hollis, A. C. *The Masai: Their Language and Folklore*. (Oxford, 1905).

Hollis, A. C. *The Nandi: Their Language and Folk-lore*. (Oxford, 1909).

Holt, P. M. *The Mahdist State in the Sudan, 1881-1989: A Study of its Origins, Development and Overthrow*. (Oxford, 1970 [1958]).

Hopkins, Elizabeth. 'The Nyabingi cult of southwestern Uganda', in R. I. Rotberg and Ali A. Mazrui (eds), *Protest and Power in Black Africa*. (New York, 1970).

Bibliography

Hopkins, Elizabeth. 'Partition in practice: African politics and European rivalry in Bufumbira', in S. Förster, W. J. Mommsen and R. Robinson (eds), *Bismarck, Europe and Africa. The Berlin Africa Conference 1884–85 and the Onset of Partition.* (London 1988).

Hopkins, Elizabeth. 'The pragmatics of ritual identity: prophet and clan in a changing imperial field'. Paper presented at the 7th Satterthwaite Colloquium on 'African Religion and Ritual', 20–3 April 1991.

Huntingford, G. W. B. 'Genealogy of the Orkoiik of Nandi', *Man*, 35 (1935).

Huntingford, G. W. B. 'Miscellaneous records relating to the Nandi and Kony tribes'. *Journal of the Royal Anthropological Institute*, 57 (1927).

Huntingford, G. W. B. 'The Nandi pororiet'. *Journal of the Royal Anthropological Institute*, 65 (1934).

Huntingford, G. W. B. *Nandi Work and Culture.* (London, 1950).

Huntingford, G. W. B. *The Nandi of Kenya: Tribal Control in a Pastoral Society.* (London, 1953).

Huntingford, G. W. B. *Ethnographic Survey of Africa: East Central Africa, Part VIII The Southern Nilo-Hamites* (London, 1953).

Iliffe, John. 'The effects of the Maji Maji rebellion of 1905–06 on German occupation policy in East Africa', in Prosser Gifford and Wm. Roger Louis (eds), *Britain and Germany in Africa: Imperial Rivalry and Colonial Rule.* (New Haven, 1967).

Iliffe, John. *A Modern History of Tanganyika.* (Cambridge, 1979).

Iliffe, John. 'The organisation of the Maji Maji rebellion', *Journal of African History*, 8, iii (1967).

Itote, Waruhiu. *Mau Mau General.* (Nairobi, 1967).

Itotia, Justin with James Dougall. 'The voice of Africa: Kikuyu proverbs', *Africa*, 1 (1928).

Jackson, Kennell. 'The dimensions of Kamba pre-colonial history', in B. A. Ogot (ed.), *Kenya Before 1900.* (Nairobi, 1976).

Jackson, Kennell. 'An ethnohistorical study of the oral traditions of the Akamba of Kenya'. (Ph.D. thesis, University of California at Los Angeles, 1972).

Jacobs, Alan H. 'The traditional political organisation of the pastoral Masai'. (Ph.D. thesis, Oxford University, 1965).

James, Wendy. *The Listening Ebony: Moral Knowledge, Religion and Power among the Uduk of Sudan.* (Oxford, 1988).

Johansen, E. *Führung und Erfahrung.* (Bethel, nd).

Johnson, Douglas H. 'C. A. Willis and the "Cult of Deng": a falsification of the ethnographic record', *History in Africa*, 12 (1985).

Johnson, Douglas H. 'Criminal secrecy: the case of the Zande secret societies', *Past and Present*, 130 (1991).

Johnson, Douglas H. and David M. Anderson (eds). *The Ecology of Survival: Case Studies from Northeast African History.* (London and Boulder, 1988).

Johnson, Douglas H. 'Fixed shrines and spiritual centres in the Upper Nile', *Azania*, 25 (1990).

Johnson, Douglas H. 'Foretelling peace and war: modern interpretations of Ngundeng's prophecies in the Southern Sudan', in M. W. Daly (ed.), *Modernization in the Sudan.* (New York, 1985).

Johnson, Douglas H. 'Ngundeng and the 'Turuk': two narratives compared', *History in Africa*, 9 (1982).

Johnson, Douglas H. *Nuer Prophets: A History of Prophecy from the Upper Nile in the Nineteenth and Twentieth Centuries.* (Oxford, 1994).

Johnson, Douglas H. 'Reconstructing the history of local floods in the Upper Nile region of the Sudan'. *International Journal of African Historical Studies*, 25, iii (1992).

Johnson, Douglas H. 'Tribal boundaries and border wars: Nuer–Dinka relations in the Sobat and Zaraf valleys, c. 1860–1976'. *Journal of African History*, 23, ii (1982).

Kabira, Wanjiku Mukabi and Mutahi, Kerega wa. *Gikuyu Oral Literature.* (Nairobi, 1988).

Bibliography

Kabiro, Ngugi. *Man in the Middle*. (Richmond, BC, 1973).

Kanyangezi, T. 'Mbatiany, 1824–1889: a biographical study of a nineteenth-century Maasai *oloiboni*'. (B.A. dissertation, University of Nairobi, nd).

Kariuki, Josiah M. *Mau Mau Detainee*. (London, 1963).

Kenny, Michael. 'Mirror in the forest: the Dorobo hunter-gatherers as an image of the Other', *Africa*, 51 (1981).

Kenyatta, Jomo. *Facing Mount Kenya*. (New York, 1965, [London, 1938]).

Kenyatta, Jomo. *Kenya: The Land of Conflict*. (London, 1944).

Kenyatta, Jomo. *My People of Kikuyu*. (London, 1942).

Kershaw, Greet. 'The land is the people: a study of social organisation in historical perspective'. (Ph.D. thesis, University of Chicago, 1972).

Kersten, O. *Von der Deckens Reisen in Ost-Afrika*. (Leipzig, 1869).

Kieran, J. A. P. 'The Holy Ghost Fathers in East Africa, 1863–1914'. (Ph.D. thesis, University of London, 1966).

Kiggen, J. *Nuer–English Dictionary*. (London, 1948).

King, Kenneth (ed.) *Harry Thuku: An Autobiography*. (Nairobi, 1970).

Kinyatti, Maina wa (ed.). *Kenya's Freedom Movement: The Dedan Kimathi Papers*. (London, 1987).

Kinyatti, Maina wa (ed.). *Thunder from the Mountains: Mau Mau Patriotic Songs*. (London, 1980).

Kipkorir, Benjamin E. (ed.) *Imperialism and Collaboration in Colonial Kenya*. (Nairobi, 1980).

Koch, K. *The Prophets. Volume 1, The Assyrian Period*, trans. Margaret Kohl. (London, 1982).

Koinange, Mbiyu. *The People of Kenya Speak for Themselves*. (Detroit, 1955).

Kopytoff, I. 'Ancestors as elders in Africa'. *Africa*, 41, i (1971).

Krapf, J. L. *A Dictionary of the Suahili Language*. (London, 1882).

Krapf, J. L. *Travels, Researches and Missionary Labours*. (London, 1860).

Krapf, J. L. *Vocabulary of the Engutuk Eloikob*. (Tübingen, 1854).

Kinuthia Mugia, D. *Urathi wa Cege wa Kibiru*. (Nairobi, 1979).

Lagae, C. R. *Les Azande ou Niam Niam*. (Brussels, 1926).

Lagae, C. R. and Vanden Las, V. H. *La Langue des Azande*. (Brussels, 1921).

Lambert, H. E. *Kikuyu Social and Political Institutions*. (London, 1956).

Lambert, H. E. 'The social and political institutions of the tribes of the Kikuyu Land Unit of Kenya'. (Unpublished manuscript, University of Nairobi Library, 1945).

Lambert, H. E. *The Systems of Land Tenure in the Kikuyu Land Unit*. (Cape Town, 1949).

Lamphear, John. 'Aspects of Turkana leadership during the era of primary resistance', *Journal of African History*, 17, ii (1976).

Lamphear, John. *The Scattering Time: Turkana Responses to Colonial Rule*. (Oxford, 1992).

Lamphear, John. *The Traditional History of the Jie of Uganda*. (Oxford, 1976).

Lane Fox, R. *Pagans and Christians in the Mediterranean World from the Second Century A.D. to the Conversion of Constantine*. (London, 1986).

Lang, B. *Monotheism and the Prophetic Minority: An Essay on Biblical History and Sociology*. (Sheffield, 1983).

Lang'at, S. C. 'Some aspects of Kipsigis history before 1914', in B. McIntosh (ed.) *Ngano: Studies in Traditional and Modern East African History*. (Nairobi, 1969).

Larken, P. M. 'Further impressions of the Azande', *Sudan Notes and Records*, 13 (1930).

Larson, Lorne E. 'A history of Mahenge (Ulanga) District, c. 1860–1957'. (Ph.D. thesis, University of Dar es Salaam, 1976).

Larson, Lorne E. 'Problems in the study of witchcraft eradication movements in southern Tanzania', *Ufahamu*, 6, no. 3 (1976).

Larson, Lorne E. 'Witchcraft eradication sequences among the people of Mahenge (Ulange) District, Tanzania'. (Unpublished paper, 1974).

Leakey, L. S. B. *Defeating Mau Mau*. (London, 1954).

Leakey, L. S. B. *The Southern Kikuyu Before 1903*, 3 volumes. (London, 1977).

Bibliography

Leonard, David. *African Successes: Four Public Administrators of Kenya's Rural Development.* (Berkeley, 1991).

Lerner, Gerda. *The Creation of Patriarchy.* (New York, 1986).

Leue, A. 'Ngura', *Deutsche Kolonialzeitung*, 28, 32, 34, 37 (1906).

Lewis, I. M. 'Spirit possession and deprivation cults', *Man*, 1, ns, 3 (1966).

Lienhardt, R. Godfrey. *Divinity and Experience: The Religion of the Dinka.* (Oxford, 1961).

Lindblom, G. *The Akamba in British East Africa.* (Uppsala, 1920).

Lindblom, J. *Prophecy in Ancient Israel.* (Oxford, 1978).

Lonsdale, John M. 'Mau Maus of the mind'. *Journal of African History*, 31, iii (1990).

Lonsdale, John M. 'La pensée politique kikuyu et les ideologies du mouvement Mau-Mau'. *Cahiers d'études africaines*, 27 (1987).

Lonsdale, John M. 'The moral economy of Mau Mau: the problem', in Bruce Berman and John M. Lansdale, *Unhappy Valley*, Volume 2. (London, 1992).

Lonsdale, John M. 'Wealth, poverty and civic virtue in Kikuyu political thought', in Bruce Berman and John M. Lonsdale, *Unhappy Valley*, Volume 2. (London, 1992).

Lugard, Frederick D. *The Rise of Our East African Empire*, 2 volumes (Edinburgh, 1893).

MacDonald, J. R. L. *Soldiering and Surveying in British East Africa 1891-1894.* (London, 1897).

MacGaffey, Wyatt. *Modern Kongo Prophets: Religion in a Plural Society.* (Bloomington, 1983).

Macpherson, R. *The Presbyterian Church in Kenya.* (Nairobi, 1970).

Magut, P. K. arap. 'The rise and fall of the Nandi orkoiyot, c. 1850-1957', in B. G. McIntosh (ed.), *Ngano: Studies in Traditional and Modern East African History.* (Nairobi, 1969).

Maji Maji Research Project. Collected Papers, 1968. (University College History Department, Dar es Salaam, 1969).

Marno, E. *Reisen im Gebiete des Blauen und Weissen Nil, im Egyptischen Sudan, 1869-1873.* (Vienna, 1874).

Mathu, Mohamed. *The Urban Guerilla.* (Richmond, BC, 1974).

Matson, A. T. 'George Wilson and Dagoretti: Kinanjui's account'. *Uganda Journal*, 30, 1 (1966).

Matson, A. T. *The Nandi Campaign Against the British, 1895-1906.* (Nairobi, 1974).

Matson, A. T. *Nandi Resistance to British Rule, 1890-1906.* (Nairobi, 1972).

McIntosh, Brian G. 'The Scottish Mission in Kenya, 1891-1923'. (Ph.D. thesis, Edinburgh University, 1969).

Meinertzhagen, Richard W. *Kenya Diary, 1902-1906.* (Edinburgh and London, 1957).

Merker, M. *Die Masai.* (Berlin, 1910).

Middleton, John. *Lugbara Religion: Ritual and Authority among an East African People.* (London, 1960).

Middleton, John. 'Prophets and rainmakers: the agents of social change among the Lugbara', in T. O. Beidelman (ed.), *The Translation of Culture.* (London, 1971).

Middleton, John. 'Spirit possession among the Lugbara', in J. Beattie and J. Middleton (eds), *Spirit Mediumship and Society in Africa.* (London, 1969).

Middleton, John. 'The Yakan or Allah Water Cult among the Lugbara'. *Journal of the Royal Anthropological Institute*, 93, i (1961).

Mockerie, Parmenas Githendu. *An African Speaks for His People.* (London, 1934).

Muchai, Karigo. *The Hard Core.* (Richmond, BC, 1973).

Mugia, Kinuthia. *Urathi*, pp. 2-7.

Munro, J. Forbes. *Colonial Rule and the Kamba: Social Change in the Kenya Highlands 1889-1939.* (Oxford, 1975).

Muriuki, Godfrey. *A History of the Kikuyu, 1500-1900.* (Nairobi, 1974).

Muthiani, Joseph. *Akamba From Within: Egalitarianism in Social Relations.* (New York, 1973).

Bibliography

Mwaniki, H. S. K. 'A political history of the Embu, c. AD 1500-1906', (MA, thesis, University of Nairobi, 1973).

Mwaniki, H. S. K. *Embu Historical Texts*. (Nairobi, 1974).

Mwaniki, H. S. K. *The Living History of Embu and Mbeere*. (Nairobi, 1973).

Mwaniki, Henry Muoria. 'The British and my Kikuyu tribe'. (Unpublished manuscript, 1982, privately held).

Mwanzi, Henry A. *A History of the Kipsigis*. (Nairobi, 1978).

Mwanzi, Henry A. 'Koitalel arap Samoei and Kipchomber arap Koilege: southern Kalenjin rulers and their encounters with British imperialism', in B. E. Kipkorir (ed.), *Imperialism and Collaboration in Colonial Kenya* (Nairobi, 1980).

Ndeti, K. *Elements of Akamba Life*. (Nairobi, 1972).

Neckebrouck, Valeer. *Le Onzième Commandement: étiologie d'une église indépendante au pied du mont Kenya*. (Immensee, 1978).

Neckebrouck, Valeer. *Le Peuple afflige: les déterminants de la fissiparité dans un nouveau mouvement religieux au Kenya central*. (Immensee, 1983).

New, Charles. *Life, Wanderings and Labours in Eastern Africa*. (London, 1873).

Ng'eny, Samuel arap. 'Nandi resistance to the establishment of British administration 1893-1906', in B. A. Ogot (ed.), *Hadith 2* (Nairobi, 1970).

Ngologoza, P. *Kigezi and its People*. (Dar es Salaam, Nairobi and Kampala, 1969).

Nimtz, August. *Islam and Politics in East Africa: The Sufi Order in Tanzania*. (Minneapolis, 1980).

Njua, Rebeka and Gideon Mulaki. *Kenya Women Heroes and Their Mystical Power* (Nairobi, 1984).

Njururi, Ngumbu. *Gikuyu Proverbs*. (Nairobi [1968], 1983).

Ochieng', William R. 'Black Jeremiah', *Journal of the Historical Association of Kenya*, 1 (1972).

Ochieng', William R. *An Outline History of the Rift Valley of Kenya up to 1900* (Nairobi, Kampala and Dar es Salaam, 1975).

Odhiambo, E. S. Atieno and Cohen, David William. *Burying 'S.M.'*. (London, 1992).

Ogot, Bethwell, A. and William Ochieng', 'Mumboism: an anti-colonial movement', in B. A. Ogot (ed.), *War and Society in Africa: Ten Studies* (London, 1972).

Ogot, Bethwell Allan. 'Politics, culture and music in central Kenya: a study of Mau Mau hymms 1951-1956', *Kenya Historical Review*, 5, 2 (1977).

Ojwang, J. B. and Mugambi, J. N. K. (eds). *The S. M. Otieno Case*. (Nairobi, 1989).

Opoku, K. A. 'Religion in Africa during the colonial era', in A. A. Boahen (ed.) *UNESCO History, Volume 7*. (Berkeley and London, 1985).

Orchardson, Ian Q. *The Kipsigis*. (Abridged by A. T. Matson, Nairobi: 1961).

Orde Browne, G. St. J. *The Vanishing Tribes of Kenya*. (London, 1925).

Overholt, T. W. 'Prophecy: the problem of cross-cultural comparison', in B. Lang (ed.), *Anthropological Approaches to the Old Testament*. (Philadelphia and London, 1985).

Overton, John D. 'The origins of the Kikuyu land problem: land alienation and land use in Kiambu, Kenya 1895-1920', *African Studies Review*, 31 (1988).

Parkin, David. *Palms, Wine and Witnesses*. (London, 1972).

Peel, J. D. Y. 'Progression and recursion in African social thought', in Christopher Fyfe (ed.), *African Futures*. (Edinburgh, 1988).

Peires, J. B. *The Dead Will Arise: Noaqqawuse and the Great Xhosa Cattle Killing Movement of 1856-7*. (Berkeley and London, 1989).

Perham, Margery and Bull, Mary (eds). *The Diaries of Lord Lugard*, 2 volumes. (London, 1959).

Perham, Margery. *Lugard, The Years of Authority, 1898-1945*. (London, 1960).

Peristiany, John G. 'The ideal and the actual: the role of prophets in the Pokot social system', in J. H. M. Beattie and R. G. Lienhardt (eds), *Studies in Social Anthropology*. (Oxford, 1975).

Peristiany, John G. *The Social Institutions of the Kipsigis*. (London, 1939).

Bibliography

Petersen, D. L. *The Roles of Israel's Prophets*. (Sheffield, 1981).

Philipps, J. E. T. 'The Nabingi: an anti-European secret society in Africa, in British Ruanda, Ndorwa and the Congo (Kivu)', *Congo*, 1 (Bruxelles, 1928).

Portal, Sir Gerald. *The British Mission to Uganda in 1893*. (London, 1894).

Porter, J. R. 'The origins of prophecy in Israel', in R. Coggins, A. Phillips and M. Knibb (eds), *Israel's Prophetic Tradition*. (Cambridge, 1982).

Prins, A. J. H. 'Islamic maritime magic: a ship's charm from Lamu', in H. J. Gerschat and H. Jungraithmayr (eds), *Wort und Religion: Kalima na Dini*. (Stuttgart, 1969).

Ranger, Terence O. 'Connections between "primary resistance" movements and modern mass nationalism in East and Central Africa', *Journal of African History*, 9, iii and iv (1968).

Ranger, Terence O. and Kimambo, Isaria (eds). *The Historical Study of African Religion*. (London, 1972).

Ranger, Terence O. 'The "New Historiography" in Dar es Salaam: an answer', *African Affairs*, 70 (1971).

Ranger, Terence O. 'The people in African resistance', *Journal of Southern African Studies*, 4 (1977).

Ranger, Terence O. 'African initiatives and resistance in East Africa 1880–1914', in A. A. Boahen (ed.) *UNESCO History, Volume 7*. (Berkeley and London, 1985).

Ranger, Terence O. 'Religious movements and politics in sub-Saharan Africa', *African Studies Review*, 29 (1986), 1–69.

Redmond, P. 'Maji Maji in Ungoni: a reappraisal of existing historiography', *International Journal of African Historical Studies*, 8 (1975).

Robertson Smith, W. *The Prophets of Israel and their Place in History*. (London, 1897).

Robins, Catherine. 'Conversion, life crises and stability among women in the East African revival', in Benetta Jules-Rosette, *The New Religions of Africa*. (Norwood, New Jersey, 1979).

Rodney, Walter. 'The colonial economy', in A. A. Boahen (ed.), *UNESCO History, Volume 7*. (Berkeley and London, 1985).

Rogers, Peter. 'The British and the Kikuyu 1890–1905: a reassessment'. *Journal of African History*, 20, 2 (1979).

Rosberg, Carl and Nottingham, John. *The Myth of Mau Mau*. (New York, 1966).

Routledge, W. S and K. *With a Prehistoric People: The Akikuyu of British East Africa*. (London, 1910).

Ruel, Malcolm. 'Kuria seers', *Africa*, 61, iii (1991).

Rwandusya, Zakayo. 'The origin and settlement of people of Bufumbira', in Donald Denoon (ed.), *A History of Kigezi in Southwest Uganda*. (Kampala, 1972).

Saberwal, Satish. *Embu of Kenya*, 2 volumes. (New Haven, Conn., 1972).

Sacks, Karen. *Sisters and Wives: The Past and Future of Sexual Equality*. (Urbana, 1982).

Samatar, Said S. *Oral Poetry and Somali Nationalism: The Case of Sayyid Mahammad 'Abdille Hasan*. (Cambridge, 1982).

Sandford, G. R. *An Administrative and Political History of the Masai Reserve*. (London, 1919).

Sandgren, David P. *Christianity and the Kikuyu: Religious Divisions and Social Conflict*. (New York, 1989).

Schmidt, Peter. *Historical Archaeology: A Structural Approach in an African Culture*. (Westport, Conn., 1978).

Schweinfurth, G, *et al.*, *Emin Pasha in Central Africa: Being a Collection of his Letters and Journals*. (London, 1988).

Sheik-'Abdi, 'Abdi. *Divine Madness: Mohammed 'Abdulle Hassan (1856–1920)*. (London and New Jersey, 1993).

Sheriff, Abdul. *Slaves, Spices and Ivory in Zanzibar: Integration of an East African Commercial Empire into the World Economy 1770–1873*. (London, 1987).

Shorter, Aylward. *African Christian Theology*. (New York, 1977).

Bibliography

Sicherman, Carol. *Ngugi wa Thiong'o: The Making of a Rebel. A Source Book in Kenyan Literature and Resistance*. (London, Munich and New York, 1990).

Sorrenson, M. P. K. *Origins of European Settlement in Kenya*. (Nairobi, 1968).

Spear, Thomas and Waller, Richard D. *Being Maasai: Ethnicity and Identity in East Africa*. (London, Athens Ohio, Nairobi and Dar es Salaam, 1993).

Spear, Thomas. *Kenya's Past: An Introduction to Historical Method in Africa*. (London, 1981).

Spencer, John. *James Beauttah, Freedom Fighter*. (Nairobi, 1983).

Spencer, Paul. 'The Loonkidongi prophets and the Maasai: protection racket or insipient state?', *Africa*, 61 (1991).

Spencer, Paul. *The Maasai of Matapato: A Study of Rituals of Rebellion*. (Manchester, 1988).

Spencer, Paul. *Models of the Maasai*. (forthcoming).

Spencer, Paul. 'Opposing streams and the gerontocratic ladder: two models of age organisation in East Africa', *Man*, 11 (1976).

Spencer, Paul. *Nomads in Alliance*. (London, 1973).

Spencer, Paul. *The Samburu*. (London, 1965).

Stigand, C. H. *Land of the Zinj*. (London, 1913).

Stollowsky, Otto. 'On the background to the rebellion in German East Africa in 1905-06' (Trans. by John W. East), *International Journal of African Historical Studies*, 21 (1988).

Stoneham, C. T. *Out of Barbarism*. (London, 1955).

Sundkler, B. G. M. *Bantu Prophets in South Africa*. (Oxford, 1961 [1948]).

Sutton, J. E. G. 'The Kalenjin', in B. A. Ogot (ed.), *Kenya Before 1900* (Nairobi, 1976).

Swantz, Lloyd. *The Medicine Man Among the Zaramo of Dar es Salaam*. (Uppsala, 1990).

Taylor, Brian K. 'The social structure of the Batoro'. (M.A. dissertation, University of London, 1957).

Temu, A. J. 'The Giriama War 1914-15', in B. A. Ogot (ed.), *War and Society in Africa: Ten Studies*. (London, 1972).

Thomas, Keith. *Religion and the Decline of Magic: Studies in Popular Beliefs in Sixteenth- and Seventeenth-Century England*. (Harmondsworth, 1973).

Thomson, Joseph. *Through Masai Land*. (London, 1887).

Throup, David W. 'The construction and deconstruction of the Kenyatta state', in M. G. Schatzberg (ed.), *The Political Economy of Kenya*. (New York, 1987).

Thurman, Judith. *Isak Dinesen: The Life of a Storyteller*. (New York, 1982).

Tignor, Robert L. *The Colonial Transformation of Kenya: The Kamba, Kikuyu and Maasai from 1900 to 1939*. (Princeton, 1976).

Tomikawa, M. 'The migrations and inter-tribal relations of the pastoral Datoga', in Katsuyoshi Fukui and David Turton (eds), *Warfare Among East African Herders*. (Osaka, 1977).

Turyahikayo-Rugyema, B. 'The British imposition of colonial rule on Uganda: the Baganda agents in Kigezi (1908-1930)', *Transafrican Journal of History*, 5, i (1976).

Vail, Leroy (ed.). *The Creation of Tribalism in Southern Africa*. (London, 1989).

Van Sambeek, J. 'Croyances et coutumes des Baha', 2 volumes. (Unpublished manuscript, Kabanga, 1949).

von Goetzen, Graf Adolph. *Deutsch Ostafrika im Aufstand*. (Berlin, 1909).

Wachanga, H. K. *Swords of Kirinyaga: The Fight for Land and Freedom*. (Nairobi, 1975).

Wagner, G. *The Bantu of North Kavirondo*. (Oxford, 1949).

Wallace, Anthony. 'Revitalization movements', *American Anthropologist*, 58, ii (1956).

Waller, Richard D. 'Emutai: crisis and response in Maasailand 1883-1902', in Douglas H. Johnson and David M. Anderson (eds), *The Ecology of Survival: Case Studies from East African History*. (London and Boulder, 1988).

Waller, Richard D. 'Interaction and identity on the periphery: the Trans-Mara Maasai', *International Journal of African Historical Studies*, 17 (1984).

Waller, Richard D. 'The Lords of East Africa: the Maasai in the mid-nineteenth century (c. 1840-c. 1885)'. (Ph.D. thesis, University of Cambridge, 1979).

Bibliography

Waller, Richard D. 'The Maasai and the British 1895–1905: the origins of an alliance', *Journal of African History*, 17, iii (1976).

Walter, B. J. 'The territorial expansion and organisation of the Nandi, 1850–1905', (MA dissertation, University of Wisconsin-Madison, 1969).

Walter, B. J. *The Territorial Expansion of the Nandi of Kenya* (Athens, Ohio, 1970).

Wamweya, Joram. *Freedom Fighter.* (Nairobi, 1971).

Wanjau, Gakaara wa. *Mau Mau Author in Detention.* (Nairobi, 1988).

Ward, Kevin. 'Uganda: the Mukono crisis of 1941', *Journal of Religion in Africa*, 19, 3 (1989).

wa Thiong'o, Ngugi. *Weep Not Child.* (London, 1964).

wa Thiong'o, Ngugi. *The River Between.* (London, 1965).

Weatherby, J. M. 'Cattle raiding in Elgon: the Nandi phase and the role of the foretellers'. (East Africa Institute of Social Research Conference, Nairobi, 1969).

Weatherby, J. M. 'Inter-tribal warfare on Mt Elgon in the nineteenth and twentieth centuries', *Uganda Journal*, 26 (1962).

Weber, Max. *Ancient Judaism.* (Chicago and London, 1952).

Weber, Max. *The Theory of Social and Economic Organisation*, trans and ed. by A. M. Henderson and Talcott Parsons. (London, 1964).

Welbourn, F. B. *East African Rebels: A Study of some Independent Churches.* (London, 1961).

White, Luise. 'Separating the men from the boys: constructions of gender, sexuality and terrorism in central Kenya, 1939–59', *International Journal of African Historical Studies*, 23 (1990).

Wright, Marcia. 'Rubber and the Kilwa hinterland, 1878–1906', (Historical Association of Tanzania, conference paper, 1974).

Wright, Marcia. 'East Africa 1870–1905', in R. Oliver (ed.), *Cambridge History of Africa, Volume 6.* (Cambridge, 1986).

Wright, Marcia. 'Kinjikitile', *Encyclopedia of Religion.* (New York, 1986).

Index

Index

'Bokero', 132-3, 135
Bokero cult, 128-31, 135-6, 139
Brazier, F. S., 145, 151, 156
Britain *see* Great Britain
Brogochut, arap, 179
Buganda, 70, 72-3, 250; Kabaka of, 278
Buha, 76-7
Bukuku, 69
Bukusu, 54
Bunyoro, 67, 70, 72-5, 77; *see also* Nyoro
Burma, 128
Burundi, 67-8, 73, 76-7; *see also* Rundi
Bushi, 73
Bushiri, 171

cargo cults, 235
Carroll, Robert, 20
Carter, Judge Morris, 244-9, 255-64, 266-9, 280, 282
Castle-Smith, District Commissioner, 182
Catholicism *see* Roman Catholicism
cattle, 36, 185, 257, 265, 279; raids, 31, 32-3, 36, 45, 47, 51, 165-8, 180, 207, 215; Xhosa Cattle Killing, 234-5
causality, attitudes to, 94-6
Central African Republic, 102, 104, 115
Chadwick, Nora, 14
Chanler, W. A., 53, 230-1
charisma, 10-13
charms, 91-2, 177, 224
Chege wa Muthemba, 260
Chepsiet, arap, 175
chiefs, 148-50, 267, 269
China, General, 272
Christianity, 7-9, 11, 15-16, 77, 83, 85, 92, 95, 104, 117-18, 135-6; Kenya, 236, 247, 270, 274-5, 279; Sudan, 6; Uganda, 79, 150-1, 156-60; *see also name of sect*
Chuka, 230
Church Missionary Society, 83-4, 87-8, 257, 260
Church of Scotland Mission, 247-8, 257, 259-61
class, social, 137
clitoridectomy, 247, 268, 280
colonialism, 3, 5, 13, 15-16, 19, 24, 45-6, 49, 53, 65, 68, 115-16; Kenya, 164-90, 221-36, 240-83; Sudan, 196-219; Tanzania, 124-39; Uganda, 143-60
cosmology, 96-7
cotton, 127-8, 130, 137, 139
Crawford, E. May, 225
Cuol Puyu, 207, 209

Cuol Yoal Abiel, 213
cursing, 29-33, 106, 224, 273, 276
Cwezi, 67, 69-70, 72, 74-5, 78

Dagoretti Fort, 245, 249-52, 254, 257, 260
Damat, 51
dancing, 234-5, 267
dang (stick), 205
Dar es Salaam, 131; University, 125
DENG, 197, 200-2, 209, 213-14, 216-17
Deng Cier, 212-14, 216-18
Deng Laka, 197-201, 203, 214-16
Denoon, D. J. W., 145, 150, 155
Dhieyier Bol Ngundeng, 209, 211, 217
DHOL, 202, 204, 206
Dinka, 5-6; Luac, 196-219; Ngok, 197; Nyarewang, 197, 213, 216; Padang, 197; Rut, 197, 212-13, 216; Thoi, 197, 212-13
DIU, 197
divination, 4, 32, 39, 92-3, 165, 170, 177, 224, 236, 243; *chebsageyot*, 184; Ebony diviners, 6, 16; *kipsachit*, 183; *kipsakeiyot*, 183-4; *kipungut*, 184; *sakeiyout*, 183-4; women, 184; Zande ghost diviners, 103-4, 108-10
Dobbs, 186
Donde, 134
Dondol, 42
Donytuli, 53
dreams, 4, 93-5, 184, 241, 266
Driberg, J. H., 159
Dundas, Charles, 225

East African Protectorate, 246
Edel, May, 145, 155
Egypt, 197
Eldama Ravine, 52, 169, 174
elders, 19, 29-31, 41, 45-50, 53, 78, 89, 107-8, 146, 167, 173, 180, 225, 230-1, 254, 264-7, 270-2, 275-6
Elgeyo, 165
Elgon, Mount, 51, 54
emandwa (spirit mediumship), 75-7, 80; *see also Kubandwa*
emandwa zabakazi ('spirits of the women'), 74
Embu, 55, 221-36
Emin Pasha, 67
Emmett, Dorothy, 12
emuron (diviner), 4
Erhardt, John James, 84, 87, 90-1
Ethiopianism, 158
Eunoto ceremonies, 48-9, 55

304

Index

Index

Index

Index

Index

OlolKakwai family, 55
Olonana, 36-7, 39-42, 47-9, 52, 55
olotuno (age-set leader), 49-50
omens, 92-3, 177
Opoku, K. Asare, 127
oracles, 7, 20, 103-5, 111, 113, 115
Orchardson, Ian Q., 184
Orde Browne, G. St J., 224-5
Oriare, 174
orkiik (prophets), 19, 21, 164-90; gene-alogy, 187-9
Otieno, 'S. M.', 282-3
Overholt, Thomas, 20

Pading, battle of (1878), 21, 196-219
Pangani shrine, 133
Parkiswaa, ole, 46
Parrit, 37
pepo (spirits), 87-8
Peristiany, John G., 4, 186
Philipps, J. E. T., 110, 145, 150-9
plants, 111, 114
Pogoro, 135
Pokot, 4, 165
Portugal, 83, 127
prediction *see* prophecy (foreknowledge)
Pringle, Captain, 255
prophecy; definition of, 2-24; foreknowl-edge, 20, 22, 94-7, 103-4, 221-36; idioms, 14, 16, 24, 55, 70, 80; tradition, 16; *see also orkoiik*
Protestantism, 104, 143, 150
Puritans, 10
Purkiss, 245, 248-56, 263
Purko, 36-7, 42, 47-9, 51, 53-4

Qur'an, 16-17

Rabai, 83-5, 91
Rafai, 106
raiding *see* cattle (raids)
railways, 169, 174, 222, 229
rainmaking, 31, 88-9, 94, 96, 177, 224
ran nhialic (man of Divinity), 5
Ranger, Terence, 65, 81, 125, 130, 138
Raurau, 52-3
Rebmann, John, 84, 87-8, 91
Rembe, 3
Ribe, 84-5, 91
Rift Valley, 35
riika (generations), 264-7, 270, 278
Robertson Smith, W., 2-3, 11
Rodney, Walter, 127, 137
Roman Catholicism, 104, 143, 150

Romans, Ancient, 7, 10
Rubaga, 72
rubber, 134, 137-9
Ruel, Malcolm, 4, 54
Rufiji, 130-1, 133, 137-9; River, 128, 131, 139
Rukiga, 75, 78
Rundi, 68; *see also* Burundi
Rutakira Kijuna, 78-9
Rwabugiri, 78-9
Rwanda, 67, 71, 73, 75-9, 127, 137, 146-7, 149, 152-3, 155-6
Rwanda Mission, 156-7
Ryangombe, 67, 69, 71-2, 74, 76-7, 79

Saaei family, 50-1
sacrifice, 89-90, 200, 202-3, 205-6, 211, 219, 225; *sadaka*, 89, 93-4, 96
Salei, 42
Samanga, 131-2
Samburu, 42, 52, 54
Samitui, 168
Samuel, 22
Sancha, 54
Sankoiyan, 46-7
Saul, 22
Sclater's Road, 169, 174
Seki, 37, 48
Semeni, 113
Senteu, 36-7, 39-43, 46-8, 52
shaitan (spirits), 88
Shambo, 78
shari'a law, 12
Sharp, Dr, 156
Sikirari, 44
Simmel, 40-1, 49
Siria, 32, 50-3
Sirtoi, arap, 174, 176
Sitonik, 50, 54
slavery, 137-9, 197
smallpox, 215
Somaliland, 17
songs *see nyimbo*
sorcery, 17, 31-2, 45, 54, 103, 116, 272, 278; *see also* witchcraft
sorghum festival, 73, 76
South Africa, 127
Spencer, Paul, 19, 29, 34, 57
Stollowsky, Otto, 130-3, 135, 138
Sudan, 6, 16-17, 24, 66, 102, 109; Anglo-Egyptian period, 196-219
Sufism, 17
Suk *see* Pokot
Supeet, 28, 34, 36, 43-4, 48, 50, 53-4

Index